New Security Challenges Series

General Editor: **Stuart Croft**, Professor of International Security in the Department of Politics and International Studies at the University of Warwick, UK, and Director of the ESRC's New Security Challenges Programme

The last decade demonstrated that threats to security vary greatly in their causes and manifestations, and that they invite interest and demand responses from the social sciences, civil society and a very broad policy community. In the past, the avoidance of war was the primary objective, but with the end of the Cold War the retention of military defence as the centrepiece of international security agenda became untenable. There has been, therefore, a significant shift in emphasis away from traditional approaches to security to a new agenda that talks of the softer side of security, in terms of human security, economic security and environmental security. The topical *New Security Challenges Series* reflects this pressing political and research agenda.

Titles include:

Natasha Underhill
COUNTERING GLOBAL TERRORISM AND INSURGENCY
Calculating the Risk of State-Failure in Afghanistan, Pakistan and Iraq

Abdul Haqq Baker
EXTREMISTS IN OUR MIDST
Confronting Terror

Raphael Bossong and Hendrik Hegemann (*editors*)
EUROPEAN CIVIL SECURITY GOVERNANCE
Diversity and Cooperation in Crisis and Disaster Management

Robin Cameron
SUBJECTS OF SECURITY
Domestic Effects of Foreign Policy in the War on Terror

Sharyl Cross, Savo Kentera, R. Craig Nation and Radovan Vukadinovic (*editors*)
SHAPING SOUTH EAST EUROPE'S SECURITY COMMUNITY FOR THE TWENTY-FIRST CENTURY
Trust, Partnership, Integration

Tom Dyson and Theodore Konstadinides
EUROPEAN DEFENCE COOPERATION IN EU LAW AND IR THEORY

Håkan Edström, Janne Haaland Matlary and Magnus Petersson (*editors*)
NATO: THE POWER OF PARTNERSHIPS

Håkan Edström and Dennis Gyllensporre
POLITICAL ASPIRATIONS AND PERILS OF SECURITY
Unpacking the Military Strategy of the United Nations

Hakan Edström and Dennis Gyllensporre (*editors*)
PURSUING STRATEGY
NATO Operations from the Gulf War to Gaddafi

Hamed El-Said
NEW APPROACHES TO COUNTERING TERRORISM
Designing and Evaluating Counter Radicalization and De-Radicalization Programs

Philip Everts and Pierangelo Isernia
PUBLIC OPINION, TRANSATLANTIC RELATIONS AND THE USE OF FORCE

Adrian Gallagher
GENOCIDE AND ITS THREAT TO CONTEMPORARY INTERNATIONAL ORDER

Kevin Gillan, Jenny Pickerill and Frank Webster
ANTI-WAR ACTIVISM
New Media and Protest in the Information Age

James Gow and Ivan Zverzhanovski
SECURITY, DEMOCRACY AND WAR CRIMES
Security Sector Transformation in Serbia

Toni Haastrup
CHARTING TRANSFORMATION THROUGH SECURITY
Contemporary EU-Africa Relations

Ellen Hallams, Luca Ratti and Ben Zyla (*editors*)
NATO BEYOND 9/11
The Transformation of the Atlantic Alliance

Carolin Hilpert
STRATEGIC CULTURAL CHANGE AND THE CHALLENGE FOR SECURITY POLICY
Germany and the Bundeswehr's Deployment to Afghanistan

Christopher Hobbs, Matthew Moran and Daniel Salisbury (*editors*)
OPEN SOURCE INTELLIGENCE IN THE TWENTY-FIRST CENTURY
New Approaches and Opportunities

Paul Jackson and Peter Albrecht
RECONSTRUCTION SECURITY AFTER CONFLICT
Security Sector Reform in Sierra Leone

Janne Haaland Matlary
EUROPEAN UNION SECURITY DYNAMICS
In the New National Interest

Sebastian Mayer (*editor*)
NATO'S POST-COLD WAR POLITICS
The Changing Provision of Security

Kevork Oskanian
FEAR, WEAKNESS AND POWER IN THE POST-SOVIET SOUTH CAUCASUS
A Theoretical and Empirical Analysis

Michael Pugh, Neil Cooper and Mandy Turner (*editors*)
WHOSE PEACE? CRITICAL PERSPECTIVES ON THE POLITICAL ECONOMY OF PEACEBUILDING

Nathan Roger
IMAGE WARFARE IN THE WAR ON TERROR

Aglaya Snetkov and Stephen Aris
THE REGIONAL DIMENSIONS TO SECURITY
Other Sides of Afghanistan

Holger Stritzel
SECURITY IN TRANSLATION
Securitization Theory and the Localization of Threat

Ali Tekin and Paul Andrew Williams
GEO-POLITICS OF THE EURO-ASIA ENERGY NEXUS
The European Union, Russia and Turkey

Aiden Warren and Ingvild Bode
GOVERNING THE USE-OF-FORCE IN INTERNATIONAL RELATIONS
The Post 9/11 Challenge on International Law

New Security Challenges Series
**Series Standing Order ISBN 978–0–230–00216–6 (hardback) and
ISBN 978–0–230–00217–3 (paperback)**
(*outside North America only*)

You can receive future titles in this series as they are published by placing a standing order. Please contact your bookseller or, in case of difficulty, write to us at the address below with your name and address, the title of the series and the ISBNs quoted above.

Customer Services Department, Macmillan Distribution Ltd, Houndmills, Basingstoke, Hampshire RG21 6XS, England

European Civil Security Governance

Diversity and Cooperation in Crisis and Disaster Management

Edited by

Raphael Bossong
Europa Universität Viadrina, Germany

Hendrik Hegemann
*Institute for Peace Research and Security Policy
at the University of Hamburg, Germany*

Selection, introduction, conclusion and editorial matter
© Raphael Bossong and Hendrik Hegemann 2015
Individual chapters © Respective authors 2015

All rights reserved. No reproduction, copy or transmission of this publication may be made without written permission.

No portion of this publication may be reproduced, copied or transmitted save with written permission or in accordance with the provisions of the Copyright, Designs and Patents Act 1988, or under the terms of any licence permitting limited copying issued by the Copyright Licensing Agency, Saffron House, 6–10 Kirby Street, London EC1N 8TS.

Any person who does any unauthorized act in relation to this publication may be liable to criminal prosecution and civil claims for damages.

The authors have asserted their rights to be identified as the authors of this work in accordance with the Copyright, Designs and Patents Act 1988.

First published 2015 by
PALGRAVE MACMILLAN

Palgrave Macmillan in the UK is an imprint of Macmillan Publishers Limited, registered in England, company number 785998, of Houndmills, Basingstoke, Hampshire RG21 6XS.

Palgrave Macmillan in the US is a division of St Martin's Press LLC,
175 Fifth Avenue, New York, NY 10010.

Palgrave Macmillan is the global academic imprint of the above companies and has companies and representatives throughout the world.

Palgrave® and Macmillan® are registered trademarks in the United States, the United Kingdom, Europe and other countries.

ISBN 978–1–137–48110–8

This book is printed on paper suitable for recycling and made from fully managed and sustained forest sources. Logging, pulping and manufacturing processes are expected to conform to the environmental regulations of the country of origin.

A catalogue record for this book is available from the British Library.

A catalog record for this book is available from the Library of Congress.

Contents

List of Tables and Figures — vii

Preface and Acknowledgements — ix

Notes on Contributors — xi

List of Abbreviations and Acronyms — xv

1 Introduction: European Civil Security Governance –
Towards a New Comprehensive Policy Space? — 1
Raphael Bossong and Hendrik Hegemann

Part I The Challenge of Diversity

2 Cooperation under Diversity? Exploring Cultural and
Institutional Diversity in European Civil Security
Governance — 27
Raphael Bossong and Hendrik Hegemann

3 Civil Security Governance Systems in the New EU Member
States: Closer to 'Old Europe' or a Distinctive Path? — 50
*Piotr Matczak, Vera-Karin Brazova, Višnja Samardžija and
Iwona Pinskwar*

4 Common Challenge – Different Response? The Case of
H1N1 Influenza — 73
Vera-Karin Brazova and Piotr Matczak

5 Regional Organizations and Disaster Risk Management:
Europe's Place in the Global Picture — 94
Daniel Petz

Part II The Challenge of Transformation

6 Preventing Disasters in Europe: Challenges and
Opportunities for Translating Global Visions into Local
Practices — 117
Simon Hollis

| 7 | Transformations in European Natural Hazard Management: There and Back Again
Timothy Prior, Florian Roth and Michel Herzog | 138 |
| 8 | Systems for Post-Crisis Learning: A Systemic Gap in Civil Security Governance?
Edward Deverell | 160 |

Part III The Challenge of Cooperation and the Role of the EU

9	Exploring the EU's Role as Transboundary Crisis Manager: The Facilitation of Sense-Making during the Ash Crisis *Sanneke Kuipers and Arjen Boin*	191
10	The EU as a Regulator of Civil Security across Europe *Han Dorussen, Evangelos Fanoulis and Emil Kirchner*	211
11	What Can EU Civil Security Governance Learn from the Common Security and Defence Policy and the European Defence Agency? *Magnus Ekengren*	233
12	Who Cares? The Relevance of EU Crisis Cooperation for EU Scholars *Mark Rhinard*	256
13	Conclusion: European Civil Security Governance between Consolidation and Contestation *Raphael Bossong and Hendrik Hegemann*	278

Index 292

Tables and Figures

Tables

3.1	Difference between the Old Member States (column 1: OMS) and the New Member States (column 2: NMS) in terms of particular types of disasters – Results of Student's t-test calculation	55
3.2	The most important type of risk as perceived by inhabitants of the EU countries	59
3.3	Difference between the Old Member States (column 1: OMS) and the New Member States (column 2: NMS) in terms of perceived risk by inhabitants of the EU countries – Results of Student's t-test calculation	62
4.1	Overall public perception of how the crisis was handled by the authorities	77
4.2	The main administrative level, which was addressing the H1N1 crisis	78
4.3	Plans for dealing with a pandemic already in place before the crisis	79
4.4	Main events in the H1N1 epidemic in Poland	82
4.5	Official review of the actions taken during the H1N1 crisis	84
4.6	The inclusion of different stakeholders in the H1N1 response	86
5.1	Indicators for regional organizations' work on disaster risk management	99
5.2	Disaster risk management indicators for four European regional organizations	109
6.1	HFA priorities for action	119
6.2	Referent points of protection in European states and international organizations	127
8.1	Crises and accidents in Sweden (1993–2013)	170
10.1	EU committees and agencies active on civil security matters	215
10.2	Signature crises in Europe (1990–2010)	216

Figures

3.1	Total number of disasters in European countries (1995–2014)	54
3.2	Number of disasters in the 28 EU countries (1995–2014)	54
3.3	Tree diagram resulting from cluster analysis, taking into account various types of disasters in the EU countries. Vertical proximity of the linked countries represents their similarity in terms of sets of occurring disasters. The horizontal axis represents Euclidean distance between countries	56
3.4	Concern of citizens in selected countries about the types of threats that are most likely to hit their country (only citizens that feel very concerned included)	58
3.5	Cluster analysis of the EU countries based on citizens' opinion on the seriousness of risks. Standardized data. Vertical proximity of the linked countries represents their similarity in terms of perception of risks. The horizontal axis represents Euclidean distance between countries	60

Preface and Acknowledgements

The present volume is the result of discussions and activities that started in the context of the international research project 'Analysis of Civil Security Systems in Europe/ANVIL', which ran from 2012 to 2014 and examined the cultural, legal, operational and institutional diversity of civil security in Europe as well as the ensuing consequences for the role of the EU as security provider. In the course of this project, we realized that new trends and patterns were emerging in the way European states and international organizations deal with diverse risks and crises, such as natural disasters, epidemics, large-scale accidents, infrastructure failure or terrorist attacks. Yet, we also became aware that these transformations show different forms and effects at different levels and in different areas, which need to be elucidated in a more systematic and social scientific manner. This led to the idea of a wider book that reviews this nascent multilevel area of what we call European civil security governance.

For this purpose, this edited volume assembled a group of distinguished scholars from different geographical and disciplinary backgrounds, including, but also going beyond, members of our initial research consortium. They kindly agreed to tackle the challenge of dealing with an emerging agenda and took our suggestions at various stages of the production process with flexibility and creativity. Each chapter addresses specific elements of European civil security governance, adding to a hopefully rich and differentiated theoretical, empirical and political engagement with the issues at hand. For this, the editors owe the authors profound gratitude.

This book has also been made possible by the substantial support from a number of people and institutions. The foundation was laid with the financial support from the European Commission under grant number FP7-SEC-2011-284678. The ANVIL project was initiated and headed by Arjen Boin and Mark Rhinard, whom we also thank for their inspiration and pioneering research in this area, and benefitted from outstanding coordination by James Rydock and the high quality of research conducted by all participants. During the project and subsequent preparation of this book, the Institute for Peace Research and Security Policy at the University of Hamburg provided a hospitable and inspiring working environment for the editors. We are particularly grateful for the research assistance by Niklas Etzel during the final stages of preparing this manuscript. Last but not least, we thank the series editor Stuart Croft and the anonymous reviewer for their helpful comments and interest in this project, while Hannah Kašpar, Emily Russell and Eleanor Davey-Corrigan at Palgrave Macmillan provided extremely professional support.

Contributors

Arjen Boin is Professor of Public Institutions and Governance at Leiden University's Department of Political Science and an adjunct professor at Louisiana State University. He is the director and co-founder of Crisisplan BV, an international consultancy firm specialized in crisis management. He is the editor of the journal *Public Administration* and has published widely on topics of crisis and disaster management, leadership, institutional design and correctional administration.

Raphael Bossong is a lecturer at the European University Viadrina, Frankfurt (Oder), Germany, and researcher at the Institute for Peace Research and Security Policy at the University of Hamburg (IFSH). He holds a BA in social and political sciences from the University of Cambridge, and an MA and PhD in international relations from the London School of Economics and Political Science. His research focuses on the intersection between EU crisis management, internal and external security policy and public administration.

Vera-Karin Brazova is a PhD candidate in public policy at Charles University in Prague, Czech Republic. She participated in several research projects, both national (Czech) and international. Her research interests cover such areas as migration, war studies and issues of security governance in the Central European countries.

Edward Deverell is an associate professor and a research fellow at the Center for Crisis Management Research and Training (Crismart) at the Swedish National Defence College in Stockholm. His research focuses on topics of organizational learning from crisis, organizational and societal crisis management and public management reform. His research has appeared in journals such as *Public Management Review, Journal of Contingencies and Crisis Management, Journal of Homeland Security and Emergency Management* and *Risk Management*.

Han Dorussen is a professor in the Department of Government at the University of Essex and a member of the Michael Nicholson Centre of Conflict and Cooperation. He is the associate editor for the *Journal of Peace Research*. His current research interests include the relationship between trade and conflict, the use of economic policies in international relations, peacekeeping operations and the governance of post-conflict societies and policy convergence in the European Union.

Magnus Ekengren is Associate Professor and Director of the Program for European Security Research (EUROSEC) at the Swedish National Defence College. He publishes in the areas of European foreign and security policy, crisis management, security sector reform and the Europeanization of the nation-state. His latest books are *The Politics of Security Sector Reform – Challenges and Opportunities for the EU's Global Role* (2011, co-edited with Greg Simons) and *The EU as Crisis Manager – Patterns and Prospects* (2013, with Arjen Boin and Mark Rhinard).

Evangelos Fanoulis is a visiting fellow at the University of Essex, Department of Government, and Lecturer in Politics at the University of Leicester for 2015. He obtained his PhD degree from the University of Essex in 2014. His main research interests lie within EU democracy, CSDP and civil and non-traditional security. He has also published on these issues, including articles in the journal *European Security*.

Hendrik Hegemann is a researcher at the Institute for Peace Research and Security Policy at the University of Hamburg (IFSH). He holds a PhD from the University of Hamburg and an MA from the University of Freiburg, both in political science. His research interests include security governance, counterterrorism, international organizations, critical security studies and international relations theory. His recent publications include a co-edited special issue on security governance in the journal *European Security*.

Michel Herzog is a researcher in the field of critical infrastructure protection and cyber-security in the Risk and Resilience Research Team at the Center for Security Studies (CSS) of the ETH Zürich. He studied political science and public law at the University of Zürich, where he received his master's degree. During his studies, he focused on security policy and legal questions in international relations as well as political risk analysis.

Simon Hollis is a postdoctoral researcher at the Swedish National Defence College and lectures on risk and disaster management in association with the Geneva Graduate School of Governance. He received his PhD in international relations from the Hertie School of Governance in 2012. His thesis examines the role of regional disaster risk management programmes. His articles have appeared in a variety of international peer-reviewed journals on various aspects of international and domestic cooperation on disaster management.

Emil Kirchner is Jean Monnet Chair and Coordinator of the Jean Monnet Centre of Excellence at the University of Essex. His current main interests include EU-China relations, European internal and external security policy and regional and global governance. His recent publications include 'Better a good neighbor than a distant friend: the scope and impact of regional security organizations', *International Relations of the Asia-Pacific* (January 2014, co-author); 'Security governance in a comparative regional perspective', *European Security* (2014, co-author); and *The Palgrave Handbook on EU-Asia Relations* (2013, co-editor).

Sanneke Kuipers is a postdoctoral researcher at Leiden University's Institute of Public Administration, Campus The Hague. She also works as a senior researcher-advisor at Crisisplan BV. She received her PhD from Leiden University in 2004. She has published on crisis and disaster management, institutionalization and path dependency, accountability and blaming after crisis.

Piotr Matczak works for the Institute of Sociology, Adam Mickiewicz University, and for the Institute for Agriculture and Forest Environment, Polish Academy of Sciences, both in Poznan, Poland. He holds PhD and Habilitation degrees from Adam Mickiewicz University, both in sociology. His research focuses on institutional dimensions of risk management, particularly related to floods and climate change, as well as on public policies in this area.

Daniel Petz is an independent consultant on disaster risk management and human rights issues. His previous work with the Project on Internal Displacement at the Brookings Institution, USA, included research on regional organizations and disaster risk management. Previously, he was a lecturer and researcher for European Studies and Peace and Conflict Studies at Gadjah Mada University, Indonesia. He currently works on his dissertation at the University of Graz, Austria, which focuses on human rights issues related to no-return policies for people displaced by natural disasters and the impacts of climate change.

Iwona Pinskwar works for the Institute for Agricultural and Forest Environment, Polish Academy of Sciences, Poznan, Poland. She holds a PhD in environmental management from the Poznan University of Life Sciences. Her research focuses on precipitation extremes, floods, droughts and modelling. Her articles have appeared in international journals such as *Acta Geophysica*, *Theoretical and Applied Climatology* and *Hydrological Sciences Journal*.

Timothy Prior is Head of the Risk and Resilience Research Team at the Center for Security Studies (CSS) of the ETH Zürich. He has been awarded a doctorate in social and environmental psychology from the University of Tasmania, Australia, a master's degree in environmental science from James Cook University, Australia, and completed his undergraduate studies in quantitative ecology. His research has focused on risk and decision-making under uncertainty, particularly in relation to individual, community and organizational preparation and response to environmental risk.

Mark Rhinard is an associate professor in International Relations at Stockholm University and Senior Research Fellow and Head of the Europe Research Program at the Swedish Institute of International Affairs. He holds MPhil and PhD degrees from Cambridge University. His areas of specialization include the EU as a global actor, the EU's rising role in societal security and institutional politics in the EU.

Florian Roth is a researcher with the Risk and Resilience Team at the Center for Security Studies (CSS) of the ETH Zurich. He holds a PhD in political science and a master's degree in political science, history, arts and media from the University of Konstanz. His research interests centre on risk and crisis communication in different domains such as disaster management and international security governance.

Višnja Samardžija holds a PhD from the Faculty of Economics, University of Zagreb. She is Head of the Department for European Integration in the Institute for Development and International Relations (IRMO) in Zagreb. She served as assistant minister in the Ministry for European Integration of Croatia (2000–2004). She lectures at the doctoral European studies programmes at the Universities of Zagreb and Osijek. Her areas of interest include the EU enlargement, civil security, Europe 2020 and communication with citizens (in particular Croatia and the EU).

Abbreviations and Acronyms

AFSJ	Area of Freedom, Security and Justice
AHA Centre	ASEAN Coordinating Centre for Humanitarian Assistance
ANVIL	Analysis of Civil Security Systems in Europe
ASEAN	Association of Southeast Asian Nations
AU	African Union
BSEC	Organization for Black Sea Economic Cooperation
CAN	Andean Community of Nations
CARICOM	Caribbean Community
CC	Country Council
CDEMA	Caribbean Disaster Emergency Management Agency
CDP	Capability Development Plans
CECIS	Common Emergency Communication and Information System
CFSP	Common Foreign and Security Policy
CMO	Chief Medical Officer
CoE	Council of Europe
COREPER II	Committee of Permanent Representatives
COSI	Standing Committee on Operational Cooperation on Internal Security
CPCP	Civil Protection Capacity Plans
CPM	Civil Protection Mechanism
CRED	Centre for Research on the Epidemiology of Disasters
Crismart	National Center for Crisis Management Research and Training at the Swedish National Defence College
CSDP	Common Security and Defence Policy
CSGS	Civil Security Governance System
DG	Directorate-General
DH ECHO	Directorate-General Humanitarian Aid and Civil Protection
DG ENVI	Directorate-General for the Environment
DG RELEX	Directorate-General for External Relations
DG SANCO	Directorate-General for Health and Consumers
DHS	US Department of Homeland Security
DIPECHO	Disaster Preparedness Programme of the EU Humanitarian Aid and Civil Protection

DM	Disaster Management
DRM	Disaster Risk Management
DRR	Disaster Risk Reduction
EACCC	Aviation Crisis Coordination Cell
EASA	European Aviation Safety Agency
ECDC	European Centre for Disease Prevention and Control
ECHO	European Community Humanitarian Office
ECOWAS	Economic Community of West African States
ECU	European Currency Unit
EDA	European Defence Agency
EERC	European Emergency Response Capacity
EFDRR	European Forum for Disaster Risk Reduction
EFSA	European Food Safety Authority
EISN	European Influenza Surveillance Network
EMA	European Medicines Agency
EMSA	European Maritime Safety Agency
EP	European Parliament
EPDRR	European Platform for Disaster Risk Reduction
ERCC	European Emergency Response Coordination Centre
EU	European Union
EUMS	EU Military Staff
Eurocontrol	European Organization for the Safety of Air Navigation
EUR-OPA	European and Mediterranean Major Hazards Agreement
EWRS	Early Warning and Response System
FAB	Functional Airspace Blocks
FLACSO	Facultad Latinoamericana de Ciencias Sociales
FMD	Foot-and-Mouth-Disease
FOI	Swedish Defense Research Agency
FP7	Seventh Framework Programme
GFDRR	World Bank's Global Facility for Disaster Risk Reduction
GMO	Genetically Modified Organism
GNDR	Global Network for Disaster Reduction
HaV	Swedish Agency for Marine and Water Management
HEOF	Health Emergencies Operations Facility
HFA	Hyogo Framework Programme for Action
HSC	Health Security Committee
ICAO	International Civil Aviation Organization
ICPR	International Commission for the Protection of the Rhine
IDNDR	International Decade for Natural Disaster Reduction

IDRL	International Disaster Response Laws, Rules and Principles
IFRC	International Federation of the Red Cross and Red Crescent Societies
IPCR	Integrated Political Crisis Response
JAIC	Joint Accident Investigation Commission
JHA	Justice and Home Affairs
Kamedo	Swedish Disaster Medicine Study Organization at the National Board of Health and Welfare
KLM	Koninklijke Luchtvaart Maatschappij voor Nederland en Koloniën
LAS	League of Arab States
LEK	Local Environmental Knowledge
LGSAT	Local Government Self-Assessment Tool
MA	Municipal Administration
MCDA	Use of Military and Civil Defense Assets to Support United Nations Humanitarian Activities in Complex Emergencies
MEP	Member of the European Parliament
MIC	Monitoring and Information Centre
MoD	Ministry of Defence
MSB	Swedish Civil Contingencies Agency
MSF	Médecins Sans Frontières
NATO	North Atlantic Treaty Organization
NATS	National Air Traffic Services
NBHW	National Board of Health and Welfare
NDMOs	National Disaster Management Organizations
NGO	Non-Governmental Organization
NMS	New Member States
OAS	Organization of American States
OMS	Old Member States
OSCE	Organization for Security and Cooperation in Europe
RO	Regional Organization
SAARC	South Asian Association for Regional Cooperation
SADC	South African Development Community
SAIC	Swedish National Investigation Authority
SARS	Severe Acute Respiratory Syndrome
SCFCAH	Standing Committee on Food Chain and Animal Health
ScVC	Scientific Veterinary Committee
SEA	Swedish Energy Authority
SEMA	Swedish Emergency Management Agency

SEPA	Swedish Environmental Protection Agency
SICA	Central American Integration System
SOU	Swedish Public Commission Inquiry
SPC	Secretariat of the Pacific Community
SPF	Swedish Board for Psychological Defence
SRSA	Swedish Rescue Services Agency
STAR	Strategic Analysis and Response Centre
SVC	Standing Veterinary Committee
SVK	Swedish National Grid
TFEU	Treaty on the Functioning of the European Union
UK	United Kingdom
UN	United Nations
UNDP	United Nations Development Programme
UNISDR	United Nations Office for Disaster Risk Reduction
USA	United States of America
VAAC	Volcanic Ash Advisory Center
VFR	Visual Flight Rules
WEU	Western European Union
WHO	World Health Organization

1
Introduction: European Civil Security Governance – Towards a New Comprehensive Policy Space?

Raphael Bossong and Hendrik Hegemann

Introduction

The post-Cold War period has witnessed a transformation from military-focused civil defence towards broader concepts of 'all-hazards' crisis and disaster management.[1] Civilian crises and disasters, it seems, are ubiquitous and 'normal' (Perrow, 1984, 2007), while the threat of major interstate war has receded from the top of the agenda of security planners and crisis managers – at least in Western Europe and before the recent confrontations in Ukraine. Thus, security challenges like large-scale industrial accidents, infrastructure failures, major terrorist attacks or global pandemics have risen to prominence in the work of security policymakers and practitioners and become merged with long-standing concerns about 'natural' disasters such as floods and storms. The paradigmatic shorthand for these developments is the emergence of the '(world) risk society' (Beck, 1992, 1999), whereby advanced societies are confronted with a multitude of increasingly complex, transnational and incalculable risks resulting from the unintended side-effects of globalization and high-tech capitalism. There is no shortage of recent examples supporting this thesis, ranging from the terrorist attacks in New York, Madrid or London and the Fukushima nuclear disaster to the 2004 Indian Ocean tsunami or the Ebola virus pandemic in Western Africa.

Both macro-sociological analyses and political science have correspondingly highlighted the growing limits to hierarchical, expert-driven and state-centred mechanisms of control. Yet, despite the growth of civil society movements in areas such as environmental protection and structural trends towards more horizontal forms of governance, citizens still demand an effective and efficient provision of core security goods by 'the state'. Even if one adopts a critical reading of exaggerated threat perceptions, such as in the case of terrorism, Western societies are not inclined to accept fatalistic interpretations of natural disasters and societal vulnerabilities. Security continues to be the quintessential value and basis for political legitimacy in modern states, apparently requiring responsible governments to take resolute action against an ever longer list of – real or imagined – threats and fears, also entailing the danger of overreaction and unintended costs and consequences (Furedi, 2005; Baumann, 2006). The US-coined concept of 'homeland security' can be seen as the most comprehensive, though highly controversial, expression of this trend. In Europe, too, the value of security can be regarded as increasingly central to political authority construction (Burgess, 2011).

In this context, the European Union (EU) has similarly built up frameworks for responding to crises, disasters and structural risks that cross both geographical and functional boundaries. Going beyond its track record as a regulator of economic infrastructures as well as the long-standing ambition to forge a Common Foreign and Security Policy (CFSP), the EU can increasingly be seen as a comprehensive security provider for its citizens. This notion is expressed in new formal norms and institutions, such as the 'Solidarity Clause' and the European Emergency Response Coordination Centre (ERCC), as well as in informal arrangements for research and best practice exchange. Furthermore, the notion of preparedness and response to crises has become central to many EU policy regimes that developed dynamically over the last decade, ranging from counterterrorism to food security and flood protection. In sum, comprehensive management of crises and disasters seems to be moving towards a distinct European policy space and research agenda (Boin et al., 2006, 2013; Attinà, 2013; Kirchner et al., 2014). Yet, functional pressures for centralization and trans-nationalization exist alongside deep rooted and potentially conflicting political interests and cultural traditions, not to forget crosscutting trends towards more decentralized societal resilience. Hence, the evolution of this hybrid governance space requires more systematic investigation.

Moreover, the potentially far-reaching economic, political, legal and operational implications of this new dimension of EU security governance have hardly attracted public or academic attention. The EU's CFSP or areas like counterterrorism and asylum, which are more directly linked to salient normative and political debates, continue to stand in the limelight (Bigo et al., 2010; Biscop, 2013). We do not want to detract from the importance of these debates. However, it is striking that the unique character and the interrelatedness of many policies and processes in the field of civilian crisis and disaster management are not awarded sufficient scrutiny – even though it has become commonplace to point to the merger of internal and external security policy (Eriksson and Rhinard, 2009; Schroeder, 2011) as well as to the EU's endorsement of a 'comprehensive approach' (Kaunert and Zwolski, 2013). From an academic perspective, the literature on EU security governance usually disregards broader policy regimes and frameworks to protect EU citizens against multiple hazards and risks rather than against intentional threats (Kirchner and Sperling, 2007; Wagnsson et al., 2009; Norheim-Martinsen, 2013). And from a political perspective, one may wonder about the agendas and interests of bureaucratic and professional actors to downplay the 'disaster-politics-nexus' and portray crisis and disaster management as a primarily technical question (Hannigan, 2012).

This edited volume, therefore, draws attention to the emerging field of 'civil security governance' in Europe. As explained further below, this volume argues that the concept of civil security governance may help to capture the emerging protection-oriented policy space, which extends beyond the EU's CFSP and Area of Freedom, Security and Justice (AFSJ) and is not adequately covered by more traditional terms like internal security. The concept further aims to highlight that EU structures and policies are placed in a complex system that involves different actors with diverse and potentially conflicting traditions, rules and institutions. Consequentially, we need a broader perspective. Member states continue to hold most competences for the provision of civil security, while one also needs to be aware of different global, regional, national and subnational actions and actors in a differentiated multilevel system dealing with the management of transnational risks and crises (de Franco and Meyer, 2011; Attinà, 2012; Hannigan, 2012). Thus, analysing civil security in and of the EU requires an appreciation for interdependence and multiple levels of governance.

In addition to students of EU security policy or European analysts of security governance, this analysis should be of relevance to researchers interested in crisis and disaster management or in the wider evolution of security studies. The former usually approach the response to concrete crisis and disasters from the perspective of functional and operational challenges impeding effective and efficient action – especially at the national level – but often disregard the broader political and conceptual dynamics in this transnational policy-field. The latter have conducted extensive analysis of the evolving concept of security in its different guises, but did not explicitly scrutinize the idea of civil security with its specific meaning and ramifications.

The remainder of this introductory chapter therefore works towards a common, though not canonical, understanding of civil security governance and how it fits in broader debates briefly alluded to above. First, it asks what 'civil security' is and which potentials and pitfalls it entails compared to related terms. Second, it raises the question of whether civil security is emerging as a new, distinct European policy space and suggests that the idea of security governance might help us understand developments in this area. The final section then briefly outlines the three parts of the book, which speak to different, but overlapping research interests and respectively address the challenge of diversity in European civil security governance; Europe's relation to global and regional processes of transformation; and the wider implications for the EU's role as a security actor.

Civil security: Just another prefix?

The definition and redefinition of security beyond conventional military-centred conceptions has been a key concern for social science research over the last two decades. The study of security has left behind its constitutive emphasis on 'national security' and added a plethora of new prefixes to security, which can be understood as parallel deepening and widening (Buzan and Hansen, 2009). These compound terms and modulations of the meaning of security have attracted intense debate, which generally revolves around the tension between the desire to 'democratize' or 'civilize' the practices of security and orient them towards the emancipatory benefit of each human being, and the dangers of eroding democracy, social cohesion and civil rights by ever expanding processes of 'securitization' (Loader and Walker, 2007; Huysmans, 2014).

By using the term 'civil security', we cannot escape this normative debate. From a critical perspective, it could be argued that civil security is guilty of unnecessarily adding to the muddy waters of academic definition. Aside from suspicions that we just seek to introduce a new buzzword, civil security could most of all be seen as yet another indicator of the securitization of all aspects of 'civil' life and the resulting claims to political authority to provide protection.

Instead of immediately staking out a normative position in this debate, we, however, first aim to open an area of investigation and pay attention to emerging empirical developments. As sketched out above, there are significant transformations in the broader field of crisis and disaster management at the EU level and beyond, which cannot readily be captured by familiar labels from security studies. On a theoretical level, we expect that the way security governance is organized and executed strongly depends upon the underlying representations and understandings of 'security' – and these representations and understandings can lead to, or accommodate, different logics of governance ranging from functional technocracy over 'normal' politics to states of emergency (Christou et al., 2010). So it matters whether a field is structured by representations that are associated with internal security, human security or civil security, but the resulting consequences do not have to automatically be read from the perspective of securitization (in its many critical variants). Following this inductive approach, the next section, therefore, surveys the existing usages of civil security before, in a second step, further discussing its possible political and normative implications, which are typically foregrounded by critical security scholars.

Civil security: What's in a name?

To date, the term civil security is used in varied geographical and functional contexts. First, some national governments advanced the concept as a way to describe the comprehensive ambitions of their reformed crisis and disaster management systems. For example, the section for Civil Security (*Sécurité Civile*) in the French Ministry of Internal Security underlines that civil security is taking place 'on all fronts' and 'for all types of disasters'.[2] In other cases, civil security also serves to capture the desired holistic and de-militarized conduct of crisis management and civil protection. Civil security, for example, was proposed as a new guiding concept for the transformation of Bulgaria's security architecture to be established as a third pillar alongside military-centred external security and police-focused internal security (Shalamanov et al., 2005). A slightly different reading becomes apparent in attempts by some analysts in the broader US discourse on 'homeland security' to suggest civil security as a useful concept to activate and inform citizens in the 'war on terror' by revitalizing and adapting experiences from civil defence programmes dating back to the Cold War (Dory, 2003). Yet, the term civil security never gained acceptance in the US context. In this comprehensive sense and through its focus on crisis and disasters within Western societies, civil security also partly overlaps with, but goes clearly beyond, the concepts of disaster relief and emergency aid as they are advanced by many international actors (Attinà, 2012; Hannigan, 2012).

Second, some actors in academia and private industry have taken up civil security to promote new research and technological agendas. For instance, the term features prominently in the EU Commission's security research programme, which highlights its goal to 'stimulate the cooperation of providers and users for civil security solutions' and 'ensure optimal and concerted use of available and evolving technologies to the benefit of civil European security'.[3] In this perspective, civil security can relate to various technological applications not only for identification, surveillance and border protection but also for warning, communication or rescue, which has resonated with the security industry to market a wider range of products to a wider range of security practitioners. The security industry members united in the 'Swedish Association of Civil Security', for example, define civil security in a broad way as 'the ability of society to handle antagonistic or non-antagonistic threats with a significant impact on the functioning of society'.[4] In general, European officials have repeatedly stressed a pragmatic need to restructure national defence industries in light of declining defence budgets, whereas military research cooperation and joint production remains fraught with numerous political obstacles and is nearly impossible in the EU context. Civil security research allowed the Commission to legitimate its fragile role as security actor beyond the contentious military sphere. Thus, *civil* security research is heuristically defined by its antonym, even if civilian-led cooperation with military actors and the development of dual use technologies is not ruled out.

Third, civil security relates to a number of broader meta-trends in security provision by Western states. A wider historical perspective brings out a loose set of family resemblances that civil security shares with some of the other terms prevalent in this discourse. A first common trend is a break with the previous Cold War tradition of 'civil defence' effectively focusing on the protection of societies against the consequences of nuclear war. During the 1990s, more comprehensive notions, such as 'civil protection', became strong as new terms to denote public activities to protect the civilian population against all kinds of disasters and emergencies in rather decentralized structures with broad societal participation (Alexander, 2002). Rather than 'the state', societies and their 'vital systems' necessary to ensure the functioning of modern societies were increasingly defined as central reference objects of security policy. This shift manifested itself in new terms like 'societal security' (Wæver et al., 1993) and 'critical infrastructure protection' (Collier and Lakoff, 2008). Another distinct attempt to advance more comprehensive concepts for the protection of societies is visible in the

US-coined concept of 'homeland security'. It appeals beyond a technical or abstract referent object of security to the politically charged or emotive term of 'homeland' that is threatened by invasion (Kaunert et al., 2012, pp. 3–4). As is well known, it also emerged directly in response to the events of 9/11 and served to justify exceptionalist political measures. The introduction and institutionalization of homeland security – most visible through the US Department of Homeland Security (DHS) – revived the Cold War idea of civil defence, highlighting the need to prepare society for the response to terrorist attacks and to increase the resilience of societies. Yet, the limits and resulting gaps on this primary focus on terrorism as well as the low levels of societal resilience and mobilization were sharply highlighted during Hurricane Katrina.

Civil security also relates to the notions of risk management, risk governance and resilience that seem to have taken hold and have come to be regarded as an almost universally applicable panacea for the assessment and management of diverse natural and man-made hazards. More recent conceptualizations of risk governance have fully incorporated the classic critiques of seminal thinkers such as Beck and seek to balance a quantitative, mathematical risk management with sensitivity to deep uncertainty, complex scenarios and the need to involve multiple societal and political stakeholders beyond technocratic experts (van Asselt and Renn, 2011). In this context, the idea of resilience further acknowledges that societies – at least within reasonable costs – cannot guarantee effective protection of all people and sights against all kinds of unforeseen crises and disasters and, therefore, need to prepare for the case of their actual occurrence. This requires steps to enable and empower societies to cope with and recover from such events (Coaffee et al., 2008; see also Prior, Roth and Herzog in this volume). Yet, resilience remains ambiguous, especially when seen as universal standard for a society. Critical scholars have increasingly seen it as a further vector or problematic norm for instilling a neoliberal logic of governmentality (Joseph, 2013; Chandler, 2014), which shifts vital responsibilities of public authorities towards the individual, irrespective of the actually available capacities for or consent to such decentred resilience. These broader debates form the background of the concept of civil security that is at the heart of this volume. This debate is much broader, however, and cannot be fruitfully addressed here. Instead of such wider social transformations this book foregrounds more readily observable, yet understudied, shifts in public governance structures for crisis, risk and disaster management with a special emphasis on Europe.

This brief overview indicates that civil security continues to be a fuzzy concept with unclear boundaries and rooted in different, but related, discourses. Moreover, the concept is seldom used explicitly and rarely, if ever, more formally defined. However, the diverse usages are held together loosely by an emphasis on the need for comprehensive and joined-up all-hazards approaches, the dissociation from civil and military security and the need to award more attention to the role of citizens and the private sector.

Such a framing appears to be especially pertinent for the EU case. Interestingly, the EU itself explicitly refers to the term civil security only occasionally and primarily in the context of its security research programme. Likewise, the academic debate on EU policies to protect its citizens is usually framed in terms of 'internal security' (Mitsilegas et al., 2003; Bossong and Rhinard, 2013a), 'homeland security' (Rhinard and Boin, 2009; Kaunert et al., 2012) or 'societal security' (Boin et al., 2007). To avoid the negative connotations of homeland security, at least in so far as they exist from a European perspective, and especially in relation to the focus on the 'war on terror', the EU particularly sought to promote the notion of 'internal security', most notably through its Internal Security Strategy (Bossong and Rhinard, 2013b). Although EU internal security has been broadened to include areas like critical infrastructure protection, most people probably still associate the term with police and judicial cooperation regarding questions of crime, asylum and border protection and, more generally, with prosecution or prevention of individual crimes, rather than with response to crises and disasters with a wider social impact. The described meaning of civil security, therefore, seems to be more conducive to analysis at the EU level where different functional competences at different levels coalesce and interact and where the domestic use of the military does not play a major role. In its communication for a 'post-2015 Hyogo Framework for Disaster Risk Reduction' the Commission, for example, underlined the goal of a 'comprehensive multi-hazard approach' and 'active engagement of civil society' while military means and actors were completely absent (European Commission, 2014, pp. 10–11).

Civilizing security or securitizing the civilian?

Despite these varied and inconclusive empirical usages, the concept of civil security can be used for the legitimation of various policies and institutions, especially by distancing them from military action and linking them to modern risks and vulnerabilities. The kind and severity of the underlying threat is not consensual and self-evident but subject to scholarly and political debate. Hence, using the term civil security can have important political and normative ramifications.

From the existing discourse, one can discern two basic positions on the potential and pitfalls of advancing civil security as a scholarly and political priority. A growing group of crisis management researchers stress the importance of increasingly complex and 'transboundary' crises, such as critical infrastructure failure or global pandemics fuelled by the growth of global travel and communication systems and the economic and technical interconnectedness of modern capitalist societies. They highlight the need for new forms of transnational cooperation dealing with these crises and search for the best way in which such cooperation should be organized in order to achieve ideal results. The EU has been at the centre of this discussion due to its high degree of economic and social integration and interdependence and its comparatively dense and advanced net of institutions and instruments (Boin et al., 2007; Boin and Ekengren, 2009; 't Hart and Sundelius, 2013). The contrary critical position mentioned earlier holds that excessive and inflated threat representations and risk constructions, for example in relation to terrorism, are used to legitimate the work of security agencies in search for a new *raison d'être* after the end of the Cold War and to justify emergency measures, which undermine the principles of democracy and civil liberty (Eriksson, 2001; Dunn Cavelty and Kristensen, 2008). The EU, in particular, is credited with a special tendency towards technocratic practices of preventive and precautionary risk management acting on the basis of knowledge representations regarding future risks and catastrophes (Bigo, 2002; Huysmans et al., 2006).

Is it necessary to take position between the functionalist and critical camp? Or can one also stake out a different, but not necessarily a compromise, position? In this perspective, one may underline the benefits of a 'civilized' definition and management of security (Loader and Walker, 2007). That is, it remains possible to conceive of public actors as crucial catalysts and guarantors, though not sole providers, of security. Security, in this context, should be understood as a 'thick' public good that cannot be reduced to individualized and only indirectly aggregated decisions and investments to increase protection (e.g. by buying safety and security equipment and services). Conversely, security cannot be defined only as an external public good to be provided by public actors, since it is also inter-subjective understandings and the engagement of citizens that make up for the shared sense of social trust and ontological security – in contrast to frightened individuals who have a potentially limitless appetite for security measures that are offered to them by public actors (by means of securitizing strategies and discourses) in exchange for docility. While the global risk society and the growth of transnational governance challenge our traditional concepts of democratic debate and control, it can remain an emancipatory project to strive for constitutionally embedded, and politically controlled and debated, security policy at the transnational level.

Empirical research on civil protection and disaster management may, thus, not typically foreground such normative debates that are normally associated with internal security and the fight against terrorism. However, the term civil security may allow to move one step beyond purely functionalist arguments for transnational cooperation and to keep an eye on the ambivalent potential to extend securitization or to promote security policies that foreground the interests and values of civilian actors and society at large. We cannot yet provide such a deeper normative defence of the concept or related goals and policies. However, we hope that our initial aim to arrive at a better grasp of the emerging political, institutional and operational governing dynamics in civil security will provide an important stepping stone in this direction.

Civil security governance: Towards a new European policy space?

We argue that a new European policy space of civil security is emerging. As illustrated above, this premise is based on the observation that many of the risks and threats subsumed under the civil security label can have significant transboundary ramifications (e.g. global pandemics), may overstress the resources of an individual country (e.g. major natural disasters) or have a strong symbolic importance for international solidarity (e.g. terrorist attacks). Moreover, the EU disposes of relevant competences in areas like transport and energy and can draw on its experience with EU-wide regulation and coordination. Hence, civil security governance may seem like an almost natural concern for EU integration and cooperation (Boin et al., 2007, 2013; Boin and Ekengren, 2009).

Yet, to move from these general considerations to the definition of, and operationalizable research on, an EU policy space is not simple. In a classic institutionalist sense, European policy spaces could be defined as 'supranational policy arenas or sites of governance, structured by EU rules, procedures and the activities of the EU's organisations' (Stone Sweet et al., 2001, p. 3). In addition to institutional and legal elements, a policy space also has a normative dimension and presupposes 'a widely shared system of rules and procedures to define who actors are, how they make sense of each other's actions, and what types of actions are possible' (Stone Sweet et al., 2001, p. 12). Such an understanding directs us to look at instances of formal rule-setting and institution-building as well as at ideational and normative processes leading to shared understandings of issues to be tackled and actors to be included.

On this account, the initial evidence seems mixed. On the one hand, civil security is increasingly formulated as a distinct EU policy goal, even if other labels may be used. Since the Treaty of Lisbon, 'preventing and protecting against natural or man-made disasters' is formally defined as a supportive competence of the EU (TFEU Art.196), whereby member states retain primary operational and regulatory competences. The EU's five year internal security programme for the period 2009–2014 ('Stockholm Programme') established the goal of 'a Europe that protects' based on 'comprehensive and effective Union disaster management' (European Council, 2010, pp. 17, 25). The EU Internal Security Strategy defines the objective to 'increase Europe's resilience to crises and disasters' as one of its key goals, including through the full implementation of the solidarity clause, the EU-wide advancement of an 'all-hazards' approach, an integrated approach to situation awareness and the development of European response capacities (European Commission, 2010a, pp. 13–15). Hence, one may think that civil security is closely linked to the EU's common identity and shared perception of threats and risks that underpin its ambition to move towards a 'secure European community' (Ekengren, 2008).

This normative commitment is backed up increasingly by processes of formal and legal institutionalization. Civil protection now has a genuine home in the Commission within the Directorate-General Humanitarian Aid and Civil Protection (DG ECHO). The EU Civil Protection Mechanism has been revised and updated, the Commission set up the new ERCC and the Common Emergency Communication and Information System (CECIS), and the Council endorsed the principle of Integrated Political Crisis Response. Moreover, the EU has advanced specific instruments and tools for implementation by member states, such as guidelines for national risk assessments (European Commission, 2010b), and agreed upon a new agenda to implement the UN's global Hyogo framework (HFA: Hyogo Framework for Action) for disaster risk reduction (European Commission, 2014).

On the other hand, protecting populations is an issue close to the core of national sovereignty where member states have historically been reluctant to delegate tasks to Brussels. Cooperation on civil protection was not initially foreseen as an integration objective, but only emerged as a literal spillover effect from the deepening economic and societal integration in Europe. In particular, the first EU activities on civil protection in the 1980s and early 1990s followed from legislative competences in the areas of industrial safety and maritime protection, whereby major chemical accidents and oil spills could not only be addressed on a regulatory level, but also as a concrete operational cross-boundary challenge for rescue services. At the same time, the transition from military-dominated civil defence to civilian-led systems for disaster management also occurred relatively recently in many member states, that is, several years after the end of the Cold War or even early into the new millennium, especially in the case of former Communist countries. The EU only acquired highly circumscribed competences in the area of military cooperation and external 'civilian crisis management' around the same time (early 2000s). Therefore, it was not to be expected that civil protection would feature prominently as a formal explicit competence of the EU, while member states clearly remain in charge of all operational resources. This is expressed in the formulation of EU Treaty Law that only briefly refers to civil protection as supportive competence.

This historical reluctance, or belated start, to move towards more supranational integration in this area reflects in the fact that legal provisions and structures for civil security remain strongly diverse across member states, depending on cultural and institutional contexts, historical experiences or exposure to specific threats (Houben, 2005; Bremberg and Britz, 2009; Krieger, 2013; Kirchner et al., 2014). In civil security, cooperation and coordination – despite the described growth of EU-level institutions and policies – eventually still mostly takes place through informal exchanges among top-ranking security policymakers and officials from national-level governments and agencies. While other policy areas that are similarly placed, such as educational or aspects of social policy, have attracted growing amounts of attention, there is hardly any comparable research on whether EU supportive action in civil security actually trickles down to the national or even local level (Hollis, 2010).

Finally, the conceptual ambiguity regarding civil security described above also casts doubt on the coherence of such a policy space as its borders by nature remain rather fuzzy. Many structures and activities take place in functional areas – ranging from counterterrorism over critical infrastructure protection to fire safety – that might be subsumed under comprehensive umbrella terms like civil security but actually follow very different traditions and do not always show much regular interaction. Even in the US, empirical research has thrown doubt over the internal cohesion and relevance of the desired integrated policy regime for homeland security (May et al., 2011). Instead, traditional policy (sub)communities remain largely isolated from each other. This suggests that even more so in the EU, civil security competences and actors are 'scattered across the EU's institutional landscape' and many of them 'were not designed with crisis management in mind' (Boin et al., 2013, p. 144). It is, thus, hard to say where this policy space ends and where it starts, and which vision, strategic concept or reference object of security is supposed to bind these different phenomena together in daily practice.

Civil security, therefore, might rather meet the more fragmented and fluid image of security governance than a coherent objective with a neatly defined policy space or institutional underpinning. A security governance approach directs us to pay attention to a broader range of phenomena beyond formal institutions and identities. In their classic definition, Webber et al. (2004, p. 8) understand security governance to include 'coordinated management and regulation of issues by multiple and separate authorities, the interventions of both public and private actors (depending upon the issue), formal and informal arrangements, in turn structured by discourse and norms, and purposefully directed toward particular policy outcomes'. Thus, security governance shares with the institutionalist notion of policy space the focus on institutional and normative features but allows for a more diverse and differentiated order below the level of more far-reaching institutionalization.

Moreover, the EU has also been more recently regarded as a leading, or most-likely case of security governance (Kirchner and Sperling, 2007; Wagnsson et al., 2009; Christou et al., 2010; Schroeder, 2011), based on its 'post-Westphalian' transfers of sovereignty, shared risks, diverse set of institutions and comprehensive notion of security. EU actions and institutions are also part of complex systems of governance at different national, regional and global levels (Sperling and Webber, 2014), while European crisis and disaster management is one aspect of the larger trend towards regional 'security complexes' (Buzan and Wæver; 2003; Hollis 2015). So security governance may capture not only different kinds of relations between diverse public and private actors but also the inclusion of local emergency response agencies or relevant regional and global organizations in the field, such as the United Nations Office for Disaster Risk Reduction (UNISDR).

Finally, the notion of security governance may be more conducive to the rather decentralized nature of EU civil security with its emphasis on informal and operational mechanisms of information exchange, network-building and best practices (Ekengren, 2006; Bremberg, 2010;

Hollis, 2010). These activities can have important consequences, or often go along with more formal supranational regulation and legislation. We do not yet have a real sense of the degree to which the recent post-Lisbon innovations lead to a sustainable transformation in practice. It may well be that they are part of a rather long-term gradual and multidimensional shift 'from sovereignty to solidarity' as some observers diagnose it for the area of EU internal security (den Boer, 2014). Yet, a security governance framework alerts us to the fact that such possible trends in the area of civil security are neither linear nor inevitable (Ehrhart et al., 2014).

Structure of the book

The structure of the book serves the central overarching objective to grasp the full dynamic and consequences of current developments in European civil security governance by providing a comprehensive analysis of diversity, transformation and cooperation in this field within its broader national, regional and global context. The volume is divided in three parts covering these different aspects, addressing different questions, challenges and research interests.

The challenge of diversity

The first part deals with diversity in European civil security governance. On the one hand, many authors diagnose a trend towards convergence and isomorphism in crisis and disaster management, mirroring the functional pressures of complex transboundary risks or the work of international organizations and standards (Quarantelli, 2000; Hollis, 2014). On the other hand, existing comparative studies find that states have implemented very different structures and policies and operate in diverse contexts with different traditions (Bremberg and Britz, 2009; Brazova et al., 2014). So far, it remains unclear which specific patterns of diversity and commonality we find in different functional and regional areas and what they imply for the challenge of cooperation under diversity. Contributions in this section therefore examine general diversity in civil security governance in different European states and regional organizations as well as more specific differences in states' response to the swine flu (H1N1) pandemic in 2009.

Raphael Bossong and Hendrik Hegemann map and examine the institutional, legal and cultural diversity in European civil security governance systems based on a novel comparative survey of twenty-two national civil security systems. The examination reveals limited similarities that could be attributed to shared needs and the changed post-Cold War context. Beyond that, administrative responsibilities, legal frameworks and operational practices continue to differ markedly, backed up by national cultural contexts and historical experiences. Some cultural and functional clusters of specific countries can be observed, but patterns of conformity and diversity are neither strong nor universal. Hence, they stress that we cannot simply presuppose strong convergence towards civil security approaches and mechanisms in response to putatively shared security challenges or widespread isomorphism following universally applicable 'best practices'. They conclude that civil security cooperation under diversity needs to take the form of flexible, reflexive and inclusive governance that shows a genuine and fine-grained appreciation for both diversity and commonality.

In the next chapter, Piotr Matczak, Vera-Karin Brazova, Visnja Samardzija and Iwona Pinskwar look at civil security governance systems in the so-called 'new' EU Member States (with focus on the post-communist countries in Central and Eastern Europe), which have been subject to special pressures for change following the end of the Cold War. They analyse these countries with regard to the types of threats that actually occurred, the public perception of these threats and the organization of civil security governance systems seeking to prevent, prepare for, respond to and recover from such risks. The chapters investigates whether the new member states constitute a specific cluster in terms of threats and risk perception and actual disaster risks and whether the shape and evolution of their systems can be attributed to these specific features. The analysis shows that the assertion about a distinctive path of civil security governance systems development in the new member states cannot be sustained. Rather, they resemble the combination of some broad overlapping trends and the persistence of case-specific contingency and diversity. The authors argue that the similarities in the countries' civil security governance systems are particularly driven by the geographic conditions and related risks.

Vera-Karin Brazova and Piotr Matczak also delve into a specific crisis, namely the so-called swine flu (H1N1 influenza) which resulted in global pandemics declared by the World Health Organization (WHO) in 2009/2010. They regard this case as a 'natural experiment' that exposed many countries to the same challenge at the same time and therefore allows for comparative inferences. The case study not only confirms the great diversity of responses to crises among European countries found in other cases studies as well, but it also elucidates the particular challenges of crisis management under conditions of inherent uncertainty, especially regarding the legitimacy of governments and experts. The authors show that the reaction among European countries displayed some similarities, such as a tendency for centralization in the particularly complex case of an epidemic, but was not uniform, for example regarding the governments' communication strategies, the kind of stakeholders involved and the ensuing reaction of the public. Moreover, there was a general tendency to rely on precautionary action in the face of uncertainty, provoking charges of overreaction, for example in regard to the purchase of vaccines. However, this seemed to be perceived as largely legitimate by the public and there were no widespread or significant reforms.

Finally, Daniel Petz draws attention to a global trend towards stronger regional cooperation in civil security governance. Regional organizations increasingly engage in joint activities to reduce disaster risk, prevent disasters, prepare for disasters and respond to disasters. Petz maps the landscape of regional organizations in disaster risk management and compares regional organizations in Europe with their counterparts around the globe along a framework of 17 indicators. He shows that the massive increase in regional activities in disaster risk management has gone hand in hand with a shift from the perception of disasters caused by natural hazards as mostly an issue of disaster response to a more comprehensive disaster risk management paradigm that sees managing natural hazards more holistically throughout the whole disaster management cycle. The chapter also confirms the heterogeneity and diversity of regional organizations as well as the special role of the EU as most advanced and comprehensive venue for regional civil security governance.

The challenge of transformation

The second part addresses the question of transformation. Civil security governance in Europe and beyond has been undergoing a period of profound change since the end of the Cold War, as reflected in new concepts, laws and institutions for all-hazards risk management or disaster resilience. As indicated above, the concept of civil security is reflective of these very changes. But still, there is not much research on the specific manifestations and degrees of transformation in different areas, its regional and global drivers and the actual levels and mechanisms of learning, diffusion and convergence across countries.

First, Simon Hollis sheds lights on the complex multilevel relationship between global standards and regional practices in Europe and the way they shape convergence and diffusion across countries and regions. He shows that transformation in civil security governance is a contingent, interrelational and contested process where the promotion of a global 'culture of prevention' faces important obstacles and challenges at the regional and national level. Reflected through the modern practice of setting global objectives, such as the HFA, global awareness on disaster reduction has clearly intensified. Visions of safer cities, societies and nation-states are often projected in these and other global conferences with reference to existing global norms such as human rights and gender equality. The EU has been a significant actor in not only promoting disaster resilience globally, but also in translating these global visions into local practices. Findings reveal that direct influence from the global or regional levels has been limited and no short-term solutions exist. However, Hollis suggests that the EU and other international venues can play an important role advancing a culture of prevention as a general ethos rather than a concrete policy, if they show long-term and sustained commitment and manage to surpass financial and institutional hurdles.

In their chapter, Timothy Prior, Michael Herzog and Florian Roth scrutinize the concept of resilience that has risen to prominence in recent debates about transformations in civil security governance. Technical natural hazard management, the traditionally dominant mode of civil security governance, has been increasingly challenged by new approaches to handling hazards that emphasize decentralized, self-organizing structures for flexible responses to challenges posed by complexity and unpredictability. The concept of resilience has been at the centre of this transformative process. Adopting a broad historical perspective on the changing interaction between people and risk environments, the chapter illustrates how the means of dealing with hazards have been characterized by a gradual centralization, systematization and technocratization since the Middle Ages before more recent experiences facilitated a partial return to rather decentralized and people-centred approaches that build upon long-standing local knowledge to deal with hazards in context- and circumstance-specific ways. This also signals a potential redistribution in the roles citizens and states. Prior, Herzog and Roth show that resilience is gaining traction in natural hazards discourse and practice, but also acknowledge that this transformations needs to deal with crucial challenges and ambivalences.

In the final chapter on the challenge of transformation, Edward Deverell turns to the question of learning from crisis, an essential task and enduring challenge for civil security governance. This aspect is important to understand how actors can direct and moderate processes of transformation. He focuses especially on public and regulated systems for accident investigation in EU member states and the organizing structures for such investigations. The argument for a more structured approach to learning from crises in EU member states emerges from a case study of crisis events and investigations in the case of Sweden. Deverell finds that such accident investigation systems are not designed to cover the more complex and diffuse notion of a crisis. In particular, the chapter highlights a systemic gap between standardized procedures for accident review, which are institutionally embedded in Sweden, and the challenges of learning from various kinds of crises that transcend regular systems for civil security governance. This is unfortunate as post hoc crisis investigation is essential for organizational crisis prevention and societal resilience.

The challenge of cooperation

Finally, the third part of this volume focuses on cooperation and more specifically asks what role the EU can and should play as actor and provider of civil security governance against the backdrop of observed patterns of diversity and transformation. This poses challenges not only for research on EU security governance, but also for questions about effective and appropriate mechanisms to facilitate cooperation as well as about the level of EU-wide coordination, regulation and standardization that is considered feasible, desirable and legitimate.

Looking at the specific functional needs, capacities and challenges for crisis management in Europe, Sanneke Kuipers and Arjen Boin examine the EU's role as transboundary crisis manager with regard to a specific capacity (sense-making) and in relation to a specific crisis (the Icelandic Ash Crisis 2010). They argue that once a threat crosses geographic and system borders, capacities to deal with these threats tend to be insufficient at the national level. They stress that national authorities will have to collaborate in order to share information, make critical decisions and communicate in a joint fashion. Studying the example of the 2010 Icelandic ash crisis, they find that the EU played a critical role in facilitating the orchestrated and joint revision of national risk perceptions, though it lacked a clear legal basis. From this, Kuipers and Boin go on to draw the conclusion that the EU can, and perhaps should, be the go-to venue for transboundary crisis management efforts. The EU has the infrastructure in place to serve and exploit such gatherings. The EU needs to prepare to speed up the process of information sharing and the search for a common interpretation of escalating events. By creating a true focal point for expertise, data collection, information sharing and international decision-making, the EU can become a hub for transboundary crisis management.

Following on from this specific management role, Han Dorussen, Evangelos Fanoulis and Emil Kirchner examine how crises in civil security have promoted EU-wide standards in civil security governance and EU authoritative actions. They note that EU institutions are increasingly engaged in civil security governance in the member states, and that a state-centric approach is no longer adequate to understand the provision of civil security across Europe. To varying degrees, the EU has acquired responsibilities to regulate the full spectrum of civil security provisions, drawing on competences from Civil Protection and the AFSJ. Comitology, in particular the role of advisory and regulatory committees and agencies, has been instrumental in providing the EU with such executive powers. The chapter examines how the EU formulated secondary EU legislation in response to a number of signature crises across different EU policy areas. The analysis demonstrates that, while intergovernmental practices and interstate cooperation remain salient features of civil security governance, the responsibilities undertaken by the EU institutions and in particular the European Commission, are more substantial than a strictly intergovernmental perspective would suggest. These cases show that the political agency of EU committees and agencies matters; faced with the need to respond to crises and given the responsibility to protect core principles of European integration, the EU institutions have been able to expand their authority and remit, creating a European space of civil security governance.

Focusing further on the organizational and institutional capacities through which EU action can and should unfold, Magnus Ekengren then discusses how the shortcomings of traditional forms of EU cooperation in the civil security area have forced the Union to invent and experiment with new methods of coordination and compliance. Specifically, he compares the EU's experience in foreign and security policy and its experience with various capacity goals with ongoing policy debates in the area of civil protection. He argues that the European Defence Agency and related 'governance by objectives' may, in fact, serve as a useful model to advance transboundary cooperation and crisis management structures under conditions of persistent national diversity and sovereignty constraints.

Reflecting the, so far, scarce scholarly attention devoted to EU civil security governance, Mark Rhinard concludes this part with an overview of supranational developments in this often neglected area of European integration. He illustrates that, over the past two decades, cooperation on issues related to protecting people and critical infrastructures from different kinds of hazards has grown rapidly. From food-borne diseases to radiation leaks, and from satellite monitoring to risk assessment, a few areas of European 'sovereignty pooling' have emerged as vividly as that taking place in civil security within the EU. Yet, such developments, Rhinard argues, have largely escaped the attention of EU scholars, thus depriving the field of a rich set of empirics that can help us understand European integration. He goes on to sketch various theoretical avenues and research agendas that could be benefit from this extended empirical basis, ranging from neo-functionalism, new institutionalism to crisis management and critical security studies. He thus submits that the EU's role in crisis management provides a strong incentive for scholars to review their empirical, theoretical and normative understandings of European integration.

Bossong and Hegemann finally review the varied empirical insights provided by this volume and set out the potential for further research beyond EU studies. We thus hope that this volume will serve as a starting point for a wider and more sustained academic as well as public engagement with this growing and increasingly multilevel field of civil security governance.

Notes

1. We thank Eva-Maria Reh for helpful research assistance.
2. http://www.interieur.gouv.fr/Le-ministere/Securite-civile, date accessed 20 June 2014.
3. http://cordis.europa.eu/programme/rcn/861_en.html, date accessed 24 November 2014.
4. http://www.civilsecurity.se/en/sacs-home, date accessed 20 June 2014.

References

Alexander, D. (2002) 'From Civil Defence to Civil Protection – and Back Again', *Disaster Prevention and Management*, 11, 209–213.
van Asselt, M. and O. Renn (2011) 'Risk Governance', *Journal of Risk Research*, 14, 431–449.
Attinà, F. (ed.) (2012) *The Politics and Policies of Relief, Aid and Reconstruction: Contrasting Approaches to Disasters and Emergencies* (Basingstoke: Palgrave Macmillan).
Attinà, F. (2013) *Merging Policies as Strategy against Emergency Threats: The EU's Institutional Response to Disasters, Risk and Emergencies*. ReShape Online Papers Series 01/13 (Catania: University of Catania).
Baumann, Z. (2006) *Liquid Fears* (Cambridge: Polity Press).
Beck, U. (1992) *Risk Society: Towards a New Modernity* (London: Sage).
Beck, U. (1999) *World Risk Society* (Cambridge: Polity).
Bigo, D. (2002) 'Security and Immigration: Toward a Critique of the Governmentality of Unease', *Alternatives: Global, Local and Political*, 27, 63–92.

Bigo, D., S. Carrera, E. Guild and R. B. J. Walker (eds.) (2010) *Europe's 21st Century Challenge: Delivering Liberty* (Farnham: Ashgate).
Biscop, S. (ed.) (2013) *The Routledge Handbook of European Security* (London: Routledge).
Boin, A. and M. Ekengren (2009) 'Preparing for the World Risk Society: Towards a New Security Paradigm for the European Union', *Journal of Contingencies and Crisis Management*, 17, 285–294.
Boin, A., M. Ekengren and M. Rhinard (2006) 'Protecting the Union: Analysing an Emerging Policy Space', *Journal of European Integration*, 28, 405–421.
Boin, A., M. Ekengren and M. Rhinard (2013) *The European Union as Crisis Manager: Patterns and Prospects* (Cambridge: Cambridge University Press).
Boin, A., M. Ekengren, A. Missiroli, M. Rhinard and B. Sundelius (2007) *Building Societal Security in Europe: The EU's Role in Managing Emergencies* (Brussels: EPC Working Paper).
Bossong, R. and M. Rhinard (2013a) 'European Internal Security as a Public Good', *European Security*, 22, 129–147.
Bossong, R. and M. Rhinard (2013b) 'The EU Internal Security Strategy: Towards a More Coherent Approach to EU Internal Security?' *Studia Diplomatica*, 66, 45–58.
Brazova, V. K., P. Matczak and V. Takacs (2014) 'Evolution of Civil Security Systems: The Case of three Central European Countries', *Journal of Risk Research* (Online First).
Bremberg, N. (2010) 'Security, Governance and Community Beyond the European Union: Exploring Issue-Level Dynamics in Euro-Mediterranean Civil Protection', *Mediterranean Politics*, 15, 169–188.
Bremberg, N. and M. Britz (2009) 'Uncovering the Diverging Institutional Logics of EU Civil Protection', *Cooperation and Conflict*, 44, 288–308.
Burgess, P. (2011) *The Ethical Subject of Security: Geopolitical Reason and the Threat Against Europe* (London: Routledge).
Buzan, B. and L. Hansen (2009) *The Evolution of International Security Studies* (Cambridge: Cambridge University Press).
Buzan, B. and O. Wæver (2003) *Regions and Power: The Structure of International Security* (Cambridge: Cambridge University Press).
Chandler, D. (2014) *Resilience: The Governance of Complexity* (London: Routledge).
Christou, G., S. Croft, M. Ceccorulli and S. Lucarelli (2010) 'European Union Security Governance: Putting the "Security" Back In', *European Security*, 19, 341–359.
Coaffee, J., D. Murakami Wood and P. Rogers (2008) *The Everyday Resilience of the City: How Cities Respond to Terrorism and Disaster* (Basingstoke: Palgrave Macmillan).
Collier, S. J. and A. Lakoff (2008) 'The Vulnerability of Vital Systems. How Critical Infrastructures Became a Security Problem', in M. Dunn Cavelty and K. Søby Kristensen (eds.) *Securing the 'Homeland': Critical Infrastructure, Risk and (In)Security* (London: Routledge), pp. 17–39.
de Franco, C. and C. O. Meyer (eds.) (2011) *Forecasting, Warning and Responding to Transnational Risks* (Basingstoke: Palgrave Macmillan).
den Boer, M. (2014) 'Policy, Polity and Politics in Brussels: Scenarios for the Shift from Sovereignty to Solidarity', *Cambridge Review of International Affairs*, 27, 48–65.

Dory, A. (2003) 'American Civil Security: The US Public and Homeland Security', *Washington Quarterly*, 27, 37–52.

Dunn Cavelty, M. and K. S. Kristensen (eds.) (2008) *Securing the 'Homeland': Critical Infrastructure, Risk and (In)Security* (London: Routledge).

Ehrhart, H.-G., H. Hegemann and M. Kahl (2014) 'Towards Security Governance as a Critical Tool: A Conceptual Outline', *European Security*, 23, 145–162.

Ekengren, M. (2006) 'New Security Challenges and the Need for New Forms of EU Cooperation: The Solidarity Declaration against Terrorism and the Open Method of Coordination', *European Security*, 15, 89–111.

Ekengren, M. (2008) 'From a European Security Community to a Secure European Community: Tracing the New Security Identity of the EU', in H. G. Brauch et al. (eds.) *Globalization and Environmental Challenges: Reconceptualizing Security in the 21st Century* (New York: Springer), pp. 695–704.

Eriksson, J. (eds.) (2001) *Threat Politics: New Perspectives on Security, Risk and Crisis Management* (Aldershot: Ashgate).

Eriksson, J. and M. Rhinard (2006) 'The Internal-External Security Nexus: Notes on an Emerging Research Agenda', *Cooperation and Conflict*, 44, 243–267.

European Commission (2010a). *The EU Internal Security Strategy in Action: Five Steps Towards a More Secure Europe*. COM (2010) 673. 22 November 2010.

European Commission (2010b) *Risk Assessment and Mapping Guidelines for Disaster Management*. SEC (2010) 1626. 21 December 2010.

European Commission (2014) *The Post 2015 Hyogo Framework for Action: Managing Risks to Achieve Resilience*. COM (2014) 216 final. 8 April 2014.

European Council (2010) 'The Stockholm Programme: An Open and Secure Europe Serving and Protecting Citizens', *Official Journal of the European Union*. 2010/C 155/01. 4 May 2010.

Furedi, F. (2005) *Culture of Fear: Risk-Taking and the Morality of Low Expectation* (London: Continuum).

Hannigan, J. (2012) *Disasters without Borders: The International Politics of Natural Disasters* (Cambridge: Polity Press).

't Hart, P. and B. Sundelius (2013) 'Crisis Management Revisited: A New Agenda for Research, Training and Capacity Building Within Europe', *Cooperation and Conflict*, 48, 444–461.

Hollis, S. (2010) 'The Necessity of Protection: Transgovernmental Networks and EU Security Governance', *Cooperation and Conflict*, 45, 312–330.

Hollis, S. (2014) 'The Global Standardization of Regional Disaster Risk Management', *Cambridge Review of International Affairs*, 27, 319–338.

Hollis, S. (2015) *The Role of Regional Organizations in Disaster Risk Management: A Global Strategy for Resilience* (Basingstoke: Palgrave Macmillan).

Houben, M. (2005) *International Crisis Management: The Approach of European States* (London: Routledge).

Huysmans, J. (2014) *Security Unbound: Enacting Democratic Limits* (London: Routledge).

Huysmans, J., A. Dobson and R. Prokhovnik (eds.) (2006) *The Politics of Protection: Sites of Insecurity and Political Agency* (London: Routledge).

Joseph, J. (2013) 'Resilience as Embedded Neoliberalism: A Governmentality Approach', *Resilience – International Politics, Practices and Discourse*, 1, 38–52.

Kaunert, C. and K. Zwolski (eds.) (2013) *The EU as a Global Security Actor: A Comprehensive Analysis Beyond CFSP and JHA* (Basingstoke: Palgrave Macmillan).

Kaunert, C., S. Léonard and P. Pawlak (2012) 'Introduction: European Homeland Security – A European Strategy in the Making?', in C. Kaunert, S. Léonard and P. Pawlak (eds.) *European Homeland Security: A European Strategy in the Making?* (London: Routledge), pp. 1–14.

Kirchner, E. and J. Sperling (2007) *EU Civil Security Governance* (Manchester: Manchester University Press).

Kirchner, E., E. Fanoulis and H. Dorussen (2014) 'Civil Security in the EU: National Persistence versus EU Ambitions?' *European Security* (Online First).

Krieger, K. (2013) 'The Limits and Variety of Risk-Based Governance: The Case of Flood Management in Germany and England', *Regulation & Governance*, 7, 236–257.

Loader, I. and N. Walker (2007) *Civilizing Security* (Cambridge: Cambridge University Press).

May, P. J., A. E. Jochim and J. Sapotichne (2011) 'Constructing Homeland Security: An Anemic Policy Regime', *Policy Studies Journal*, 39, 285–307.

Mitsilegas, V., J. Monar and W. Rees (2003) *The European Union and Internal Security: Guardian of the People?* (Basingstoke: Palgrave Macmillan).

Norheim-Martinsen, P. (2013) *The European Union and Military Force: Governance and Strategy* (Cambridge: Cambridge University Press).

Perrow, C. (1984) *Normal Accidents: Living with High-Risk Technologies* (New York: Basic Books).

Perrow, C. (2007) *The Next Catastrophe: Reducing Our Vulnerabilities to Natural, Industrial, and Terrorist Disasters* (Princeton: Princeton University Press).

Quarantelli, E. L. (2000) *Disaster Planning, Emergency Management and Civil Protection: The Historical Development of Organized Efforts to Plan for and to Respond to Disasters.* University of Delaware. Disaster Research Center. Preliminary Paper 301.

Rhinard, M. and A. Boin (2009) 'European Homeland Security: Bureaucratic Politics and Policymaking in the EU', *Journal of Homeland Security and Emergency Management*, 6, 1–17.

Schroeder, U. C. (2011) *The Organization of European Security Governance: Internal and External Security in Transition* (London: Routledge).

Shalamanov, V., S. Hadjitodorov, T. Tagarev, S. Avramov, V. Stoyanov, P. Geneshky and N. Pavlov (2005) 'Civil Security: Architectural Approach in Emergency Management Transformation', *Information & Security*, 17, 75–101.

Sperling, J. and M. Webber (2014) 'Security Governance in Europe: A Return to System', *European Security*, 23, 126–144.

Stone Sweet, A., W. Sandholtz and N. Fligstein (2001) 'The Institutionalization of European Space', in A. Stone Sweet, W. Sandholtz and N. Fligstein (eds.) *The Institutionalization of Europe* (Oxford: Oxford University Press), pp. 1–28.

Wæver, O., B. Buzan, M. Kelstrup and P. Lemaitre (1993) *Identity, Migration and the New Security Agenda in Europe* (London: Pinter).

Wagnsson, C., J. Sperling and J. Hallenberg (eds.) (2009) *European Security Governance: The European Union in a Westphalian World* (London: Routledge).

Webber, M., S. Croft, J. Howorth, T. Terrif and E. Krahmann (2004) 'The Governance of European Security', *Review of International Studies*, 30, 3–26.

Part I
The Challenge of Diversity

2
Cooperation under Diversity? Exploring Cultural and Institutional Diversity in European Civil Security Governance[1]

Raphael Bossong and Hendrik Hegemann

Introduction

The recent increase in EU activities for crisis and disaster management has led to the emergence of a hybrid EU policy space for civil security governance (see Bossong and Hegemann in the introduction). As demonstrated in other contributions to this volume, the EU has created a growing number of institutions, policies and best practices to protect its citizens from various risks. This emerging field has been cast as an ambivalent mix of policies and institutions trying to reconcile the imperative for transnational cooperation and solidarity in the face of increasingly complex transboundary crises with the need to respect national desires for sovereignty and subsidiarity (Ekengren et al., 2006; Boin et al., 2013b; Kirchner et al., 2014).

The preservation of sovereignty is not only an inherent interest of member states, but also reflects the fact that they are no uniform bloc when it comes to the organization of civil security governance systems and the possible benefits of supranational integration. For example, especially 'Southern' and 'Northern' EU member states have frequently disagreed over the exact depth and scope of European civil security cooperation and coordination, especially when it moves to operational and regulatory questions beyond the identification of common risks. These differences relate to very diverse institutional and cultural structures and traditions shaping crisis and disaster management within member states (Bremberg and Britz, 2009). Thus, the future development of EU civil security policy strongly depends on the capabilities and ideas that member states bring to the table. Before well-grounded assessments of the limits and opportunities facing European cooperation in the civil security field can be made, it is essential to first examine the situation at the level of nation-states.

Greater knowledge of the existing level of diversity is also necessary in light of the fact that we cannot simply presuppose a strong convergence of civil security approaches and mechanisms in response to putatively shared security challenges. In the field of crisis and disaster management, some analysts have pointed to increased cross-national convergence due to the growing threats from natural and technological disasters in the globalized post-Cold War world (Quarantelli, 2000) and to growing isomorphism spurred by the activities of global and regional standard-setting organizations in the 'world polity' (Hollis, 2014; see also Hollis, in this volume). This research, thus, accentuates the surprising similarity of general approaches to civil security governance across different Western jurisdictions. Consequentially, they do not study patterns of diversity and divergence in any detail and 'local differences often appear as little more than an inconvenient exception to the general trend' (Zedner, 2003, p. 166). However, the debate could also be framed the other way around. In this case, the question becomes why we still see so many differences when looking at the details of national security architectures and cultures despite the alleged rise of new transnational risks in the 'world risk society'. Some scholars have pointed in this direction and stressed the persistence of cultural and institutional fragmentation and diversity in European security, notwithstanding broader global transformations towards new conceptions of comprehensive security (Burgess, 2009). Hence, patterns of national similarity or diversity remain an open question to be answered by empirical research and cannot be assumed at the outset.

Overall, we still do not very well understand the national underpinnings of European civil security governance. The limited number of comparative studies usually either select a very limited number of countries (Bremberg and Britz, 2009; Brazova et al., 2014) or focus on rather narrow functional areas like flood management (Krieger, 2013) or the response to specific crisis events, such as the H1N1 epidemic (Brazova et al., in this volume), or a special dimension of crisis management systems, such as countries' rules and mechanisms for international assistance and cooperation (Houben, 2005). We, therefore, lack a systematic and comprehensive analysis of European civil security governance systems as a whole.

An emphasis on comprehensiveness seems especially pertinent with a view to the notion of civil security governance underpinning this volume. Civil security is a 'hybrid area' (Kirchner et al., 2014, p. 2) that cuts across functional boundaries and administrative levels and may be more a matter of emergent governance patterns than clear political design. Keeping in mind the increasingly blurred divide between internal and external security as well as the shift from military-focused civil defence systems to broader notions of crisis and risk management, civil security policy now stretches across various functional, legal and political sectors. Civil security further includes different formal as well as more informal institutional structures and processes, features a range of public but also private actors, ranging from technology companies to voluntary rescue organizations. Finally, it touches upon various normative and cultural views, for example regarding state–society relations and the use of the military. It thereby meets the common understanding of security governance as described in the recent literature (Kirchner and Sperling, 2007a; Hollis, 2010; Schroeder, 2011), which highlights the aspects of actor and regulatory complexity as well as the need for a shared, if limited, normative underpinning.

In other words, security governance highlights coordination processes with regard to challenges that cannot be contained by standard operating procedures, fixed sets of actors and hierarchical legal structures. In this context, we do not intend to draw a categorical distinction between flexible governance regimes that arise from the 'bottom-up' and more complex forms of overarching steering, which involves various hierarchical and network approaches as expressed by the notion of 'meta-governance' (Jessop, 2011; Bossong, 2014). Instead, we expect a mix of explicit strategies and tools to deal with the boundary-spanning problems of civil security provision, such as by the creation of new coordination structures, as well as more diffuse processes of adaptation and coordination, as in the case of ad hoc consultations and response mechanisms between shifting actor networks for various crises scenarios. At the same time, claims about the universal blessings of purportedly consensual, flexible and functional security governance at various political levels should not be accepted uncritically. Depending on the specific cultural and institutional predispositions, security governance can take very different forms in different geographic contexts (Kirchner and Sperling, 2007b; Norheim-Martinsen, 2013) and also implies patterns of exclusion, incompatibility and possibly conflict between different governance regimes (Ehrhart et al., 2014).

With these aims in mind, this chapter presents key findings from a novel and comprehensive empirical comparison of European civil security governance systems conducted by an international collaborative research project.[2] In this context, 'civil security governance systems' are defined as institutional structures, laws and societal arrangements that jointly determine how a given country typically handles major crises and disasters that challenge the physical integrity of its economy or critical infrastructures and endanger the personal security of its citizens. The available data on 22 such governance systems does not cover all EU member states and includes three non-members (Norway, Serbia and Switzerland), of which the former two participate in the EU Civil Protection Mechanism. Hence, it remains limited in its generalizability. The comparison is also not designed on the basis of a theoretical model explaining patterns of policy and institutional convergence and diffusion across cases. Yet, the analysis offers a broad and structured comparison of hitherto unavailable depth and scope, and thus charts out some of the main coordinates for different European national civil security governance systems.[3]

Specifically, we trace three major dimensions. First, we analyse the formal administrative and legal structures that set the basic parameters for crisis and disaster management (e.g. the degree and form of (de)centralization). Second, the chapter delves into the cultural and normative foundations affecting views and attitudes towards civil security, such as traditions of state–society relations. Third, we elucidate the operational procedures and practices, such as mechanisms for risk assessment, which determine how civil security is organized and implemented in practice. This follows common practice in institutionalist comparisons of systems for security and risk governance (Krieger, 2013, p. 244). Still, these three dimensions primarily serve as heuristic clusters and there is some overlap. It is, therefore, not our intention to make a case for the dominance of one cluster or perspective over another.

In conclusion, we find a high degree of diversity on all comparative dimensions. However, the observed differences give only limited support for archetypical contrasts between 'Northern' and 'Southern' or 'old' and 'new' member states, whereas case-specific structural, historical and cultural influences appear more important. At the same time, one can also identify some basic shared themes across all national case studies, such as the challenge to move towards more risk-based forward planning and how to review or learn from past crises. Overall, we are faced with multiple, yet largely equivalent or equifinal, governance regimes for civil security, which are generally a synthesis of several logics and legacies. Instead of strong convergence and harmonization across European countries, this also suggests that flexible, hybrid forms of transnational coordination and cooperation may well be possible.

Institutional and legal structures: Some broad trends, but diverse ways of organizing civil security

The first category of our analysis is a classic – and even for a governance perspective highly relevant – comparison of formal legal and institutional structures, as is also expressed in levels of political and administrative centralization and decentralization. This also applies to the operational responsibilities of the different public agencies involved in crisis and disaster management, which relates to an ongoing debate on the benefits of central lead agencies versus flexible and less hierarchical governance models (Boin et al., 2013a).

Legal structures for civil security

The post-Cold War period has witnessed a basic change from military-oriented civil defence towards genuinely civilian and comprehensive concepts for risk and disaster management. While this process has been identified as a broad trend in Western countries, the exact implementation of civilian control and the adaptation of legal structures remains an important challenge (Quarantelli, 2000; Alexander, 2002). This goes along with debates about the changing domestic role of militaries in the context of blurring divides between internal and external security, which have intensified since the attacks of 9/11 (Burgess, 2009; Weiss, 2013). Our analysis shows that all studied countries underwent corresponding major reform processes over the last 15–20 years. Thus, one can identify a general move towards civilian-led all-hazards risk management, but the extent and form of changes vary considerably and reflect the diverse national legal systems.

Classic legal frameworks for crisis management have typically condensed in conceptions of a state of emergency, understood as an exceptional constitutional provision in order to respond to foreign violent/armed threats and (in some cases) internal uprisings. Thus, a declaration of a state of emergency typically includes the possibility of derogation from civil liberties and the constitutional separation of powers. As an international counterpart, the European Convention on Human Rights (of which all studied states are parties of) restricts extensive derogation from human rights to the existence of a public emergency that threatens the life of the nation. Only 3 of the 22 studied countries do not have provisions for such a formal emergency declaration, namely Austria, Sweden and Switzerland. The two latter states have not been part of the major European Wars of the 20th century and all three states officially embrace the principle of neutrality, which may explain these divergent legal rules.

Since the end of the Cold War, these established frameworks were considered inadequate in light of new security challenges, which replaced the dominant fear of nuclear war in Europe. Crisis management became increasingly geared towards dealing with natural disasters and other 'civilian' crises, including new and complex risks like critical infrastructure failure. Such a situation triggers different needs than a state of war or conflict, though some limiting measures might be more important, as for example the derogation from property rights. Therefore, the majority of studied countries made separate provisions for declaring a state of disaster that primarily enable facilitated operational coordination and more limited civil rights constraints. For instance, the new Polish and Hungarian constitutions separate between the state of emergency and the state of natural disaster. The Nordic countries stand out due to their principle of 'conformity', which underlines that authorities have to abide by regular legal standards as far as possible. In other countries, such as Germany, one can find a greater willingness to use blanket clauses that empower public authorities to take 'necessary measures' to avert and to respond to an exceptional crisis or threats in conformity with the proportionality principle and constitutional rights. Six of the studied countries (France, Ireland, Malta, Netherlands, Sweden and UK) lack an overall legal framework for the declaration of peacetime disasters and emergencies, which is, however, compensated to varying degrees in sector-specific legislation on health emergencies.

The scope and depth of reforms in civil security law differed considerably across European countries. The civil security reform process in former communist countries went along with the formulation of fundamentally new constitutional and legislative structures. In many Western European states – among them Germany, the Netherlands and Switzerland – debates instead revolved around the distribution of competences in multilevel governance and the development of specialized networks and coordination functions for new threat scenarios. This means that in a few major countries, including Germany and Italy, the inherited difference between civil defence and civil protection remains encoded in formal laws and competences. Thus, these countries still have separate systems of legislations for civil defence and civil protection including respective constitutional prescriptions.

At the same time, it must be recognized that the phrasing and understanding of core concepts for civil security remain diverse across different cases and languages. National definitions typically stress that a crisis refers to situations that affect a large number of people, infrastructures, goods or other values and require some form of coordination above normal emergency structures. Beneath these broad commonalities, however, differences across case studies are considerable, ranging from mere terminological divergences to different formal procedures for crisis management that hinge on specific definitions. While general terms like 'disaster', 'accident' or 'emergency' are often used for open-ended, everyday use, 'crisis' is often used as a more programmatic concept to activate different mechanism. Yet, the threshold of what is labelled a crisis is interpreted very differently, which is linked to different degrees of formalization and legal consequences, as discussed above. These terminological and conceptual differences are not trivial and can have important legal and political consequences (Zedner, 2003), such as for cooperation and coordination across levels and borders. In this context, the US federal emergency management system and its efforts and challenges to develop a more standardized doctrine for response management may be used as an illustrative comparison (Birkland and DeYoung, 2011).

Against this background, the currently dominant legislative frameworks for civil security governance across cases are umbrella laws for emergency coordination that leave many more sectors and geographically specific tasks open to more detailed regulation. Most studied countries have central statutory frameworks with one to two key laws, which typically go hand in hand with more narrow sets of legislation regulating distinct sectors, where crisis management is only one of several considerations. For example, in Sweden there are two main civil security laws, which are accompanied by various other laws and ordinances that regulate more specific aspects, such as health issues or the role of the armed forces. Six countries (Austria, Croatia, Germany, Lithuania, Norway and Switzerland) have highly fragmented civil security legislation with more than six key laws. This fragmentation is mainly, but not only (see unitary states such as Lithuania), due to the existence of separate legal frameworks at national and regional levels. In line with the importance of the subsidiarity principle in these legal systems, the legislative competence for peacetime crisis management in some of these countries lies primarily on the regional levels whereas federal competences originated from wartime civil defence, which results in a fragmented legislation. In Austria, for example, the federal level has the legislative competence regarding disaster prevention and preparedness, while the regional *Länder* have the competence relating to crisis response (with the exception of some areas, such as epidemics and mining disasters).

Institutional centralization and decentralization

Related debates about the necessary and optimal degree of centralization or decentralization have a long tradition in the civil security field. While actual crisis experiences often facilitate public calls for the creation of central authorities and lead agencies with visible responsibility and traditional approaches to crisis management praised the advantages of clear lines of authority, scholars of modern governance and public management for the last two decades have tended to highlight the benefits of decentralization, flexible networks and local solutions ('t Hart et al., 1993; Boin et al., 2013a). Our findings indicate a mixed picture across all studied cases, without clear evidence on the advantages or disadvantages of either position. Crisis and disaster management is often more decentralized than other policy fields, but the specific arrangements still reproduce the diverse basic setups of member states. At the same time, civil security governance systems in Central/Northern countries on average tend to be more decentralized than those in Eastern/Southeastern countries.

In 16 of the 22 countries that were investigated, the levels used for crisis management purposes are identical with general governmental levels and structures. Most of these countries usually have three or four tier systems of administration.[4] Moreover, in many countries, the specific patterns and structures can vary internally with regard to different functional areas. Following on from these internal multilevel structures, countries differ with regard to the rules and arrangements for up- and downscaling of crisis management responsibilities. In most countries, lower levels of government formally retain the authority to upscale responsibilities and request assistance from higher levels only if they choose to do so. This means that operational civil security governance is in many cases out of the hand or sight of national administrations. This could be compared to the challenges of EU regional policy, which has to account for an extremely high diversity of organizational capacities and nature of administrative units. Thus, it is far from clear who the appropriate political and operational counterpart is when dealing with transboundary crisis cooperation, since national agencies, international organizations or the EU often need to interact with local or regional authorities in a third state.

Whereas the preference for bottom-up solutions is very marked in federalist countries, many other countries eventually evolve into more mixed systems of rather central and rather decentralized elements. For instance, in the Czech Republic crisis management is taken up automatically by higher levels when a crisis cuts across regions while similar mechanisms are phrased more loosely in other countries, such as in Norway, Poland and France, leading to a more regularized and somewhat more centralized crisis management system. Yet, there are also counterexamples for development from centralized to more decentralized systems in several countries, such as Italy, Poland and Serbia. Looking across all cases, one can note that operational crisis management is a shared responsibility of several local agencies and emergencies responders, most notably fire brigades, emergency medical services, police and voluntary emergency organizations. When it comes to special, complex risks that demand particular expertise, such as epidemics but also large-scale forest fires, a number of functional agencies kick in and may resume overall leadership. Yet, there is no clear pre-determined or discernible logic in most countries, so that coordination structures are often organized on an ad-hoc basis and differ depending on the crisis situation authorities are confronted with.

However, many countries have created single lead agencies with an integral responsibility for crisis management. For example, the Croatian National Rescue Board is in charge of overall coordination from the central level and the National Directorate General for Disaster Management in Hungary has supervisory competence for other agencies. Where existent, the powers of national lead agencies are more constrained in less centralized countries. The Norwegian Directorate for Civil Protection and Emergency Planning or the Swedish Civil Contingency Agency might be considered 'lead agencies' but implementation remains mostly in the hand of the local level of emergency services. To operate comparable compromise arrangements is a special challenge for countries with strong federalist traditions and a legally mandated separation of civil defence and civil protection (Austria, Germany and Switzerland), where the coordination of a common approach across levels is difficult and usually requires some kind of formal, threat-specific differentiation. Still, some of these countries pride themselves of new overarching concepts, such as Austria's 'comprehensive security provision' or Switzerland's 'integrated system for the protection of the population'. This indicates a growing consensus on the need for conceptual and procedural integration, but should not be taken as evidence for a strong substantive convergence of governance systems.

In light of these mixed trends for further national coordination structures vs. a high degree of decentralization, we can sketch four heuristic groups among the 22 studied countries[5]: The first group has a clear and explicit preference for decentralized and localized bottom-up solutions placing responsibility at the lowest possible levels of government in all or most respects. This applies fully only to the federal countries Austria, Germany and Switzerland who embrace a strong interpretation of the principle of 'subsidiarity'. A second group of countries (Czech Republic, Finland, Ireland, Italy, Netherlands, Norway, Sweden and the UK) tend towards rather decentralized, bottom-up systems but also include some elements of centralization, though to different degrees. Within this rather diverse group, Finland, Netherlands, Norway and Sweden show a clear preference for decentralized arrangements, but also display limited elements of centralization. Thirdly, four countries (Croatia, Estonia, France, Poland and Romania) generally take rather centralized forms that constitute the basis for their civil security governance framework, but they have also taken significant steps to induce some forms of decentralization, such as the creation of so-called the 'Defence and Security Zones' in France. Finally, there is a group of six countries (Hungary, Latvia, Lithuania, Malta, Serbia and Slovakia) with more or less fully centralized systems. The borders between these groups are not always clear-cut, but this clustering indicates that decentralization is most established in Central/Northern European countries, whereas many 'new' and candidate countries in Southeastern Europe and the Baltic region have a higher propensity to adopt centralized models.

Cultural and normative foundations of civil security governance: Between common cultural clusters and case-specific traditions and experiences

The second dimension our survey looks at pertains to the cultural and normative foundations of civil security governance. It is an established finding in studies of risk assessment and perception that collective cultural beliefs and identities shape the scope of risks a society regards as important and the responses it considers appropriate (Douglas and Wildavsky, 1982). Moreover, scholars of security governance have argued that different systems of security governance depend on wider or deeper normative and cultural foundations (Kirchner and Sperling,

2007b; Norheim-Martinsen, 2013). However, culture is notoriously difficult to measure and has many facets, especially if one ascribes it such a foundational role. For the purposes of this contribution, we therefore cannot offer more than some broad heuristic findings and selective examples on cultural diversity. After providing a brief overview of potential cultural clusters in European civil security governance, we turn to two more specific features. First, we examine state–society relations in civil security as this depends on and reflects fundamental ideas, such as conceptions of security or views on the legitimacy of the state (Zedner, 2003). Taking up the debate on the more military-focused concept of strategic culture in Europe (Meyer, 2006), we, in a second time, take a look at the use of and attitudes towards the military in domestic crisis and disaster management and its effect on civil security governance.

Basic patterns of cultural diversity

As a first heuristic orientation, our 22 cases could potentially be grouped into several conventional cultural clusters, if one recognizes that there are numerous cross-cutting findings and that cultural stereotypes are not helpful. With these caveats in mind, a typical cross-country cultural influence is visible in the distinct Nordic principle of 'conformity', according to which state and society operate under normal legal and political standards even during crisis situations. This reflects the cultural proximity among Scandinavian countries, which also cooperate strongly on issues of civil security. In a similar vein, civil security in the primarily German-speaking countries (i.e. Austria, Germany and Switzerland) shows a great deal of similarity in many respects, such as the emphasis devoted to the principle of subsidiarity and the strong differentiation between military-focused civil defence and civilian oriented civil protection. It also appears that egalitarian, individualistic and secular societies, such as the Netherlands and the Nordic countries, demonstrate a preference for openness, local solutions and a critical attitude towards authorities also during crises. In contrast, some former communist countries, such as Latvia or Slovakia, do not prioritize active citizen participation, as taken up further below.

Citizens' security perceptions (see also Matzcak et al., in this volume) broadly correspond to this picture. Based on Eurobarometer data (European Commission, 2012), the generally lowest levels of concern regarding natural disasters, man-made disasters and terrorist attacks can be observed in three rather decentralized, high-capacity, North-Western member states (Finland, the Netherlands and Sweden). Conversely, the highest rates of concern were found in the Czech Republic, Hungary, Italy, Latvia, Poland, Romania and Slovakia. Thus, in general, many new member states – but also Italy – tend to be especially concerned while citizens in the Netherlands and Scandinavian countries are least concerned. However, several case studies, including those with countries with comparatively high levels of concern, underline that concern about civil emergencies and crisis in general remains low in comparison to other national issues for concern, such as economic decline, unemployment or environmental protection. That means that different levels of concerns about disaster may not necessarily tell us much about the shape of the national civil security governance system, but rather reflect an overall degree of popular trust or satisfaction. National, rather than regional, differences in threat perceptions are furthered by the experience of distinct signature crises that are kept as a central feature of the collective memory and often lead to political and institutional change. Examples of signature crises include the 2005 London bombings, the L'Aquila earthquake and the Oslo/Utøya attacks. These experiences led to a significant crisis in national legitimacy and are typically referred to as models or negative examples for national crisis management practitioners. This also shows that case-specific and contingent historical experiences and cultural influences ultimately appear more important than stereotypical cultural groupings. The described heuristic clusters, hence, should be treated with caution and not be overgeneralized.

State–society relations

Culture may also condition the different involvement of individual citizens as well as of organizations from the societal and private sector. In most countries, citizens are ready to actively assist, though in different formats. Forms of voluntary engagement vary significantly depending on cultural and historical background. Many countries, especially those with corporatist state traditions, highlight the formal inclusion of officially registered voluntary organizations whereas other countries with a more libertarian heritage prefer more flexible arrangements. Voluntary fire brigades, for example, are particularly significant and in some cases, such as in many areas of Austria and Germany, even largely complement professional forces. In contrast, the UK, for example, defines the participation of citizens in much less formal and institutionalized ways.

In this context, national civil protection organizations – which previously fulfilled armed-conflict-focused responsibilities in some countries – have increasingly taken up new roles as providers for emergency management as well as catalysts for wider citizen involvement in civil security governance. For example, the Swedish Voluntary Defence Organization and the Austrian Civil Protection Association focus on training and education to activate citizens and stimulate self-help with regard to various disasters and emergencies. The Irish 'Civil Defence' has come to encompass numerous specialized emergency voluntary services dealing with the civil security issues, such as the Cave Rescue Teams and River Rescue Units. The German Federal Technical Relief Agency offers personnel, extensive training as well as heavy equipment, such as water treatment units or bulldozers, for domestic and international disaster assistance.

Further systematic evidence on societal involvement in civil security governance is hard to come by, however. Less than half of the countries considered maintain official registers for volunteers and the numbers are often approximations or even not available. Moreover, the status of volunteers can be unclear and many volunteers work in several organizations, while some governments may over-report on the number of volunteers in contrast to genuine popular involvement. With these limitations in mind, one may set the overall number of volunteers in relation to the overall population, at least for those 15 out of the total of 22 cases where some figures are available. This provides indicative evidence for deeper historical legacies and path-dependencies in civil security governance systems or state–society relations. The highest numbers of volunteers per 1,000 capita can be recorded for Austria (49), Hungary (43), Czech Republic (31), Slovakia (31), Germany (22) and Switzerland (20).[6] Interestingly, Austria is followed by three countries with which it has close historical ties and two other primarily German-speaking countries. These countries share a certain neocorporatist tradition that benefits the emergence of formalized structures for societal participation through officially registered membership organizations. At the same time, some 'new' member states, which may have formally high number of volunteers – most notably in Hungary, Poland, Romania and Serbia – are still struggling with some of these legacies since many citizens have ambivalent attitudes regarding voluntary engagement in emergencies, going back to volunteerism campaigns during communist rule. As taken up below, this results in a limited shift to for-profit solutions to civil security tasks. But also in 'old' EU member states, voluntary organizations face deep challenges from societal meta-trends, such as domestic migration, growing workloads and demographic change.

Yet, one cannot detect a major and pervasive opposite trend for extensive privatization or outsourcing of security tasks to make up for declining civil society participation. In all studied cases, the basic approach towards the private sector is one of legal compliance rather than voluntary participation. Corporate actors have to observe extensive legal requirements for safety regulations, emergency plans or the maintenance of private fire fighting and rescue services for hazardous production sites. In many cases, this also entails the partial delegation of some emergency rescue services with regard to private assets, vessels, installations and related personnel, while exceptional crisis may trigger mechanisms for forced cooperation or use of private assets. Again, countries with a strong civil defence tradition, most notably the Nordic and Central European countries, often mandate companies to store specific goods and maintain stockpiles for the case of sustained emergencies, which are a rare occurrence. In some cases, this also includes mandatory logistical services by railway, telecommunications or trucking companies as well as the duty to maintain critical services, such as energy and water supply, during crisis. Many of the relevant companies are former state-owned monopolists and, hence, have traditionally close ties to the government.[7]

Beyond that, we see a varied pattern and limited evidence for public–private partnerships in civil security governance. This confirms earlier research finding that private sector involvement can take 'markedly different forms, even in neighboring jurisdictions' (Zedner, 2003, p. 169). Some smaller, new member states seem to have been more willing to outsource civil security tasks. For example, the three Baltic countries pay particular importance to the role of the private sector at all levels of preparedness and response. In Croatia and Poland, public civil security agencies actively outsource civil security tasks to private companies through subcontracting and tenders. This includes special tasks like the response to oil spills and mining disasters, but also the provision of shelters and sanitary equipment. Other small states, such as Malta, are also heavily reliant on active involvement of private actors to muster sufficient crisis management capacities. In the UK, with its traditional economic liberalism, engagement with the private sector is usually not formalized and legally mandated, but public agencies can and often do subcontract private actors for specific tasks through voluntary ad-hoc agreements. In the future, however, there may be more potential for convergence across countries on the role of public–private partnerships, as new functional pressures and growing EU activities in areas like critical infrastructure protection and 'cyber-security' have demanded the inclusion of specialized knowledge and enhanced outreach to private companies (Bossong, 2014).

Civil security governance and the contested domestic role of the military

As discussed above, civil defence systems geared towards the response to war and armed conflict have changed to primarily civilian risk management. This transformation relates to the literature on strategic cultures, which highlights very different and deep-seated attitudes towards the use of the military in European countries and the resulting limitations and challenges for EU security governance (Meyer, 2006; Norheim-Martinsen, 2013). One might expect that this also conditions the domestic role of national armed forces in responding to civilian crises. Across most studied countries, military forces more or less regularly contribute manpower and logistical capacities to large-scale emergency management operations, such as helicopters, to civil security efforts at the behest of civilian authorities, at least when it comes to exceptional and prolonged crises such as large-scale floods.

However, the frequency and ease with which the military is employed domestically varies considerably between countries. One logical difference lies in the overall resources of a country rather than its historical legacy and cultural context. Smaller countries or those with fewer resources might be more inclined or even forced to rely on the military for assistance during complex crisis response operations. For instance, in Malta the military reserve forces are an important auxiliary for crisis management operations in light of overall limited capacities and human resources. In countries that have not made the full transition from conscription system to professional armies the role of the military in civil security is also debated with a view to capacity and size. In Austria, the scenario that a professional army might lack the personnel to provide disaster assistance was used as a central – and eventually decisive – argument by supporters of the conscription system during a political referendum in January 2013. For militaries searching for new definitions and justifications of their role in a post-Cold War environment presenting themselves as crisis managers piling up sandbags rather than intervention armies in controversial overseas operations might thus be a promising strategy.

Non-functionalist, cultural factors accounting for the differential use of the military are divergent national traditions. The Nordic countries of Finland, Sweden and Norway have a tradition of total defence going back to their position during World War II and the Cold War, which is still visible in their ability to mobilize civil defence components to facilitate rescue operations today. In other countries, such as the Netherlands, military assistance is a rare occurrence as citizens expect the state to handle crises with civilian means. In some countries, the domestic role of the military continues to be a contentious political issue. Germany's federal armed forces have provided much applauded assistance during recent flood crises, but there has been a controversial debate about the deployment of the army for counterterrorist purposes since 9/11, including genuinely military equipment like combat aircrafts. This goes back to the country's special historical experiences that led to a strong separation of civilian and military spheres.

Practices and processes of civil security governance: Global trends meet local traditions

The finding of diverse institutional and legal structures as well as different cultural and normative foundations raises the question through which practices and processes civil security 'works' within these broader contexts. In particular, this section focuses on two broader trends in civil security and their implementation at the national level. First, practices and procedures for risk assessment and forward planning are promoted as global standard for rational governance (Power, 2004) and have gained increasing attention in the civil security field (Hollis, 2014; see also Hollis and Prior et al., in this volume). Second, processes for evaluation and quality assessment are considered critical for the evolution and improvement of civil security governance (see Deverell, in this volume).

Risk assessment and forward planning

The development and implementation of increasingly sophisticated and scientific models of risk management and forward planning have been a major fashion in post-Cold War civil protection (Quarantelli, 2000, pp. 18–20). Recent academic contributions also argue that comprehensive national risk assessments and risk registers for internal security policy constitute an important trend (Hagmann and Dunn Cavelty, 2012). As a leading example, Switzerland has taken a number of steps to advance explicit risk-based planning for natural hazards management at various levels of government, including through special tools and guidelines, and requires agencies to check their investments based on risk calculations.

Yet, other country case studies suggest that risk-based planning beyond conventional contingency plans at local and regional levels are faced with severe obstacles. A number of case studies suggest fragmented or uneven implementation across issue-areas (Norway) or regional units

(Germany, Austria), while other cases do not accord any weight to such processes. In fact, the majority of studied countries does not feature integrated and coherent budgetary planning for, or aggregate figures on, their national civil security governance systems, which presents an additional obstacle to steering preventive and preparatory efforts on the basis of new risk indicators. Furthermore, the experience of implementing common EU guidelines on national risk mapping underlines the importance of language barriers and different institutional, legal and cultural contexts. In spring 2014, the EU Commission presented a long-delayed report which highlighted the fragmented and uneven national risk mapping practices, with only 11 member states having reported full or substantial adoption of the common guidelines (European Commission, 2014, p. 4). This chimes in with more recent comparative work on national risk governance processes, which highlights 'slow, complex and often contradictory' developments (Rothstein et al., 2013, p. 231).

Evaluations and reviews in civil security governance

Evaluations and reviews of civil security systems are an important feature and challenge of contemporary crisis and disaster management. Scholars and practitioners continue to grapple with the search for effective mechanisms to assess the effectiveness and efficiency of civil security governance systems and draw lessons for reform and improvement, such as through crisis-induced learning (see Deverell in this issue). The popularity of these questions in many quarters mirrors the broader move towards 'evidence-based policy' and performance assessments in Western countries. There have been calls and attempts to apply this kind of thinking to a number of areas, including crime prevention and counterterrorism (Lum and Kennedy, 2012). Aside from fundamental criticism pointing to the contested and fallible nature of policy expertise and technocratic tendencies towards de-politicization, assessments of policy effectiveness and efficiency also have to struggle with intricate conceptual and methodological challenges, such as the search for appropriate indicators and the attribution of causal effects (Hegemann et al., 2013).

These challenges may explain why countries vary considerably in the frequency, systematization and formalization of review and evaluation processes, but also find it hard to develop accepted quality indicators and benchmarks. The number of professional and political inquiries differs due to diverse evaluation cultures as well as varying exposures to disasters. While some countries, such as the Netherlands and Sweden, feature a strong investigation culture in public policy and also a high density of evaluations and inquiries in the civil security field, the number in most countries is rather low. This can be due to the absence of major crises sparking strong pressure for reform or the generally rather low level of societal politicization in the civil security field, but it can also stem from legalistic and consensus-oriented traditions (e.g. Switzerland) or a fragile balance between political actors (e.g. Serbia). This does not mean, however, that inquiries, where they occur, cannot occasionally have major effects. In Norway, the 2011 Utøya and Oslo attacks, for example, served as a trigger event that shook the entire civil security system and initiated a series of investigations that produced a number of recommendations and initiated important changes. There are also differences in style and methodology. Civil security agencies in some countries conduct internal inquiries whereas others hire external experts and consultants or have independent review bodies, such as the Finish Safety Investigation Authority and the Swedish National Audit Office.

The diverse and intermittent evaluation practices underline the difficulties of providing grounded, accurate and unambiguous assessments of the overall level of effectiveness and efficiency of a country's civil security governance system. There are no common standards for effectiveness assessment in Europe, which could be expected to command wide acceptance and support. Some countries occasionally refer to technical international standards, such as the Hyogo Framework for Action, or to formalized thresholds like reaction times for emergency services. Yet, most evaluations generally follow case-specific questions and benchmarks set by political interests or reflecting recent crisis experiences leading to extended narratives of successes and failures in certain crisis management operations rather than general systematic evaluations of the quality of civil security governance systems. Keeping in mind the underlying methodological challenges as well as political implications and cultural differences, this is unlikely to change fundamentally.

Efficiency assessments are an especially difficult and underdeveloped feature of civil security governance. Only a few countries have even begun to collect more systematic data and to use investment review instruments; implementation of financial reviews remains sketchy and uneven. Similar findings have been noted for the field of counterterrorism (Mueller and Stewart, 2011). Even governments do not have a clear overview of civil security spending. This is due to inherent difficulties of measurement but also to the fact that civil security is not a coherent political and administrative field. Rather, it is a cross-cutting task with fuzzy borders and its widespread decentralization leads to complex multilevel financing. The scarcity of efficiency assessments also seems to indicate normative and political pitfalls. Mundane, run-of-the-mill bureaucratic politics complicates the allocation of scarce resources among competing agencies and levels according to clear agreed-upon indicators. Applying cost-effectiveness criteria to the protection of life and other essential goods may also create discomfort among many citizens as well as politicians trying to circumvent the delicate balance between the need to protect societies and prevalent fiscal constraints. Hence, any general baseline for desired or 'optimal' spending levels is likely to be contested on normative and functional grounds.

Conclusion

European civil security governance systems have undergone parallel, yet not necessarily strongly convergent, reform processes since the end of the Cold War. Civil defence provision has given way to more comprehensive, fully civilian-controlled civil protection and crisis management, even though the armed forces in most countries regularly provide important assistance services during major crises. This trend is matched by a tendency towards 'all-hazards' civil security governance, whereby diverse and often changing configurations of civilian authorities need to cooperate across functional boundaries to address the evolving nature of contemporary threats. However, one should not overstate the extent of convergent modernizations across the studied cases, since there is often a gap between rhetoric and practice, as illustrated with regard to the use of new forms of risk assessment and forward planning. Overall, different national administrative and legal structures as well as distinct cultural contexts and historical experiences continue to play a dominant role. Even though one can make out more hybrid arrangements that seek to match the benefits of centralization and decentralization in civil security governance different national structures and traditions remain decisive. Another, if not more important, difference between national civil security governance systems regards state–society relations and the role of the private sector. Observed governance regimes range from the highly formalized inclusion of officially registered emergency organizations with large capacities and hierarchical regulations and laws to very informal mechanisms and self-regulation. This may be related to some indicative cultural and historical clusters between Northern, Central, Southern and Eastern European countries, while some overlap and inconsistencies remain. This gives at least some credence to the utility of smaller, more regional forums for civil security cooperation, which also reflects the limited geographical reach of many physical hazards. Yet again, these possible clusters should not be reified and specifically national security cultures and idiosyncratic experiences remain of great, if not greatest, importance.

While attesting diversity among countries with different traditions, experiences and political-administrative systems might not be a very unusual finding, it has important ramifications for scholarly and political arguments about global convergence and the diffusion of new concepts for civil security governance. As alluded to in the introduction to this contribution, many authors stress processes towards isomorphism and the impact of global meta-trends, such as all-hazards risk management and the fusion of internal and external security. In the emerging transnational field of civil security governance, experts from governments, international organizations, industry or academia have advanced various standards, 'best practices', benchmarks and 'lessons learned' for effective, efficient and legitimate policy, often portraying them as technical, evidence-based and apolitical (Hannigan, 2012; Hollis, 2014). Indicators like the Hyogo Framework might offer some orientation and are also increasingly used in the European context, as evidenced by the recent EU peer evaluation of the UK according to the Hyogo Framework.[8] As with the related concept of 'resilience' (Chandler, 2014; see also Prior et al., in this volume), these standards are increasingly used as global gold standards and linked to normative debates about 'good governance' and 'human security'.

Yet, our discussion on evaluations and quality assessments in civil security governance showed that it is extremely difficult to develop accepted indicators. It is also not clear that there are obvious and shared functionalist pressures to converge on a particular, or supposedly most 'effective', model of civil security governance. Aside from exceptional 'signature' crises that have challenged the legitimacy of some national systems, such as the L'Aquila earthquake, the comparative study of 22 European countries suggests a high degree of flexibility and equivalent paths to addressing the most pressing concerns of contemporary crisis management. Diversity, hence, seems to be a reality to be dealt with rather than a problem to be solved. A narrow functional understanding of security governance propagating the non-reflexive implementation of specific governance forms for civil security without proper attention to underlying rifts, tensions and incompatibilities seems inappropriate (Ehrhart et al., 2014).

However, a governance perspective might still provide a basis for the EU to facilitate cooperation under diversity. Instead of advocating a 'best practice' on how to structure and organize a system, we should be inclined to trust in the emergent and diverse adaptive capacity of existing arrangements across countries and different levels of government. A more flexible and inclusive form of steering exchange and coordination, for example following the concept of meta-governance (Jessop, 2011; Bossong, 2014), might be more suitable to account for the discovered diversity and complexity. As the EU moves forward in finding its role in enhancing security through effective and legitimate civil security governance, a genuine and fine-grained appreciation for both diversity and commonality thus promises to pay dividends not just in cooperation, but also the end-goal: improving the security of the European population.

Notes

1. Parts of the work on this article were co-funded by the European Commission within the Seventh Framework (FP7) Programme [grant number FP7-SEC-2011-284678] (ANVIL – Analysis of Civil Security Systems in Europe).
2. ANVIL country studies covered ten interview-based case studies (Croatia, Finland, France, Germany, Italy, the Netherlands, Poland, Serbia, Sweden and UK) and 12 desk studies (Austria, Czech Republic, Estonia, Hungary, Ireland, Latvia, Lithuania, Malta, Norway, Romania, Slovakia and Switzerland). The detailed country studies and the analytical framework are available on the ANVIL project website: www.anvil-project.net.
3. Due to space limitations, this article only presents and discusses the most important and pertinent findings and patterns emerging from ANVIL. It cannot provide an exhaustive comparison of the systems that were covered by the detailed ANVIL case studies. A broader and more descriptive synthesis report of the project, which includes parts of the content presented in this contribution, is available elsewhere (Bossong and Hegemann, 2013). For detailed evidence and references on the specific cases, see the respective ANVIL country studies.
4. Only two cases deviate most clearly from this state of affairs through special arrangements for security and crisis management purposes that have no correspondence in regular administration: the Netherland's 25 'Security Regions' and France's seven 'Defence and Security Zones'.
5. For a more detailed map and further explanations on how these heuristic groups were assigned, see Bossong and Hegemann (2013, pp. 14–15).
6. For a more detailed discussion and visualization of these numbers and the data on which they are based, see Bossong and Hegemann (2013, p. 34) and the coded data schemes attached to the ANVIL case studies.
7. Serbia is a somewhat special case as the industry is still undergoing a process of privatization and many critical companies remain publicly owned.
8. http://www.unisdr.org/we/inform/publications/32996, date accessed 8 December 2014.

References

Alexander, D. (2002) 'From Civil Defence to Civil Protection – And Back Again', *Disaster Prevention and Management*, 11, 209–213.

Birkland, T. A. and S. E. DeYoung (2011) 'Emergency Response, Doctrinal Confusion, and Federalism in the Deepwater Horizon Oil Spill', *Publius: The Journal of Federalism*, 41, 471–93.

Boin, A., M. Busuioc and M. Groenleer (2013a) 'Building European Union Capacity to Manage Transboundary Crises: Network or Lead-Agency Model?', *Regulation & Governance* (EarlyView).

Boin, A., M. Ekengren and M. Rhinard (2013b) *The European Union as Crisis Manager: Patterns and Prospects* (Cambridge: Cambridge University Press).

Bossong, R. (2014) 'The European Programme for the Protection of Critical Infrastructures: Meta-governing a New Security Problem?', *European Security*, 23, 210–226.

Bossong, R. and H. Hegemann (2013) ANVIL Deliverable 4.1: Synthesis Report on Comparison of Civil Security Systems. http://anvil-project.net/wp-content/uploads/2013/12/Deliverable_4.1.pdf, date accessed 17 October 2014.

Brazova, V. K., P. Matczak and V. Takacs (2014) 'Evolution of Civil Security Systems: The Case of three Central European Countries', *Journal of Risk Research* (Online First).

Bremberg, N. and M. Britz (2009) 'Uncovering the Diverging Institutional Logics of EU Civil Protection', *Cooperation and Conflict*, 44, 288–308.

Burgess, P. (2009) 'There is No European Security, Only European Securities', *Cooperation and Conflict*, 44, 309–328.

Chandler, D. (2014) *Resilience: The Governance of Complexity* (London: Routledge).

Douglas, M. and A. Wildavsky (1982) *Risk and Culture: An Essay on the Selection of Technological and Environmental Disasters* (Berkeley and Los Angeles: University of California Press).

Ehrhart, H.-G., H. Hegemann and M. Kahl (2014) 'Towards Security Governance as a Critical Tool: A Conceptual Outline', *European Security*, 23, 145–162.

Ekengren, M., N. Matzén, M. Rhinard and M. Svantesson (2006) 'Solidarity or Sovereignty? EU Cooperation in Civil Protection', *Journal of European Integration*, 28, 457–76.

European Commission (2012) *Special Eurobarometer 383: Civil Protection*. http://ec.europa.eu/echo/sites/echo-site/files/CP.pdf, date accessed 28 October 2014.

European Commission (2014) *Overview of Natural and Man-Made Disaster Risks in the EU*. SWD (2014) 134 final. 8 April 2014.

Hagmann, J. and M. Dunn Cavelty (2012) 'National Risk Registers: Security Scientism and the Propagation of Permanent Insecurity', *Security Dialogue*, 43, 79–96.

Hegemann, H., R. Heller and M. Kahl (eds.) (2013) *Studying 'Effectiveness' in International Relations: A Guide for Student and Scholars* (Opladen: Barbara Budrich).

Hannigan, J. (2012) *Disasters without Borders: The International Politics of Natural Disasters* (Cambridge: Polity).

't Hart, P., U. Rosenthal and A. Kouzmin (1993) 'Crisis Decision Making: The Centralization Thesis Revisited', *Administration & Society*, 25, 12–45.

Hollis, S. (2010) 'The Necessity of Protection: Transgovernmental Networks and EU Security Governance', *Cooperation and Conflict*, 45, 312–330.

Hollis, S. (2014) 'The Global Standardization of Regional Disaster Risk Management', *Cambridge Review of International Affairs*, 27, 319–338.

Houben, M. (2005) *International Crisis Management: The Approach of European States* (London: Routledge).

Jessop, B. (2011) 'Metagovernance', in M. Bevir (ed.) *The SAGE Handbook of Governance* (London: Sage).

Kirchner, E. and J. Sperling (2007a) *EU Security Governance* (Manchester: Manchester University Press).

Kirchner, E. and J. Sperling (eds.) (2007b) *Global Security Governance: Competing Perceptions of Security in the 21st Century* (London: Routledge).

Kirchner, E., E. Fanoulis and H. Dorussen (2014) 'Civil Security in the EU: National Persistence versus EU Ambitions?', *European Security* (Online First).

Krieger, K. (2013) 'The Limits and Variety of Risk-Based Governance: The Case of Flood Management in Germany and England', *Regulation & Governance*, 7, 236–257.

Lum, C. and L. W. Kennedy (eds.) (2012) *Evidence-Based Counterterrorism Policy* (New York: Springer).

Meyer, C. (2006) *The Quest for a European Strategic Culture: Changing Norms on Security and Defence in the European Union* (Basingstoke: Palgrave Macmillan).

Mueller, J. and M. G. Stewart (2011) *Terror, Security and Money: Balancing the Risks, Benefits and Costs of Homeland Security* (Oxford: Oxford University Press).

Norheim-Martinsen, P. (2013) *The European Union and Military Force: Governance and Strategy* (Cambridge: Cambridge University Press).

Power, M. (2004) *The Risk Management of Everything: Rethinking the Politics of Uncertainty* (London: Demos).

Quarantelli, E. L. (2000) *Disaster Planning, Emergency Management and Civil Protection: The Historical Development of Organized Efforts to Plan for and to Respond to Disasters*. University of Delaware. Disaster Research Center. Preliminary Paper 301.

Rothstein, H., O. Borraz and M. Huber (2013) 'Risk and the Limits of Governance: Exploring Varied Patterns of Risk-Based Governance in Europe', *Risk & Regulation*, 7, 215–235.

Schroeder, U. C. (2011) *The Organization of European Security Governance: Internal and External Security in Transition* (London: Routledge).

Weiss, T. (2013) 'Fighting Wars or Controlling Crowds? The Case of the Czech Military Forces and the Possible Blurring of Police and Military Functions', *Armed Forces & Society*, 39, 450–66.

Zedner, L. (2003) 'The Concept of Security: An Agenda for Comparative Analysis', *Legal Studies*, 23, 153–176.

3
Civil Security Governance Systems in the New EU Member States: Closer to 'Old Europe' or a Distinctive Path?[1]

Piotr Matczak, Vera-Karin Brazova, Višnja Samardžija and Iwona Pinskwar

Introduction

Natural and man-made risks cause substantial and growing losses in Europe and the world (Howell, 2013; Smith, 2013), which poses challenges for national civil security governance systems (CSGSs), understood here as the organizations and processes engaged in the prevention of, preparedness for, mitigation of, response to and recovery from crises and disasters (see Bossong and Hegemann, in the introduction to this volume). Yet, even across European countries such systems have only fully emerged over the last three decades in a rather uneven manner (Quarantelli, 2000). In Western European countries, an important shift occurred in the last quarter of the 20th century when more attention was paid to the protection of civilians during peacetime, which we call civil security, rather than to military defence. In the New Member States of the EU and especially in Central European states, however, civil security started to gain importance in national policy-making and post-Communist transition only since the very late 1990s (Brazova et al., 2014).

Against this background, little is known about the evolution and possible convergence of patterns among European CSGSs (see also Bossong and Hegemann, in this volume). Comprehensive comparative analyses are still lacking, particularly those which would differentiate between post-communist and other Old and New EU Member States. Therefore, this chapter reviews various dimensions and parameters that are likely to impact on the evolution of CSGSs with a particular focus on the post-communist countries. In particular, our analysis encompasses the countries covered by the 'big-bang' EU 2004/07 accession, namely the eight post-communist countries of Central and Eastern Europe (Czech Republic, Estonia, Hungary, Latvia, Lithuania, Poland, Slovakia and Slovenia), which joined the EU in 2004 together with Malta and Cyprus. The two latter states do not share the specific characteristics of the post-communist countries and are therefore not included in the set of the New Member States for the purpose of this chapter. Furthermore, the study covers Bulgaria and Romania, which joined the EU in 2007, as well as Croatia, which joined the EU in 2013 as its 28th member state. These eleven countries are referred to below as the New Member States (NMS). For the purposes of comparison, the Old Member States (OMS) are therefore logically states that were members of the EU before 2004.

In our analysis, we set the scene regarding possible factors for convergence and divergence in civil security governance in Europe and then look at three specific dimensions: the types of threats which European countries predominantly face; their matching or diverging perceptions of these threats; and the organization of national CSGSs. The first two aspects are analysed quantitatively including both Old and New Member States, using cluster analysis based on the Emdat.be disaster database and Eurobarometer (public opinion surveys commissioned by the European Commission) data, respectively. The third part features an illustrative qualitative analysis that focuses on the NMS and specifically on Croatia as the latest EU member. During communist times, what is now widely understood as civil security was typically part of a military-based centralized system. Thus, one could expect certain similarities between the NMS systems developed after 1990, following the model set by the OMS. However, our analysis also shows that the NMS cannot be treated as a singular block in terms of threats and risk perception and that we may observe wider processes than could be specifically attributed to the path dependent development as a NMS.

Stability and change of civil security governance systems

Currently, national CSGSs do seem to converge globally as decision-makers plan for international responses and disaster assistance (Aldrich, 2013, p. 3). At the level of the EU, more pronounced convergence might be expected due to so-called 'Europeanization', which refers to processes of 'domestic change caused by an EU-generated influence' (Major, 2005, p. 176). Such influences in the civil security realm may take the form of, for instance, relevant EU directives, such as the Flood Directive that requires all member states to undertake advanced risk and preparedness planning for regular flood events.

Moreover, the relative importance of risk management has generally started to grow at the EU level. Particularly in the case of industrial risks one can point to a long-running process of mutual accommodation in reaction to several accidents, such as the Seveso chemical accident in 1976. A tension exists, however, between the importance of collective efforts to deal with disasters on the one hand, and a relative unwillingness of the member states to perceive civil security as a supranational matter (Ekengren et al., 2006). Even in a leading case like industrial risk management, where the Seveso accident marked the beginning of supranational thinking about civil security governance in Europe, countries differ with respect to their specific conceptualization and practices and remain largely influenced by local accidents and circumstances (van Eijndhoven, 1994, pp. 114–130). This could be read as an indication that civil security is still treated as a matter of national sovereignty.

Hence, one can hypothesize that the Europeanization in civil security governance does not demonstrate itself as a clear trend. Instead one can expect to find persistent differences both in terms of actual risks and in terms of the CSGSs structures, designed to react to different disasters. Differences also lie in the administrative levels at which civil security is mainly addressed (i.e. local/regional/federal/national), as divisions of responsibilities vary among countries (Vanneuville et al., 2011). The local government's position differs comparably to other levels of administration, as the local power structures in civil security governance (i.e. whether the leading role is assumed by a professional or by a public administration official) are sometimes regarded crucial (Wolensky and Wolensky, 1990). Despite the overall trend towards decentralization in disaster management (Cheong, 2011), one can expect a comparatively less developed process in the post-communist NMS[2] as a (relinquishing) relic of the centralized organization during the communist times.

Another important aspect relevant for CSGSs' evolution is presented by the growing importance of public participation and involvement. Public participation is increasingly considered an effective means to enhance general disaster awareness and encouraging citizens to take more responsibility in coping with risks (Wachinger et al., 2013). Yet, despite the importance of the role of civil society in civil security governance, little research on the topic exists and it typically focuses only on immediate citizen involvement during and after a crisis (Aldrich, 2013). Generally, the European post-communist countries are characterized by a rather weakly developed civil society (Howard, 2003), which is likely to exist in the field of civil security governance as well. Therefore, the scale of public participation in civil security governance – be it in an organized form through non-governmental organizations (NGOs) involved in the provision of civil security or through unorganized volunteering – is another factor to be taken into the analysis.

Disasters and threat perceptions in Europe

Beyond these general structural and political factors that shape our expectations of convergence and difference of European CSGSs, we need to consider the possible functional relation between, on the one hand, threats and the perception of threats in a given state territory and, on the other hand, the organization of national CSGSs. In other words, both actual risks and their perception, which can be biased, influence the shape and evolution of CSGSs. Therefore the following sections first describe the distribution of disasters in Europe, followed by a discussion of risks as perceived by European societies. In both cases, patterns of similarities and differences among both Old and New EU Member States are investigated, which further allows defining the possible room for convergence or divergence between CSGSs.

Distribution of disasters in Europe

The types of threats analysed below include both natural and man-made disasters, such as floods, forest fires, storms, earthquakes, droughts and industrial and transportation accidents. For each country, varying sets of risks and disasters are observed. Based on the Emergency Events Database EM-DAT,[3] the number of actual disasters in European countries varies considerably. In general, however, the bigger a country is, the more disasters it experiences (Figure 3.1).

In Europe, natural disasters are the most frequent and devastating type of crisis. They often affect large areas and cause significant damages. This is particularly the case with floods, storms, forest fires and earthquakes. Major floods have been an especially frequent phenomenon in the EU countries (Figure 3.2).

In order to explore the difference between the OMS and the NMS in terms of disaster occurrence, we use Student's t-test. This tool allows us

54   *The Challenge of Diversity*

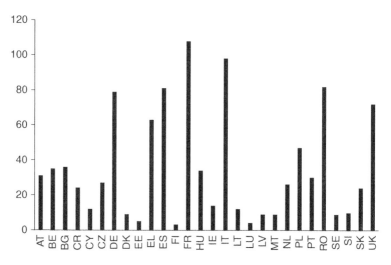

Figure 3.1   Total number of disasters in European countries (1995–2014)
Source of data: emdat.be.

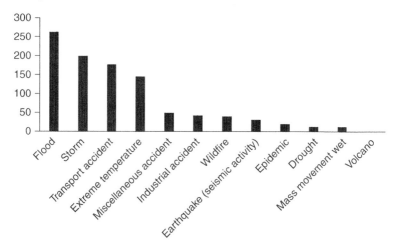

Figure 3.2   Number of disasters in the 28 EU countries (1995–2014)
Source of data: emdat.be.

to look for statistically significant differences between the two groups of countries for each of the disasters type. The analysis suggests no major differences in the number of disasters. Only in the case of extreme temperature a higher occurrence in NMS compared to OMS could be found (Table 3.1).

Table 3.1 Difference between the Old Member States (column 1: OMS) and the New Member States (column 2: NMS) in terms of particular types of disasters – Results of Student's t-test calculation

Risk type	Mean 1 (OMS)	Mean 2 (NMS)	t	df	P	N 1 (OMS)	N 2 (NMS)
Epidemic	0.03568	0.01342	1.09657	26	0.28288	17	11
Drought	0.01189	0.01767	−0.5805	26	0.56654	17	11
Extreme temperature*	0.10524	0.27722	−4.8688	26	0.00004	17	11
Wildfire	0.03250	0.03282	−0.0139	26	0.98901	17	11
Earthquake (seismic activity)	0.02455	0.02969	−0.2592	26	0.79752	17	11
Volcano	0.00060	0.00000	0.79899	26	0.43153	17	11
Flood	0.17026	0.28392	−1.8716	26	0.07255	17	11
Mass movement wet	0.00995	0.00110	1.39194	26	0.17573	17	11
Storm	0.28125	0.15957	1.76807	26	0.08878	17	11
Industrial accident	0.04385	0.03745	0.30989	26	0.75911	17	11
Miscellaneous accident	0.04960	0.06584	−0.5047	26	0.61797	17	11
Transport accident	0.23457	0.08125	1.96074	26	0.06070	17	11

Group 1: Old Member States.
Group 2: New Member States.
* – significant difference.
Results of Levene test for homogeneity of variance are not presented in the table.
Source of data: emdat.be.

Although the analysis shows overall very little difference between the NMS and the OMS in terms of a particular disaster-type occurrence, one could, in reverse, expect more pronounced similarities between subsets of the EU countries. For this purpose, we use cluster analysis as a classifying technique to organize multiple attributes data, such as the emdat.be data on disasters, in order to show more fine-grained similarities and patterns. However, as the following graphic analysis shows, no pronounced clustering effect can be observed (Figure 3.3).

The cluster analysis shows a general heterogeneity of the European countries in terms of disaster-type occurrence and therefore no overriding pattern can be identified. Nevertheless, relative similarity in threat exposure – or similar disaster experience – can be observed between Romania and Slovakia, as well as Hungary and Austria. These four countries constitute one, more general cluster. Other clusters link: Belgium with France; Poland with Lithuania; Greece with Italy and Spain. Malta is the most visible outlier. In addition, some Scandinavian countries cluster together (Finland, Denmark, Estonia).

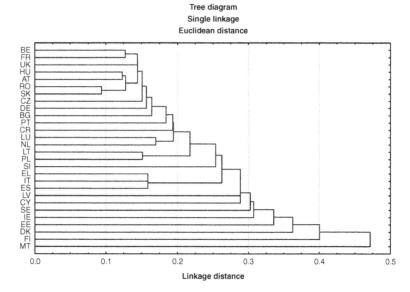

Figure 3.3 Tree diagram resulting from cluster analysis, taking into account various types of disasters in the EU countries. Vertical proximity of the linked countries represents their similarity in terms of sets of occurring disasters. The horizontal axis represents Euclidean distance between countries
Source of data: emdat.be, calculation based on standardized data.

To summarize, disasters in Europe are unequally distributed. Generally, clusters of countries are not very marked. Certain similarities of the groups of countries shown by the cluster analysis (e.g. Slovakia, Romania, Austria and Hungary; or Greece, Italy and Spain) can be attributed to the proximity of geographical conditions. Beyond that, however, the NMS do not constitute a coherent set that could be differentiated from the OMS on the basis of clustered disaster and threat experience.

Threat perceptions in Europe

Besides the structural characteristics and actual threats faced by CSGSs, threat perceptions are likely to exercise an important influence on policy decisions that shape national CSGS (Sjoberg, 1999). Empirical research on comparative risk perception shows significant differences across countries (de Zwart et al., 2007; Renn and Rohrmann, 2000) although the variance is not always easy to explain (Viklund, 2003).

Perceived threats are only partially determined by real or statistically significant risks (Renn and Rohrmann, 2000). Instead, differences in threat perception are frequently attributed to cultural differences (Douglas and Wildavsky, 1982). Yet, analyses of systematic differences in risk preferences among nations by Ding et al. (2012, p. 1846) do not lead to a typology or clusters of countries. So threat perceptions tend to vary unsystematically from one country to another, even among the OMS, as shown in a comparative analysis across Sweden, Spain, UK and France (Viklund, 2003). Results of a study among five European countries conducted in the wake of the avian influenza (de Zwart et al., 2007) suggest, however, a potential difference between the OMS and NMS. Compared to four OMS, namely Denmark, the Netherlands, UK and Spain, Poland displayed markedly different results in threat perceptions. Still, these limited indications do not show up in a wider comparison across threats and all EU member states (Table 3.2).

In most of the countries, natural risks are ranked the highest. Moreover, perception of risks broadly corresponds with actual threats present in the respective country, which, as shown above, could not be systematically clustered together either. Correspondingly, post-communist countries or NMS cannot be treated as one bloc as their level of concern towards threats and related risk perception vary.

Citizens' perceptions of the most threatening risks also vary among all EU countries (Figure 3.4). Yet, here one can observe more structured differences between countries where the level of concern is generally high and where citizens are less concerned.

According to data from Eurobarometer (2012) polls, citizens in the post-communist NMS and countries of Southern Europe feel most threatened by natural disasters. The highest levels of concerns are indicated in the Bulgaria (66 per cent of citizens feel very concerned), the Czech Republic and Greece (in both countries 51 per cent feel very concerned). Poland (46 per cent) and Slovakia (45 per cent) followed by Latvia, Hungary and Romania rank above the EU 27 average (31 per cent). The mid to lower levels of concern are indicated in Lithuania and Estonia – together with France, Malta, Austria, Ireland, Germany and UK; while the lowest levels of concern are in some Northern OMS. In Finland, only 5 per cent of citizens feel very concerned; in the Netherlands and in Sweden, 4 per cent.

Additionally, the countries could be divided on the basis of citizens' concern regarding natural disasters, man-made disasters and threat of terrorism. In most of the NMS there is a high level of citizens' concern regarding man-made disasters, namely in Latvia (49 per cent very

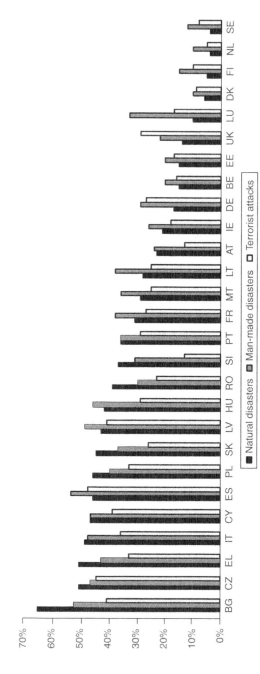

Figure 3.4 Concern of citizens in selected countries about the types of threats that are most likely to hit their country (only citizens that feel very concerned included)[4]
Source of data: Eurobarometer, 2012.

Table 3.2 The most important type of risk as perceived by inhabitants of the EU countries

Post-communist New Member States	Type of risk	Old Member States (plus CY and MT)	Type of risk
Bulgaria (BG)	Earthquake	Cyprus (CY)	Earthquake
Romania (RO)	Earthquake	Greece (EL)	Earthquake
Czech Republic (CZ)	Flooding	Italy (IT)	Earthquake
Poland (PL)	Flooding	Austria (AT)	Flooding
Slovakia (SK)	Flooding	Ireland (IE)	Flooding
Estonia (EE)	Forest fire	Netherland (NL)	Flooding
Latvia (LV)	Forest fire	UK	Flooding
Lithuania (LT)	Forest fire	Portugal (PT)	Forest fire
Hungary (HU)	Violent storm, with gale	Spain (ES)	Forest fire
Slovenia (SI)	Violent storm, with gale	Finland (FI)	Industrial accident (Chemical accident, etc.)
		Malta (MT)	Marine pollution (oil spill, etc.)
		Sweden (SE)	Marine pollution (oil spill, etc.)
		Belgium (BE)	Violent storm, with gale
		Denmark (DK)	Violent storm, with gale
		France (FR)	Violent storm, with gale
		Germany (DE)	Violent storm, with gale
		Luxembourg (LU)	Violent storm, with gale

Note: Croatia is not included because the country was not an EU member in 2009.
Source of data: Eurobarometer, 2009.

concerned), Czech Republic (47 per cent), Hungary (46 per cent) as well as in Poland (40 per cent), Lithuania (38 per cent) and Slovakia (37 per cent). Romania (30 per cent) and Estonia (20 per cent) show mid- to lower levels of citizens' concern, while the countries with the lowest levels of concern regarding man-made disasters are again some OMS (Finland, Sweden and the Netherlands).

60 *The Challenge of Diversity*

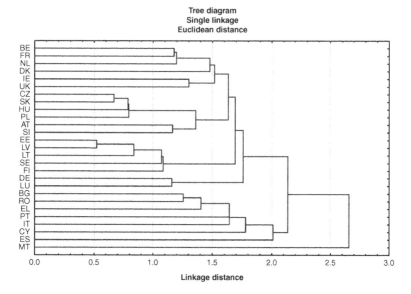

Figure 3.5 Cluster analysis of the EU countries based on citizens' opinion on the seriousness of risks. Standardized data. Vertical proximity of the linked countries represents their similarity in terms of perception of risks. The horizontal axis represents Euclidean distance between countries
Source of data: Eurobarometer, 2009.

Despite some emerging groupings, this short survey of European risk perceptions does not allow for a clear delineation between NMS and OMS. To what extent does the distinction between the post-communist countries and the OMS take into account patterns of diverging risk perceptions within particular countries? Here, a cluster analysis enables us to classify objects (countries) into groups, taking into account multi-dimensional characteristics, in which countries being the closest in terms of 'the syndromes' of the perceived risks are linked together. Yet, this analysis also reveals that the post-communist countries do not constitute a distinct group (Figure 3.5).

The closest countries concerning various risks perceived are: Estonia and Latvia together with Lithuania, Sweden and Finland form the 'Nordic' bloc (Figure 3.5). Besides, the Czech and Slovak Republics constitute a close pair with Hungary and Poland linked into a larger, Central European (or Visegrad) group. Other pairs of similar countries are: Belgium and France (plus the Netherlands); Ireland and the UK; Bulgaria and Romania; Germany and Luxemburg; Austria and Slovenia.

It can be noted that the close pairs in risk perception often are neighbours in a geographical sense. Moreover, for the pairs, the risk perceived as the most eminent is not always the same. For instance, for Austrians flooding is the biggest risk while for Slovenians it is violent storm with gale. Nevertheless, taking the whole set of risks, these two countries (as well as other pairs mentioned above) constitute a close pair.

Malta appears to be the most distinctive country. Marine pollution is perceived by the Maltese as the most dangerous risk, followed by earthquake, flooding and storms. It can be assumed that risk perception in Malta is specific due to its nature as a small, densely populated island. Taking into account the post-communist vs. the OMS distinction, it can be noticed that the post-communist countries do not constitute a separate group. Slovenia 'joins' neighbouring Austria. Estonia, Latvia and Lithuania are within the Scandinavian group. Bulgaria and Romania are within the Southern circle (together with Greece, Portugal, Italy, Cyprus and Spain). The most specific cluster of the post-communist countries is Central Europe, namely the Czech Republic, Hungary, Slovakia and Poland.

Thus, one could conclude that geographical proximity and the geographical conditions behind it are the most important factors explaining the similarity of risk perceptions in the European countries.

This conclusion is supported by the analysis of differences between OMS and NMS for particular types of risk. Tests show no statistically significant difference between the two groups of countries in any of the risk types (Table 3.3). Apparently, the risk perception in the NMS has no specificity compared with the OMS.

Organization of civil security governance systems in the New Member States

Based on the foregoing analysis we cannot deduce a clear functionalist or perception-based argument for a convergent transformation of CSGSs in NMS when compared to OMS. This needs to be set against alternative historical and political factors that might be adduced for expecting convergence or common trends in NMS.

The transition context of the civil security governance systems reforms in the New Member States

Similarly to those in the OMS, the CSGSs in the NMS have passed through considerable reforms and transition since the end of the Cold War. The issues at stakes were complex, taking into account the shift

Table 3.3 Difference between the Old Member States (column 1: OMS) and the New Member States (column 2: NMS) in terms of perceived risk by inhabitants of the EU countries – Results of Student's t-test calculation

Risk type	Mean 1 (OMS)	Mean 2 (NMS)	t	df	P	N 1 (OMS)	N 2 (NMS)
Earthquake	0.21329	0.11450	0.20636	25	0.83818	17	10
Forest fire	0.34431	0.80966	−1.1519	25	0.26026	17	10
Flooding	1.06441	1.37766	−0.9302	25	0.36112	17	10
Violent storm, with gale	0.96153	1.27997	−1.1467	25	0.26234	17	10
Tsunami	−0.8195	−0.7512	−1.6812	25	0.10516	17	10
Volcano eruption	−0.8199	−0.7602	−1.1895	25	0.24541	17	10
Landslide	−0.4921	−0.4249	−0.4062	25	0.68804	17	10
Industrial accident	0.63881	0.17156	1.93317	25	0.06461	17	10
Nuclear accident	−0.1119	−0.3564	1.10438	25	0.27994	17	10
Marine pollution	0.43382	0.05549	1.06002	25	0.29927	17	10
Other	−0.8580	−0.7749	−1.8425	25	0.07728	17	10
None	−0.5546	−0.7409	1.74146	25	0.09389	17	10

Group 1: Old Member States.
Group 2: New Member States.
The number of New Member States equals 10, since at the moment of the survey Croatia was not the EU member yet.
Results of Levene test for homogeneity of variance are not presented in the table.
Source of data: Eurobarometer, 2009.

from military to non-military threats and the increasing awareness of modern society about disasters and emergencies (Shalamanov et al., 2005). Yet, the transformation of CSGSs in the post-communist countries has been more comprehensive than in the OMS. The reasons for this could be found in the profound political, economic and societal changes in the post-communist countries during their turbulent recent history and also in some relatively recent military conflicts in South-Eastern Europe. It needs to be noted that the reforms were introduced with a lack of consensus of political elites about the directions of changes and the concrete solutions.

Generally speaking, CSGSs in most NMS changed from the Soviet-type system of civil defence, based on the idea that civil society should be fully mobilized in the support of the country's defence in case of war, towards a model of civil protection focused on protecting the population against natural and man-made disasters. The overall process of the post-communist transformation brought along serious political, economic and societal adjustments to the new standards in every field, including civil security governance (Knezović and Vučinović, 2013). The old, defence driven systems were abandoned but, somewhat contradictory, the transformation of the CSGSs was not the top priority during the reforms in the NMS and has remained an issue of low importance.

Notably, EU accession did not have a major impact on the CSGSs of the NMS, if compared with such sectors as agriculture, water management, environment protection and so on. While in the latter sectors the implementation of EU legislation (directives) required the transposition of EU laws, in civil security governance the EU plays a coordinative role only.

Rather, the modernization of the CSGSs resembled or followed general changes made in the broader process of transition in these countries. Firstly, the public administrations were the subjects of substantial changes. Starting from an omnipotent administration regulating most aspects of life, including the economy, public administrations were transformed into a system based on the Western European examples. Civil service legislation and administrative courts were introduced along with substantial reforms decentralizing tasks and competences. Dismantling the bureaucratic party states included the reconstruction of local government structures and reorganization of the central government. As the CSGSs were moved under civil supervision they needed to be adjusted to the evolving shape of public administrations. In effect, this led to a marginalization of the CSGSs.

Secondly, the democratic transformation aimed at building accountability of public administration and re-establishing the vital role of civil society. Grassroots-type social activity was seen as a pillar of a democratic society. It revealed that revitalizing civil society is a difficult task. The civil society development indicators show that NMS are hardly catching up the Western model (see also Bossong and Hegemann, in this volume). It involves not only smaller numbers of NGOs but also lower popular trust towards governmental institutions. Nevertheless, civil society organizations have had an important role within the third sector in the NMS. Voluntary fire brigades and rescue organizations have constituted an important part of the sector. Moreover, they have been trusted and were largely incorporated to the CSGSs.

Despite many similarities, there were also differences in terms of CSGS development among the NMS. In most NMS, for instance in Estonia, the CSGS was rebuilt from the ground up after 1991. In some the process was more complicated. The CSGSs in the Czech and the Slovak republics diverged after the separation in 1993. In Lithuania, the civil protection and rescue system has become an integral part of the national security, with no clear distinction between external and internal security. Furthermore, the role of military differs as well. For instance, although in most of the countries military forces play a small role in CSGSs, in Romania the Ministry of Defence has a significant role in the management of emergency situations. These differences can also be attributed to historical factors, such as conflicts in the Balkan Peninsula.

General features of civil security governance systems in the New Member States

The foregoing section illustrated that the historical transformation processes in NMS have been deep, turbulent, diverse and beset by persistent challenges. The following discussion presents these qualitative differences in a more structured comparative, rather than historical, perspective and also pursues again the difference between NMS and OMS. These differences could be noticed through major concepts that are applied, the degree of organizational centralization and societal involvement in civil security governance, and finally the role of the military sector, which in some NMS had stronger involvement for a longer period than in the OMS. Nevertheless, in NMS, similarly to OMS, today there is a civilian primacy and control of the CSGSs. In most of the NMS, military forces still regularly contribute to civil security needs, particularly when it comes to exceptional and prolonged crisis (Bossong and Hegemann, 2014). Development of the new organizational forms was – at least partially – initiated by big disasters, revealing the weakness of existing systems (Brazova et al., 2014).

Most of the NMS generally developed an 'all-hazards' (or multi-hazard) approach for their CSGSs, rather than a 'specific threat' approach. In practice, though, they mostly implemented a combination of both these approaches. This means that they have defined comprehensive approaches in their civil security strategies and other documents, but also have additional strategies for some specific types of crises. Romania and Slovakia are among the countries that put strong emphasis on the all-hazards approach while Lithuania and Poland tend towards the specific threat approach. The practice shows that the organizational structures have elements of flexibility meaning that very often the all-hazards crisis management systems represent a common coordination platform. In practice, however, the response activities are undertaken by specialized agencies (Bossong and Hegemann, 2014).

The degree of centralization varies considerably due to different administrative traditions and institutional arrangements. While the North-Western countries (e.g. Sweden and Germany) mostly implement decentralized forms of organization, the NMS in Central, Eastern and South-Eastern Europe tend towards more centralized and top-down systems (the examples are Hungary, Slovakia, Romania, Latvia and Lithuania) or modestly centralized systems (Poland and Croatia) (Boin et al., 2014; Bossong and Hegemann, 2014). In the Baltic States, the organizational structures are centralized. They are coordinated and mostly organized by the central national civil protection authority. Other NMS have created specialized agencies or platforms responsible for overall civil protection and disaster management. The example here is the National Protection and Rescue Directorate in Croatia, or the Czech Integrated Rescue System. Some other NMS have established several agencies, such as Romania, where various central and local administrations, public institutions and NGOs take responsibility for policy implementation.

Civil security governance is primarily the responsibility of public agencies, but in several NMS, citizens are expected to contribute and to bear their share in response efforts. In general, the essential citizens' obligation is to comply with the authorities' ordinances when a disaster occurs. In most of the NMS (Croatia, the Czech Republic, Estonia, Lithuania, Poland, Romania and Slovakia), citizens are legally obliged to temporarily and actively contribute in the event of disaster upon request by public authorities. In Hungary, citizens have even wider formal obligations regarding crisis preparedness and responses, which includes responsibility to temporarily participate in disaster management (Samardžija et al., 2014).

In most European countries, citizens tend to actively assist in crisis situations. In general, they are directly included in crisis management activities, mostly through their participation in voluntary organizations dealing with civil security issues, such as the firefighting brigades and/or the national Red Cross organizations. Generally, the countries with centralized organizational structures tend to have a rather low use of voluntary organizations and higher-level civil-military cooperation in the peacetime civil protection activities. Croatia, the Czech Republic, Hungary, Lithuania, Romania and Slovakia are the countries with a high percentage of citizens who are generally willing to help and volunteer in the case of disaster. Estonia is an interesting example of wide-spread citizen's initiatives through the Estonian Neighbourhood Watch which is a unique association aimed to increase the sense of security of the citizens in their homes (Samardžija et al., 2014). On the other hand, in Poland, the level of voluntary engagement in emergencies is lower, compared with countries like the Czech Republic or Estonia.

There are specific features regarding the organization of the CSGSs that are common for some groups of NMS, or – on the other hand – are unique in individual NMS. In the case of the Baltic States, their civil protection systems differ from one another, but it seems that the post-Soviet countries do share common features within certain variables related to civil-military cooperation, the use of voluntary organizations and public–private cooperation (Pursiainen et al., 2005). Romanian experience shows that the adoption of new norms and break from the previous 'traditional' values created some uncertainties about responsibilities and accountability as well as some coordination problems (Chifu and Ramberg, 2007). Croatia had a specific experience due to the fact that it emerged in the context of the dissolution of the Yugoslav Federation and the so-called 'Homeland War'. Yet, as is also discussed in more detail further below, the Croatian system has evolved from a system that focuses on the military to a system focusing on the protection of citizens against natural and man-made disasters.

Civil security governance system in a post-conflict country: The case of Croatia

Croatia is a case, which shares the transition features (political, economic and administrative transformation, civil society development, transposing the EU legislation, etc.) with other NMS. At the same time, it also faces particular challenges that have not been experienced by the other NMS, for example the post-war legacy. In other words, Croatia's CSGS has been shaped by path-dependence from the former Yugoslav CSGS and cultural values of the Croatian society but also by legacies of the recent war of independence (1991–1995) and the transition process during the 1990s and 2000s (Knezović and Vučinović, 2013, p. 169). As such, Croatia serves as an illustrative case of the particular dynamics of transformation of national CSGS, set against the assumed shared experiences of NMS, such as EU enlargement or threat perceptions in Central and Eastern Europe that were critically discussed above.

The basis for developing civil security capabilities in Croatia was an administrative tradition of well-developed and organized CSGS in the former Yugoslav federation, which was functional, despite its ideological shape and massive size. However, the Croatian War of Independence (1991–1995), which emerged from conflicts between the former Yugoslav republics, led to the need of re-organizing the crisis management system to protect citizens from conflicts in the war-torn country (Knezović and Vučinović, 2013, p. 174). During the war, the CSGS played an important role in the provision of shelters, civilian evacuations, refugee acceptance, humanitarian assistance and other tasks. Subsequently, in the post-war period the system needed to be adapted in order to function as a part of democratic society. Accessing NATO and the EU required further development of the CSGS.[5] Moreover, regional cooperation in South-Eastern Europe has revealed a necessity for greater civil security cooperation and positively impacted the Croatian strategic culture.

The legacy of the war forced the country to develop strong humanitarian demining capacities. The remaining risk from landmines was constantly present after the war, threatening the civil security of the country. Croatia is today one of 59 countries in the world facing a mine problem. In the period of 1991–2012, almost 2,000 people were affected by mines in Croatia, out of which 508 people died. By the signing of the Ottawa Convention (1997), Croatia was recognized as one of the leading humanitarian demining countries in the world. Croatia's demining capacities include physical demining, equipment, know-how and assistance to rehabilitation of mine victims. Special attention is given to educating and informing citizens about the risk of mines. In this respect, Croatia is a particular case for risk education, communication and perceptions among the EU countries.

Despite the recent war experience, Croatia features further similarities to other NMS. As elsewhere in Europe, the management of civil security in Croatia is shifting to civilian authorities. The armed forces may be deployed to assist in police, firefighting and rescue operations as well as in surveillance and protection of the country's rights at sea in the case of serious disasters. However, the managerial reform process is ongoing, following the reform of national institutions for functioning civil security governance. The reforms started in 2005 with the establishment of a main executive protection and rescue body, and they are still underway aiming to strengthen coordination, strategic planning and risk management at the national level, building an integrated system for horizontal and vertical linkage of actors for natural disaster risk reduction, and involve stronger local and regional self-government (Samardžija et al., 2013, p. 37).

Conclusion

The end of the Cold War together with technological progress contributed to a shift in the type of threats countries face and perceive as well as in their underlying understanding of security. CSGS, organizations and processes designed to deal with threats, were adapted accordingly. In the European perspective, the post-communist countries are likely to constitute a particular group of countries in this respect. Not only did they have to adjust their CSGSs to the changing post-Cold War environment, but they also had to profoundly reshape their wider economic and political systems. As initially the CSGSs in these countries shared certain characteristics, most notably centralization and close links of the CSGSs with defence systems, one could have expected a similar path of transformation of these systems, ultimately leading to convergence with the OMS.

To explore the likelihood or plausibility of convergence, or treating the NMS as a block of similar national CSGS, this chapter first analysed the actual risks and risk perceptions among the European countries. It was found that natural disasters are the most frequent and devastating type of crisis in the NMS as well as the OMS. In terms of actual disasters, geographical proximity clearly takes the main role. Typically, neighbouring countries, which obviously may include both Old and New Member States, experience the same patterns of disasters. In addition, threat perception – based on the test of the difference between OMS and NMS for particular types of risk – cannot be regarded as a differentiating factor between these two groups of countries. Again, geography, rather than any other influence, tends to be the factor that can most easily explain similarities in opinion about the seriousness of risks. Nonetheless, two groups among the NMS stand out in terms of overall threat perceptions: the Central European Visegrad Group and the Baltic States. Generally, the citizens' perception of risks (although this varies across the EU counties) tends to be higher among NMS.

Alongside the profound transformation in the national CSGSs in NMS after 1990, the CSGSs in OMS also underwent significant changes due to the end of the Cold War and to the appearance of the so-called new threats. The structures of the CSGSs in both the OMS and the NMS seem to converge gradually, which reflects itself for example in the civilian control over the CSGSs or in the involvement of other stakeholders, such as NGOs or volunteers. The old military-type of approach was abandoned while the new organizational forms were developed to face large disasters, new threats, or to overcome the weaknesses of the previous systems. Most of the NMS and OMS generally tend towards an 'all-hazards' (or 'multi-hazards') approach in their CSGSs rather than a 'specific threat' approach, but in practice mostly implement a combination of mentioned approaches. To summarize, the assertion about a distinctive path of CSGSs development in the NMS cannot be sustained.

Yet, the analysis also suggests diverse and persistent administrative traditions and institutional arrangements between OMS and NMS, as well as between NMS themselves. The systems of NMS are relatively more centralized compared to the OMS. This can be attributed to the legacy of the communist system. Moreover, there is a difference in risk perception. The level of anxiety is higher in NMS than in OMS. Yet, it can be argued that the similarities in the countries' CSGSs are mainly driven by the geographic conditions and related risks. Still, the Europeanization thesis, therefore, cannot fully explain the development of the CSGSs in the NMS.

The results of this analysis might have implications for future cooperation of the countries with the aim to increase the effectiveness and efficiency of the CSGSs. Our findings suggest rather bilateral or sub-regional cooperation of relatively small groups of neighbouring countries facing similar threats, for instance cooperation in issues related to river flooding or maritime risks. An all-European approach could have a facilitative role in this respect but – based on the differences between and within the OMS and the NMS – it cannot be expected to pave the way for a unified one-size-fits-all model.

Notes

1. This research was partially funded by the EU Seventh Framework Programme for research, technological development and demonstration under grant agreement no 284678, ANVIL – Analyses of Civil Security Systems in Europe; co-financed by Poland's Ministry for Science and Higher Education from funds for science in 2013–2014 granted to an international project, and by the Specific Research Grant of the Charles University in Prague, Faculty of Social Sciences Nr. SVV 2014 260 112.
2. It has to be noted that (de)centralization is used here as a descriptive category only. We intentionally refrain from using it in a normative sense, as decentralized disaster management is not necessarily more successful in all aspects of the disaster response (Cheong, 2011).

70 *The Challenge of Diversity*

3. The EM-DAT database has been established in 1988 and is maintained by the Centre for Research on the Epidemiology of Disasters at the Université catholique de Louvain. The EM-DAT contains data on the occurrence and effects of more than 18,000 mass disasters in the world from 1900 to the present.
4. Figure 3.4 shows the distribution of citizens that feel 'very concerned' regarding natural disasters, man-made threats and terrorist attacks across selected countries for this research (The Eurobarometer question: 'How concerned are you personally about certain type of disasters?' Answers: very concerned, fairly concerned, not concerned; don't know).
5. Croatia became a member of NATO in 2009, while in 2013 the country joined the European Union.

References

Aldrich, D. P. (2013) *The Role of Governmental Capacity and Citizens' Input in Disaster Management*. The East Asia Institute's Working Paper No. 40. http://eai.or.kr/data/bbs/kor_report/2013052714345232.pdf, date accessed 13 October 2014.

Boin, A., R. Bossong, V.-K. Brazova, F. Di Camillo, F. Coste et al. (2014) *Civil Security and the European Union: A Survey of European Civil Security Systems and the Role of the EU in Building Shared Crisis Management Capacities*, UI Papers 2, April 2014. http://www.ui.se/eng/upl/files/102569.pdf, date accessed 12 December 2014.

Bossong, R. and H. Hegemann (2014) *Anvil Final Analytical Report: Critical Findings and Research Outlooks*, ANVIL Deliverable 4.2. February 2014. http://anvil-project.net/wp-content/uploads/2014/02/Deliverable_4.2.pdf, date accessed 12 December 2014.

Brazova, V. K., P. Matczak and V. Takacs (2014) 'Evolution of Civil Security Systems: The Case of Three Central European Countries', *Journal of Risk Research* (OnlineFirst), DOI: 10.1080/13669877.2014.913659.

Cheong, S. M. (2011) 'The Role of Government in Disaster Management: The Case of the Hebei Spirit Oil Spill Compensation', *Environment and Planning C: Government & Policy*, 29, 1073–1086.

Chifu, J. and B. Ramberg (eds.) (2007) *Crisis Management in Transitional Societies: The Romanian Experience* (Crisis Management Europe Research Programme Volume 33) (Stockholn: Swedish National Defence College and CRISMART).

de Zwart, O., I. K. Veldhuijzen, G. Elam, A. R. Aro, T. Abraham et al.(2007) 'Avian Influenza Risk Perception, Europe and Asia', *Emerging Infectious Diseases*, 13. http://www.cdc.gov/eid/content/13/2/290.htm, date accessed 13 October 2014.

Ding, P., M. D. Gerst, A. Bernstein, R. B. Howarth and M. E. Borsuk (2012) 'Rare Disasters and Risk Attitudes: International Differences and Implications for Integrated Assessment Modeling', *Risk Analysis*, 32, 1846–1855.

Douglas, M. and A. Wildavsky (1982) *Risk and Culture: An Essay on the Selection of Environmental and Technological Dangers* (Berkeley: University of California Press).

Ekengren, M., N. Matzén, M. Rhinard and M. Svantesson (2006) 'Solidarity or Sovereignty? EU Cooperation in Civil Protection', *European Integration*, 28, 457–476.

Eurobarometer (2009) *Special Eurobarometer 328 Civil Protection Report*, European Commission, November 2009. http://ec.europa.eu/public_opinion/archives/ebs/ebs_328_en.pdf, date accessed 13 October 2014.

Eurobarometer (2012) *Special Eurobarometer Report 383 Civil Protection*, European Commission, November 2012. http://ec.europa.eu/echo/files/eurobarometer/reports/CP.pdf, date accessed 13 October 2014.

Howell, L. (ed.) (2013) *Global Risks 2013*, World Economic Forum Report. http://reports.weforum.org/global-risks-2013/, date accessed 13 October 2014.

Howard, M. M. (2003) *The Weakness of Civil Society in Post-Communist Europe* (Cambridge: Cambridge University Press).

Knezović, S. and Z. Vučinović (2013) *Croatian Civil Security System between Historical Legacy, Political Transition and Regional Cooperation*, Proceedings of the International Conference Crisis Management Days, University of Applied Sciences Velika Gorica, pp. 169–180.

Major, C. (2005) 'Europeanisation and Foreign and Security Policy: Undermining or Rescuing the Nation State?', *Politics*, 25, 175–190.

Pursiainen, C., S. Hedin and T. Hellenberg (2005) *Civil Protection Systems in the Baltic Sea Region: Towards Integration in Civil Protection Training*, Eurobaltic Publications 3. http://www.helsinki.fi/aleksanteri/english/projects/files/eurobaltic_report3b.pdf, date accessed 13 October 2014.

Quarantelli, E. L. (2000) *Disaster Planning, Emergency Management and Civil Protection: The Historical Development of Organized Efforts to Plan for and to Respond to Disasters*. University of Delaware. Disaster Research Center. Preliminary Paper 301.

Renn, O. and B. Rohrmann (eds.) (2000) *Cross-Cultural Risk Perception: A Survey of Empirical Studies* (Heidelberg: Springer).

Samardžija, V., S. Tišma, S. Knezović and I. Skazlić (2013) *Country Study: Croatia*. http://anvil-project.net/, date accessed 12 December 2014.

Samardžija, V., H. Butković and I. Skazlić (2014) *Do Citizens Feel Safe? Expectations, Information and Education on Civil Security: A Comparative Perspective*, Proceedings of the International Conference Crisis Management Days, 2014. University of Applied Sciences Velika Gorica, pp. 1413–1431.

Shalamanov, V., S. Hadjitodorov, T. Tagarev, S. Avramov, V. Stoyanov, P. Geneshky and N. Pavlov (2005) 'Civil Security: Architectural Approach in Emergency Management Transformation', *Information & Security. An International Journal*, 17, 75–101.

Sjoberg, L. (1999) 'Risk Perception in Western Europe', *AMBIO: A Journal of the Human Environment*, 28, 543–543.

Smith, K. (2013) *Environmental Hazards: Assessing Risk and Reducing Disaster* (New York: Routledge, 6th edition).

van Eijndhoven, J. (1994) 'Disaster Prevention in Europe' in S. Jasanoff (ed.) *Learning from Disaster: Risk Management after Bhopal* (Philadelphia: University of Pennsylvania Press), pp. 113–132.

Vanneuville, W., W. Kellens, P. De Maeyer, G. Reniers and F. Witlox (2011) 'Is "Flood Risk Management" Identical to "Flood Disaster Management"?', *Earthzine*. http://www.earthzine.org/2011/03/21/is-flood-risk-management-identical-to-flood-disaster-management/, date accessed 13 October 2014.

Viklund, M. J. (2003) 'Trust and Risk Perception in Western Europe: A Cross-National Study', *Risk Analysis*, 23, 727–738.

Wachinger, G., O. Renn, C. Begg and C. Kuhlicke (2013) 'The Risk Perception Paradox: Implications for Governance and Communication of Natural Hazards', *Risk Analysis*, 33, 1049–1065.

Wolensky, R. P. and K. C. Wolensky (1990) 'Local Government's Problem with Disaster Management: A Literature Review and Structural Analysis', *Review of Policy Research*, 9, 703–725.

4
Common Challenge – Different Response? The Case of H1N1 Influenza[1]

Vera-Karin Brazova and Piotr Matczak

Introduction

Dealing with epidemics constitutes an undisputable part of civil security governance. Of all communicable diseases, the pandemic influenza is probably the most feared by both policymakers and health practitioners (Kamradt-Scott, 2012, p. 90). However, due to high levels of uncertainty which require contentious political choices it also challenges the most common view of disaster management, which typically focuses on technical and natural disasters in a narrow sense. Pandemics are a type of risk of a supranational and sometimes even of a global scale. In case of an emergency, coordinated action is needed in order to control the spread of the illness within and across borders. At the same time, actions are undertaken basically within the national jurisdictions. Thus, there is a tension between nationally focused efforts and coordinative demands.

Although the European Union (EU) and the World Health Organization (WHO) have played an important role in enhancing uniformity and coherence of national pandemic strategies across Europe, significant differences still exist in pandemic influenza policies of the European countries (Martin and Conseil, 2012). Agencies such as the European Centre for Disease Prevention and Control are instrumental in the harmonization of disaster management, but when it comes to pandemics there is little interaction between the policies and legislations of many member states. Among the European countries, various types of civil security governance systems have developed and are also responsible for dealing with special risks, such as pandemics (see Bossong and Hegemann, in this volume).

This chapter focuses on the so-called swine flu (H1N1 influenza), which resulted in global pandemics declared by the WHO in 2009/2010. The virus appeared first in Mexico being a new strain of an earlier known influenza virus. Despite containment efforts, it spread globally and evoked various reactions of governments and responsible bodies. In the history of mankind, pandemics have caused enormous losses. For this reason, governments put a significant emphasis on preventing and dealing with such events. In the case of H1N1, the 1918 flu epidemics was a sinister reference point.

Usually, the H1N1 pandemic is portrayed in terms of an overreaction, be it on the side of the WHO which, according to many, has exaggerated the pandemic alert (Kamradt-Scott, 2012), or on the side of nation states who tended to apply precautionary approaches *en masse* (Seetoh et al., 2012). In this respect, the case of H1N1 does seem to showcase an example of a 21st century global risk where decisions often have to be taken 'on the basis of more or less unadmitted not-knowing' (Beck, 2006, p. 335), and where the boundary between rational response and an overreaction becomes blurred. In cases of pandemics, it is the fear, rather than the disease itself, which threatens to break the society apart, thus posing a high challenge for governments and emergency responders trying to retain public trust (Upshur, 2005; Lagadec, 2009, p. 483). In a situation where the pandemic risk cannot be interpreted accurately, the necessity to manage uncertainty arises (Seetoh et al., 2012; see also Kuipers and Boin, in this volume).

This has an important implication for legitimacy. On the one hand, risks alienate people from expert systems as they cannot be controlled fully rationally even by scientists or governments (Beck, 2006, p. 336). On the other hand, current crises often pose a challenge to the legitimacy of governance structures and processes, which sometimes turn out to be inadequate (Boin, 2009). Such a decrease in legitimacy leads to declining societal, political or legal support for extant decision-making procedures, instruments or ideas in the given policy domain (Nohrstedt, 2008).

Due to the nature of the crisis, which was assumed to be uncontainable within smaller geographical areas, central coordination mechanisms were in place in most of the countries, including those where disaster response typically rests at the regional or local level. The disease created a 'natural experiment' as it posed a similar threat for national civil security systems in parallel and in many countries. That is, the case of the swine flu allows us to analyse the reaction in the European countries all of which were hit by the same kind of crisis at the same time. Based on these similarities, preparedness and response actions are compared in this chapter, employing the notions of overreaction and precaution (Beck, 2006). The chapter builds on data for 22 European countries that was compiled the collaborative European research project ANVIL,[2] covering both the 'old' (joining the EU before 2004) and the 'new' member states (accessing the EU in 2004 and later), as well as all geographical regions of Europe.

The first part of the chapter touches upon the general functioning of the civil security governance systems and their overall legitimacy in the context of the H1N1 crisis. We examine such issues as the level at which the crisis was addressed, main actors, the overall reaction of the government, as well as the overall public perception of the authorities' reaction. Taking into account the implications for legitimacy, we analyse whether there were any official reviews of the actions taken during the H1N1 crisis and, consequently, whether the H1N1 crisis resulted in any changes in the countries' civil security governance systems in order to 're-legitimize' them in the eyes of the public.

The second part, then, goes into more practical aspects of crisis management and focuses on the actual procedures. As it was pointed out by Martin et al. (2010) based on a survey of national public health laws concerning pandemic influenza, differences among European countries exist when it comes to the legitimacy of their conduct of crisis management in this field. Here, we focus on some core factors which are typically described in the crisis management literature as potentially determining the success of policies to fight pandemics. In particular, these are the involvement of a large array of stakeholders and communication with the public.

Theoretical underpinnings

Suchman (1995) distinguishes three forms of legitimacy: a pragmatic, a moral and a cognitive one. The first one is based on self-interested calculation; the second one on positive normative evaluation; the third one is connected with permanent, structurally legitimate organizations, such as nation states (Suchman, 1995, pp. 578–584). These three forms can be well associated with different levels of policy-making: politics, policy and polity (see for example Hajer, 2003).

To study the response to the H1N1 influenza pandemic, we focus on the 'moral legitimacy', that is, one based on normative approval and on judgements about whether an activity promotes values of the respective society. Thus, we focus largely on the policy domain with which relevant operational responsibilities are connected. Although there are also important questions concerning responsibility which are related to the internationalization of the H1N1 issue, we focus here exclusively on the national responses and legitimacy connected with them.[3]

From the viewpoint of the moral legitimacy in policy-making, both outputs and procedures can be examined[4] (Suchman, 1995, p. 579). The outputs are mostly associated with effectiveness and correspondence with desired ideas and values (Schmidt, 2013, p. 8). Hence, our operative definition of legitimacy is based on the absence of political crisis and/or the need to make significant changes to the system in the aftermath of the pandemic as a post hoc reaction. When seen as unsuccessful, we might expect the civil security governance systems dealing with the influenza in some countries to attempt a 'relegitimation through (…) restructuring' (Suchman, 1995) and thus to undergo structural changes. Below, we review the reaction of the European countries to the pandemics – whether the legitimacy of those in authority or of the governance system was shaken.

Procedures, or 'throughput' (Schmidt, 2013), touch upon a more practical level as legitimacy is also linked to the success of the actions undertaken by the agencies and officials dealing with disasters (Quarantelli, 1988). Here, the 'openness and inclusiveness in institutional processes and constructive interactions' (Schmidt, 2013, p. 8) are particularly important. A survey conducted in Canada in the aftermath of the H1N1 pandemic revealed that – although there was not any single best model of how to handle the crisis – the comprehensive planning, the involvement of multiple stakeholders and communication (both among the official bodies as well as with the general public) were crucial to address the crisis successfully (Masotti et al., 2013). Similarly, the literature on disaster management stresses also the inclusion of various stakeholders and both internal and external distribution of information as factors crucial for success (Harrald, 2006; Moe and Pathranarakul, 2006; Fitzgerald et al., 2012; Schemann et al., 2012). Thus, these are the aspects we deal with in the second part of the chapter, where the inclusion of stakeholders and communication are discussed.

Response to H1N1: Similarities and differences

In most of the countries, addressing the H1N1 pandemic involved significant efforts of bodies responsible for public health and crisis management. The issue reached media headlines and was politically discussed in several cases. Interestingly, the material effects of the crisis

Table 4.1 Overall public perception of how the crisis was handled by the authorities

Public perception of handling the crisis	Country
Positive	Croatia, Estonia, Finland, Malta, Norway, Sweden
Negative	France, Switzerland, UK

Source: Authors' compilation based on ANVIL project data.

were often sidelined and, in most cases, did not lead to the perception of the H1N1 management as a failure. As the human losses were relatively low, the actions were commonly perceived neither as a success nor as a failure.

In some countries, however, a positive overall perception was reported (Table 4.1). In Croatia, the public continued to view the governmental reaction in a positive light, despite the fact that there was mistrust towards the vaccines and their potential negative effects. Positive citizens' perception was reported also for Malta, Norway and Sweden. Also in Estonia and Finland, no public criticism of the governmental reaction arose and, especially in the latter country, the population complied with the vaccination strategy. Contrastingly, the authorities' reaction in France, Switzerland and in the UK was seen as rather problematic.

As it was argued in the introductory section, preventing and responding to a pandemic influenza represents an integral, yet somewhat special part of civil security governance. In this section, we look into how the crisis was addressed by the analysed European countries and what implications these reactions had for legitimacy as discussed above.

The level at which the crisis was addressed

Despite the fact that the main responsibility for crisis management rests at different levels in different countries of Europe and is quite often decentralized (see Bossong and Hegemann, in this volume), the H1N1 crisis was addressed by the central level in almost all the countries (Table 4.2). The only exception was Germany, where the level of federal states was the most important one. This applies to both decision-making and bearing the costs of purchasing antiviral vaccines as the central government refused to provide any financial support here, despite the recommendation to start the vaccination campaign that came from the Permanent Vaccination Commission, a body resting under the Federal

Table 4.2 The main administrative level, which was addressing the H1N1 crisis

Main administrative level addressing the crisis	Countries
Central	Austria, Croatia, Czech Republic, Estonia, France, Hungary, Ireland, Latvia, Malta, the Netherlands, Norway, Poland, Romania, Serbia, Slovakia, Switzerland
Central and Regional	Italy
Central and Municipal	Finland, UK
Federal states	Germany
All levels largely involved	Sweden

Source: Authors' compilation based on ANVIL project data.

Ministry of Health (Hegemann and Bossong, 2013a). In Germany, the lack of central coordination during a nationwide epidemic was criticized as a weakness and the need for emergency decision-making at the central level in such cases was stressed (Hegemann and Bossong, 2013a). Similarly, in the UK – which is otherwise perceived as a rather centralized state – the responsibility of the local authorities in decision-making concerning the epidemics was relatively large. This was also regarded a weakness, and it was suggested that the active involvement of the Cabinet Office should have been larger (Fanoulis et al., 2013a).

In most of the countries, the main body governing the crisis was the Ministry of Health or, alternatively, the Ministry of Social Affairs (where it is also responsible for the public health agenda) in Estonia, Finland and Sweden. In France, the crisis was a test for a new joint crisis management organization driven by the Ministry of Interior – a result of the changes following the 2008 White Paper on Defence and National Security. The Ministry of Health, however, played an important role here as well. Although there were several deficiencies in the management of the crisis in France (see further below), the system setup was not questioned (Coste et al., 2013). In some countries where the overall civil security governance system also tends to be centralized, such as in Romania, Slovakia and the UK, the role of the government and/or Prime Minister in dealing with the H1N1 pandemics was significant.

The European countries were prepared to meet such crisis as the H1N1 pandemic. The preceding years were marked by growing concerns stemming from the experience with the so-called bird flu (H5N1) in the late 1990s. There had been substantial activity on both international

Table 4.3 Plans for dealing with a pandemic already in place before the crisis

Plans for pandemics already extant	Country (year when the plan was drafted)
Yes	Austria (2005), Czech Republic (2006), Finland (2007), France (2004), Ireland (2001), Italy (2006), Norway (2006), Serbia (2006), Slovakia (2006), Sweden (2007), Switzerland (January 2009)
No	Hungary, United Kingdom

Source: Authors' compilation based on ANVIL project data.

and national levels aimed at preparation for the next pandemic. This included the drawing up of contingency plans and training of critical personnel, as well as large investments in procuring and/or securing access to antiviral pharmaceuticals in many Western countries (Kamradt-Scott, 2012, p. 90). Worldwide, expenditures on pandemic influenza preparedness and control tripled between the years 2004 and 2009 (Seetoh et al., 2012, p. 717), driving many countries into a 'pandemic overdrive' (Kamradt-Scott, 2012, p. 95).

Looking across European countries, most of them had plans for dealing with pandemics in place, typically drafted between 2005 and 2007 (Table 4.3). The countries lacking such plans were made to issue them when the crisis started. In Hungary, a new decree was issued on coordination of H1N1 related tasks. A National Pandemic Plan was adopted in August 2009 (Takacs and Matczak, 2013). While the crisis was not perceived as mismanaged in Hungary, giving rise to no large criticism (Takacs and Matczak, 2013), a different situation occurred in the UK. Here, the government was largely blamed for missing out on a five-year period which it had at disposal for preparation for a pandemic crisis. Consequently, the authorities – especially the Cabinet Office – were criticized for having been very poor on such issues as the procedural details of coping with the influenza pandemic (Fanoulis et al., 2013a).

Priority groups

The already existing research on the topic points to a mixed policy landscape when it comes to the identification of priority groups to access antiviral vaccines. This is especially marked in situations of limited supply (Martin and Conseil, 2012). The need to decide on priority groups over longer term and over the whole of the population also makes the issue more politically challenging compared to a 'classical' disaster management, where for example the criteria for evacuation are much more clear-cut (as in a case of floods).

Although commonalities exist (such as the health care workers being included among the priority groups in all the countries), differences concern the size of the target population as well as ranking of priority groups. Not all countries took the decision to regard the protection of everyone as their public health goal (Martin and Conseil, 2012, pp. 1106–1107). In our sample, the majority of states indeed opted for the strategy of vaccinating specified target groups first and – eventually – the entire population later on demand. Vaccines were typically procured to cover a certain percentage of the population (for example, in the Czech Republic this was 40 per cent; in Slovakia 20 per cent; in Italy, the purchased pandemic vaccine would cover 4 per cent of the population but there was already a stockpile of 40 million doses of antiviral drugs stored by the Ministry of Health and distributed during the H1N1 alert). Outliers from this approach were Serbia, where the focus was on priority groups only and – on the other side of the reaction scale – Finland, where the decision was taken to immunize the entire population. In the Netherlands, there were set priority groups but vaccines were eventually purchased for the entire population – an action criticized later on as unnecessary.

As it turns out, even the plans to vaccinate (some of) the priority groups met specific challenges, which needed to be overcome when designing a vaccination strategy. This concerned the decision to make the vaccination compulsory for some groups crucial for the functioning of the security system in particular. Such decision was reported for example in the USA in some hospitals where the medical staff was threatened with sanctions if not getting vaccinated (Winston et al., 2014).

From the countries under study, such a decision was made in the Czech Republic with respect to the army (as one particular priority groups), causing a large controversy. While other priority groups (such as medical staff or politicians) were encouraged (but not ordered) to get vaccinated, thousands of soldiers were obliged to get vaccinated at the beginning of January 2010 by an order stemming from the resolution of the chief sanitary inspector of the Ministry of Defence (MoD). Non-compliance was to be sanctioned. The first to intervene against such practice was the president of the country. Thereafter, the issue was discussed at the State Security Council and, eventually, the government reached the decision that such a declaration legally rests only in the competences of the Chief Sanitary Inspector of the country, who is subordinated to the Ministry of Health. Hence, the professional soldiers and employees of the MoD were to be also vaccinated upon their request only (Nový, 2013).

Governmental (over)reactions

The H1N1 was not the first example where an overreaction could be observed. During a pandemic emergency in the USA in 1976, for example, strong precautionary measures were applied despite the lack of strong scientific evidence for the severity of the threat (Seetoh et al., 2012). As 'the political costs of omission are much higher than the costs of overreaction' (Beck, 2006, p. 336), we can assume that in the case of H1N1, the strong precautionary approach was perceived by the decisionmakers in the European countries as an adequate strategy.

Of all the countries under study here, only two did not seem to overreact with respect to the purchasing and using of the antiviral vaccines. These were Estonia and Poland. On the other side of the spectrum, Finland and Sweden represented examples of a precautionary principle applied. In Sweden, not only was there a massive vaccination campaign, and the decision was taken to opt for the maximum quantity order, but also – as it was revealed later – the key officials were in possession of information suggesting that the pandemic would be milder than anticipated. The Swedish public, though, appreciated the governmental actions and the approach was justified by it being better than neglecting the issue (Bakken and Rhinard, 2013).

With respect to the countries where an overreaction did not occur, in the case of Estonia, after a certain delay, only a limited number of vaccines were purchased by the Estonian government. In the case of Poland, the final decision was taken by the government not to purchase the vaccines at all. These findings seem to correspond with general patterns of national cultural differences as grasped for example by the World Values Survey: while both Poland and Estonia belong to the same group of countries concentrated more on survival values; both Finland and Sweden belong to another category which is concentrated on secular-rational values on the one hand and self-expression (as opposed to survival) on the other hand (Bossong and Hegemann, 2013, p. 16).

It has to be noted, however, that there were other factors than the cultural ones at play. In Estonia, it was the economic crisis that hit the country quite severely and heavily impacted on the public sector (Purfield and Rosenberg, 2010). The main reason for the hesitation and for the limited vaccine purchase, therefore, was found to be the economic downhill of that time rather than other considerations related to the national security culture (Hellenberg and Vissuri, 2013).

Excursion: The exceptional case of Poland

In terms of the crisis management conduct during the H1N1 crisis, Poland revealed to be an exceptional case among the European countries. The government did not buy the vaccines. Eventually, this strategy appeared to be appropriate and efficient. Not only did it avoid unnecessary expenses, but also the post-vaccination side effects, which in several countries caused severe criticism of the governmental strategies. Thus, what was the path to reaching this strategy in Poland?

At the end of April 2009, the Chief Sanitary Inspectorate announced that despite reports from around the world there was no imminent threat of influenza in Poland, but appropriate protective measures were undertaken. A special hotline providing information on the virus was established. In early May 2009, the first case of H1N1 was detected in Poland, which was confirmed by the Minister of Health at a press conference (Table 4.4). On 11 June 2009, the WHO declared there was an influenza pandemic in the world. An increase in cases of influenza occurred in early November, and on 13 November 2009, the first fatal case of the virus in Poland occurred. In mid-November 2009, the Minister of Health summarized the spread of the virus, confirming 344 cases

Table 4.4 Main events in the H1N1 epidemic in Poland

Date	Description
26.04.2009	Poland takes initial steps (Chief Sanitary Inspector)
04/2009	Hotline launched providing information about the virus
06.05.2009	first case of A/H1N1 in Poland detected – 58-years-old female
11.06.2009	WHO declares flu pandemic
13.11.2009	The first case of death, 37-year-old man
17.11.2009	Meeting of the Minister of Health with Ombudsman – delaying the purchase of vaccines
19.11.2009	Summary of the Minister of Health – 344 cases of flu in Poland, 4 deaths, 101 people in hospitals, 644 people under the epidemiological supervision
17.02.2010	World Report – in Poland 2521 cases and 178 deaths
24.06.2010	Resolution of the Parliamentary Assembly of the Council of Europe – approves the government position on the purchase of vaccines
10.08.2010	WHO announces entry into post-pandemic phase

Source: Authors' compilation based on ANVIL project data.

of infection in Poland. At the same time, the Minister of Health met the Ombudsman, and it was decided to postpone the purchase of vaccines against H1N1. In the end, the purchase was not made.

The issue of the purchase of vaccines was debated. The previous health ministers criticized the conduct of the Ministry of Health. The Ombudsman firmly recommended purchasing the vaccines and so did the parliamentary opposition. The president of the Polish Chamber of Physicians and Dentists also demanded the purchase of vaccines (Gazeta Wyborcza, 2010). Polish officials explained that the postponing of the purchase was due to the fact that there had not been sufficient testing of the vaccines. The Minister accused the pharmaceutical companies of pressing for the purchase and hiding the information about potential side effects (Polskie Radio, 2009). These statements were criticized by the European Medicines Agency, accusing the Polish ministry of populism. The Ministry of Health contacted the Swedish and Hungarian officials to buy surpluses of vaccines. Therefore, the reluctance of the Polish government was supposedly caused by facing a lack of supply caused by a surprisingly large demand. At the end of June 2010, the Parliamentary Assembly of the Council of Europe passed a resolution confirming the validity of the position of the Polish Minister of Health of not purchasing the vaccine (Ministry of Health, 2010). On 10 August 2010, the WHO (2010) declared that the pandemic had entered its post-pandemic phase.

Despite a fierce political conflict in Poland, the decision of the Ministry of Health not to buy the vaccines was not strongly criticized by the parliamentary opposition (Dmochowski, 2012). The parsimony of the government met a cool headed public reaction. Overall, the outstanding conduct of the Polish government can hardly be explained by the excellence of the civil security governance systems and procedures. Instead, it was seemingly the result of contingent factors combined with the general expectation that the issue should be dealt with by the responsible governmental bodies.

Consequences of the H1N1 pandemic for the civil security systems

Despite the large political and media attention to the H1N1 pandemic, only very limited change could be observed in the aftermath of the crisis. This corresponds with the finding that the crisis was perceived neither as a success (especially due to economic overspending on the response) nor as a failure (due to the low number of fatalities) in many countries.

Only in few countries was the H1N1 pandemic followed by changes to the civil security governance system. In Estonia, better support of the inter-agency cooperation between the authorities in charge of epidemics was introduced. This included both the budgeting of additional financial resources and the creation of administrative solutions, such as improved monitoring and communication systems (Hellenberg and Vissuri, 2013). In Sweden, only minor changes took place, based on recommendations for more flexible agreements with the vaccine providers (Bakken and Rhinard, 2013).

The only country which underwent considerable changes to the security system was Switzerland. It was the only country where a revision of epidemic law took place after the H1N1 crisis, resulting in a stronger lead position of the central government (Hegemann and Bossong, 2013b). This change in the Swiss civil security system contrasts with Germany. Here, coordination problems also occurred, yet – despite intensive discussions – the H1N1 crisis did not lead to any major revision of the decentralized approach in place (Hegemann and Bossong, 2013a).

While – with the exception of Switzerland – no restructuring took place after the pandemic, in several countries political and/or professional inquiries occurred, investigating the appropriateness of the authorities' reaction (Table 4.5). Yet, generally speaking, the H1N1 pandemic does not seem to have provoked many public inquiries – neither political nor professional ones. In Italy, Norway, Slovakia and Sweden only an evaluation took place, typically concerning the influenza as such and not questioning the actions taken by the authorities.

Among the countries where more rigorous inquiries occurred were representatives of both the old and the new member states of the EU. In the Netherlands and the UK, the operational response to the H1N1

Table 4.5 Official review of the actions taken during the H1N1 crisis

Professional or political inquiries applied	Country
No	Austria, Croatia, Czech Republic, Estonia, Finland, Germany, Ireland, Latvia, Malta, Romania
Evaluation only	Italy, Norway, Slovakia, Sweden
Yes	France, Hungary, the Netherlands, Poland, Serbia, Switzerland, UK

Source: Authors' compilation based on ANVIL project data.

influenza (including the lead authorities) was in the focal point of the inquiries. In France and Hungary, the financial issue was stressed. The use of funds was examined in the former case; while the agreement conditions with vaccine supplier were explored in the latter one.

Serbia and Poland were an exception. In Serbia, the inquiries were undertaken by the Anti-corruption Council of the Serbian government and took the form of a criminal affair regarding frauds in vaccine procurement of which the ex-director of the National Institute for Health Insurance was accused, together with three of her associates (Kešetović, 2013). Thus, in the Serbian case the crisis also accentuated some otherwise salient issues such as corruption. In the case of Poland, on the other hand, it was the Parliamentary Assembly of the Council of Europe which examined the validity of the opposition to the purchase of the vaccines by the Polish Minister of Health. A resolution confirming this position was passed in June 2010. Finally, in Germany, Transparency International called for a public investigation on the appropriateness of the reaction to the pandemic and the related costs in 2011, yet this has not been conducted yet.

Defining success: The importance of 'throughput'

'Success' of the actions undertaken by the authorities dealing with a crisis is another aspect crucial for legitimacy (Quarantelli, 1988). For moral legitimacy in policy-making, procedures are also important, including the openness of the processes and their inclusiveness. As suggested by a relatively large body of literature on crisis management, the inclusion of various stakeholders is among the key conditions for handling an influenza pandemic successfully (see for example Harrald, 2006; Schemann et al., 2012).

The array of stakeholders involved

The pandemic influenza can be treated as a global risk and the activation of diverse stakeholders and their connections across borders – what Beck (2006, p. 340) terms 'enforced cosmopolitanization' – could be expected. Therefore, for a successful management of the crisis we might expect a rather large array of stakeholders to be involved in the planning, prevention and response actions.

Yet, with respect to the stakeholders, including individuals, groups or organizations having the interest and the potential to influence the respective policy-making and implementation (Brugha and Varvasovszky, 2000), the EU countries varied substantially (Table 4.6).

Table 4.6 The inclusion of different stakeholders in the H1N1 response

Array of stakeholders	Country
Narrow	Croatia, Czech Republic, Estonia, Hungary, Poland, Romania, Slovakia
Broad	Ireland, Malta, the Netherlands, Sweden

Source: Authors' compilation based on ANVIL project data.

In Eastern Europe, the response to the pandemic was almost entirely left in the hands of public administration at the central level. This does not mean that no role was played by lower levels, but that they usually only took part in the implementation of the plans and decisions. With the exception of Poland (as portrayed above), the centralized reaction did not prevent the countries from an overreaction to the H1N1 crisis. In some cases, such as the Czech and French ones, however, the exclusion of some of the stakeholders seems to have had an adverse effect upon the legitimacy of the government's conduct.

Contrastingly, relatively broad array of stakeholders took part in the reaction to the pandemic in Ireland, Malta, the Netherlands and Sweden. This included not only independent experts, but also for example non-governmental organizations and others. In Ireland, tackling the crisis was not limited to the Irish state only but included also cross-border cooperation with the public authorities of Northern Ireland in pre-planning the management of the influenza pandemic (Fanoulis et al., 2013b). In Malta, the involvement of the voluntary sector was relatively large and the Red Cross, in particular, played an important role there (Fanoulis et al., 2013c).

A broad range of stakeholders was included in governmental action also in the Netherlands. These came from both the private sector (such as private medical practitioners) and from the non-governmental one (such as the Dutch Red Cross). Medical experts from the private sector were also invited by the government to join the Outbreak Management Team advising the Minister (Kuipers and Boin, 2013). In Sweden, the inclusion of different stakeholders reflected the variety of entities typically involved in the Swedish civil security governance system where – due to the responsibility principle – a large number of authorities, agencies and institutions have key executive responsibilities (Bakken and Rhinard, 2013).

In some countries, a consensus among stakeholders was not reached when it comes to the governmental reaction. This made the implementation of the vaccination strategy particularly difficult and shed a negative light on the appropriateness of the official approach addressing the pandemic. While the media were reportedly exaggerating the pandemic threat and – later on – the negative effects of the vaccines in many countries, it was the medical professionals in particular who questioned the official approach.

In the Czech Republic and Serbia, a large number of medical practitioners were actively opposing vaccination, which also undermined the credibility of the vaccination in the eyes of the public (Brazova and Matczak, 2013; Kešetović, 2013). Besides the potential side effects, the main argument here was that the vaccination was beginning too late to be effective. In the Czech Republic, many practitioners were claiming the H1N1 influenza to be a media bubble (Brazova and Matczak, 2013). Interestingly, however, these two countries differed when it comes to consensus at the political level. While the decision to purchase the antiviral vaccines was agreed unanimously in the Czech Republic, in Serbia, there was an opposition also among the politicians.

Dissatisfaction of the health professionals with the management of the H1N1 crisis occurred also in France. Here, however, the criticism was not questioning the vaccines (as it was in the two cases above) but rather the system setup. Independent medical doctors and nurses in particular criticized the fact that they were not sufficiently involved in the preparation process. The decision of public authorities to resort to vaccination centres instead of relying on the existing structures, such as general practitioners, was deemed to be an unfortunate one (Coste et al., 2013).

The role of the media and the medical staff deserves further distinction with respect to civil security governance during the H1N1 crisis. While all these voices were potentially undermining the legitimacy of authorities' conduct, their role with respect to the governance issue was different. The alarmist approach of the media (see further below) could be said to have made the crisis management more difficult and to contribute significantly to the overreaction, making the political cost of a more sober approach very high. The role of the medical staff, on the other hand, was very different in some cases as discussed above, providing a more practical perspective and thus representing a positive feature of the civil security governance system.

Communication

Providing information is crucial in crisis management (Lagadec, 2009, p. 482), as conflicting or confusing information can be destructive during emergencies (Fitzgerald, 2012, p. 162). The role of the media proved to be particularly ambiguous during the H1N1 crisis. On the one hand, the information had to be disseminated to the population and some countries, such as the Netherlands, launched large information campaigns. On the other hand, however, in many countries (notably in Austria, Czech Republic, Estonia, Germany, Italy, Latvia, Slovakia and the UK) the media were reported to exaggerate the severity of the pandemic threat and thus to alarm and confuse the population.

Slovakia and Latvia are examples of countries where the media portrayed the government as not doing enough. In Slovakia, the media presented the amount of vaccines to be purchased as low and was comparing the situation to other states where the decision was taken to buy larger quantities. Somewhat similarly, in Latvia, the media at first reported that the government was not going to purchase vaccines at all – a message which created a lot of concern among the citizens (Hellenberg and Vissuri, 2013b).

Even the countries that involved traditional media channels, such as TV and radio, in their crisis management – as France did – were facing challenges from 'open' media (especially the internet) through which negative information about the vaccines were spread. The authorities then were not able to adopt an efficient strategy to deal with the rumours launched in this way, which were competing with the official communication (Coste et al., 2013). The growing role of the Internet poses a challenge for civil security governance. On the one hand, it can help in information dissemination, but, on the other hand, it also can undermine the credibility of governmental bodies' decisions and provoke panic reactions.

Leaving the interfering role of the media aside, the way in which the authorities themselves communicated with the public during the crisis was crucial. Here, Germany can serve as an example of a rather sober and informing approach. The official bulletin provided recommendations to the media and the public, yet it was stressed that the advice was based on relatively less certain data and predictions (Hegemann and Bossong, 2013a). Contrastingly, the communication with the public was characterized as poor in Switzerland and the UK. In both cases, the public was rather confused, receiving inconsistent and often even contradicting information from various official sources (Hegemann and Bossong, 2013b; Fanoulis et al., 2013a). In the UK, the exchange of information was also problematic, not only as far as the public was concerned, but also among different participants involved in the management of the H1N1 crisis (Fanoulis et al., 2013a).

Conclusion

Analysing the responses to the H1N1 influenza in Europe, both diversity and similarities of the actions can be observed. Starting with similarities, the actions of the states (with few exceptions) were serious and can be characterized as strongly precautionary. The pressures from the media, the public and possibly from the pharmaceutical industry led the governments and the responsible bodies to purchase vaccines and to implement vaccination as well as other measures. The actions were clearly presented as proper in a situation of high uncertainty. It helped building an image of the situation being under control.

At the beginning, the chapter set out to focus on the legitimacy of the authorities' conduct, operationalized through output and throughput. In none of the countries, the legitimacy seems to have been shaken dramatically (or even at all). In most of the cases (with the exception of Switzerland and, to a lesser extent, Estonia), there were no important changes to the national civil security governance systems in the aftermath of the crisis.

Among the different European countries, the reaction was not completely uniform. Poland did not purchase the vaccines and Estonia purchased only a (comparably) small number. In most of the cases, stakeholders (such as medical professionals) were involved in decision-making; but different ones, and in different positions. Some were criticizing the governmental actions while others were more directly involved in the decision-making. Also the public reaction varied: in some countries, the governments and the responsible bodies were criticized; in others, the public remained relatively calm. In some countries, the governments put a significant emphasis on communication with the public (by launching information campaigns), while in others the communication with the public was modest.

Furthermore, civil security governance systems are differently organized in terms of dealing with pandemics. In most of the countries, the response was highly centralized, although exceptions could be found. The countries used different procedures to react – some of them equally effective – without any single best model to be drawn. Coordination deficits were noted within both centralized (UK) and decentralized (Germany) systems dealing with the H1N1.

While coordination (or a lack thereof) is a typical feature for crisis management in general, the uncertainty and the related overreaction are specific to pandemic crises. The reaction to the H1N1 influenza caused (as became clear eventually) most of the European countries to overreact. The only states not overreacting to the crisis were Estonia and Poland. As for the former, other factors were also at play, such as economic ones. Thus, the differences here seem to correlate with cultural and economic differences rather than with different civil security institutions and governance processes.

It could be summarized that the H1N1 pandemic showed that despite a significant diversity in terms of the organization scheme of civil security governance system, and particular courses of action, there is a general tendency to rely on precautionary action in the European countries. This seems to have been perceived as legitimate by the public as well. Although the cases showed that the response was indeed exaggerated, this did not lead to widespread or significant reforms. Similarly, a few countries launched political or professional inquiries in the aftermath of the crisis. Thus, there seems to be a consensus that the reaction was largely acceptable and appropriate.

Except for Serbia, where a H1N1-related corruption scandal took place, the overreaction did not seem to have had more far-reaching consequences. In the cases where the reaction was perceived as rather mismanaged (Switzerland and the UK), the problems were mainly associated with the tasks performed in crisis management in general – that is poor coordination and poor communication, especially with the public, which was receiving conflicting information from different official sources during the crisis. By the same token, in Estonia – one of the countries not overreacting with its limited vaccines purchase – the changes in the aftermath of the crisis included the budgeting of additional financial resources to deal with such crises in the future. Hence, across Europe, economic overspending seems to be much less critical to legitimacy than the (potential) fatalities.

Notes

1. The analysis was funded by the Specific Research Grant of the Charles University in Prague, Faculty of Social Sciences Nr. SVV 2014 260 112.
2. The international governance issues concerning the H1N1 pandemic have been already addressed elsewhere (see for example Wilson et al., 2010) and are beyond the scope of this chapter.
3. ANVIL stands for Analysis of Civil Security Systems in Europe. All country studies and reports are available on the project website, http://www.anvil-project.net.
4. Moral legitimacy in Suchman's terms does not directly focus on the 'inputs' in the policy process in the sense of representative participation in decision-making. In this chapter, we somewhat overcome this by discussing the array of stakeholders involved in the H1N1 decision-making and response actions.

References

Bakken, M. and M. Rhinard (2013) Country Study: Sweden. http://anvil-project.net/wp-content/uploads/2014/01/Sweden_v1.0.pdf, date accessed 15 December 2014.
Beck, U. (2006) 'Living in the World Risk Society: A Hobhouse Memorial Public Lecture Given on Wednesday 15 February 2006 at the London School of Economics', *Economy and Society*, 35, 329–345.
Boin, A. (2009) 'The New World of Crises and Crisis Management: Implications for Policymaking and Research', *Review of Policy Research*, 26, 367–377.
Bossong, R. and H. Hegemann (2013) *ANVIL Deliverable 4.1: Synthesis Report on Comparison of Civil Security Systems*. http://anvil-project.net/wp-content/uploads/2013/12/Deliverable_4.1.pdf, date accessed 15 December 2014.
Brazova, V.-K. and P. Matczak (2013) *Country Study: Czech Republic*. http://anvil-project.net/wp-content/uploads/2014/01/Czech-Republic_v1.0.pdf, date accessed 15 December 2014.
Brugha, R. and Z. Varvasovszky (2000) 'Stakeholder Analysis: A Review', *Health Policy and Planning*, 15, 239–246.
Coste, F., E. Nexon and J.-F. Daguzan (2013) *Country Study: France*. http://anvil-project.net/wp-content/uploads/2014/01/France_v1.0.pdf, date accessed 15 December 2014.
Dmochowski A. (2012) 'Czy rząd PO odpowiada za śmierć 2000 osób?', *Gazeta Polska*, 2, 11 January 2012.
Fanoulis, E., E. Kirchner and H. Dorussen (2013a) *Country Study: United Kingdom*. http://anvil-project.net/wp-content/uploads/2014/02/United-Kingdom_v1.1.pdf, date accessed 15 December 2014.
Fanoulis, E., E. Kirchner and H. Dorussen (2013b) *Country Study: Ireland*. http://anvil-project.net/wp-content/uploads/2014/01/Ireland_v1.0.pdf, date accessed 15 December 2014.
Fanoulis, E., E. Kirchner and H. Dorussen (2013c) *Country Study: Malta*. http://anvil-project.net/wp-content/uploads/2014/01/Malta_v1.0.pdf, date accessed 15 December 2014.
Fitzgerald, G., P. Aitken, R. Z. Shaban, J. Patrick, P. Arbon et al. (2012) 'Pandemic (H1N1) Influenza 2009 and Australian Emergency Departments: Implications for Policy, Practice and Pandemic Preparedness', *Emergency Medicine Australasia*, 24, 159–165.
Gazeta Wyborcza (2010) Trzy razy więcej chorych na grypę niż rok temu. Dominuje wirus A/H1N1. http://wiadomosci.gazeta.pl/wiadomosci/1,114873,8503451,Trzy_razy_wiecej_chorych_na_grype_niz_rok_temu__Dominuje.html, date accessed 15 December 2014.
Hajer, M. (2003) 'Policy without Polity? Policy Analysis and the Institutional Void', *Policy Sciences*, 36, 175–195.
Harrald, J. R. (2006) 'Agility and Discipline: Critical Success Factors for Disaster Response', *The Annals of the American Academy of Political and Social Science*, 604(1), 256–272.
Hegemann, H. and R. Bossong (2013a) Country Study: Germany. http://anvil-project.net/wp-content/uploads/2013/12/Germany_v1.0.pdf, date accessed 15 December 2014.

Hegemann, H. and R. Bossong (2013b) *Country Study: Switzerland*. http://anvil-project.net/wp-content/uploads/2014/01/Switzerland_v1.0.pdf, date accessed 15 December 2014.
Hellenberg, T. and P. Vissuri (2013) *Coutry Study: Estonia*. http://anvil-project.net/wp-content/uploads/2013/12/Estonia_v1.0.pdf, date accessed 15 December 2014.
Hellenberg, T. and P. Vissuri (2013b) *Country Study: Latvia*. http://anvil-project.net/wp-content/uploads/2014/02/Latvia_v1.1.pdf, date accessed 15 December 2014.
Kamradt-Scott, A. (2012) 'Changing Perceptions of Pandemic Influenza and Public Health Responses', *American Journal of Public Health*, 102, 90–98.
Kešetović, Ž. (2013) *Country Study: Serbia*. http://anvil-project.net/wp-content/uploads/2014/01/Serbia_v1.0.pdf, date accessed 15 December 2014.
Kuipers, S. and A. Boin (2013) *Country Study: The Netherlands*, http://anvil-project.net/wp-content/uploads/2013/12/Netherlands_v1.1.pdf, date accessed 15 December 2014.
Lagadec, P. (2009) 'A New Cosmology of Risks and Crises: Time for a Radical Shift in Paradigm and Practice', *Review of Policy Research*, 26, 473–486.
Martin, R., A. Conseil, A. Longstaff, J. Kodo, J. Siegert, et al. (2010) 'Pandemic Influenza Control in Europe and the Constraints Resulting from Incoherent Public Health Laws', *BMC Public Health*, 10, 532.
Martin, R. and A. Conseil (2012) 'Public Health Policy and Law for Pandemic Influenza: A Case for European Harmonization?', *Journal of Health Politics, Policy and Law*, 37, 1091–1110.
Masotti, P., M.E. Green, R. Birthwistle, I. Genmill, K. Moore, K. O'Connor, A. Hansen-Taugher, and R. Shaw (2013) 'pH1N1 – A Comparative Analysis of Public Health Responses in Ontario to the Influenza Outbreak, Public Health and Primary Care: Lessons Learned and Policy Suggestions', *BMC Public Health*, 13, 687.
Ministry of Health (2010) Komunikat: Rezolucja Zgromadzenia Parlamentarnego Rady Europy dot. pandemii grypy AH1N1 potwierdza słuszność stanowiska rządu RP w sprawie zakupu szczepionek, http://www.mz.gov.pl/wwwmz/index?mr=m99&ms=915&ml=pl&mi=915&mx=0&mt=&my=708&ma=015404, date accessed 25 March 2013.
Moe, T. L. and P. Pathranarakul (2006) 'An Integrated Approach to Natural Disaster Management: Public Project Management and its Critical Success Factors', *Disaster Prevention and Management*, 15, 396–413.
Nohrstedt, D. (2008) 'The Politics of Crisis Policymaking: Chernobyl and Swedish Nuclear Energy Policy', *Policy Studies Journal*, 36, 257–278.
Nový, D. (2013) 'Analýzasystémuvnitřníchpředpisů a řídícíchaktů v ozbrojenýchsilách', *Vojenskérozhledy* [Czech Military Review], 22 (54), 4, 113–123.
Polskie Radio (2009) Minister nie ulegnie, poczekamy na szczepionkę. http://www.polskieradio.pl/5/3/Artykul/180624/, date accessed 12 November 2014.
Purfield, C. and C. B. Rosenberg (2010) *Adjustment under a Currency Peg: Estonia, Latvia and Lithuania During the Global Financial Crisis 2008–2009*. International Monetary Fund. https://www.imf.org/external/pubs/ft/wp/2010/wp10213.pdf, date accessed 15 December 2014.
Quarantelli, E. L. (1988) 'Disaster Crisis Management: A Summary of Research Findings', *Journal of Management Studies*, 25(4), 373–385.

Schemann, K., J. A. Gillespie, J. A. Toribio, M. P. Ward and N. K. Dhand (2012) 'Controlling Equine Influenza: Policy Networks and Decision-Making during the 2007 Australian Equine Influenza Outbreak', *Transboundary and Emerging Diseases*, 61, 449–463.

Schmidt, V. A. (2013) 'Democracy and Legitimacy in the European Union Revisited: Input, Output and "Throughput"', *Political Studies*, 61, 2–22.

Seetoh, T., M. Liverani and R. Coker (2012) 'Framing Risk in Pandemic Influenza Policy and Control', *Global Public Health*, 7, 717–730.

Suchman, M. C. (1995) 'Managing Legitimacy: Strategic and Institutional Approaches', *Academy of Management Review*, 20, 571–610.

Takacs, V. and P. Matczak (2013) *Country Study: Hungary*. http://anvil-project.net/wp-content/uploads/2013/12/Hungary_v1.0.pdf, date accessed 15 December 2014.

Upshur, R. E. (2005) 'Enhancing the Legitimacy of Public Health Response in Pandemic Influenza Planning: Lessons from SARS', *The Yale Journal of Biology and Medicine*, 78, 335.

Wilson, K., J. S. Brownstein and D. P. Fidler (2010) 'Strengthening the International Health Regulations: Lessons from the H1N1 Pandemic', *Health Policy and Planning*, 25, 505–509.

Winston, L., S. Wagner and S. Chan (2014) 'Healthcare Workers under a Mandated H1N1 Vaccination Policy with Employment Termination Penalty: A Survey to Assess Employee Perception', *Vaccine*, 32, 4786–4790.

World Health Organization (2010) H1N1 in post-pandemic period, 10 August, http://www.who.int/mediacentre/news/statements/2010/h1n1_vpc_20100810/en/, date accessed 25 March 2015.

5
Regional Organizations and Disaster Risk Management: Europe's Place in the Global Picture[1]

Daniel Petz

Introduction: The rising wave of regionalism and regions' engagement with disaster risk management

Together with globalization, regionalization has been one of the most transformative processes in the international domain since the end of the Cold War. By now, almost all regions in the world have some sort of regional organization, in many cases there are even further sub-regional divisions of organizations that focus on more specific issues or even numbers of overlapping organizations. While regional integration almost everywhere initially started out as cooperation on political, economic or security issues, the activities of regional organizations have steadily expanded to a wide array of issues (Fawcett, 2004). One of these domains regional organizations have expanded into is cooperation on managing disasters caused by natural hazards,[2] which particularly gathered speed in the late 1990s/early 2000s and has continued unabated ever since. There is a range of possible explanations for the expansion of regional cooperation into that particular area.

(1) Natural hazards do not stop for national boundaries: As disasters caused by natural hazards often affect a number of countries, disaster risk management issues seem to be a logical area of cooperation between countries that face a similar set of hazards. Once regional frameworks for cooperation are being developed they allow for a (maybe more effective) alternative to bi-lateral cooperation.

(2) Benefits of assistance from neighbours: Major disasters can overwhelm national capacities for response and reconstruction. Assistance from neighbours is close by and can in many cases be faster and cheaper than assistance that comes from further away. It often is also seen as culturally more appropriate or politically more acceptable.[3]
(3) Rise in number and impact of disasters caused by natural hazards: The number of reported disasters caused by natural hazards has almost doubled since the 1980s.[4] Among the reasons for this are rising exposure to natural hazards by growing global populations, adverse impacts of economic development on natural protection mechanisms such as forests, mangroves, climate change, which leads to the changes in frequency and ferocity of certain natural hazards (IPCC, 2013), and better monitoring and reporting. Particularly rising economic damage by natural disasters has become a severe threat to economic development for a growing number of countries. In several regions, triggering events (for example the Indian Ocean Tsunami for Southeast Asia) have led to deepening and widening of integration on disaster risk management.
(4) International enabling environment: International actors have taken up the issue of disaster management and created an enabling environment that is supporting regional organizations in expanding into the area of disaster risk management (compare Hollis in this volume). Of particular importance is the Yokohama/Hyogo process managed and supported by the United Nations Office for Disaster Risk Reduction (UNISDR) and the World Bank's Global Facility for Disaster Risk Reduction (GFDRR), which actively engage with regional actors on disaster risk reduction (UNISDR, 2007). Other important initiatives are the work of the International Federation of the Red Cross and Red Crescent Societies (IFRC), particularly on International Disaster Response Law.
(5) Low hanging fruit: Particularly in the initial stages, cooperation on disaster risk management does not require big political or financial commitments, as much of the cooperation is on the technical rather than political level and compared to issues such as conflict disaster risk management is often seen as politically less sensitive.
(6) Shifts in technology: Rise in information technology and other technologies opened up cooperation on a regional scale, particularly regarding disaster monitoring and early warning systems. Systems that might be difficult to afford and maintain for single, particularly

small and/or low income countries can be managed at scale at the regional level.

Another important observation is that the massive increase in regional activities in disaster risk management has gone hand in hand with the shift from seeing dealing with disasters caused by natural hazards as mostly an issue of disaster response to a more comprehensive disaster risk management paradigm that sees managing natural hazards more holistically throughout the whole disaster management cycle (risk reduction, preparedness, early warning, response, reconstruction). This shift opens up a wider area of activities on which cooperation is possible and, as countries within a region often face similar hazards, generates incentives to engage in processes such as the exchange of experiences or 'best practices' and peer learning. This broad range of issues and coordination processes matches the notion of civil security as an emergent governance regime at multiple levels and with a variety of governance instruments. Previous studies on security governance similarly placed a particular emphasis at intersection institutions and hybrid regimes at the regional level (Kirchner and Sperling, 2007; Sperling and Weber, 2014), even though these studies mainly focused on conflict management and 'traditional' security policy.

So while there certainly has been a quantitative shift in regional organization's engagement with disaster risk management, it is not all clear if the engagement of those bodies with the issue makes a qualitative difference in terms of reducing disaster losses on the ground, however. Some authors see regions as uniquely suited to provide important functions in disaster risk management, such as Sumonin (2005, p. 7) who notes that:

> [r]egional organizations are particularly well-equipped to carry out today's threat management functions. They have solid information and expertise on their regions, inherently tailor their responses to the regional realities, and can get on the ground fast. ROs [regional organizations] are also innately compelled to continue their engagement and monitoring of the scene when the other actors depart. And having reshaped their policies and plans over the years to meet newly emerging challenges, ROs have a record of responsiveness and institutional flexibility.

Others see large gaps between what is promised and what is actually delivered, so for example Harvey (2010, p. 17):

By and large, the rhetoric of many regional organizations is ahead of the reality. Actors in many regions have called attention to the importance of strengthening national capacities for disaster response, and to developing relationships between international and national disaster management officials, but there remain significant gaps between 'what is established in principle and what happens in practice'.

Unfortunately, there is still very little empirical research on the issue of ROs engagement with disaster risk management. In particular, there have been a few systematic attempts to look at the global picture of regional organization's work. This is particularly true about the question on the added value that ROs bring to the multitude of actors that are engaged in disaster risk management, from governments, the UN system, development banks, IFRC, NGOs, universities and research institutions, civil society and so on.

Seventeen indicators on regional organizations' work on disaster risk management

Before this chapter comes to introduce and discuss the 17 indicators on ROs in disaster risk management, two major definitional issues need to be raised. Firstly, there is no agreed upon definition about what counts as a region or not. Many definitions include geographical criteria, noting that regions are defined by certain geographic boundaries. Others highlight more the fact of some kind of shared history, community or shared interests. Different definitions are also contentious about the question if regions are based on states or if smaller geographical and political units, such as municipal areas, can also be defined as regions. One definition that makes good sense for the purpose of this chapter is given by Joseph Nye, who defines a region as a group of states linked together by both a geographical relationship and a degree of mutual interdependence (Fawcett, 2004). This makes particular sense when talking about ROs, which consist of a group of states that have decided to cooperate on certain issues, creating a set of institutions to manage that cooperation, but are not necessarily confined to narrow geographical definition. One only has to look at Europe, where the European Union (EU), Organization for Security and Cooperation in Europe (OSCE) and Council of Europe (CoE) have different notions of the boundaries of Europe. It also allows for the integration of organizations such as the League of Arab States and OSCE which are spread over more than one continent.

In addition, as for the purpose of dealing with disaster caused by natural hazards action overwhelmingly is organized based on states, a statist definition is useful. One further definitional issue is the differentiation of regional and sub-regional organizations. As in several continents there are organizations that include most if not all states on the continent, those organizations are often termed ROs, while smaller sub-sets of organizations are termed sub-regional organizations. This includes, for example, the cases of the African Union (AU) and the Economic Community of West African States (ECOWAS) in Africa. As this definition is not clear-cut, this chapter refers to all such organizations as ROs.

Secondly, terminology defining activities dealing with disasters caused by natural hazards is often used unclearly and interchangeably, particularly the terms disaster management (DM), disaster risk reduction (DRR) and disaster risk management (DRM).[5] Genealogically, the term disaster management is the oldest and has a connotation to describe activities that are mostly focused on disaster response. DRR came to the fore through the Yokohama and Hyogo processes and is mostly used to describe activities that are pre-emptive to disasters and aiming at reducing disaster risk. Recently, the term DRM has become an umbrella term comprehensively including all activities that deal with managing disasters from natural hazards (pre-, during- and post-disaster). This chapter follows this distinction.

As stated previously, ROs have taken on a wide range of activities in DRM, but there is little comparative research on this issue. The following framework for analysing ROs' involvement in DRM was developed by looking at more than 30 ROs. The original study by Ferris and Petz (2013) deliberately cast a wide net and tried to include all relevant ROs that had engaged in some way in DRM, the minimum being a mission statement that they planned to engage with DRM. This was followed by a more in-depth analysis of 13 ROs[6] that displayed more substantive activity. This narrower sample was also defined by additional considerations, namely to include at least one organization from each global region and cases that could highlight intra-regional diversity to DRM.

Overall, the aim was to provide a first sense of the existing empirical diversity that could be explored further in subsequent studies as well as to shed light on the question of effectiveness of regional disaster management (RDM). The result is a list of 17 indicators that guided extensive desk research on the surveyed ROs (Ferris and Petz, 2013, p. 8). Their organization is summarized in Table 5.1.

In the following, each indicator is briefly elaborated and illustrated with reference to current developments.[7]

Table 5.1 Indicators for regional organizations' work on disaster risk management

Does the regional organization have:

1. regular intergovernmental meetings on DRM
2. a regional DRR framework/convention
3. a RDM framework/convention
4. a specific organization for DRM
5. a regional/sub-RDM centre
6. a regional disaster relief fund
7. a regional disaster insurance scheme
8. a way of providing regional funding for DRR projects
9. a means to provide humanitarian assistance
10. a regional rapid response mechanism
11. regional technical cooperation (warning systems)
12. joint DM exercises/simulations
13. regional capacity building for national disaster management organizations (NDMO) staff/technical training on DRM issues
14. research on DRM issues
15. regional military protocols for disaster assistance
16. a regional web portal on DRM
17. a regional International Disaster Response Law, Rules and Principles (IDRL) treaty/guidelines

The first indicator looks at the holding of regular intergovernmental meetings on DRM. This can be seen as a minimum requirement for cooperation as usually intergovernmental forums are the main policy and decision-making bodies in ROs. One main qualifying factor for this indicator is the frequency of those meetings, which serves as an indication of the importance that member states give to the issue. Organizations that closely cooperate on DRM usually hold meetings on both technical and ministerial levels. All 13 organizations that were researched more closely were holding regular intergovernmental meetings on DRM issues. In Europe, the EU, CoE and Organization for Black Sea Economic Cooperation (BSEC) hold regular intergovernmental meetings on DRM. The OSCE does not.

The second and third indicators look at the existence of a RDM or DRR framework. DRR frameworks were mostly developed with the rising importance of the issue through the 2005 Hyogo Framework for Action. The frameworks also take very different legal forms, with only a small number of regional treaties dealing primary with DRM.

The fourth indicator looks at the question if ROs have a specific organization for DRM issues. Several ROs have formed a distinct entity that deals with DRM. This is particularly prevalent in Latin America and the Caribbean, where the Caribbean Community (CARICOM), Central American Integration System (SICA) and the Andean Community all have formed specific agencies, centres or committees focusing on disaster issues. Other ROs have subsumed the DRM agenda within larger departments, mostly dealing with humanitarian and social issues. For example, the EU has integrated the Civil Protection Mechanism within the Commission's European Community Humanitarian Office (ECHO).

The fifth indicator is about the existence of a regional/sub-regional DM centre. Several organizations have developed DM centres. There are two types of centres. The first type with distinct operational capacities monitors natural hazards, collects data, provides information management and facilitates humanitarian assistance. Prime examples are the Emergency Response Coordination Centre of the EU and the ASEAN Coordinating Centre for Humanitarian Assistance (AHA Centre). The second type of centres focuses mostly on training and research, such as the Disaster Management Centre of the South Asian Association for Regional Cooperation (SAARC).

The sixth indicator is looking at the existence of a regional disaster relief fund. Several organizations have disaster relief funds. The most significant fund is the EU's Solidarity fund, which spent more than Euro 3.7 billion for 63 major disasters in Europe since 2002.[8] A number of other funds were already developed in the early stages of regional cooperation. For example, the AU Special Emergency Assistance Fund was already active in 1984 and has since dispersed 40 million US dollars for risk reduction and relief activities. In light of these sums, those other funds often have symbolic character or are not sufficiently replenished.

Indicator seven looks at the existence of regional disaster insurance schemes. Risk finance and risk insurance have become a rather trendy topics in recent years, with several organizations such as the Secretariat of the Pacific Community (SPC), Association of Southeast Asian Nations (ASEAN), AU and Indian Ocean Commission having recently made forays into that area. The predecessor of all those efforts is the Caribbean Catastrophe Risk Insurance Facility, which provides emergency funding for countries affected by hurricanes and earthquakes. These insurance schemes are not only important mechanisms for countries to pool risk and access insurance markets, they also lead to underlying data collection such as detailed risk assessments that can be used for other DRM interventions. European ROs have not yet developed disaster insurance schemes, but the European Commission published a Green Paper on the insurance of natural- and man-made disasters (European Commission,

2013). It also sponsored related academic studies and organized a conference on prevention and insurance of natural catastrophes.

The provision of regional funding for DRR projects, which is indicator number eight, looks at those organizations that provided direct financial assistance for DRR programs. The study found that only two organizations fulfilled that criterion, the AU via the above-mentioned fund and the EU through both the Civil Protection Mechanism (CPM) and EU's structural funds. In the EU, the CPM provides funding for multi-member projects, while the structural funds have several billion Euros allocated for DRM projects. Given that most ROs' efforts on DRM are mostly donor funded, it is not surprising that most do not have large emergency relief funds or provide direct funding for DRR projects. In DRR, they can rather be seen providing technical assistance and/or work on joint donor funded projects with member states.

Indicator nine specifies whether ROs provide humanitarian assistance and number ten relates to regional rapid response mechanisms. There is a dividing line between ROs that have invested strongly in response capacity, and others, putting a stronger focus on risk reduction activities. ROs that have invested in response capacities often take roles in monitoring and relaying disaster information as well as coordinating regional response efforts. Prime examples are the EU's CPM, where in case of a disaster member states communicate assistance needs to the CPM, which then links up the affected state with capacities available from other member states and supports the logistical and legal deployment of assistance. In 2013, the mechanism had 16 requests for assistance only four of which were within the EU. ASEAN's AHA Centre aims to play a similar role. Not surprisingly, both organizations have developed DM centres that are equipped to monitor regional hazards and are equipped with modern information systems.

Several organizations also have developed more specific rapid response capacities. For example, the EU through the CPM can dispatch a small team of experts to disaster areas, the ECOWAS has created an Emergency Response Unit Team and ASEAN has developed Emergency Rapid Assessment Teams. Those teams or units work on coordinating and supporting aid delivery from other member states and/or provide damage and needs assessments. Other ROs provide direct humanitarian assistance in emergencies, too, but usually not on large scale and within their region only.

Indicators 11, 13 and 14 respectively refer to issues of technical cooperation; regional capacity building for NDMO staff and technical training on DRM issues; and the provision of research on DRM issues done by the regional organization. ROs play an important role in fostering technical cooperation on DRM issues, with ten out of 13 organizations engaged in that area and more than half engaged in technical training and capacity building. Also about half of the organizations were performing research on DRM issues. Again, there is a great variety among organizations. Several organizations have specialized technical centres and units; others rely on regional networks. For example, the CoE supports research on DRM issues through its EUR-OPA network of over 20 Euro-Mediterranean Centres. These centres are based on a network of cooperation between member states governments, universities and international agencies. On the intersection between capacity building and the provision of humanitarian assistance is the role that some organizations play in pooling and training response capacity from member states. Again, the EU is a prime example, where the CPM facilitates the creation of disaster modules, which are thematic clusters of experts and equipment. The Caribbean Disaster Emergency Management Agency (CDEMA) has created the Caribbean Disaster Relief Unit, comprising DM experts from military forces within CARICOM. The unit provides logistical support in disaster areas, in particularly pertaining to the handling of relief goods.

Indicator 12 analyses whether regions have joint DM exercises or simulations. A growing but still small number of ROs organize regularly DM exercises and simulations. While some regions, like ASEAN hold region-wide exercises, the EU has a more indirect role, supporting multi-country thematic civil protection exercises that are organized by member states. For many organizations, training for member states' national disaster management organizations (NDMO) is an important part of their core function (see also indicator 13). For example, CDEMA makes training an important part of its framework and SAARC's DM Centre, which is its core institution, mainly focuses on training and research activities. ROs in this realm often collaborate with international actors and actors within the region.

Indicator 15 looks at the existence of regional military protocols for disaster assistance, spelling out the rules for military assistance and/or developing rules for civil-military cooperation. The main international instruments on the issue are the 'Oslo guidelines' (Guidelines on the Use of Military and Civil Defence Assets in Disaster Relief) and the Guidelines on the Use of Military and Civil Defence Assets to support United Nations Humanitarian Activities in Complex Emergencies (MCDA). The EU was strongly engaged in the review of the MCDA guidelines and the EU Commission published a communication on the adherence to the promotion of the guidelines in the EU (European Commission, 2014a). In addition, the EU developed a framework for military disaster relief assistance and a civil-military cell within the EU Military Staff (EUMS) to support civil-military coordination.

The next indicator, number 16, looks at the existence of a web portal on DRM. About half of the organizations had regional DRM portals. The portals have different shapes. While some, like ASEAN's AHA Centre website, directly relay real-time hazard and disaster information, others focus more on being resource portals for member state governments and international actors. Pacific Disaster Net, for example, supports national action planning and decision-making and includes information as detailed as risk management plans. The EU's Common Emergency and Communication Information System (CECIS) is aimed at member states, providing web-based alerts and notifications, aiming at facilitating emergency communication between participating states. The other European ROs researched do not have web portals on DRM.

The seventeenth and final indicator refers to the existence of a regional International Disaster Response Laws, Rules and Principles (IDRL) treaty or guideline. The earliest is the Inter-American Convention to Facilitate Disaster Assistance adopted by the Organization of American States (OAS) in 1991. While it has only been ratified by five member states yet, it has already entered into force. Furthermore, guidelines for the domestic facilitation and regulation of international disaster relief and initial recovery assistance were developed by the International Federation of Red Cross and Red Crescent Societies (IFRC) and unanimously adopted by the state parties to the Geneva Conventions in 2007. In addition, three UN General Assembly resolutions encourage states to make use of the guidelines. The guidelines mostly aim at implementation on the national level, and therefore not many ROs have yet taken on the issue. Nonetheless, there are some activities surrounding the issue of IDRL. In Europe, the EU developed guidelines for host nation support, aiming to support the affected country to receive international assistance in an effective and efficient manner. In addition, BSEC's Agreement on Collaboration in Emergency Assistance and Emergency Response to Natural and Man-Made Disasters is largely an IDRL treaty.

Taken together, the organization fulfilling the most indicators was the EU with 16, followed by CARICOM with 12, SPC with nine, then ASEAN and SICA with eight of the listed indicators. The CoE fulfilled six indicators (BSEC and OSCE that were not part of the initial study would fulfil six and two, respectively). In terms of indicators, not surprisingly all organizations held intergovernmental meetings (indicator 1) and all had a DRR framework/convention and 12 out of 13 had a DM framework/convention (indicator 3), with eight organizations having a single comprehensive framework. Ten organizations engaged in technical cooperation (indicator 11), seven in technical training and capacity building (indicator 13), six have developed regional DRM web portals (indicator 16) and also six performed research on DRM and climate change adaptation issues (indicator 13). Five ROs had specific organizations for DRM (indicator 4) and four RDM centres (indicator 5). Three organizations had a regional disaster relief fund (indicator 6), two a regional disaster insurance scheme (indicator 7), two provided substantial regional funding for DRR projects (indicator 8) and only one organization provided large scale humanitarian assistance (indicator 9). Five organizations had regional response mechanisms (indicator 10), three organizations joint DM exercises/simulations (indicator 12), three organizations regional military protocols for disaster assistance (indicator 15) and two organizations regional IDRL treaties/guidelines (indicator 17).[9]

The European picture

Against this background, the final section of this paper deepens this picture of a European lead in terms of (partly overlapping) regional organization and governance structures for civil security. First and foremost, the EU is clearly *the* leading regional organization in terms of DRM, and for most European countries it is also the main regional actor in terms of DRM. This does not mean that the EU was one of the first organizations that engaged with the issue; particularly organizations in the Americas were way ahead in cooperating on DRM before the EU developed its work on civil protection. Members of the European Community started to coordinate on civil protection issues in the mid-eighties, but only in 1997, after the formation of the EU, a civil protection program was started. The CPM was developed after the 9/11 terror attacks in 2001.[10] Current membership includes all 28 member states, plus Iceland, Norway and the Republic of Macedonia.[11] Core of the mechanism is the 24/7 Emergency Response Coordination Centre (ERCC), which monitors emergencies and coordinates the response of the participating countries in case of a crisis. The CPM also developed protection modules, which can be deployed during emergencies both within and outside the EU. Another key tool is the CECIS, a web-based alert and notification system providing the participating states and the ERCC a necessary communication tool for responding to disasters. The mechanism also provides capacity and training for member states and broadly supports their prevention and preparedness efforts through exercises, research, information management and so on. Also in light of other contributions to this volume, there is no need to give a detailed account of EU civil protection and crisis management capacities here.

Beyond that, the list of 17 indicators discussed above illustrates the breadth of additional activities undertaken by the EU. Beyond that it is also interesting to note that the EU aims to address the whole range of natural and man-made disasters, while the majority of ROs outside of Europe avoid mixing issues of 'natural disasters' and conflict and therefore rarely develop comprehensive civil security programs. The EU certainly has the structural advantage that its member states are developed countries and on average well off, which is not a given in most of the other ROs engaged in DM. Of course, the principle of subsidiarity guides and at some point limits the further expansion of all EU activities, including in the area of crisis and DM, not least since its member states have generally well-developed domestic systems for these purposes (compare Bossong and Hegemann in this volume). However, as seen with the 2013 revision of the European CPM, there is still scope for widening and deepening of joint activities. Strong domestic systems coupled with a (comparatively) rather benign hazard environment in terms of natural hazards in Europe also mean that much of the EU's work on natural disasters response can happen outside its boundaries, which makes the decision to house the CPM within DG ECHO understandable. As seen from the study discussed above, the only area where the EU has not developed work is the field of disaster finance and insurance, which again can be explained by the fact that member states on average have sufficient access to financial and insurance markets. Nevertheless, the EU, as mentioned, has started to explore options to engage in that area in the future.

The strength of the EU should, however, not distract attention from the view that other European organizations also play a significant role. In terms of membership, the CoE with its 47 member countries is one of the most comprehensive organizations in Europe. The CoE is mostly recognized for its protection of human and civil rights based on the European Convention of Human Rights. However, already in 1987, the CoE developed the European and Mediterranean (EUR-OPA) Major Hazards Agreement to promote cooperation between member states in terms of DRM, focusing on major natural and technological disasters. The date unsurprisingly falls shortly after the Chernobyl disaster, which marked a decisive shock with regard to the mutual environmental and technological vulnerability of European states. The agreement currently has 26 members, which also include non-member states such as Algeria, Lebanon and Morocco.[12] Cooperation happens at two levels. First, at the political level with the Committee of Permanent Correspondents, which meets at least once a year; and the ministerial meeting, which convenes at least every four years. At the scientific and technical level, the CoE, secondly, has developed a network of (currently 28) specialized Euro-Mediterranean Centres, which develop projects aiming to improve the awareness and resilience to risks in member states. Projects usually involve a lead organization and a number of supporting/partner organizations from within the designated centres.[13] The CoE's work on DRM under the treaty has a budget of about 5.7 million Euros, of which 1.5 million Euros are funded by the EU with which the CoE is cooperating on EUR-OPA.[14]

EUR-OPA is one of the earliest agreements by a regional organization on DRM and it has a clear but narrow focus on research, awareness raising and training, meaning that is does not engage with the whole complex of operational work of DRM. While several other ROs also engage with regional research resources such as universities, research institutes and think tanks, the CoE is unique in building such a wide network of institutions, based on a small central organizational platform. It seems that the aim is more to foster cooperation between member states and to build capacity through that cooperation, instead of building specialized capacity on the regional level like the EU does. Another issue of interest is the inclusion of the non-European Mediterranean area, as again, a few ROs usually transcend their membership when it comes to work on DRM. Highlighting the Euro-Mediterranean cooperation, the treaty is designed to engage non-CoE member states. Yet, this strength of inclusiveness can also be read as a downside. Given the fact that only about half of the CoE member states have ratified the agreement, one could in fact infer the treaty holds limited appeal, particularly to member states in central and northern Europe, where other frameworks are available.

The OSCE is another institutional regime that reflects the strengths and weaknesses of wider inclusiveness. It was institutionalized in 1994, stemming from the Conference for Security and Cooperation in Europe (since 1975).[15] It remains the world's largest regional security organization and with its 57 members stretches the boundaries of what is usually considered to be geographical Europe, including the USA and Canada in the west and the Central Asian countries in the east. Formed to support the East-West détente that started in the 1970s, the organization became a big regional tent for addressing a range of security issues after the Cold War. The organization promotes a comprehensive view of security, covering three dimensions: the politico-military, the economic and environmental and the human security. Interesting enough, given the broad range of activities of the organization, it has only recently started to engage with the issue of DRM and does so under the umbrella of its work on environmental issues. Among other activities, it held a workshop on the potential role of the organization in natural disaster relief in 2011 and designated the 22nd OSCE Economic and Environmental Forum in 2014 to focus on regional cooperation in managing disasters. These efforts, however, have so far not led to major efforts in the area aside from some project areas related to DRM. On the project level, the OSCE has been active in building capacity for wild fire management in the South Caucasus and Western Balkans, which has been ongoing since the OSCE conducted environmental emergency assessments to fire-affected areas in the South Caucasus region in 2006 and 2008. In 2014, the organization also held a workshop on the protection of electricity networks from natural disasters.[16] The OSCE's work on DRM seems rather project oriented than comprehensive. Being still relatively unsure of its role in Europe's regional architecture in terms of DRM, and given that much ground is already covered, this is understandable.

Shifting perspective from larger to smaller regional structures for DRM issues, BSEC provides an instructive example of another layer of cooperation in Europe. Founded in 1992, it currently has 12 member states[17] and mainly focuses on economic cooperation in the region. One additional area of cooperation for BSEC is emergency assistance, based on the Agreement on Collaboration in Emergency Assistance and Emergency Response to Natural and Man-Made Disasters, which was signed in April 1998 (with an additional protocol adopted in 2005). The agreement lays down the ground rules for mutual aid and emergency assistance in case of disasters. Based on the agreement, the organization has formed a working group on cooperation in emergency assistance. This group in turn has formed several ad hoc working groups on specific hazards, which are on seismic risk, massive forest fires and floods and torrents, and foster cooperation between technical experts of member states.[18] Based on the treaty and working groups, BSEC's activities have included several workshops, seminars and trainings dealing with DRM issues, as for instance a seminar on disaster prevention measures jointly organized by BSEC and Japan in 2013.[19]

The core of BSEC's engagement with DRM issues is certainly the 1998 treaty, which focuses on IDRL questions related to facilitating emergency assistance between member states and is coupled with technical cooperation and capacity building on hazard-specific issues. As most member states of BSEC are not members of the EU's CPM (with the exception of Greece and Romania), there seems to be a commitment to regional engagement on DRM issues in the Black Sea region, albeit, given a number of political difficulties between member states (for example the recent Ukraine-Russia conflict), integration is on a rather low level compared to many other ROs engaging in DRM.

Having looked at a variety of ROs in Europe in more detail, we can now make a couple of observations on how the work of European ROs fits into the global picture in the area of DRM (Table 5.2). A first observation shows that the European regional landscape is far from homogenous. There is no single major regional actor that includes (almost) all states in a DRM framework (such as in the Pacific, the Caribbean and Africa), but a number of actors, who work in the area of DRM on different levels and with widely differing mandates and capacities. If we take the indicators introduced above as a template, we can see that the EU would fulfil 16 out of 17 indicators, CoE six out of 17, OSCE two and BSEC six. Based on this picture, we can say that there is only one comprehensive actor in regional DRM in Europe, which is the EU. While its membership and membership in the Civil Protection Mechanism is limited to EU member states and a small number of partner countries, the CPM reaches far beyond the region and makes it unique in terms of the scope of work for a regional organization.

The CoE is interesting in the sense that it early found a well-defined niche in the DRM field and prudently developed it, and by that it is one of few organizations not joining the rush of other ROs to push into new areas of cooperation in the field. While the scope of this chapter does not reach far enough to describe those mechanisms in more detail, there seems to be a good level of cooperation between the EU and the CoE's work on disaster issues, showing that there is some kind of division of tasks between those two organizations, with the CoE covering the area of research on DRM, which is less prominently covered by the EU's CPM.

Given their comprehensive membership, both the CoE and OSCE could fulfil the role of an umbrella organization in Europe in terms of DRM. Therefore, it is very interesting that neither of them does so, with the CoE mainly focusing on the Mediterranean area and the OSCE having only recently discovered that DM issues might fit their description of security. Given its late entry into the field, the OSCE

Table 5.2 Disaster risk management indicators for four European regional organizations

Indicator \ Regional organization	BSEC	EU	CoE	OSCE
1. Regular intergovernmental meetings on DRM	☒	☒	☒	☐
2. Regional DRR framework/convention	☒	☒	☒	☐
3. RDM framework/convention	☒	☒	☒	☐
4. Specific organization for DRM	☐	☒	☐	☐
5. RDM centre	☐	☒	☐	☐
6. Regional disaster relief fund	☐	☒	☐	☐
7. Regional disaster insurance scheme	☐	☐	☐	☐
8. Regional funding for DRR projects	☐	☒	☐	☐
9. Provides humanitarian assistance	☐	☒	☐	☐
10. Regional rapid response mechanism	☐	☒	☐	☐
11. Regional technical cooperation	☒	☒	☒	☒
12. Joint DM exercises/simulations	☐	☒	☐	☐
13. Technical training on DRM issues/capacity building	☒	☒	☒	☒
14. Research on DRM/CCA issues	☐	☒	☒	☐
15. Regional military protocols for disaster assistance	☐	☒	☐	☐
16. Regional web portal on DRM	☐	☒	☐	☐
17. Regional IDRL treaty/guidelines	☒	☒	☐	☐
Total	6	16	6	2

might find that most other seats have already been taken by other ROs so far and that it might be difficult to escape a risk of replication of other organizations' work, and therefore only certain niches remain available.

BSEC shows that there is clearly an appetite for cooperation on DRM in smaller regional formations as well as along the periphery of the EU. Still, cooperation on DRM issues in BSEC clearly has not evolved above a basic level, with the exemption of the relatively comprehensive IDRL treaty.

Nevertheless, an interesting feature of several European organizations is that they also include non-member states in their work on disaster issues, which is rather uncommon outside of Europe. While we have no ready answer for this phenomenon, it could suggest that DRM issues are seen as a good area to foster cooperation with the 'near abroad' of ROs as they usually bring good public relations and are politically less sensitive or controversial than other areas.[20]

Conclusion

The indicators introduced in this chapter sketched out a wide range of diversity among ROs engaging with DRM. Specifically, this showed in terms of mandates and (political) integration, DRM capacity and resources. As a result, ROs' engagement with DRM needs to be understood as a complex phenomenon that does not conform to a singular template or trajectory, but is also a dynamically evolving picture. Turning to the empirical focus on European civil security governance of this volume, one can, however, make out the following developments and patterns that stand out against this global context.

First, Europe has a heterogeneous landscape in terms of ROs working on DRM. The modus Vivendi among those organizations on a first look seems to be on cooperation, but it would be interesting to further research if and how that heterogeneity creates cooperation and competition between European ROs.

Second, the EU is by far the largest actor in DRM in Europe, and while it has a global scope, the membership of its CPM leaves gaps particularly in South-Eastern and Eastern Europe as well as the South Caucasus that allow other organizations such as the BSEC, OSCE and CoE to step in. Nonetheless, efforts by those organizations have a very different scope than the work done by the EU.

Third, the EU runs the most comprehensive and best-funded DRM program in a global perspective, but might be a difficult example to emulate. By looking at the issue through the lens of subsidiarity, the EU can be seen a showcase for the added benefits of a regional organization among a group of countries with relatively well-developed DRM systems. These benefits are mainly defined by providing regional services such as information management, coordination between member states, the pooling of assets and capacity building through joint projects/exercises and peer learning. However, given its unique features and the high level of integration yet unmatched by other ROs, the EU model will hardly become a global template in the near future.

Fourth, both European and other ROs display an overarching trend towards more engagement with DRM issues, which could be traced further over time by means of the comprehensive set of indicators. For instance, EU has just 'upgraded' its emergency response centre and reformed the CPM, BSEC is strengthening cooperation in the field and the OSCE is also trying to stronger engage with natural disaster issues.

Many other dynamic developments for RDM in Europe and worldwide remain open at the time of writing. For instance, we currently witness an ongoing shift in terminology and focus on different phases of the crisis management cycle. In some regions, ROs have mainly followed the global discourse on DRR; whereas others are cautiously making forays into that area (compare Hollis in this volume). This underlines that we need to extend our efforts to track trends and diversity in regional civil security governance over time. The set of indicators presented here should serve as a useful conceptual operationalization and empirical baseline for that purpose that could be built upon in future comparative studies.

Notes

1. The idea for this chapter and most of the data on ROs are based on a 2013 research report that I co-authored with Elizabeth Ferris for the Brookings-LSE Project on Internal Displacement titled 'In the Neighborhood: The Growing Role of Regional Organizations in Disaster Risk Management'. It is available at http://www.brookings.edu/research/reports/2013/02/regional-organizations-disaster-risk-ferris, date accessed 3 December 2014.
2. For convenience reasons, this paper will at times refer to these disasters as natural disasters.
3. See, for example, the case of Cyclone Nargis in Myanmar.
4. For more details, see the International Disaster Database by the Centre for Research on the Epidemiology of Disasters, CRED. It is available at http://www.emdat.be/, date accessed 3 December 2014.
5. UNISDR defines DRR as: 'The concept and practice of reducing disaster risks through systematic efforts to analyse and manage the causal factors of disasters, including through reduced exposure to hazards, lessened vulnerability of people and property, wise management of land and the environment, and improved preparedness for adverse events.' Available at: http://www.unisdr.org/we/inform/terminology, date accessed 1 December 2014.
6. The Association of Southeast Asian Nations (ASEAN), African Union (AU), Andean Community of Nations (CAN), Caribbean Community (CARICOM), Council of Europe, Economic Community of West African States (ECOWAS), EU, League of Arab States (LAS), Organization of American States (OAS), South Asian Association for Regional Cooperation (SAARC), South African Development Community (SADC), Central American Integration System (SICA) and Secretariat of the Pacific Community (SPC).
7. Again, this follows the original study by Ferris and Petz (2013), while some data has been updated because of more recent developments.
8. For more details, see http://ec.europa.eu/regional_policy/thefunds/solidarity/index_en.cfm, date accessed 1 December 2014.
9. For a detailed breakdown, see Ferris and Petz (2013, p. 23). Of course, the indicators have to be taken with a number of caveats. While they indicate areas of work of ROs, they do not clearly indicate the scope of cooperation in each area and they also cannot judge the effectiveness with which activities are done by ROs. Given the rapid development of cooperation on

DRM, some of the information based on the publication might no longer be accurate.
10. There were major revisions to the mechanisms in 2007 and 2014. The most recent revision allowed for a further strengthening of the mechanism. The revised legislation creates a European Emergency Response Capacity, allowing for better planning. A voluntary pool of response capacities and experts will be established and available for immediate deployment as part of a collective European intervention. Member states provide resources for standby which are certified by the EU. It also demands member states to share risk assessments and refine risk assessment planning (European Commission, 2014b).
11. Montenegro is in the process of joining the CPM as its 32nd member.
12. For a list of member states see: http://conventions.coe.int/Treaty/Commun/ListeTableauAP.asp?AP=6&CM=&DF=&CL=ENG, date accessed 1 December 2014.
13. For a list of centres see: Council of Europe, Network of Specialized Euro-Mediterranean Centres, http://www.coe.int/t/dg4/majorhazards/centres/default_en.asp, date accessed 25 October 2014.
14. According to the CoE's budget 2014/2015. For details, see https://wcd.coe.int. The overall budget of the CoE in 2014 is around Euro 400 million.
15. It was institutionalized as Conference on Security and Cooperation in Europe in 1975 and became a fully fledged organization called OSCE in 1994.
16. For more details see http://www.osce.org/secretariat/124372, date accessed 1 December 2014.
17. Member States are: Albania, Armenia, Azerbaijan, Bulgaria, Georgia, Greece, Moldova, Romania, Russian Federation, Serbia, Turkey and Ukraine.
18. For more details see http://www.bsec-organization.org/aoc/cooperationemergency/Pages/information.aspx, date accessed 1 December 2014.
19. For the Plan of Action 2013–2015 of the BSEC Working Group on Cooperation in Emergency Assistance see http://www.bsec-organization.org/aoc/cooperationemergency/Pages/Action.aspx, date accessed 1 December 2015.
20. There is evidence that spending on DRM is one of the more popular areas of spending for a state as for example a recent survey in Austria showed. For details see http://derstandard.at/2000007286249/Katastrophenhilfe-ist-die-populaerste-Staatsausgabe, date accessed 1 December 2014.

References

Ahrens, J. and P. M. Rudolph (2006) 'The Importance of Governance in Risk Reduction and Disaster Management', *Journal of Contingencies and Crisis Management*, 14.

Collymore, J. (2011) 'Disaster Management in the Caribbean: Perspectives on Institutional Capacity Reform and Development', *Environmental Hazards*, 10, 6–22.

European Commission (2014a) *Annual Report on the European Union's Humanitarian Aid and Civil Protection Policies and Their Implementation in 2013*, 28 August 2014, COM(2014) 537 final (Brussels: European Union).

European Commission (2014b) *EU Civil Protection: ECHO Factsheet.* http://ec.europa.eu/echo/files/aid/countries/factsheets/thematic/civil_protection_en.pdf, date accessed 1 December 2014.

European Commission (2013) *Green Paper on the Insurance of Natural and Man-Made Disasters,* COM/2013/0213 final.

Fawcett, L. (2004) 'Exploring Regional Domains: A Comparative History of Regionalism', *International Affairs,* 80, 429–446.

Ferris, E. and D. Petz (2013) *In the Neighborhood: The Growing Role of Regional Organizations in Disaster Risk Management* (Washington, D.C.: Brookings-LSE Project on Internal Displacement).

Harvey, P. (2010) 'The Role of National Governments in International Humanitarian Response', *ALNAP Meeting Paper,* 26th Annual Meeting, 16–17 November 2010, Kuala Lumpur, Malaysia.

Kirchner, E. and J. Sperling (2007) *EU Security Governance* (Manchester: Manchester University Press).

Sumonin, K. (2005) 'Globalizing Regionalism: Harnessing Regional Organizations to Meet Global Threats', *UNU- CRIS Occasional Papers,* 2005/11.

Sperling, J. and M. Weber (2014) 'Security Governance in Europe: A Return to System', *European Security,* 23, 126–144.

UNISDR (2007) 'Hyogo Framework for Action 2005–2015: Building the Resilience of Nations and Communities to Disasters', *Final Report of the World Conference on Disaster Reduction.*

Part II
The Challenge of Transformation

6
Preventing Disasters in Europe: Challenges and Opportunities for Translating Global Visions into Local Practices

Simon Hollis

Introduction

At the end of the 20th century, the UN Secretary-General, Kofi Annan, noted in his annual report: 'political and organizational cultures and practices remain orientated far more towards reaction than prevention' (1999, p. 6). This, he insisted, had to be changed. There was a need for a 'transition from a culture of reaction to a culture of prevention' (Annan, 1999, p. 7). This statement came at the end of the International Decade for Natural Disaster Reduction (IDNDR), a global framework agreement designed to increase awareness on the need to reduce risk from natural hazards.

More than 15 years has passed since Annan's call for a culture of prevention was made. During this time, many international organizations and NGOs have sought to expand the IDNDR's mission, instilling a culture of protection in the minds of policymakers. The UN's International Strategy for Disaster Reduction (UNISDR), the International Federation of Red Cross (IFRC), the World Bank's Global Facility for Disaster Reduction and Recovery (GFDRR) and the EU's Strategy for Supporting Disaster Risk Reduction are examples of this growing community of organizations committed to increasing the resilience of states to natural hazards (Hannigan, 2012). Has Annan's call for a transition to a culture of prevention been answered? To what extent have global prescriptions on Disaster Risk Reduction (DRR) – seen, for example, in the Millennium Declaration and the Hyogo Framework Programme for Action (HFA) – impacted the capacity of states to prevent and prepare for disasters?

These questions guide the contours of this chapter that aims to examine the extent to which global prescriptions on DRR have influenced European civil security systems. This region of the world receives particular attention because it raises an ostensible paradox. On the one hand, we can observe a highly developed and prosperous system of states that have been robust supporters of the HFA, as reflected in the EU's external strategy on DRR. Internally, member states have also taken on an increased role in supporting the EU mechanism for civil protection: a framework agreement that aims to increase the regions resilience to transboundary disasters. On the other hand, European commitment to implement global prescriptions on disaster prevention appears fairly weak. European states appear to be less willing to adopt the very prescriptions that they eagerly promote to developing countries. While a wavering commitment to implement such prescriptions might be more understandable in regions that have limited access to financial resources and are marked by unstable regimes, the economic, social and political conditions of European civil security systems ought to encourage a more inclusive approach to disaster management that emphasizes the importance of prevention.

The theme of this chapter – understanding the diffusion of DRR-based norms – is grounded on normative, theoretical and substantive goals. The former aims to arrive at a deeper understanding of how societies can become more resilient to disasters: how a society can become more secure. This is a more general aim that exists in the background of the text. The theoretical aim is to understand the scope conditions of norm diffusion from the global to the local level. Substantively, this chapter aims to shed light on an important yet understudied policy space that straddles the global, regional and local levels of risk governance together into a single conceptual framework.

These aims are achieved through a comparative study of civil security systems in Europe. Much of the empirical data comes from an EU co-funded research project that collated and compared political, institutional and cultural features of 21 European disaster management systems (ANVIL, 2014). This source material is complemented by similar comparative studies conducted by international organizations, such as the HFA progress reports and the European Forum for DRR (EFDRR) surveys.

The following study is divided into three sections. First, an empirical sketch of the global community on DRR is provided, with particular attention to the role of the EU as a mediator of ideas. Second, various mechanisms found in diffusion theory that reflect necessary conditions for the diffusion of ideas, or expected outcomes, are discussed and applied to the empirical material. These include an analysis on (i) the sites of diffusion, (ii) the language of DRR and (iii) institutional change.

The global community and the EU on disaster risk reduction

The concept of prevention is a rational credo that denotes the importance of acting in the present to establish a secure future. This logic is expressed well by Benjamin Franklin's iconic phrase, 'an ounce of prevention is worth a pound of cure', and has formed an important rationale for the construction of prevention strategies by states. The last two decades have seen this idea transcend the state and become a global norm propagated and reified by the international community under the term DRR.[1]

International advocacy on DRR has been active at least since the IDNDR in the 1990s and has become increasingly prolific since 2000 with the creation of particular institutions and global policy instruments and prescriptions. The event that has perhaps been most important for setting DRR on the global scene is the second world conference on DRR held only a few months after the 2004 Asian Tsunami. The outcome of this conference was the HFA, which lists five priorities for action that states ought to implement in the period 2005–2015 (see Table 6.1). The underlying theme of this document is to instil a culture of prevention in regional, state and sub-state institutions.

Various organizations have emerged in the last decade to support this global call for prevention. The World Bank, for example, established the GFDRR in 2006, which aims to mainstream DRR and climate change adaption in developing states along the lines of the HFA (GFDRR, 2013).

Table 6.1 HFA priorities for action

1. Ensure that DRR is a national and a local priority with a strong institutional basis for implementation
2. Identify, assess and monitor disaster risks and enhance early warning
3. Use knowledge, innovation and education to build a culture of safety and resilience at all levels
4. Reduce the underlying risk factors
5. Strengthen disaster preparedness for effective response at all levels

Source: UNISDR, 2005.

A multi-stakeholder enterprise designed to implement the HFA in Asia and the Pacific has been established, the International Federation of Red Cross and Red Crescent (IFRC) have been active in promoting the HFA and a network of NGOs and not-for-profit organizations – the Global Network for Disaster Reduction (GNDR) – conducts important independent progress reviews on state resilience to disasters.

Regional organizations have been quick to 'download' international prescriptions on DRR according to the HFA, producing highly similar framework agreements albeit with little actual cooperation (Hollis, 2015b). The Southern African Development Community (SADC, 2006) and the League of Arab States (LAS, 2011), for example, have copied parts or all of the HFA into their framework agreements on disaster risk management while others such as the Association of Southeast Asian Nations (ASEAN, 2005) bear a canny 'family resemblance' to the HFA.

An exception to this general trend is the EU, which has provided considerable capacity at the regional level, at least, in terms of coordinating responses to disasters. For example, in 2012 the European Emergency Response Centre (EERC) facilitated requests for assistance to Italian and Greek forest fires and floods in Bulgaria; it provided specialized forecasts and risk maps to Slovenia; and it assisted in writing a report on the aftermath of the Italian earthquake. Additionally, the EU encourages states to provide national and regional modules, such as an 'aerial forest fire fighting module using helicopters', 'heavy urban search and rescue' or an 'advanced medical post' that can be deployed in the event of a crisis (European Commission, 2010). The production of such modules means that the EU has ad hoc capacities that can be used in the event of a crisis although the final word remains with the state.

The EU has also become increasingly active in its promotion of DRR principles – along the lines of the HFA – to developing countries (see Hollis, 2014). This is clearly seen in the various activities conducted through the Disaster Preparedness Programme of the EU Humanitarian Aid and Civil Protection (DIPECHO) department and the EU's strategy for supporting DRR in developing countries (European Commission, 2009).

The EU thus appears to be acting as a legitimate 'teacher of norms' on DRR (Hollis, 2015b; see Finnemore, 1993) externally and appears to have established a considerable internal role in supporting civil protection among its member states. Yet, it would be wrong to assume that its external activity on DRR is matched by its internal role as a supporter of disaster prevention. As this chapter demonstrates, it remains highly unclear whether the EU has increased member state awareness on ex-ante disaster management. Indeed, until the revised version of the civil protection mechanisms in 2014, focus on prevention has been explicitly sidestepped. The original framework agreement in 2001 notes that while prevention is 'of significant importance for the protection against natural, technological and environmental disasters... [it] require[s] further action to be considered' (Council of the European Union, 2001, preamble §5). The re-cast framework agreement in 2007 repeats this ambivalent statement and mentions the word 'prevention' only twice in the entire document (Council of the European Union, 2007, preamble §7).

The 2014 version of the civil protection mechanism is significantly different. The term prevention appears 41 times and it has an entire chapter on prevention. The document even includes the specific phrase 'culture of prevention', perhaps indicating some 'light' form of diffusion from the global to the regional level. It aims is to: 'achieve a high level of protection against disasters by preventing or reducing their potential effects, by fostering a culture of prevention and by improving cooperation between the civil protection and other relevant services' (Council of the European Union, 2014, Art.3, 1(a)).

This substantial increase in discourse by the EU on prevention may be the start of a more inclusive position on disaster management that includes not only response and recovery, but also prevention and preparedness. However, this has to be assessed against the stubborn norm of national sovereignty. The aims expressed in the latest agreement on civil protection is conditional upon Article 346 of the Treaty on the Functioning of the European Union, which 'guarantees that no Member State should be obliged to supply information, the disclosure of which it considers contrary to the essential interests of its security' (Council of the European Union, 2014, preamble §8). The decision also notes that this 'should not affect Member States' responsibility to protect people, the environment, and property on their territory' (Council of the European Union, 2014, §5). Compounding this issue is the financial division of labour whereby only 20 per cent of the budget for disaster management is earmarked for prevention activities (Council of the European Union, 2014, Annex 1). This means that while more attention is now being placed on developing a culture of prevention, there are clear financial and normative obstacles to any interference by the Union on its member states. Achieving greater resilience to disaster remains fully in the hands of the state.

This brief overview of the international and regional scene on DRR for Europe leaves us with two questions. First, have norms on DRR diffused to European states despite the limited role of the EU? Second, even with its restricted position has the EU been able to support member states' prevention capacities? The following section first looks at how we can understand norm diffusion before taking a closer look at the extent to which states in Europe have translated global norms enshrined in the HFA.

Norm diffusion

The analytical focus of this chapter aims to understand the diffusion of transnational norms on disaster management. Based on previous studies that have outlined the emergence of global norms on DRR (as set out in the HFA), this chapter takes a holistic view on the diffusion of norms, recognizing that a comprehensive account of diffusion necessarily includes the global, regional and local levels of analyses (Solingen, 2012). This neatly merges the so-called waves of norm scholarship that respectively focus on international and domestic processes of diffusion (Cortell and Davis, 2000).

Norm diffusion is defined as a process where 'collective expectations about proper behaviour for a given identity' (Jepperson et al., 1996, p. 54) are 'communicated through certain channels over time among the members of a social system' (Rogers, 1983, cited in Strang and Meyer, (1993) 2009, pp. 136–137). A number of important scholarly contributions have shed light on these social systems, the types and channels of communication and the formation of collective behaviour. The various processes involved, from norm formation to its emulation, localization, congruence or convergence is usefully reflected in Finnemore and Sikkink's well-versed model on the life cycle of norms (1999). Like all good ideal types, research has since expanded and critiqued this cycle producing alternative (Krook and True, 2012) and more fine-grained analyses on the formation (Hyde, 2011), advocacy (Carpenter et al., 2014), congruence (Checkel, 2001), localization (Acharya, 2004) and emulation (Meyer, 2010) of norms.

These and other contributions offer an appealing smorgasbord of mechanisms – such as learning, coercion, competition and emulation – that assist in explaining (non) diffusion. However, instead of concentrating on one particular mechanism, attention is rather focused on a general precondition and two expected outcomes of diffusion, allowing the existing literature to provide insight wherever possible. This approach is thus geared towards a general overview on the diffusion of norms, allowing others to 'dig deeper' into particular issues.

The general precondition for diffusion analysed in this chapter examines 'sites of diffusion'. It has been argued that when members of a social system meet at particular 'sites of diffusion', such as the global UN conference on the environment, norms can be set through the outcome of deliberation and subsequently diffused by a league of transnational actors to states, communities and people (Schofer et al., 2004; Lechner and Boli, 2005). These sites of diffusion that foster inter-subjective exchange are understood as a necessary but not sufficient condition for the diffusion of a norm. It is thus expected that at the global level of analysis one will find sites of diffusion that aid in the formation and diffusion of DRR.

The partial or whole diffusion of a norm from the global to more local levels of risk governance is expected to alter the way organizations and individuals talk about issues related to DRR (see Berger and Luckmann, 1967, p. 22; Hollis, 2015b). Depending on the congruence between existing local customs and the new global language used to explain and promote DRR, states will modify existing language to accommodate ideas related to DRR. When there is little diffusion, language will remain largely connected to existing cultural and path-dependent practices. When there is partial diffusion, one may detect a family resemblance in key definitions on DRR. Full diffusion would reveal high similarities across countries.

While language provides a fairly deep expression of cultural change, one can also look to more technical or institutional changes as a result of norm diffusion. Indeed, institutional change is understood as one of the main outcome of diffusion (Acharya, 2004, p. 240). It is assumed that by examining institutional change in states' societal security strategies over time will offer insight into how, and the extent to which, global norms have influenced societal security in Europe.

The following section thus examines (i) 'sites of diffusion', (ii) the language of DRR and (iii) institutional change to orientate an analytical overview on the diffusion of DRR.

Sites of diffusion

Much literature on norm diffusion either implicitly or explicitly notes that interaction in specific locales is a necessary (but not sufficient) precondition for the diffusion of ideas. Sites that encourage relational exchange among its participants such as UN world conferences or the football World Cup provide useful platforms for construction and diffusion of norms (Lechner and Boli, 2005, pp. 84–88). This is achieved through deliberation whereby different countries and participating international organizations and NGOs construct a common agenda (Schofer et al., 2004; Lechner and Boli, 2005, pp. 84–88).

This type of activity can be clearly seen in the production and diffusion of the principles underlying the HFA (see Table 6.1): a direct outcome of the second global forum on DRR held in 2005 at Hyogo, Japan. In an effort to enforce the spread of these principles, the UNISDR has encouraged states to establish regional and national platforms defined as 'multi-stakeholder national mechanism that serves as an advocate of DRR at different levels. It provides coordination, analysis and advice on areas of priority requiring concerted action' (UNISDR, 2007, p. 1).

At the regional level, a European Platform for Disaster Risk Reduction (EPDRR) was established in 2009. Since its establishment, it has encouraged European states to establish national platforms and participate in the UNISDR campaign on resilient cities. The members meet annually to discuss, for example, how to stimulate exchanges of information among national platforms, standardization, post-crisis learning and identifying common needs (EPDRR, 2013).

If the EPDRR is designed to support national implementation, the 25 existing national platforms in Europe (including Russia) are designed to implement DRR policies at the local level while linking into international efforts (UNISDR, 2013). These platforms typically include representatives from NGOs, universities, the private sector and relevant ministries.

At first glance, the number of states now directly engaged in regional and national platforms is fairly impressive. However, there are a number of prominent European states that have not established a national platform and do not participate in the regional platform. While this may not be an issue for countries that have few natural hazards and thus low risk levels, it is difficult to understand why other countries with higher levels of risk have not been more active in adopting a culture of prevention.

As we shall see in the following sections, country participation in regional and national platforms does not necessarily equate to any real change in the behaviour of states. Sites of diffusion may be a precondition for successful diffusion, but this must also be matched by effective translation requiring political will. Analysing the language of DRR in various European states is one method of uncovering whether states have or are in the process of making such changes according to global calls to build a culture of prevention.

The language of disaster risk reduction

If global ideas on DRR have been diffused to the state level, it would be expected that the type of language used would bear similarities (see Berger and Luckmann, 1967, p. 22). Reasons for this may be based on the concept of isomorphism, whereby states adopt similar definitions because that is what states *ought* to do. Another, more practical reason, may be driven by an interest to increase coordination among likeminded states. This more rational explanation of diffusion is well summed up in a progress report on DRR by Germany, which explicitly mentions the importance of having similar definitions whereby the 'notion of "disaster"' represented an obstacle for an accomplishment of the decade targets (IDNDR, 1999, p. 3). A more recent gathering of stakeholders on DRR echoed a similar problematique, noting that 'concepts matter' and are necessary to establish a 'common point of orientation' especially in the arena of joint operations, underlining the need for smooth interoperability (Bossong and Hegemann, 2014, p. 6).

A recent example of the diffusion of key terms on disaster management can be observed in disaster management agreements published by various regional organizations across the world. Key terms such as 'disaster', 'prevention' and 'hazard' share a close resemblance despite their cultural and political differences (Hollis, 2015b). For example, the ASEAN, the Caribbean Community (CARICOM) and the SADC use almost identical language in their definitions of DRR. Other terms such as 'disaster' and 'early warning' are also very similar (Hollis, 2015b). These similarities can be traced to a single publication from the UNISDR that defines concepts related to DRR (UNISDR, 2009). Furthermore, these agreements express strikingly similar goals that closely resemble the five aims of the HFA. In other words, there is strong empirical support for the diffusion of norms related to DRR in regional organizations. While the EU does not seem to be as influenced by the HFA, choosing instead to construct its own specific mandate on civil protection, it does provide references to the HFA and some of its definitions are comparable to the UNISDR handbook on DRR terminology. Such examples of diffusion are largely absent among European states.

Definitions of key concepts on disaster management in European states are highly dissimilar. A comparison of 15 states and 4 organizations reveals a high variance in how they define a crisis, disaster, emergency or civil protection. The only similarity in the construction of definitions is found between the World Bank and the UNISDR, which have identical sentence construction.

While numerous definitions abound in Europe, the actual content of most definitions are highly similar. In most cases, a disaster is understood to overwhelm existing capacities and functions of a state and affect people, the environment, property and critical societal functions.[2] Sweden and Romania also include fundamental values to this list of values.

Table 6.2 identifies the main values that ought to be protected according to the self-definitions of European states or organizations. This depiction may not be fully inclusive, as the values have only been forged out of the country definitions of disaster, crisis, emergency and civil protection. Some countries may also include other referent points that do not feature in their definitions of a crisis. It is nevertheless considered a satisfactory account of the values that each country holds close to its heart. The related referent points of life and health are placed under *people*; cultural heritage, material goods and the economy are included under the rubric of *property*; and essential services and vital interests of society are included under *societal functions*.

It is unlikely that the similar referent points of protection shared by global organizations and European states (Table 6.2) reflect a diffusion of DRR principles. If states have been influenced by any global changes, it would presumably be from the shift in global discourse since the end of the Cold War, where many states and organizations have shifted from 'civil defence' – with a focus on traditional security issues – to civil protection, where a wider set of reference points have been included in what ought to be protected, such as fundamental values and the environment (see ANVIL, 2014). At a more fundamental level, it has also been argued that these referent points of protection are rather defined within a historically path-dependent stream of thought heavily influenced by the Enlightenment and the recent global focus on the environment and global warming (Hollis, 2015a).

From a more pragmatic perspective, the comparative study conducted by the ANVIL consortium emphasizes the problem of diversity and even confusion among European states on basic terminology. A pertinent example is the overarching term used to describe disaster management, which comes in a number of colourful varieties such as 'civil security', 'societal security', 'civil protection', 'civil defence' and 'crisis management' (Bossong and Hegemann, 2014, pp. 6–7; see also the introduction to this volume). The meanings of these broad terms and the way DRR

Table 6.2 Referent points of protection in European states and international organizations

		\multicolumn{5}{c}{Referent points of protection}
		People	Environment	Property	Fundamental values	Societal functions
Organization	UNISDR	✓	✓	✓		✓
	World Bank	✓	✓	✓		✓
	IFRC	✓	✓	✓		✓
	EU	✓	✓	✓		
State	Sweden	✓			✓	✓
	Czech Republic	✓	✓	✓		
	Poland	✓	✓	✓		
	Slovakia	✓		✓		
	Serbia	✓	✓	✓		
	Netherlands	✓	✓	✓		
	Malta	✓	✓	✓		
	Croatia	✓	✓	✓		
	Hungary	✓		✓		
	Finland	✓		✓		
	Germany	✓		✓		
	Netherlands					✓
	Ireland	✓	✓	✓		✓
	Romania	✓	✓	✓	✓	
	Latvia	✓	✓	✓		

Source: UNISDR, 2009; World Bank, 2013; ANVIL, 2014; Council of the European Union, 2014; IFRC, 2014.

is perceived – such as through the lens of resilience or vulnerability – appear to be socially constructed with little influence from an external or global source. Indeed, DRR seems to be a term reserved for 'developing' states, featuring less prominently within disaster management discourse in the EU and European states.

Analysing similar patterns in discourse thus provides little evidence for any fundamental transfer of ideas from the global and/or regional level to states in Europe. When contrasted to other regional organizations and states in the developing world, a different picture emerges, whereby global prescriptions appears to have made a larger impact, at least according to the language used in constructing framework agreements and definitions on DRR. While the EU has incorporated parts of a global terminology into its framework agreements, it has not been successfully diffused to its member states. Even if language has not significantly altered, the behaviour and institutional changes may still be taking affect due to external support. This aspect of possible diffusion is now turned to.

Institutional change

If the principles enshrined in the HFA have had an effect on the resilience of states, by increasing their capacity to prevent disasters, institutional change should also be apparent. Successful or partial diffusion of the HFA ought to reveal particular changes in a state's emergency strategy and corresponding implementation plan. As will be shown, a few distinct casual links between the adoption of the HFA and institutional change can be observed. It would seem that most states assimilate pre-existing agreements, strategies and operational practices in line with the HFA goals rather than adjust their behaviour. It appears more an act of window dressing old products that already existed to appease the new clientele rather than enact any fundamental changes; a process that is similar to what norm scholars would call adaption or grafting (Acharya, 2004, p. 251).

A good place to begin an analysis on institutional change is by examining self-assessment reports filled in by European states on their level of progress on fulfilling the HFA priorities for action. The UNISDR have encouraged all states to periodically submit these standardized reports on three separate occasions (2007–2009; 2009–2011; and 2011–2013). Out of 45 European states: 14 have submitted reports on all 3 occasions; 6 have submitted on 2 occasions; 5 have submitted on 1 occasion; and 19 have not submitted any reports. Some of the latter countries include: Denmark, Austria, Belgium, Estonia, Latvia, Lithuania and Slovakia. This immediately reflects a significant variation across Europe on support for the HFA. So what signs of progress do these reports reveal?

A general synthesis of 65 reports, submitted in the period 2007–2013, reveals no significant progress according to the coding system the UNISDR uses between 1 (minor progress with few signs of forward action in plans or policy) and 5 (comprehensive achievement with sustained commitment and capacities at all levels). That is, the level of graded commitment does not increase substantially in the period 2007–2013. HFA priority 2 increased from an average of 3.6 to 3.8, HFA priority 5 increased from an average of 3.6 to 3.9 and all other priority issues (1, 3 and 4) remained stagnate at 3.7, 3.5 and 3.5, respectively. Of course, this lack of quantitative proof is checked against other qualitative measures in the synthesis report, where evidence of progress is demonstrated. However, according to the general scaling system, these changes are fairly insignificant as many European states have already established functioning, albeit diverse, prevention systems. Indeed, the detail provided by those countries that completed self-assessment reports seem to reflect what the country has done prior or in parallel to global activity on DRR, making it difficult to assess if there is any real connection between ideas from the global to the local.

A similar situation is also apparent when looking at the level of commitment made by European states in implementing the resilient cities campaign. In line with the HFA goals, this campaign encourages cities to build a culture of prevention and establish interrelational exchanges with the UNISDR. Part of this entails the adoption of a Local Government Self-Assessment Tool (LGSAT); a template designed to help cities identify gaps and establish minimal standards of disaster prevention. These include establishing a budget for DRR, encouraging a culture of prevention in school curricula and efficient land-use planning (UNISDR, 2012). However, less than half of European countries have signed up to this campaign. Of the countries that are part of the campaign only three countries (Italy, Serbia and Austria) can boast more than 20 cities that have joined the campaign, while the remaining countries have only two or three cities in the campaign (UNISDR, 2012). Moreover, out of the cities that have committed to the campaign very few have actually implemented the LGSAT (EFDRR, 2013).

Instances of institutional change can nevertheless be seen that have direct links to the HFA. Armenia, for example, has with the assistance of the external support of the United Nations Development Programme (UNDP) developed a Capacity Development Methodology for DRR and a DRR National Strategy and action plan. Some outcomes include the creation of an educational package on DRR that has been distributed to 915 communities and have been testing a Community Risk Certificate in some communities (UNISDR, 2013). While these examples reveal a clear transference of ideas, albeit through clear external support, from the global to local level, such explicit and welcome changes are not widespread.

One reason for the apparent lack of commitment by European states is the different cultural traditions and learning methods of each state. This aspect of European societal security is well reflected in the findings of the ANVIL study. The results of this comparative study depict a large diversity among European states' disaster management systems and their approach to DRR. Key concepts emphasized in the HFA, such as decentralization (subsidiarity) and risk analysis, do not align to a global script but are orientated to and constructed through historical and cultural belief systems. While the issue of (de)centralization contains some sub-regional similarities – such as decentralization in North/North-western Europe and centralization in East/South-eastern Europe – even these divisions are not homogenous (Bossong and Hegemann, 2014, p. 5). Likewise, risk analysis and risk assessment are generally seen as positive aspects for DRR, however, their implementation, level of commitment and oversights vary greatly across countries (Bossong and Hegemann, 2014, p. 13).

Another reason for limited activity is a general lack of financial commitment. The main commonality mentioned by most states is their apparent lack of financial resources to make their society more resilient. However, for many European states it is not necessarily the lack of financing, but a rational choice informed through the short-term opportunity cost of investing in prevention vis-à-vis the expected benefits. This is not just a common feature across almost all countries in Europe, but an endemic issue for the entire policy field of DRR. It is simply difficult to persuade states, organizations or the private sector to insure against a contingency that will produce diffuse financial returns. Kofi Annan expressed this point nicely when he quoted an old aphorism: 'it is difficult to find money for medicine, but easy to find it for a coffin' (1999, p. 7).

A third reason is the incredibly complex process involved in providing a well-built and efficient prevention strategy. A resilient community is a community where all tiers of society are strong and well functioning: the equivalent of a brick house where all pieces must be in place to enable a strong structure (Wisner et al., 2004). It is difficult to place this complexity within five general points that are common enough for all to agree upon. Yet, it is only through the construction of abstract principles that HFA can successfully diffuse as a norm. The reinterpretation of these norms according to local contexts, and in the absence of enforcement mechanisms, reveal hard challenges for implementation. It should be noted, however, that knowledge and awareness of this multi-sectorial aspects of DRR is making headway in Europe. This is apparent in a recent review of national platforms that, at least on paper, reveal and awareness of including a large number of ministries in DRR (UNISDR, 2013).

Post-HFA and the limits of diffusion

The international community has been going through a period of reflection as they prepare for the third world conference on DRR: the post-HFA era. While awareness of the need for greater DRR capacity has certainly increased, for the case of Europe it has been difficult to perceive any direct causal linkages between the global promotion of the HFA and changes in the behaviour of states. This is partly due to the generally high level of DRR capacity prevalent in many European countries, meaning that any change over time is going to appear fairly stagnant particularly as change is measured on a standard format for all countries in the world. Nevertheless, as the previous analysis illustrates, even though sites of diffusion have been established, there is little evidence that these sites have led to any substantial changes in the language of DRR or institutional design. Instead, it would appear that cultural and particular local histories prevent any change from 'above': local-based learning and indigenous knowledge appears to be the way forward (Bossong and Hegemann, 2014). If this is the case, then further study is needed on the particular aspects of norm localization, whether there is evidence only of prelocalization, local initiative or adaption (Acharya, 2004, p. 251).

Yet, one should be wary in concluding that different local histories prevent the diffusion of DRR. Indeed, practitioners and stakeholders within Europe are largely positive to finding a more common language and are certainly interested in obtaining the HFA goals. Success stories like Armenia and Germany's commitment in its national platform are good examples of such propensity towards achieving the HFA goals (UNISDR, 2013). While local cultural traditions are certainly part of the issue, it is also important to take a more holistic perspective that includes complex technical issues at the global, regional and national level of risk governance.

Globally, one of the main issues is the design of the HFA. Reducing the HFA to a set of simplified goals means that while it may be more easily diffused, there is also more room for interpretation by states, regional organizations and civil society. While on one level, this can provide for a 'better fit' theoretically, it also raises some confusion of what type of policies ought to be implemented. This is reflected in the results of a 'learning needs assessment' survey conducted by RedR, a humanitarian NGO that aims to strengthen the resilience of societies to disasters. Based on the responses by 146 participants from the international community (UN bodies, Red Cross, MSF, OXFAM, USAID, etc.), the results found that: there was a general lack of unified information on DRR which reduced their ability to properly implement DRR programmes; there was a need for a DRR manual to connect theory and practice; and a wish for information sharing between the local and international level (RedR, 2012).

Regionally, the main issue – at least for the EU – is the importance of national sovereignty. This has a direct effect on the extent to which the community can play an important role in supporting states' resilience to disasters. Although the EU is often seen as one of the most developed supranational authorities on the planet, and while its civil protection mechanism is impressive, the importance of DRR has remained in the shadow of state interests. This is regrettable as the EU could provide an additional source of support to local communities through the supply of knowledge and financial resources. At least to a greater degree than it is currently the case. From a comparative perspective, it is also interesting to note that other regional organizations that do not have the same supranational stature as the EU have nevertheless advanced a more ambitious DRR agenda, although implementation of this agenda remains limited.

Nationally, the main impediment noted across many national self-assessments and other reports on the implementation of HFA goals, is a lack of financial resources (Bossong and Hegemann, 2014, p. 17; EFDRR, 2014, p. 17). This is less a reflection of political will or cultural issues, but the *multi-sectorial* nature of DRR. If DRR and its emphasis on a multi-hazard approach is taken seriously, then an effective DRR strategy will require a holistic approach by the state. It is less a single policy and more an ethos that ought to be implemented and encouraged in all areas of society and correspondingly to all government sectors, from education to the environment. It thus needs to comply with the notion of civil security governance underpinning this volume (see Bossong and Hegemann in the introduction). A research report prepared by the EFDRR working group on governance and accountability for DRR notes that one of the reasons for a lack of awareness on DRR-based spending is due to this multi-sectorial issue (EFDRR, 2013, p. 6). Out of a comparative study of 25 European countries, only seven countries could provide some indication of the per cent of funds that are dedicated to DRR as financing is often divided into particular policy fields (EFDRR, 2013, p. 6). This creates issues for establishing any reliable cost-benefit calculus for the state which is vital for encouraging a strong incentive structure to invest in a DRR policy/ethos.

Conclusion

Prevention is the poor man of disaster management. Compared to preparation, response or recovery, this important aspect of making societies more resilient to future disasters tends to get the least amount of attention. This was a central concern for scholars in the 1970s (Hewitt, 1983; see Wisner et al., 2004) and a driving impetus for the IDNDR and world conferences on DRR. Perhaps the most influential set of global prescriptions that have emerged in an attempt to create more resilient societies has been the HFA. In the last decade numerous NGOs, states and organizations have supported the implementation of the HFA priorities, which have certainly produced a number of success stories and helped build knowledge and awareness of DRR. Have these initiatives helped to take prevention out of its chains of poverty? Not entirely.

The analysis on European disaster management systems and their inclination to adopt global prescriptions on DRR does not reflect any significant increase in Europe's commitment to ensure regional and local societal resilience. However, this may be the wrong way of framing the issue. There are many states and cities that are now actively discussing how to increase societal resilience through regional and national platforms. The recent framework agreement from the European Parliament and Council has also addressed prevention directly for the first time, perhaps indicating a broadening of its agenda, albeit in the face of guarded sovereignty. It is yet to be seen, however, if the EU's positive development towards a more inclusive approach to disaster management will trickle down to member states.

Resistance instead seems to emanate from more fundamental issues of the actual policy field of DRR. First, is the issue of limited financing. This is apparent in the EU's regional agreement that has set aside 20 per cent towards prevention and 80 per cent on response and recovery. Nationally, the results of most self-assessments reports reveal a lack of financial investment for DRR activities. There are two possible reasons for this: (i) that states hold the perception that the short-term costs of DRR investment do not provide suitable long-term benefits; (ii) that the holistic and inclusive nature of DRR means that it is difficult to assess and thus provide general figures that would promote an increase in financing.

Second, the highly simplified form of the HFA priorities for action mean that they may 'travel' well, but have trouble settling in different cultural contexts. Generalized goals provide a large space for different interpretations. The incredibly complex field of DRR that is in fact more an ethos than a real policy field means that general goals are difficult to implement.

Adding to these explanations is the high variance found among European states' DRR systems, such as the different institutional structures that favour either centralization or decentralization. Different definitions also abound in European states that may prohibit effective cooperation and interoperability. Such path-dependent concepts with European states may also prevent the introduction of DRR as an additional concept that appears similar to the standing concepts of prevention and preparedness.

Do European states then need DRR? Yes. Concepts matter because they help to establish boundaries of acceptable activity and increase interoperability. In the case of European civil security, the plethora of definitions, and the limited voice of DRR, means that prevention may remain confined to a sub-section of the infamous disaster cycle that guides disaster management practice, instead of becoming an integrated and multi-sectorial approach that is encouraged at a global and increasingly regional level. If one were to push the integrated concept of DRR towards the idea of an ethos rather than a single policy area, the likelihood of greater resilience for the long-term development of states could be enhanced. The adaption of an ethos, or 'risk lens', that colours the agendas of government sectors, would require active engagement and advocacy from within national emergency management agencies alongside the support of the EU. This would not mean an additional framework agreement, but more informal support in creating awareness among government ministries and the private sector. The regional and national DRR platforms seem like a valuable tool to encourage a DRR ethos that would require greater commitment by member states and a closer EU–UN relationship. Such a method would not jeopardise state sovereignty – an issue when dealing with prevention – but complement the principle of subsidiarity and encourage solidarity.

The charge that European states are less willing to adopt the very prescriptions that they promote to developing countries is unfounded. DRR is a complex issue area that is highly challenging to implement. No short-term solutions appear to exist, rather long-term and sustained commitment will see increased change particularly if financial and institutional hurdles can be surpassed. Indeed, if awareness among all relevant sectors of society increases, choosing to see DRR as an ethos rather than a specific policy space, Europe may move one step closer towards a more secure region where a culture of prevention can be fully realized.

Notes

1. DRR is defined as 'the concept and practice of reducing disaster risks through systematic efforts to analyse and manage the causal factors of disasters,

including through reduced exposure to hazards, lessened vulnerability of people and property, wise management of land and the environment and improved preparedness for adverse events' (UNISDR, 2009).
2. For exceptions, see the Netherlands, Czech Republic and Malta, where emphasis is placed on coordination.

References

Acharya, A. (2004) 'How Ideas Spread: Whose Norms Matter? Norm Localization and Institutional Change in Asian Regionalism', *International Organization*, 58, 239–275.
Annan, K. (1999) *Report of the Secretary-General on the Work of the Organization General*, Assembly Official Records Fifty-fourth Session, Supplement No. 1 (A/54/1).
ANVIL (2014) *Analysis of Security Systems in Europe*. http://anvil-project.net, date accessed 7 November 2014.
ASEAN (2005) *Agreement on Disaster Management and Emergency Response*. http://www.jus.uio.no/english/services/library/treaties/13/13-02/asean_disaster_management.xml, date accessed 30 November 2010.
Berger, P. L. and T. Luckmann (1967) *The Social Construction of Reality: A Treatise in the Sociology of Knowledge* (New York: Anchor Books, Random House).
Bossong, R. and H. Hegemann (2014) ANVIL Deliverable 4.2: Final Analytical Report Critical Findings and Research Outlooks. http://anvil-project.net, date accessed 27 November 2014.
Carpenter, C., S. Duygulu, A. H. Montgomery and A. Rapp (2014) 'Explaining the Advocacy Agenda: Insights from the Human Security Network', *International Organization*, 68, 449–470.
Checkel, J. (2001) 'Why Comply? Social Learning and European Identity Change', *International Organization*, 55, 553–588.
Cortell, A. P. and J. W. Davis (2000) 'Understanding the Domestic Impacts of International Norms: A Research Agenda', *International Studies Review*, 2, 65–87.
Council of the European Union (2001) *Council Decision of 23 October 2001 Establishing a Community Mechanism to Facilitate Reinforced Cooperation in Civil Protection Assistance Interventions*, 2001/792/EC, Euratom.
Council of the European Union (2007) *Council Decision Establishing a Community Civil Protection Mechanism (recast)*. 2007/779/EC.
Council of the European Union (2014) *Decision of the European Parliament and of the Council on a Union Civil Protection Mechanism*. PE-CONS 97/13.
European Forum for Disaster Risk Reduction (2013) *Working Group 2, Local-Level Implementation of HFA*, 4th EFDRR Meeting Oslo, 24 September 2013. http://www.preventionweb.net/files/32998_08efdrr24sep2013norwaywglocalleveli.pdf, date accessed 24 November 2014.
European Forum for Disaster Risk Reduction (2014) *Governance and Accountability of the Hyogo Framework for Action: The European Perspective. Draft*. http://www.preventionweb.net/files/37472_draftoutcomeefdrrgovernanceeuropedr.pdf, date accessed 24 November 2014.

European Commission (2009) *EU Strategy for Supporting Disaster Risk Reduction in Developing Countries: Communication from the Commission to the Council and the European Parliament,* COM (2009) 84 final.

European Commission (2010) *Commission Decision of 29 July 2010 Amending Decision 2004/277/EC, Euratom as Regards Rules for the Implementation of Council Decision 2007/779/EC, Euratom Establishing a Community Civil Protection Mechanism.* 2010/481/EU, Euratom.

Finnemore, M. (1993) 'International Organizations as Teachers of Norms: The United Nations Educational Scientific, and Cultural Organization and Science Policy', *International Organization,* 47, 567–597.

Finnemore, M. and K. Sikkink (1999) 'International Norm Dynamics and Political Change', *International Organization,* 52, 887–917.

Global Facility for Disaster Reduction and Recovery (2013) *Partnership Charter: Global Facility for Disaster Reduction and Recovery* (Washington, D.C.).

Hannigan, J. (2012) *Disasters without Borders* (Cambridge: Polity Press).

Hewitt, K. (ed.) (1983) *Interpretations of Calamity* (Winchester, Mass.: Allen & Unwin Inc.).

Hollis, S. (2014) 'The External Construction of EU Development Policy', *Journal of European Integration,* 36, 549–566.

Hollis, S. (2015a) 'Competing and Complimentary Discourses in Global Disaster Risk Management', *Risk, Hazards & Crisis in Public Policy,* 5, 342–363.

Hollis, S. (2015b) *The Role of Regional Organizations in Disaster Risk Management: A Strategy for Global Resilience* (Basingstoke: Palgrave Macmillan).

Hyde, S. D. (2011) 'Catch Us If You Can: Election Monitoring and International Norm Diffusion', *American Journal of Political Science,* 55, 356–369.

International Decade for Natural Disaster Reduction (1999) *Assessment of Achievements During the Decade, German INDR Committee* (Bonn: German Red Cross).

International Federation of Red Cross (IFRC) (2014) What is a Disaster? https://www.ifrc.org/en/what-we-do/disaster-management/about-disasters/what-is-a-disaster/, date accessed 24 November 2014.

Jepperson, R. L., A. Wendt and P. J. Katzenstein (1996) 'Norms, Identity, and Culture in National Security', in P. J. Katzenstein (ed.) *The Culture of National Security: Norms and Identity in World Politics* (New York: Colombia University Press), pp. 33–72.

Krook, K. L. and J. True (2012) 'Rethinking the Life Cycles of International Norms: The United Nations and the Global Promotion of Gender Equality', *European Journal of International Relations,* 18, 103–127.

League of Arab States (2011) *Arab Strategy for Disaster Risk Reduction 2020.* http://www.unisdr.org/we/inform/publications/18903, date accessed 2 June 2011.

Lechner, F. J. and J. Boli (2005) *World Culture: Origins and Consequences* (Malden, Mass.: Blackwell).

Meyer, J. W. (2010) 'World Society, Institutional Theories, and the Actor', *Annual Review of Sociology,* 36, 1–20.

RedR (2012) Disaster Risk Reduction: Are We Doing Enough? http://www.redr.org.uk/en/News/Latest_News.cfm/disaster-risk-reduction-are-we-doing-enough, date accessed 24 November 2014.

Southern African Development Community (2006) *Building the Resilience of Southern Africa to Disasters: SADC Disaster Risk Reduction Strategic Plan*

2006–2010, Review Process of the SADC Strategy for DRR Policy Framework, Power Point Presentation by Masamvu, Kennedy, SADC Council Secretariat. http://ochaonline.un.org/OchaLinkClick.aspx?link=ochaanddocId=1095645, date accessed 18 May 2011.

Schofer, E., A. Hironaka, D. J. Frank and W. Longhofer et al. (2004) 'Sociological Institutionalism and World Society', in E. Amenta, K. Nash and A. Scott (eds.) *The New Blackwell Companion to Political Sociology* (New York: Wiley-Blackwell), pp. 57–69.

Solingen, E. (2012) 'Of Dominoes and Firewalls: The Domestic, Regional, and Global Politics of International Diffusion', *International Studies Quarterly*, 56, 631–644.

Strang, D. and J. W. Meyer [1993] (2009) 'Institutional Conditions for Diffusion', in G. S. Drori and G. Krücken (eds.) *World Society: The Writings of John W. Meyer* (Oxford: Oxford University Press), pp. 136–156.

United Nations Office for Disaster Risk Reduction (2005) *World Conference on Disaster Reduction*, 18–22 January 2005, Kobe, Hyogo, Japan. http://www.unisdr.org/eng/hfa/docs/Hyogo-framework-for-action-english.pdf, date accessed 7 June 2011.

United Nations Office for Disaster Risk Reduction (2007) *Guidelines: National Platforms for Disaster Risk Reduction*. http://www.unisdr.org/we/inform/publications/601, date accessed 24 November 2014.

United Nations Office for Disaster Risk Reduction (2009) *Terminology on DRR*. http://www.unisdr.org/we/inform/terminology#letter-e, date accessed 3 February 2011.

United Nations Office for Disaster Risk Reduction (2012) *Making Cities Resilient: My City is Getting Ready*. http://www.unisdr.org/campaign/resilientcities/toolkit/essentials, date accessed 24 November 2014.

United Nations Office for Disaster Risk Reduction (2013) *Overview of National Platforms for Disaster Risk Reduction in Europe: Fact Sheets on European National Platforms*. http://www.unisdr.org/files/19617_overviewnpeuropeefdrr20130802.pdf, date accessed 24 November 2014.

Wisner, B., P. M. Blaikie and T. Cannon (2004) *At Risk: Natural Hazards, People's Vulnerability and Disasters*, 2nd edition (Oxon: New York: Routledge).

World Bank (2013) *Building Resilience: Integrating Climate and Disaster Risk into Development: The World Bank Group Experience* (Washington, D.C.: International Bank for Reconstruction and Development), p. 644.

7
Transformations in European Natural Hazard Management: There and Back Again

Timothy Prior, Florian Roth and Michel Herzog

Mitigating risk: There and back again

Today, technical natural hazard management represents the central mode of governance for coping with natural and man-made hazards in many parts of the world. In most European states, it is primarily organized through specialized agencies at the national or sub-national level, which analyse and assess risks to society, organize preventive and responsive measures and inform the public. In recent years, however, this mode of security governance has been increasingly challenged by new approaches to handling hazards that emphasize decentralized, self-organizing structures for flexible responses to challenges posed by complexity and unpredictability (see also Hollis in this volume). Resilience is an oft-used concept (and sometimes buzzword) arguably lying at the centre of this transformation in civil security that seems to cherry-pick elements of natural hazard management's long and varied history. This transformation has been triggered by several obvious failures and shortcomings of technical natural hazard management, in particular to effectively prevent or mitigate major large-scale, cascading disasters such as the 2004 Indian Ocean Tsunami, Hurricane Katrina in 2005 and the Great Eastern Japan Earthquake and Tsunami in 2011 (which resulted in the Fukushima Daiichi Nuclear Power plant meltdown).

The dynamic nature of hazard management approaches, when viewed throughout history, reflects the evolving human relationship with the environment. However, what is interesting at the moment is that current approaches to safety and security in the context of natural hazard management increasingly reflect practices that were evident historically. It is therefore important to explore why, after a strong focus on very technical and quantitative natural hazard management approaches in the 19th and 20th centuries, should governments increasingly favour 'people-centred' or 'societal security approaches' to natural risk hazard management in the 21st century. While it is common that the proponents of 'modern' natural hazard management practices often claim their approaches are superior to their predecessor(s), this may not always be the case, especially if we assume that the dynamic relationships between society and hazards change over time. In this context, it is important to recognize that traditional cultures often developed highly effective adaptive mechanisms to cope with natural hazards at the local level (Hernández-Morcillo et al., 2014). For example, the residents of the Doñana wetland in South-west Spain developed a detailed Local Environmental Knowledge (LEK) of flooding hazards that could affect agricultural practices there and extends at least as far back as the 16th century (Gómez-Baggethun et al., 2012). Based on this knowledge, the residents established practices to forecast, avoid and otherwise cope with the threat of seasonal or extreme flooding episodes (resource storage, rationing, pooling and so on), some of which remain in use. Cases like this illustrate that traditional approaches to natural hazard management can still yield life-saving benefits to modern societies, so it is timely to explore the ways in which modern natural hazard security governance mechanisms might draw off traditional cultural approaches and practices in the future.

This chapter will explore transformations in natural hazard management in Europe, especially in relation to the rise of 'resilience' as a central paradigm. In order to look towards the future of natural hazard management in Europe, we first step backward to explore the history of natural hazard management in Europe, showing that change and transformation is by no means a new feature of the civil security landscape. We demonstrate that evolutionary or adaptive processes of transformation in hazard management have reflected both the dynamic society and changing environmental characteristics. The current trend towards 'resilience thinking' is no different, and we find that the historical lens provides an informative backdrop to explore this transformation. The rise of this concept is associated with distributed governance, self-organization and people-centred approaches to natural hazard management based on individual responsibility, characteristics that we show are reminiscent of medieval-style natural hazard civil security. By describing this history, we lay the groundwork for an exploration of why history seems to be repeating itself.

This historical exploration begins with a focus on three historical periods when important social or environmental changes have shaped the practices of hazard management: beginning with the Middle Ages, followed by the Early Modern Period, through to the hazard management heyday of the 19th and 20th centuries. We then examine how a changing risk environment, characterized by increased complexity, uncertainty, unpredictability and rising disaster losses, is influencing a 21st-century transformation in natural hazard management in Europe. We suggest that the most recent evolutionary step in civil protection processes in Europe retreats partly from solely technical and quantitative approaches established since the 18th and 19th centuries, to one that draws off local knowledge, local experience, action and bottom-up organization, which is in many ways more similar to the hazard management of the Middle Ages. We argue that 'resilience' is a central element of this current transformation, and describe how this concept and approach has gained popularity in the context of the changing risk environment, particularly exploring some important issues that must be considered in any meaningful practical application of the resilience approach in natural hazard management. We also discuss in how far alternative modes of governance, such as resilience, can replace or supplement technical natural hazard management as the central form of organizing civil security measures.

Natural hazard management: A brief history of nearly everything

The way in which natural hazard risk has been defined and addressed has a long history in the context of civil security. In many ways, how risk has been managed through this history reflects the way people have conceptualized risks objectively and subjectively, and how these conceptualizations have contributed to the evolution of natural hazard management practices and process. This section provides a very basic history of natural hazard management through the ages, highlighting how the social conceptualization of risk at different points in history influenced how risks were dealt with. We acknowledge that risk from natural hazards is fundamentally considered in the context of the social consequences that the interaction of natural hazards and society promulgate. For this reason, we focus on time periods where distinct social changes or technical developments loosely coincide with developments in, or changes to, attitudes, practices and techniques of natural hazard management (as we loosely label the practices, even though the term was not used to classify these practices prior to the 19th century). We do not aim to describe the evolution of natural hazard management in its entirety, but to illustrate very broadly how European society, risk and hazard management have evolved together. Consequently, the time periods we examine do not flow together in a seamless manner.

We define natural hazard management as a process involving the identification, assessment and prioritization of risk that culminates in the proposition of risk mitigation or treatment practices and techniques. This conceptualization has a fundamentally forward-looking element: that knowledge concerning the nature of potential risk, its consequence and its prospective occurrence can be used to develop a future picture of what might happen, how and where. This information is then used to establish risk mitigating or risk prevention structures or behaviours.

In Europe, this modern practice has evolved as a result of extensive social experience with natural hazards and with historical applications of different methodologies or techniques. We illustrate this history very broadly in three sections, beginning with the very experiential and localized nature of medieval 'risk management'. We then describe the arrival of probabilistic, mathematical treatments of risk in the innovative Early Modern Period. We close this section with a discussion of the post-19th century technical, command-and-control style of natural hazard management that we are familiar with today.

Medieval risk experience as understanding

The Middle Ages, or medieval period (roughly 5th to the 15th century), saw the development of many modern cities through burgeoning urbanization, the establishment and expansion of kingdoms and population growth supported by technical innovations and methods of production. The period saw new philosophical beginnings in Scholasticism, for example, that sought to bridge the heretofore-distinct realms of faith and reason, and which was the predominant teaching style in the newly established universities of Bologna and Paris. From the Feudal system developed the major European monarchies, which ultimately birthed the modern European states as we know them today.

The social dynamics of the period was matched, and confronted, by an equally dynamic disaster record. The list of natural disasters during the medieval period, especially the late Middle Ages, was long and consequential. Earthquakes (Basel, 1356; Austria/Italy, 1348), volcanoes (Sicily, 1408, 1537), floods and wild weather (Bavaria, 1301;

Cologne, 1372) were some of the historically recorded natural hazards that resulted in disasters during the medieval period. The ways in which these disasters were experienced and perceived by different elements of the medieval European societies provides an early glimpse of how those disasters were managed.

During this period, natural hazard risk was perceived largely through the lens of the Bible and other religious texts, which often described the disasters of Antiquity in the contexts of the Apocalypse and the death of Christ. For example, fear at the unintentional ringing of bells simultaneously across towns in northern Italy and southern Austria during the Carinthian earthquake of 1348 reflected this faith-based hazard perception prevalent during the period (Rohr, 2003). While the assumption that this fatalistic 'natural hazards as acts of God' framing of the perception of risk is a common one, it is not the whole story in the context of early natural hazard management. Gerrard and Petley (2013, p. 1051) suggest that societies of the Middle Ages were not helpless, but often exhibited 'complex, considered and, at times, surprisingly modern' approaches to natural hazards. This proposition is illustrated by a growing literature that documents long-established local forms of natural hazard management from around the globe (for example, Cronin et al., 2004; Becker et al., 2008).

The new era of scholarship that flowered during the late Middle Ages meant that once faith-dominated beliefs about disasters were slowly being complemented by reasoned explanations. The result was a very active process of post hoc incident description and documentation. While these activities were obviously undertaken in the aftermath of an event (and often a long time after, thus affecting their accuracy), they nevertheless served to establish a written record of environmental features evident in the lead up to a hazard event and pseudo-scientific accounts of the event's consequences. These efforts were often made by members of the clergy or local intellectuals, were experiential, or at least informed by eyewitness accounts, and arguably constituted the first qualitative natural hazard analyses (even if only post hoc).

Documented experiences influenced the adoption of early natural hazard risk mitigation, protection and adaptation practices during this time (Covello and Mumpower, 1985). Non-structural mitigation actions like relief and rehabilitation (tax reductions or food relief, for example) were adopted in direct response to repeated natural hazards: flooding in Florence; famine in England; earthquakes in Greece and Italy and so on. Typically, medieval risk mitigation practices were characterized by cooperative and collective endeavours, and Keene (2011) presents evidence that much of the responsibility for mitigation lay with the citizen, not with the monarch. Structural actions, like raising floors in flood prone areas, hardening vulnerable structures in earthquake risk areas and the construction of sea break walls along coasts are all examples of hazard protections, informed by experiences, that were evident during the medieval period (Gerrard and Petley, 2013; Hernández-Morcillo et al., 2014). Lastly, Gerrard and Petley (2013) provide many examples of medieval hazard adaptation, where hazard experience-informed behaviours of citizens and states helped at-risk populations to avoid, or at least tolerate the consequences of natural hazards.

During the Middle Ages, the crude foundations of 'risk management' reflected extensive locally experienced natural hazard activity, where individuals, households and communities were largely responsible for their own safety and security. While the Middle Ages were seen as a relatively static time in history, the subsequent Early Modern Period was comparatively dynamic. Importantly for natural hazard management, and particularly the attribution of responsibility in hazard security, the relationship between the citizen and the state changed fundamentally after the Middle Ages with corresponding implications for perceptions about risk and the way it was treated. These changes are examined in the following section.

Early modern risk measurement

The Early Modern Period was an age of geographic and scholarly discovery and of political reinvention. Europe's great powers of the time supported explorations that led to the colonization and exploitation of the globe's furthest corners. Universities flourished and deep innovations in society, the sciences and politics were the by-products of the Age of Enlightenment. The geographic globalization that characterized the period has perhaps had the most significant influence on the quantitative nature of natural hazard management that would develop in the 20th century. As new, but uncertain trading opportunities and enterprises were established, so too was the concept of risk applied in the context of the probabilities associated with profit and loss.

Although the etymological origin of the word 'risk' is unclear, it most likely comes from the Greek word 'ρίζα' (meaning cliff). It is largely uncontested that the term's first applications came along the development of naval trade during the Early Modern Age. During this period, the term risk was used to describe opportunities where profit could only be achieved at the cost of a potential loss. In the wake of the fast growing global naval trade, the first risk calculations were developed, multiplying the estimated probability of a disruptive event with the value of goods at risk. Accordingly, risk was defined as 'the probability of an adverse future event multiplied by its magnitude'. As this statistical thinking associated with risk began to spread to other social domains, so the conception of risk as a probabilistic phenomenon began to triumph.

During this period, the first attempts were made to find a scientific definition of the concept of risk and to delineate it from other related concepts. In early applications, risk was regarded as something desirable in contrast to uncertainty, which was conceived (and still often is) in a negative light. Risk was seen to be calculable; this 'knowability' gave risk managers a perceived element of control over risk situations. From the domain of economics, risk spread to domains like medicine and criminology. In contrast to the earlier economic conceptions, in disease and crime prevention risk was for the first time conceptualized exclusively in a negative sense.

While the feudal system was to be supplanted by monarchical systems throughout Europe (which were themselves also largely removed during the Age of Revolutions), both influenced political philosophizing during the Age of Enlightenment. This was especially in the case of Thomas Hobbes' theoretical proposition concerning the establishment of a 'social contract' between state and citizen (1651), and further elaborated by scholars including Jean-Jacques Rousseau (1762). The social contract described the relationship between the citizen and overlord or monarch where the former yielded all or some freedoms to the latter in exchange for protection or an assurance of security. The origin of this tacit contract, and the philosophy it embodied, was consequential in the context of civil security, and arguably for hazard management, during the Early Modern Period because of the assumed roles of the state as assurer of civil safety and security and the citizen as a contributor to the state (through the fief or tax). Together with the new technical specialization that was developing in the context of risk management, and a desire to measure risk, a focus on the state's responsibility to assure civil security was a marked difference from the Middle Ages, when natural hazard management actions and behaviours were seen as a civil responsibility.

Changes in governance, and the technical difficulty of new statistical risk analyses, ensured that natural hazard management processes were situated squarely under the responsibility of government organizations. As the role of government structures continued to strengthen during this period and further into the long 20th century, so did perceptions about the role of the state in assuring the security of the citizen. This role was reinforced by technical specializations in hazard analysis and the measurement and discourse concerning hazard probability that developed during the subsequent centuries.

The long 20th century and risk analytical precision

Between the 18th and 20th centuries modern risk measurement, analyses and management processes and practices were developed, systematized and institutionalized. These developments were influenced by significant changes in the nature of real and perceived risks, the context in which society interacted with those risks and the political will and capacity to assure civil security (Covello and Mumpower, 1985). The period was characterized largely by industrialization, and following from this, the technical modernization of many elements of life and society. Social and demographic changes during the period coincided with precipitative transformations in the way natural hazards were measured and managed.

During the late 18th and 19th centuries, modern conceptions of 'risk' and 'probability' were developed. These developments followed an active period of probability theory scholarship, which culminated in perhaps the first quantitative risk assessment, conducted by LaPlace, and examining how the probability of death from a smallpox was influenced by a vaccination (LaPlace, 1812, cited in Covello and Mumpower, 1985). By improving their mathematical techniques to increase the accuracy and precision of the probability predictions, the belief that the probabilities of uncertain events in the future could be made more knowable became an attractive goal (Bernstein, 1996). With the belief of improved predictability came the realization that, once predicted, uncertain events could also be managed. However, this realization also shined a glaring light on the need to ensure that these predictions were based on trustworthy data and unquestionable analyses. In addition, precise and accurate analyses could only be made in the context of clear risk conceptions (Klüppelberg et al., 2014), and the term 'risk' became closely associated with the idea that 'apparent uncertainties [could] be measured or quantified probabilistically' (Zachmann, 2014, p. 3).

Faster population growth, industrialization, modernization and urbanization significantly influenced the risk landscape of the 19th and 20th centuries. The structural and innovation changes in society during this era also influenced the way society thought about and dealt with natural or technical risk (Beck, 1992; Giddens, 2013; Zachmann, 2014). Around this time, Aaron Wildavsky noted that the social view of risk in the second half of the 20th century was mired in contradiction: there could 'be no safety without risk' (1988, p. 1), and, that in seeking safety through advances in technology and medicine 'unintended consequences [became] a staple of social life' (1988, p. 69). Yet, while the era was characterized by a strong focus on quantitative and technocentric approaches to managing the consequences of hazards, there was little systematic administrative focus on ensuring safety by managing risks, apart from in the sanitation and health sectors. Only by the late 1970s were government risk management agencies being established to focus on assessing and treating risks across the broader modern society (Covello and Mumpower, 1985; Stallings and Quarantelli, 1985). This rather late government organization of specialized risk management agencies was especially due to the increasing need to dedicate extensive intellectual, financial and technical resources to natural hazard management in order to satisfactorily estimate the probabilities and consequences of hazards within the vastly more complex society (Zachmann, 2014). Being deployed by government organizations, natural hazard management processes were specifically established on the basis of technical capacities and expertise, with a centralized and hierarchical model of management. The 'command-and-control' model was founded on the assumption that 'only by firm coordination and effective command [would] resources be deployed efficiently and effectively' (Alexander, 2008, p. 137), reflecting the need to manage risks under circumstances of increasing complexity, event intensity and length, and the numbers of people involved in disaster planning, response and recovery.

At the same time, because of the perceived potential (negative) effects of technological innovations on public health and safety, risk began to develop a communicative dimension in the context of public and political discourses. Advocates of new technologies were keen to demonstrate to the public that their technologies were reasonably safe and the 'residual risks' were negligible, or at least under the control of professional risk managers. In order to achieve this goal, many risk analyses and assessments were conducted with a clear focus on precision and accuracy: practices that technical risk managers expected would assure the public that the new technologies were safe, and that public fears of industrial risks were unjustified. Yet, the technical understanding of risk and the intended message to the public were neither well communicated nor well received. In retrospect, these early attempts to establish a public understanding of risk based on a technical application of risk management processes largely failed, as they were generally unable to convince the public to trust in the risk calculations of experts and remove the fears of the new technologies (Wardman, 2008). Unfortunately, major catastrophes including the nuclear accidents of Three Mile Island (1979) and Chernobyl (1986) and the mismanagement of the 'Mad Cow Disease' (Bovine Spongiform Encephalopathy – first recorded in 1986) did nothing to nourish the public's trust in 'expert' risk managers. Ultimately, the controversies over technological side effects of modern technologies triggered growing attention to the psychological components of risk (for example, Lopes, 1987).

A changing risk environment and hazard management focus

The processes of industrialization and modernization influenced the nature of risks during the long 20th century. Yet arguably, these developments, started two centuries ago, and defining modern society, continue to influence some of the major natural hazards of the 21st century, particularly those associated with anthropogenic changes in the climate (for example, flood, wildfire, landslides, droughts, tropical storms and so on). Importantly, there is abundant evidence to suggest that climate-associated hazards in Europe are likely to become more extreme and more frequent (IPCC, 2014). While quantitative natural hazard management techniques (risk analyses, assessments, risk mapping, risk registers and so on), as mechanisms that help to gain 'intelligence and control' in a hazard management process (Kasperson and Pijawka, 1985, p. 8), still remain important tools in the risk manager's practical toolbox, they are increasingly being complemented by practices like local public participation, community engagement and methods of incorporating LEK into hazard management decisions. These elements of 'people-centred' or distributed approaches are steadily gaining recognition as important practices to improve hazard management under conditions of heightened uncertainty and unpredictability in the risk environment of the 21st century.

Although a long tradition of risk measurement and technical hazard accuracy and precision in Europe has certainly contributed to the natural hazard knowledge base and improved natural hazard management practice (Kasperson and Pijawka, 1985; White et al., 2001), disaster losses continue to increase[1] (Shreve and Kelman, 2014). While the character of 'natural hazard chains' are well understood and remain relatively stable (Kasperson and Pijawka, 1985, p. 8), the society they interact with has changed dramatically since the middle of the 20th century and continues to be highly dynamic (Liu et al., 2007; Coaffee, 2013).

Any change in hazard characteristics (intensity or frequency) and consequences must therefore be considered in the context of a global society that has grown substantially in complexity: relying on extensive and complicated economic and technical infrastructures and technology; and on greater connectivity through communications, transport, supply chains and urbanization.

The resulting uncertainty associated with hazard event activity and unpredictability of event consequences are challenging the appropriateness of top-down, technocratic natural hazard management practices and the utility of technical and quantitative risk analytic techniques.[2] In particular, uncertainty and unpredictability influence the technical capacity to determine event probabilities of future events (Dessai and Hulme, 2004), the fundamental linchpin on which modern technical natural hazard management is founded (Lopes, 1987). Together with factors like the increasing costs (social, financial and so on) associated with protection measures, higher population densities and urban development in higher risk areas and more complex critical infrastructure systems, these challenges diminish the capability (even willingness) of governments to guarantee the safety of citizens all the time (Coaffee and Wood, 2006; Stark and Taylor, 2014).

Particularly during the second half of the 20th century, risk analyses and management practices were heavily focused on the hazards themselves. Gaining a technical and probabilistic understanding of the risk posed by natural hazards (intelligence), which could inform causality, was seen to be fundamental in supporting the prioritization of natural hazard management activities (control) in the form of mitigation, protection or encouraging behavioural change (Covello and Mumpower, 1985). However, increasing disaster losses, despite a better understanding of natural hazard activity (White et al., 2001), has seen the focus of natural hazard management shift away from understanding hazards, towards better understanding disasters and the vulnerabilities that exacerbate them: social, economic and structural. Seemingly, as Covello and Mumpower (1985, p. 118) predicted, 'improved risk management capabilities' have indeed been 'outstripped by improved risk identification capabilities', resulting in a situation where knowing better about hazards is not actually improving mitigation or response, especially in the context of a society growing in complexity (FLACSO and UNISDR, 2013).

In order to reduce disaster losses by addressing vulnerability, a strong focus in the disaster risk reduction community (particularly) has advocated a stronger role for civil society in natural hazard management processes (Thomalla et al., 2006). This has come in part as a response to the recognition that quantitative and technical risk analytic approaches were clearly not delivering sufficient or appropriate hazard 'intelligence' to inform hazard 'control' for effective hazard mitigation. Emergent community action has been embraced nationally and internationally to address growing natural hazard vulnerability and increasing disaster losses since at least the middle of the 1990s when the UN's intergovernmental Yokohama Strategy was established to address natural hazard vulnerability and growing disaster loss by integrating hazard prevention, mitigation and preparedness measures (United Nations, 1994). This integration provided a basis for, but also required, multi-stakeholder interaction in natural hazard management processes. Since this time, the increased relevance of participation has been reflected in a huge variety of policy documents, including the Hyogo Framework for Action (HFA) 2005–2015. The HFA explicitly called for the 'development and strengthening of institutions, mechanisms and capacities at all levels, in particular at the community level, that can systematically contribute to building resilience to hazards' (UNISDR, 2005). While not the first step, the HFA has further influenced a shift from government-lead natural hazard management undertaken by technical specialists, back towards the civil society, and a somewhat more distributed approach to DRM that is increasingly being bundled under the broad notion of resilience.

Resilience: The future of disaster natural hazard management in Europe?

During the last decade, the concept of resilience has become closely associated with the integrated, but more distributed, approach to natural hazard management that has developed as the focus of DRM has shifted from the hazard towards addressing vulnerabilities. Resilience in natural hazard management has been framed in many ways (Klein et al., 2003; Zhou et al., 2010; Zebrowski, 2013; Prior and Hagmann, 2014), but the concept's use has nevertheless burgeoned. In many ways, the popular conceptions of resilience seem to dovetail closely with the very characteristics of the 21st century that have limited the suitability of other existing approaches to natural hazard management. Given that the use of resilience in Europe's civil protection and natural hazard management is already well established (for example, European Commission, 2013), it seems clear that this shift represents the most recent transformation in European civil natural hazards security governance. However, while many governments and international organizations highlight the necessity of 'being resilient', the ubiquity of the concept overshadows a rather simplistic and poorly articulated practical application of 'the' resilience approach to date. The limitations of the approach must be addressed if this latest of civil security transformations can be meaningful now and into the future.

The word resilience originates from the Latin *resiliere*, meaning to spring or bounce back. The concept's modern usage originated in the technical and natural sciences (particularly engineering and ecology) during the 1960s and 1970s and was at the time applied in relation to an entity or system's ability to return to normal functioning (a point of equilibrium) quickly following a disturbance. More recently, the concept has been applied in a more nuanced fashion that discarded the idea of equilibrium in favour of change through adaptation and learning to ensure the system's functions persist following disturbance. In this vein, the United Nations Office of Disaster Risk Reduction (UNISDR) defines resilience as 'the capacity of a system, community or society potentially exposed to hazards to adapt, by resisting or changing in order to reach and maintain an acceptable level of functioning and structure' (UNISDR, 2009). Also, the European Commission frames resilience as 'the ability of an individual, a household, a community, a country or a region to resist, adapt and quickly recover from a disaster or crisis' (European Commission, 2014). While these definitions seem relatively clear, the diverse disciplinary background of the modern conception of resilience may nevertheless pose difficulty in applying resilience in a robust and meaningful manner in practical natural hazard management situations (Walker and Cooper, 2011; Prior and Hagmann, 2014).

From a problem solving perspective, the ubiquity of resilience has perhaps increased as a result of the confluence of three important changes: uncertainty and unpredictability challenge traditional natural hazard management practices; governments are consequently less able or willing to guarantee safety; and therefore seek to encourage or piggy-back on emergent community-lead hazard mitigation activities. In the following, we provide greater detail regarding these three factors and illustrate some of the challenges these elements of resilience may pose in a process of civil security transformation.

Firstly, the perception of increasing uncertainty and unpredictability in future natural hazard threat scenarios presents a growing challenge for accurate and precise quantitative natural hazard management approaches. Under these circumstances, it is difficult to obtain data for a risk assessment that is complete and accurate if the frequency and intensity of future hazards is unknown and cannot be assumed based on historical experience. Modern mathematical modelling approaches can in many cases assist in these situations, but even these sophisticated predictive tools introduce uncertainty into natural hazard management decisions. Proponents of resilience highlight that resilience approaches should introduce more flexibility and adaptive capabilities into traditional natural hazard management processes because they can draw on a range of information (quantitative and qualitative) and on diverse stakeholders to inform hazard management decisions (Norris et al., 2008; HM Government, 2010; National Emergency Management Committee, 2011; The National Academies, 2012). However, the application of resilience approaches can be hindered by the difficulty of quantifying resilience (Prior and Hagmann, 2014), raising a difficult conundrum for government-lead natural hazard management agencies, whose operations and decisions about risk planning and response have been strongly based on quantitative data for at least the last 40 years.

Secondly, conditions of uncertainty and unpredictability, coupled with the need to coordinate hazard planning within significantly more complex, populous and interdependent societies, mean traditional government natural hazard management agencies are now less able and willing to guarantee the safety and security of citizens all the time (Coaffee and Wood, 2006). The suitability of technical expert-dominated natural hazard management approaches is being diminished by the very changes in society that increase social exposure and vulnerability to natural hazards. As a leading advocate of the resilience approach to safety and security, the government of the UK recognizes that:

> we cannot prevent every risk as they are inherently unpredictable. To ensure we are able to recover quickly when risks turn into actual damage to our interests, we have to promote resilience, both locally and nationally. Ensuring that the public is fully informed of the risks we face is a critical part of this approach.
> (HM Government, 2010, p. 23)

The Strategy goes on to point out that:

> Of course, the Government has a crucial role to play, and we will certainly fulfil our responsibilities. But we all have a part to play in keeping the country safe – be it from terrorists, cyber attack or natural disasters.
> (HM Government, 2010, p. 5)

The UK government is not alone in this philosophy of a distributed or devolved approach to natural hazard management (UNISDR, 2005; National Emergency Management Committee, 2011; The National Academies, 2012). The need to plan for and respond to natural hazard events with an approach that draws on society-wide distribution of hazard prevention and mitigation activities at once recognizes the diminishing capacity of technical natural hazard management processes (Alexander, 2008; Bulley, 2013; Welsh, 2014), but also the necessity to share an increasing hazard mitigation burden across all members of at-risk societies, especially if antecedent natural hazard vulnerabilities within society are to be addressed rather than attempting to prevent hazards. While the rhetoric of devolution in government 'command-and-control' powers of natural hazard managers seems a clear policy directive, critical authors recognize that this element in a prospective security transformation towards resilience still faces practical hurdles (Stark and Taylor, 2014).

Thirdly, while Stallings and Quarantelli (1985) were surprised by the public's interest in becoming involved in natural hazard mitigation decisions pre-1970, emergent hazard mitigation behaviour among at-risk populations is now very common and encouraged (Adger, 2003; Morrison, 2003; Bihari and Ryan, 2012; Prior and Eriksen, 2013). The 'deficit' model of risk communication[3] philosophy of government hazard managers has been replaced with a recognized necessity to engage members of civil society in hazard management planning and decision-making processes. Indeed, many resilience scholars recognize that one of the more valuable aspects of the modern conceptualization of resilience is its focus on self-organization (for example, Klein et al., 2003; Kaufman, 2013). Part of the value of emergence and diverse involvement of civil society can be associated with the way people-centred elements can complement traditional hazard management outcomes by drawing off the experiences and knowledge of local people to directly improve their hazard coping capabilities. While this civil participative element of hazard planning and management has been enshrined in both national and international frameworks for disaster risk reduction for two decades (United Nations, 1994; UNISDR, 2005), the practical success of participation and emergent process remains patchy at best in many instances (for example, Schmid, 2013). Some authors argue that this focus on citizen participation or local involvement represents a hazard mitigation responsibility shift (even active 'responsibilization') from governments to civil society (Bulley, 2013; Coaffee, 2013; Welsh, 2014), which, if accurate, will likely present challenges in the development of effective resilience approaches (Roth and Prior, 2014). Given that attempts to improve the local level and bottom-up activities of civil society in disaster risk reduction (DRR) will likely be a central element in future supragovernmental DRR frameworks, the necessity to clarify and improve the practical applicability of the relationship between emergent or self-organized hazard mitigation activities among the public, and process of building resilience, will remain centrally important element of this transformation in civil security.

More critical perspectives associate the rise of resilience in natural hazard management with the spread of neoliberal attitudes in governance practices (for example, Evans and Reid, 2013; Joseph, 2013; Zebrowski, 2013). Authors who highlight his perspective tend to suggest that resilience represents the practical delivery of a political agenda that seeks to subjectify the citizen by spreading fear and breeding uncertainty. In reality, resilience proponents highlight a variety of practical activities (including preparedness, household planning, risk dialogue and information sharing with technical experts and so on) that can empower people and help them to personally control their experience of hazard consequences. In general, natural hazard managers (as distinct from political representatives) and the policies they develop and implement tend to be practical in nature and designed to solve a problem. Current transformations in the relationship between the modern global society and natural hazards are presenting new challenges for natural hazard managers and for society. Whether or not resilience is the paradigmatic answer to these challenges is yet to be determined, but actions that are known to increase social resilience in the face of natural hazards suggest that at least developing a better understanding of resilience is worth some effort.

Conclusion

The chapter illustrates that processes and practices of ensuring or assuring civil security in Europe have undergone significant transformation throughout history. Interestingly, not only have practices changed, but also assumed roles of civil society and governance structures seem to be cycling. In early history, before modern governance structures were established, civil society was expected to assume responsibility for implementing natural hazard mitigation. As kingdoms and democracies evolved, the establishment of the social contract fomented a shift in mitigation responsibility to governing structures or organizations. Yet, under the influence of a number of factors that are encouraging rising popularity of resilience as an outcome and approach in natural hazard management, a shift in responsibility back towards the citizen, enacted through a stated requirement for local involvement, self-organization and/or emergent public mitigation behaviour, is becoming evident. This change is the latest in a series of civil security transformations, which will influence the way natural hazard civil security can be (and will be) generated in the 21st century and beyond. However, while the popularity of the resilience approach continues to snowball in the context of a changing risk environment, it is important to examine the ways this approach and forms of resilience 'thinking' (Berkes, 2007) might influence the way we perceive natural hazards and achieve civil security in places prone to natural hazard risk.

One important issue is the fundamental conception of 'risk' could become outdated under conditions that favour the resilience approach. Accurately describing what a risk is has been a major discourse in the context of natural hazard management since the technical accuracy and precision of risk assessments and analyses gained dominance in the 19th and 20th centuries. For many users, 'risk' 'refers to situations in which a decision is made whose consequences depend on the outcomes of future events having known probabilities' (Lopes, 1987, p. 255). This widely used conception (see also Zachmann, 2014) reflects a technical objectivity that could well be challenged by the increasing uncertainty and unpredictability of natural hazards in modern times. *If* increasing uncertainty and unpredictability of natural hazard consequences (influenced by the complex, dynamic and interdependent modern society) limit the capability to know the probabilities of future events, then can we confidently say we are still looking at situations of risk? If we are unable to attribute probabilities to hazard events, will the accuracy and precision of technical analytic practices in natural hazard management become obsolete? Certainly, a transformation from technical and quantitative natural hazard management to a more qualitative resilience approach is unlikely to be a black-to-white transition, but a diversification in natural hazard management practices, which are executed in a complementary fashion, will likely contribute to better hazard mitigation outcomes for civil society and government into a future characterized by social complexity. Similarly, while a technical probability-focused definition of risk may be less relevant in a 21st-century natural hazard context, the notion of risk will retain its currency with regard to its more general association with uncertainty, which is a fundamentally social conception. Even so, it seems timely that a transformation in the relationship between society and natural hazards, that determines how we cope with these events and secure our lives and lifestyles, should be adopted.

Another challenging issue associated with the apparent transformation towards resilience is the organization of command-and-control, and shifts in responsibility attribution, among natural hazard management actors (public, private and civil society). The social contract between state and citizen established a clear relationship between those who govern and those who are governed in the context of civil security and safety: some civil freedoms were surrendered in return for protection and safety from an overlord or monarch. If citizens are increasingly asked, encouraged or made to take greater responsibility for their own hazard mitigation, as was the case in the Middle Ages, does this indicate an erosion of the social contract under a resilience approach, or just an evolution? It would be naïve to assume that the social contract as described above has not changed in the last 300 years. Instead, it has gradually evolved to reflect the changing value systems, norms and perceived uncertainties within a dynamic society. While some governments may want to devolve responsibility to citizens, it is also important to accept that a society that is well informed, more interested in policy decision-making and keen to take on greater control over some aspects of their lives or lifestyles is likely to also *want* to take on more responsibility. So establishing how best to accommodate these (possibly) mutual desires arising from different sectors of society will become increasingly important. However, the implications of shifting responsibility for both society and government must be mapped and well understood before resilience approaches can present realistic alternatives to (or complement) existing modes of natural hazard management. The question of how to re-organize natural hazard management and mitigation then becomes a central element in properly establishing resilience approaches, but should it occur at the individual, community, organizational or societal scales? Responsibility shifts may well characterize a new social contract in a transformed civil security context, where neither 'draconian measures and excessively authoritarian command-and-control procedures' (Alexander, 2008, p. 138), nor distributed and devolved governance arrangements predominate, but are balanced against one another.

Applying resilience is not yet (and may never be) a 'hard' and fast science like risk analysis, statistics or their associated natural hazard management practices. However, in the context of the changing society and the dynamic risk environment, the flexible and qualitative approach that resilience embodies is gaining considerable traction. The very characteristics of resilience approaches to civil security in the context of natural hazards – public participation, responsibility sharing, flexible and adaptive governance and so on – represent decentralization in the approach to natural hazard security. Similar patterns of decentralization can be seen in other areas of security, such as policing social unrest. At the same time, approaches to civil security in other domains, particularly in the linked fields of counterterrorism and homeland security, appear to be increasingly centralized. This simultaneous centralization and decentralization across the various civil security fields is highlighted by Bossong and Hegemann in the introduction to this volume. Whether useful or not, such dichotomy in practice likely reflects a recognized necessity to modify security approaches to suit perceived conditions of civil security or risk. It may also reflect differences in the national or international drivers behind different security areas. For instance, natural hazard civil security may be increasingly decentralized because of a growing influence from international organizations' perspectives (for example, from the UN, NGOs or other development and humanitarian help agencies and so on), which are typically more deliberative, as opposed to national perspectives on terrorism and homeland security, which can be more decisive and prescriptive. As Cerny identifies (1998, p. 41), the growing complexity of society, partly influenced by globalization, interdependence and dynamism, creates a situation of 'multiple potential equilibria' and the 'interaction of differences', which influence governance structures and places transformative and differentiated pressure on the way different forms of civil security are ensured and assured in the complex society of the 21st century.

Notes

1. Not only is this a result of increasing value and complexity in the infrastructure that supports modern societies, it also reflects the increasing likelihood that these assets are insured (at least in developed states).
2. The dynamic and interdependent global society adds complexity to the traditional hazard management calculus, influencing the uncertainty and unpredictability of hazard consequences (but not necessarily hazard activity).
3. Where information was provided by technical specialists or government officials to the civil society in order to 'correct' risk related misunderstanding or misperceptions in the population.

References

Adger, W. N. (2003) 'Social Capital, Collective Action, and Adaptation to Climate Change', *Economic Geography*, 79, 387–404.

Alexander, D. (2008) 'Emergency Command Systems and Major Earthquake Disasters', *JSEE-Journal of Seismology and Earthquake Engineering*, 10, 137–146.
Beck, U. (1992) *Risk Society: Towards a New Modernity* (London: Sage).
Becker, J., D. Johnston, J. Lazrus, G. Crawford and D. Nelson (2008) 'Use of Traditional Knowledge in Emergency Management for Tsunami Hazard: A Case Study from Washington State, USA', *Disaster Prevention and Management*, 17, 488–502.
Berkes, F. (2007) 'Understanding Uncertainty and Reducing Vulnerability: Lessons from Resilience Thinking', *Natural Hazards*, 41, 283–295.
Bernstein, P. L. (1996) *Against the Gods: The Remarkable Story of Risk* (New York: John Wiley & Sons).
Bihari, M. and R. Ryan (2012) 'Influence of Social Capital on Community Preparedness for Wildfires', *Landscape and Urban Planning*, 106, 253–261.
Bulley, D. (2013) 'Producing and Governing Community (through) Resilience', *Politics*, 33, 265–275.
Cerny, P. G. (1998) 'Neomedievalism, Civil War and the New Security Dilemma: Globalisation as Durable Disorder', *Civil Wars*, 1, 36–64.
Coaffee, J. (2013) 'Rescaling and Responsibilising the Politics of Urban Resilience: From National Security to Local Place-Making', *Politics*, 33, 240–252.
Coaffee, J. and D. M. Wood (2006) 'Security Is Coming Home: Rethinking Scale and Constructing Resilience in the Global Urban Response to Terrorist Risk', *International Relations*, 20, 503–517.
Covello, V. T. and J. Mumpower (1985) 'Risk Analysis and Risk Management: An Historical Perspective', *Risk Analysis*, 5, 103–120.
Cronin, S. J., D. R. Gaylord, D. Charley, B. V. Alloway, S. Wallez and J. W. Esau (2004) 'Participatory Methods of Incorporating Scientific with Traditional Knowledge for Volcanic Hazard Management on Ambae Island, Vanuatu', *Bulletin of Volcanology*, 66, 652–668.
Dessai, S. and M. Hulme (2004) 'Does Climate Adaptation Policy Need Probabilities?', *Climate Policy*, 4, 107–128.
European Commission (2013) *Disaster Risk Reduction: Increasing Resilience by Reducing Disaster Risk in Humanitarian Action*. http://ec.europa.eu/echo/files/policies/prevention_preparedness/DRR_thematic_policy_doc.pdf, date accessed 2 December 2014.
European Commission (2014) *Factsheet – Resilience*. http://ec.europa.eu/echo/en/factsheets, date accessed 2 December 2014.
Evans, B. and J. Reid (2013) 'Dangerously Exposed: The Life and Death of the Resilient Subject', *Resilience*, 1, 83–98.
FLACSO and UNISDR (2013) *The Future of Disaster Risk Management: Draft Synthesis Document, Meeting Notes, Background Papers and Additional Materials from a Scoping Meeting for the GAR 2015*. http://www.desenredando.org/public/2013/2013-08-14_UNISDR_FLACSO_GARscoping_Document_LaRed.pdf, date accessed 2 December 2014.
Gerrard, C. M. and D. N. Petley (2013) 'A Risk Society? Environmental Hazards, Risk and Resilience in the later Middle Ages in Europe', *Natural Hazards*, 69, 1051–1079.
Giddens, A. (2013) *Modernity and Self-Identity: Self and Society in the Late Modern Age* (Chichester: John Wiley & Sons).

Gómez-Baggethun, E., V. Reyes-Garcia, P. Olsson and C. Montes (2012) 'Traditional Ecological Knowledge and Community Resilience to Environmental Extremes: A Case Study in Doñana, SW Spain', *Global Environmental Change*, 22, 640–650.
Hernández-Morcillo, M. J. Hoberg, E. Oteros-Rozas, T. Plieninger, E. Gómez-Baggethun and V. Reyes-García (2014) 'Traditional Ecological Knowledge in Europe: Status Quo and Insights for the Environmental Policy Agenda', *Environment: Science and Policy for Sustainable Development*, 56, 3–17.
HM Government (2010) *A Strong Britain in an Age of Uncertainty: The National Security Strategy*. http://www.official-documents.gov.uk/, date accessed 2 December 2014.
IPCC (2014) *IPCC WGII AR5 Summary for Policymakers*. http://ipcc-wg2.gov/AR5/images/uploads/IPCC_WG2AR5_SPM_Approved.pdf, date accessed 2 December 2014.
Joseph, J. (2013) 'Resilience in UK and French Security Strategy: An Anglo-Saxon Bias?', *Politics*, 33, 253–264.
Kasperson, R. E. and K. D. Pijawka (1985) 'Societal Response to Hazards and Major Hazard Events: Comparing Natural and Technological Hazards', *Public Administration Review*, 45, 7–18.
Kaufman, M. (2013) 'Emergent Self-Organisation in Emergencies: Resilience Rationales in Interconnected Societies', *Resilience*, 1, 53–68.
Keene, D. (2011) 'Crisis Management in London's Food Supply, 1250–1550', in B. Dodds and C. D. Liddy (eds.) *Commercial Activity, Markets and Entrepreneurs in the Middle Ages: Essays in Honour of Richard Britnell* (Woodbridge: The Boydell Press).
Klein, R. J. T., R. J. Nicholls and F. Thomalla (2003) 'Resilience to Natural Hazards: How Useful Is This Concept?', *Environmental Hazards*, 5, 35–45.
Klüppelberg, C., D. Straub and I.M. Welpe et al. (eds.) (2014) *Risk: A Multidisciplinary Introduction* (Berlin: Springer International Publishing).
Liu, J., T. Dietz, S. R. Carpenter, M. Alberti, C. Folke, E. Moran, A. N. Pell, P. Deadman, T. Kratz, J. Lubchenko, E. Ostrom, Z. Ouyang, W. Provencher, C. L. Redman, S. H. Schneider and W. W. Taylor (2007) 'Complexity of Coupled Human and Natural Systems', *Science*, 317, 1513–1516.
Lopes, L. L. (1987) 'Between Hope and Fear: The Psychology of Risk', *Advances in Experimental Social Psychology*, 20, 255–295.
Morrison, N. (2003) 'Neighbourhoods and Social Cohesion: Experiences from Europe', *International Planning Studies*, 8, 115–138.
National Emergency Management Committee (2011) *National Strategy for Disaster Resilience: Building our Nation's Resilience to Disasters* (Canberra: Australian Government).
Norris, F. H., S. P. Stevens, B. Pfefferbaum, K. F. Wyche and R. F. Pfefferbaum (2008) 'Community Resilience as a Metaphor, Theory, Set of Capacities, and Strategy for Disaster Readiness', *American Journal of Community Psychology*, 41, 127–150.
Prior, T. and C. Eriksen (2013) 'Wildfire Preparedness, Community Cohesion and Social – Ecological Systems', *Global Environmental Change*, 23, 1575–1586.
Prior, T. and J. Hagmann (2014) 'Measuring Resilience: Methodological and Political Challenges of a Trend Security Concept', *Journal of Risk Research*, 17, 281–298.

Rohr, C. (2003) 'Man and Natural Disaster in the Late Middle Ages: The Earthquake in Carinthia and Northern Italy on 25 January 1348 and its Perception', *Environment and History*, 9, 127–149.
Roth, F. and T. Prior (2014) 'The Boundaries of Building Societal Resilience: Responsibilization and Swiss Civil Defense in the Cold War', *Behemoth: A Journal on Civilisation*, 7, 91–111.
Schmid F. (2013) Switzerland: National Progress Report on the Implementation of the Hyogo Framework for Action (2011–2013). http://www.preventionweb.net/english/countries/europe/che/, date accessed 2 December 2014.
Shreve, C. M. and I. Kelman (2014) 'Does Mitigation Save? Reviewing Cost-Benefit Analyses of Disaster Risk Reduction', *International Journal of Disaster Risk Reduction*, 10, Part A, 213–235.
Stallings, R. A. and E. L. Quarantelli (1985) 'Emergent Citizen Groups and Emergency Management', *Public Administration Review*, 45, 93–100.
Stark, A. and M. Taylor (2014) 'Citizen Participation, Community Resilience and Crisis-Management Policy', *Australian Journal of Political Science*, 49, 1–16.
The National Academies (2012) *Disaster Resilience: A National Imperative* (Washington, D.C.: The National Academies Press).
Thomalla, F., T. Downing, E. Spanger-Siegfried, G. Han and J. Rockström (2006) 'Reducing Hazard Vulnerability: Towards a Common Approach Between Disaster Risk Reduction and Climate Adaptation', *Disasters*, 30, 39–48.
UNISDR (2005) *Hyogo Framework for Action 2005–2015: Building the Resilience of Nations and Communities to Disasters.* http://www.unisdr.org/we/inform/publications/1037, date accessed 2 December 2014.
UNISDR (2009) Prevention Web: Resilience. http://preventionweb.net/go/501, date accessed 23 October 2014.
United Nations (1994) *Yokohama Strategy and Plan of Action for a Safer World: Guidelines for Natural Disaster Prevention, Preparedness and Mitigation*, World Conference on Natural Disaster Reduction, 1994 Yokohama, Japan, 23–27 May. http://www.preventionweb.net/english/professional/publications/v.php?id=8241, date accessed 2 December 2014.
Walker, J. and M. Cooper (2011) 'Genealogies of Resilience: From Systems Ecology to the Political Economy of Crisis Adaptation', *Security Dialogue*, 42, 143–160.
Wardman, J. K. (2008) 'The Constitution of Risk Communication in Advanced Liberal Societies', *Risk Analysis*, 28, 1619–1637.
Welsh, M. (2014) 'Resilience and Responsibility: Governing Uncertainty in a Complex World', *Geographical Journal*, 180, 15–26.
White, G. F., R. W. Kates and I. Burton (2001) 'Knowing Better and Losing Even More: The Use of Knowledge in Hazards Management', *Global Environmental Change Part B: Environmental Hazards*, 3, 81–92.
Wildavsky, A. B. (1988) *Searching for Safety* (New Brunswick: Transaction Publishers).
Zachmann, K. (2014) 'Risk in Historical Perspective: Concepts, Contexts, and Conjunctions', in Klüppelberg, C., D. Straub and I. M. Welpe (eds.) *Risk: A Multidisciplinary Introduction* (Berlin: Springer International Publishing), pp. 3–35.
Zebrowski, C. (2013) 'The Nature of Resilience', *Resilience*, 1, 159–173.
Zhou, H., J. Wang, J. Wan and H. Jia (2010) 'Resilience to Natural Hazards: A Geographic Perspective', *Natural Hazards*, 53, 21–41.

8
Systems for Post-Crisis Learning: A Systemic Gap in Civil Security Governance?

Edward Deverell

Introduction

Increasing the capacity of governments to learn from harmful events, such as for instance pandemics, hurricanes, terrorist attacks or large-scale accidents, is of importance for civil security and organizational safety (Stern, 1997; Deverell, 2010). A frequently used strategy by governments and public organizations in this regard is to launch a crisis investigation after an event. This chapter deals with such forms of investigations and especially the importance of organizing structures for post hoc crisis investigations. The chapter argues that a lack of structured arrangements regarding post hoc crisis investigations will have negative effects on organizational and governmental lesson drawing from crises, and thus on long-term EU civil security. We depart from the premise that taking structured and deliberate steps after crisis events to restore legitimacy and to make sure that historic mistakes are not repeated is an important part of civil security governance (see Sulitzeanu-Kenan and Holzman-Gazit, 2013). At the same time, civil security governance can also be seen as a problem for learning. Civil security governance involves a wide variety of actors and confronts ambiguous policy problems and fuzzy boundaries. As such it tends to work against systemization and standardized organizational processes required for effective post hoc crisis investigations.

Post hoc crisis investigation is a key concept of this chapter. Nested in this concept are a number of more or less organized ways of investigating crisis events such as the after action report, the crisis inquiry or the lessons learned document. According to the work of prior scholars, a lessons learned document is the most basic and straightforward approach of a post hoc crisis investigation. It is understood as 'a post-event review of what worked and what did not, resulting in recommendations for changes to current practice' (Rostis, 2007, p. 198). The after action report is focused more on the evaluation process. After action reports have been described as 'tools for gathering and documenting evaluations of key processes during the response to both real-incidents and fictional exercises' (Savoia, 2012, p. 2949). The crisis inquiry is the most comprehensive of the post hoc crisis investigations. It is assigned by some form of government and usually works according to a broader and more public fact finding mission (Resodihardjo, 2006; Sulitzeanu-Kenan and Holzman-Gazit, 2013). These different approaches to crisis investigations highlight the divergences in scope, authority and political influence that surround these processes and arrangements in the practitioners' realm.

Based on a review of previous crisis events and investigations, three problems tied to the crisis-induced learning process are outlined in this chapter. First, there is a lack of automatic instigation of investigations. Investigations are not always carried out after crisis events. Some events are thoroughly investigated, while others are not. Second, a systematic approach is lacking. As a result, investigations are carried out by different actors and in different ways, which leads to anecdotal rather than systematic lessons being drawn by agencies and other organizations. Thirdly, there is a lack of objectivity. Investigations are only rarely carried out by truly independent and neutral bodies. Taken together, these shortcomings hamper systematic organizational learning from crises on a societal basis. Before presenting the review of crisis events and investigations, however, the analysis is framed by outlining and defining the central concepts of the study. In particular, it is shown how the concept of 'learning' could be understood in relation to crises as well as in organizational contexts. Such a more refined conceptual understanding highlights the difficulties of linking observed policy changes and official documents on lessons learning. The next step is to present a case study of crises events and investigations in the case of Sweden. Sweden is selected as an illustrative case study of an EU member state and a potential high-capacity country for learning systems. Put more specifically, Sweden serves as a good case to explore the use of systematic review and learning processes, since it has an established and permanent framework of a designated Accident Investigation Authority and generally features a strong culture of governmental transparency.

The review of crisis events is conducted on the basis of theoretical accounts of crisis investigations as well as empirical data and reviews of previous crisis events over the last two decades. From this case analysis, the analytical argument for a more structured approach to learning from crises in EU member states at large is constructed. In particular, the chapter highlights a systematic gap between standardized procedures for accident review, which are institutionally embedded in Sweden, and the challenges of learning from varied kinds of crises that transcend regular systems for civil security governance.

Framing the analysis: Crises and major accidents

Crises are focusing events (Kingdon, 2003). This means that a crisis gathers the attention of the public, media and policymakers alike. The actual event then centres this attention on problems tied to the crisis and the context in which it occurred, as well as on solutions to those very problems.

What then is a crisis for an EU member state? Recent crises with repercussions on the EU sphere include a variety of events such as financial and sovereign debt crises, pandemics, volcanic ash clouds, hurricanes, earthquakes, tsunamis, floods, terrorist bombings, school shootings, urban riots, contaminated water, chemical explosions and infrastructure collapses (McConnell, 2010). It should be acknowledged, however, that a list of events that may be understood as crises will only provide partial insight into the elusive crisis phenomenon. A variety of events can develop into crises depending on the circumstances for the case in point. A crisis is often unforeseen. Thus the next crisis may be an event that is not included in a list of crises constructed from past experience. The list of events mentioned above indicates that some crises may also be accidents. Nonetheless, managing crises involves much more than handling major accidents and other emergencies that occur at an everyday basis. The fact that an accident often is the triggering event that sets a crisis into motion (Turner, 1976) pinpoints the difference in the scale of complexity between the concepts of an accident and a crisis.

Another distinguishing factor between what is a crisis and what is not can be found in the separation of crisis management from normal and everyday work. For many public agencies, such as for instance emergency response organizations, managing a major accident is part of 'normal' day-to-day management. Accidents and serious incidents tend to be closer to normalcy and on a lower level of complexity than crises. For instance they tend to have an, at least in hindsight, distinguishable cause, such as a human, technical or organizational error and, in some cases, a more underlying root cause, that if dealt with will neatly diminish the risk of that specific accident from reoccurring. Moreover, the concept of an accident seems more easily and objectively defined than a crisis. For instance, a major accident has, according to practitioner's jargon at least, been defined as an accident with five or more casualties (MSB, 2010, p. 13). Given these diversities in how we perceive the nature of major accidents in relation to crises, it is not surprising that systems for investigating and evaluating the former tend to be more developed than systems for investigating the latter.

The lack of organized systems for crisis investigation and lessons learned relates to the level of complexity embedded in the crisis concept. In the words of Mitroff et al. (2004), a crisis is an 'ill-structured mess – a highly interactive set of problems, each of which is ill-structured' (Mitroff et al., 2004, p. 175). The crisis concept is encompassed by a number of questions such as: What is a crisis? According to what criteria can it be defined? In addition, who gets to define it? Crises are the product of several interrelated and interacting processes and problems that coincide in complex and often haphazard ways. A crisis is defined as a crisis 'precisely because something out of the ordinary happens' (Boin and Lagadec, 2000, p. 186). One way to define a crisis is therefore to frame it in relation to some sort of normalcy. The crisis is understood as something 'abnormal' that breaks up a given 'normal' organizational routine. Inadequacy in terms of the organizations' own ability, knowledge and resources to handle the situation thus characterizes a crisis from this perspective.

Crisis management requires managing dynamic processes that take place before, during and after the most acute phase of the emergency in question, which may but need not be an accident. The temporal crisis management trilogy of before, during and after may also be structured according to four phases: prevention and mitigation; preparation and planning; response and decision-making; and recovery, reconciliation and change (Comfort, 1988). This process view of a crisis means that crisis management poses challenges to crisis leaders, urging them to excel in prevention and preparedness before, sense making, decision-making, meaning making, and collaborating during, and learning and reforming after the crisis (Boin et al., 2005). Further, crises put pressure on decision makers to act promptly despite high uncertainty regarding the course of events (Rosenthal et al., 1989). A crisis thus requires that individuals or groups perceive the situation at hand as permeated by values at play, uncertainty and time pressure and thus as a crisis. In taking on this subjective and elite decision maker perspective to crisis management, this study posits that different crises can differ extensively in terms of, for instance, more objective facts such as the number of dead or injured and the extent of damages to property, the environment or the legitimacy of authorities.

Structures and systems for accident investigation are essential for accident learning and social safety, but they are not sufficient for crisis-induced learning. Not all accidents turn into crises and not all crises originate in accidents. By design then, accident investigation systems do not automatically cover the diffuse notion of a crisis. Accidents and crises are different although related events. Both are complicated phenomena occurring rapidly through unexpected interactions between many interplaying underlying factors (Perrow, 1984). Usually there are no simple explanations as to why they occur. Crises, however, differ from serious accidents such as fires and traffic accidents. A major accident is in many ways a routine event, although it may have a large impact. First responders manage major accidents according to their everyday routines and working ways. Crises, on the other hand, are the very opposite of routine. They are unpredictable and often unthinkable. The daily routines, working methods and organization need to be adjusted by flexibility and even improvization to meet the crisis challenge. As Topper and Lagadec (2013, p. 8) write, 'The core of crisis is precisely the fact that an event, a dynamic, does not fit into the conventional references, formats and codes – and moreover, is threatening to destroy those very references, formats and codes.' In practice, the concept of a crisis covers a variety of serious phenomena that can be handled at local, regional, national or international level. The value of communities and authorities systematically drawing lessons from the relatively few experiences of crises that they are tasked to manage is emphasized in the academic world as well in the practitioners' realm. The lack of such a system may have serious repercussions for societal safety as systematic lessons learned from crises help us understand causal mechanisms leading to accidents and crises. Such investigation is necessary for safe and resilient organizations and communities, and for preventing crisis recurrence (Argyris and Schön, 1978; Deverell, 2010; Stoop and Roed-Larsen, 2011).

In order to put a crisis definition to work on empirical data, we need to reduce the subjectivity built into the crisis definition. In short, we need to use more objective criteria for our crisis categorization. One way to do this is to build our definition not only on scholarly conceptualizations. We need also to integrate conceptualizations used by practitioners in our crisis definition. Hence, here a crisis is understood as an 'event that affects many people and large parts of society, and threatens fundamental values and functions' (Proposition 2007/08: 92, p. 7), thus necessitating key members of government authorities to make critical decisions amidst time pressure and highly uncertain circumstances (Rosenthal et al., 1989, p. 10). This definition will serve as guiding hand when events that qualify as a crisis are selected. Further, the selected empirical examples will provide the basis for a typology of crises developed from the case study presented below.

Investigations and learning

In most EU member states, after action reports and lessons learned documents are carried out within a regulated system for accident investigation. Such systems often include several learning arrangements. For instance, in the case of Sweden, learning from everyday rescue service incidents is carried out in the form of operating procedures for routine emergency management incident reports. In addition, learning from large-scale civil and military accidents on land, by sea and in the air are achieved through reports carried out by the permanent Swedish Accident Investigation Authority. Similar major accident investigation arrangements are established in, for instance, the Netherlands, Finland and Austria. Other EU members such as Ireland, Germany, France and Italy have more specialized agencies focusing specifically on for instance air traffic incidents. All these major accident investigation systems, however, are not designed to cover the more complex and diffuse notion of a crisis. By consequence, then, critical post hoc crisis investigations are, if carried out at all, performed in a non-systematic way and in an ad hoc fashion. The unstructured way of organizing crisis investigation may have repercussions on the long-term learning capacities of government agencies in EU countries.

Crisis-induced investigation is defined in this chapter as purposeful activities carried out within the framework of an organized crisis inquiry that lead to new understanding and that aims at establishing new behaviour based on that understanding (cf. Deverell, 2010, p. 37). Crisis-induced investigation and crisis-induced learning are closely connected phenomena. The most important aim of an investigation of this kind is to learn from the event at hand in order to prevent recurrence (Cedergren and Petersen, 2011, p. 1238). Crisis-induced investigation is, in this context, a systematic and structured learning process in which information about the crisis and how it was managed is identified, collected, analysed and used in an effort to assist members of authorities in prevention and improvement. The actual learning in this process takes place inside individual minds. However, learning may also expand beyond the individual as knowledge is shared and disseminated to organizational members through processes of participation and interaction (Elkjaer, 2003). Learning then becomes organizational. Like individual learning, this type of organizational learning entails cognition as well as behaviour (Argyris and Schön, 1978; Fiol and Lyles, 1985, p. 803; Carley and Harrald, 1997). From a crisis-induced learning perspective, cognition signifies a change in the states of knowledge as new knowledge is added. Behaviour, on the other hand, refers to a change in actual behaviour as new knowledge is put into practice. Learning agents must understand what they did not previously understand, and then they need to act on the basis of that understanding. New cognition that guides behaviour will result in cognitive and behavioural change (Dekker and Hansén, 2004).

The potential effects of post-crisis investigations

It is notoriously difficult to measure effects of policy change and reform in the public sector (Pfeffer and Salancic, 1978; Christensen et al., 2005). The effects of post-crisis investigations are no different in this regard. External as well as internal pressures will impact on any government agency involved in post-crisis investigations. An important question is what the actual effects of post-crisis investigations may be. Most research to date takes a pessimistic stance on the issue of the effects of crisis investigations. One such example is Thomas Birkland who describes post-crisis investigations as 'fantasy documents' dealing not with 'real causes and solutions to disasters' but with proving that authorities have 'done something' in regard to a disaster. In addition, these reports are 'generally ignored after they are published' (Birkland, 2009, p. 146). In sum, fantasy documents 'are created and disseminated for rhetorical purposes, even if their authors somehow *believe* that learning has really occurred' (Birkland, 2009, p. 146; emphasis in original).

According to Birkland, there are three basic mechanisms behind such so-called fantasy documents. The first is the desire to learn quickly, which leads to hasty and unfounded lessons (Birkland, 2009, p. 151). The second mechanism is self-interest. This bias draws attention to policy issues and solutions that are important for some, but not necessarily for a larger population. The third and final mechanism is the human tendency to search for simple solutions and explanations for complex social and political issues (Birkland, 2009, p. 152). In a similar vein previous research on accident causation and modelling has identified a shift 'from linear to more complex interactions' and more specifically from 'technological failures to human error, and later to organizational factors' (Cedergren and Petersen, 2011, p. 1239). Yet, practice does not seem to follow these developments. Savoia et al. (2012) analysed 91 after action reports. Recommendations found in inquiries were, according to their study, 'often rather generic and could not be translated into concrete actions' (2012, p. 2960). Further, they lacked root cause analysis as well as specific examples of mentioned problems and errors (Savoia et al., 2012, p. 2960). Another interesting piece of research in this regard is presented by Rostis (2007, p. 209), who studied local emergency management in Canada. He concluded that poor understanding of lessons learned techniques rendered these practices largely ineffective. The main problem was that the agencies in question lacked 'a process through which lessons can result in meaningful organizational change' (Rostis, 2007, p. 208).

A slightly more optimistic side in this debate is supported by research with an instrumental approach to crisis inquiries. The effects of crisis inquiries from this perspective may not be substantial from a democratic or social perspective, but rather from an elite self-interest point of view. From this instrumental perspective, crisis inquiries are seen as tool at the crisis managers' disposal, underscoring their control of the situation and creating a peaceful post-crisis environment, as officials will refrain from commenting on sensitive issues as long as an inquiry is going on. Following that approach, they will also cool down critique as attention will possibly be directed at new issues at the time when the report is published (McConnell, 2003; Resodihardjo, 2006). Real learning, on the other hand, occurs when 'policy changes in a way that is reasonably likely to mitigate the problem revealed by the focusing event' (Birkland, 2009, p. 150). For such change to be a result of investigation findings, these need to be specific, which is rarely the case (Savoia et al., 2012, p. 2960). Another critical factor that increases the inquiry's viability for shaping the debate and introducing a reform agenda for the future is high public trust for the investigation. Resodihardjo (2006, p. 204) found empirical evidence underscoring that factors such as a strong chair, innovative procedures adopted by the inquiry, and distance from political actors could lead to high public trust and an increase of post-crisis investigations effectiveness.

With these prior research findings in mind, the following analysis departs from the premise that lessons learned processes need to incorporate more than the production of a single overarching report. The actual context of the investigation, the composition, mandates, beliefs and competences of the investigating unit are vital indicators for systematic crisis learning processes. Another critical indicator is the actual methods used by the investigating unit. Although every crisis event is in one sense unique, there are enough circumstances regarding crises and crisis management to suggest that a post hoc crisis investigation can be conducted by analysing generic crisis indicators linked to, on the one hand, the perception of a crisis, the characteristics of an event and its consequences, and on the other hand to response-related features activated by crisis managers as a reaction to the actual event (Deverell and Stiglund, forthcoming).

A review of crises past

In light of the foregoing discussion that highlighted the dual challenges of defining 'crises' and 'learning', this chapter now takes a more empirical approach to crises and post hoc investigations. First, we clarify the type of event that we regard as a crisis and which thus should be covered by an organized system for lessons learned from crisis. This is accomplished by presenting a number of crisis categories. These categories are then applied to an illustrative case study of crisis and post hoc investigations. Put more specifically, a historical review of Swedish crisis events in recent years is conducted. From the review we build the claim that there is indeed a need for an organized system for lessons learned from crisis. We end by suggesting a few building blocks required to establish such a system.

By conducting an historical review of incidents and events that have taken place in recent years, we try to bring clarity to the issue of what a crisis is and what it is not. Before presenting such a list, however, a reservation is in order. Rear view mirror management will not suffice for future crisis management (Lagadec, 2006, p. 489). At the same time, the knowledge that experience may provide us with is probably our best and definitely our most available teacher (March, 2010). Therefore, knowledge in the form of experience based on past events needs to be utilized. To be able to make sense of past experiences, it is feasible to organize the events into different categories.

Categorizing or making typologies is beneficial for structuring the crisis phenomenon and for demystifying the crisis concept (Deverell and Olsson, 2010). Arguably, one of the most used crisis dichotomies is the natural disaster versus the man-made crisis. Man-made crises are created by some form of human action compared to more natural events that occur without direct influence of human behaviour. It should be noted, however, that modern technology and society have blurred the lines between crises that may be induced by actions or inactions of governments and other organizations and natural disasters 'to which governments can simply respond' (Birkland, 2006, p. 3). For instance, a train accident caused by rails buckled from a scorching sun can be blamed on regulating and supervising bodies rather than on natural forces. Likewise a natural disaster like a flood does not only happen out of the blue, leaving governments only to respond once the crisis has occurred. In most EU countries governments will receive their share of blame after a natural event as citizens expect agencies to act by preventing, preparing and planning to mitigate potential natural disasters (Boin et al., 2005, p. 138). Policy issues such as land development in risk areas, flood preparedness, early warning and evacuation go hand in hand with political accountability. In fact, previous research questions the value of constructing crisis typologies based on for instance the man-made and natural disaster distinction. In the words of Rosenthal et al.:

> these efforts have failed to cover the entire range of crisis events. Furthermore, research has shown that they are too simple: The idea of a compound disaster often involving a combination of natural (an earthquake) and man-made (dam-failures, floods, collapsing buildings, gas fires, congestion) contingencies, has replaced simple distinctions.
> (1989, p. 11)

Still, however, accident investigations are preoccupied with cases understood as primarily man-made, rather than natural accidents or disasters. Therefore, it is apt to distinguish between crises that are determined by their initial cause and this crisis type (cf. Birkland, 2006).

From prior research on crisis typologies and previous Swedish crises, Table 8.1 presents a list of crises that affected authorities in Sweden over the last two decades. The following review effort is guided by previous categorizations of crises into natural disasters and man-made disasters, where the latter category is further splintered into six groups. The table also presents the location of the event, its cause and its consequence as well as a brief description of how it was evaluated. The compilation of events considered by national crisis management scholars and experts to be the most influential crises to occur in Sweden in recent years is based on previous studies of and open source data about

Table 8.1 Crises and accidents in Sweden (1993–2013)*

Crisis (N: 36)	Location affected	Cause	Type	Consequence	Investigation**
JAS air crash 1993	Stockholm	Man-made as JAS Gripen crashed during air show	Accident	Damage to reputation of the JAS project and Armed Forces	SAIC ML 1993:3, Crismart Vol. 13
Sinking of Jan Heweliusz 1993	Baltic Sea	Man-made as Polish ferry sank on journey from Swinoujscie to Ystad	Accident	54 dead, 7 Swedes	National Polish investigation
Sinking of MS Estonia 1994	Baltic Sea	Man-made as MS Estonia sunk on journey from Tallinn to Stockholm	Accident	852 dead, 501 Swedes	JAIC, SOU1998:132, SOU 1999:48, Kamedo Rept 68
Gothenburg discotheque fire 1998	Gothenburg	Man-made as arsonists started a fire in a discotheque for juveniles organized by the Macedonian Association	Accident	63 dead, more than 200 injured. Psychosocial and politico symbolic challenge for authorities	SAIC RO 2001:02 O-07/98, SOU 1999:68, SPF Rept 179, Crismart Vol. 15, Kamedo Rept 75
Linate air crash 2001	Milan, Italy	Man-made as SAS airliner crashed with Cessna during takeoff in foggy weather	Accident	118 dead, 20 Swedes	Italian official investigation N/A1/04
Ängelsberg Bus crash 2003	Ängelsberg Fagersta	Man-made as bus drove off icy road and overturned	Accident	6 dead, 30 injured	SAIC RO 2004:01, SEMA 061015

Event	Location	Description	Type	Consequences	Source
Arboga bus crash 2006	Arboga	Man-made as a bus overturned after driver collapsed	Accident	9 dead, 50 injured	SAIC RO 2007: 1, CC Investigation
Kista blackout 2001	Stockholm	Fire in cable tunnel	Accident, infrastructure breakdown	50,000 people, 800 companies lost power for 37 hrs	Self-assessment by coordinating body SBF 2001, Crismart Rept 20
Kista blackout 2002	Stockholm	Fire in cable tunnel	Accident, infrastructure breakdown	50,000 people, 800 companies lost power for 54 hrs	Self-assessment by coordinating body, investigation by contract by energy company and SEA ER2005:14, Crismart Rept 27
Danish/Swedish blackout 2003	Southern Sweden	Network overload as part of nuclear power plant shut down and substation failed. Power cut for 1–2 million people in South of Sweden for 5 hrs	Accident, infrastructure breakdown	5 hr blackout over south of Sweden and Själland and Bornholm affected	Self-assessments by SvK 1:2003, by contract by SEA ER 4:2004, SPF Rept 2004
Kälarne derailment 1997	Kälarne, Jämtland	Train with 17 carriages carrying ammoniac, acetic acid and ethane oxide, derailed due to buckled rails	Accident, dangerous substances	Residents evacuated. No leakage reported	SAIC RJ 2000:01
Borlänge train crash 1998	Borlänge	Two freight trains collided while changing tracks. Train and three carriages derailed	Accident, dangerous substances	7 tons of nitric acid leaked. Parts of city center cordoned off, 1,000 evacuated, 4 injured	Railway Inspectorate Authority, SPF 146, SPF 158

Table 8.1 (Continued)

Crisis (N: 36)	Location affected	Cause	Type	Consequence	Investigation
Borlänge train derailment 2000	Borlänge	Train carrying 500 tons LPG derailed due to intoxicated driver and high speed (70 in a 40 zone), 5 carriages overturned	Accident, dangerous substances	No leakage. 700 evacuated	Self-assessments by train company, Railway Inspectorate Authority and others, SPF 158
Environmental scandal 1997	Hallands-åsen	Substance used to fix leakage during construction of a tunnel contained acrylamide which spilled into surrounding environment	Accident, dangerous substances	Poison spread to groundwater, fish and livestock	SOU198:137, SPF Repts 175:1, 175:2, 175:3, 175:4
Bohuslän oil spill 2011	Bohuslän, Tjörn	Man-made accident as Maltese freighter and Belgian fishing vessel collided in September 2011	Accident, dangerous substances	500 tons of oil spilled into the waters of the Swedish west coast. During 18 days the Coast Guard removed 644 m^3 oil	SAIC S-149/11, MSB & HaV
Jämtland water crisis 2010	Jämtland	Household sewage accidentally discharged in Lake Storsjön in connection to a major downpour. Cryptosporidium found in the water	Dangerous substances	Contaminated drinking water, 20,000 people affected by Cryptosporidium infection	Self-assessment led by Östersund County Administration's Dept. for Environment and Health and Jämtland CC's Dept. of Infectious Diseases and Infection Control

Anthrax letters 2001	Sweden	Spread of Anthrax letters in the US led to fear of substances in letters and packages	Risk, fear of dangerous substances	Public fear, media pressure on agencies	Self-assessment FOI Report 0877 SE
Vagnhärad landslide 1997	Vagnhärad	Heavy rain in landslide prone area cause 200 m landslide	Natural accident	7 houses destroyed, 3 came down with the landslide. 5 people in need of medical care. Eventually 100 evacuated and 29 houses demolished, large area turned into park	SAIC Report O 1998:1
Gävle snowstorm 1998	Gävle	3 days of snowfall and hard winds	Natural accident	City of Gävle cut off from transports and supplies, schools closed for days, ban on cars in city for a week, blackouts	Self-assessment by Gävle MA, SPF 151
Tyresta forest fire 1999	Tyresta	Unknown, warm and dry summer, 2 weeks without rain prior to fire	Natural accident	450 hectares damaged by fire (10% of national reserve). Fire lasted 11 days, 800 people involved in rescue service mission	Self-assessment by Fire Dept, SEPA Rept 20

Table 8.1 (Continued)

Crisis (N: 36)	Location affected	Cause	Type	Consequence	Investigation
Arvika flood 2000	Arvika	More than 3 times normal rainfall in October and November raised water levels more than 3 m above normal in Glafsfjorden	Natural accident	Damage to roads, infrastructure, private property and agricultural land	Self-assessments by Arvika MA Rept 20010814, SvK Rept 1:2001 BE 90, SRSA, Kamedo Rept 76
Hurricane Gudrun 2005	Southern Sweden	2 day storm struck 9 counties in south Sweden, local winds of 42 m/s	Natural disaster	7 dead in storm, damage to roads, railways, power cut for 730,000 homes, telecom cuts for 300,000 homes, 250 million trees fell, 11 dead in clearing up	Self-assessments by Jönköping and Kronoberg County Boards, SEA ER 2005:16, SEA ER 2006:8, ET 2006:02 Parliamentary Rept 2007/08:RFR5
Hurricane Per 2007	Southern Sweden	Storm over Götaland, local winds of 40 m/s	Natural accident	5 dead, 16 million m^3 of trees fell, power cuts for 440,000 homes, telecom cuts for 37,000 homes	Self-assessment by Kronoberg CC, SPF 2008:1, SEA Rept ER 2007:37, SEA Dnr 17-07-2831
Southeast Asian tsunami 2004	Sweden	Earthquake off the coast of Sumatra caused tsunami, Swedes on holiday in Thailand were among the victims	Natural disaster, consular crisis	230,000 dead, 543 Swedes dead, 1,500 injured; local, regional and central level crisis management activated	SOU 2005:104, Kamedo Rept 91, self-assessment by SRSA, NBHW 2006-131-33

Evacuation from Lebanon 2006	Sweden	Armed conflict between Hezbollah and Israel in July 2006. Visiting Swedes in need of evacuation	Armed conflict, consular crisis	Government spent 100 million SEK on evacuating 8,400 people	Self-assessment by Foreign Ministry PM 2006-10-02, Kamedo Rept 92
Falun shootings 1994	Falun	Intoxicated Lieutenant killed 7 people	Psychosocial, mass shooting	7 dead, 3 injured	SPF 171
Stureplan shootings 1994	Stockholm	4 men denied entrance to nightclub opened fire at nightclub entrance	Psychosocial, mass shooting	4 dead, 20 injured	Stockholm CC investigation 1996-10-18 Dnr 871-94-44567
Malexander police murders 1999	Malexander	Robbers killed 2 police men	Psychosocial, murder	2 dead	Self-assessments by National Police Board RPS 1999, 2001
Murder of Foreign Minister Anna Lindh 2003	Sweden	Sweden's FM stabbed at department store	Psychosocial, murder	The FM died the following morning, challenge for government offices and the police	No known official investigation into the crisis besides criminal investigation and SBHW investigation on the medical care, SEMA Communication Repts 2004:4, 2006:3, SOU 2004:108 on personal protection of ministers

Table 8.1 (Continued)

Crisis (N: 36)	Location affected	Cause	Type	Consequence	Investigation
Stockholm bombings 2010	Stockholm	Shortly after a car exploded, a suicide bomber detonated an explosive device in midtown busy street	Psychosocial, terrorist attack	1 dead, 2 injured	No known official investigation besides criminal investigation (closed in October 2014)
Tidaholm prison riots 1994	Tidaholm	Some 100 prisoners involved in riots	Riot	Buildings set on fire	Government Rept (Ministry of Justice) Ds 1994:140
Gothenburg riots 2001	Gothenburg	50,000 activist demonstrated during EU summit and US President George W. Bush's visit	Riot	Some 50 police officers and some 80 activists injured	SOU 2002:122, Self-assessments by Local Police AL 199–5993/01 and National Police RPS 2001
Volcanic ash cloud 2010	Sweden	Icelandic volcano Eyjafjallajökull erupted and spread ash plume over Europe	Natural accident, infrastructure breakdown	Ban on air traffic	No known official national investigation
Bird flu 2006	Sweden	Migrating birds brought Bird flu AH5N1 into Sweden	Infectious disease	Culling of birds, information management	Self-assessment by SEMA Dnr 0442/2006

A(H1N1) New influenza 2009	Sweden	New Influenza A(H1N1) spread from Mexico and US	Infectious disease	Some 11,000 verified cases of the disease, 31 dead (23 in risk groups), nationwide mass vaccinations implemented, increased risk of narcolepsy among young vaccinated people (some 155 cases)	Self-assessment by MSB & SBHW: 2011-3-3
Financial crisis 2008	Sweden	Global financial crisis peaked in Fall 2008	Financial		SOU 2013:6, Growth Analysis Dnr 2012/006

*Data on the investigations was collected from searches in the MSB database RIB http://rib.msb.se/, the database for natural accidents http://ndb.msb.se/, the database of SAIC reports, the database of SOU reports, Google, the Global Terrorism Database, the Swedish university and research libraries database (Libris) and the website of the Swedish National Police www.polis.se.

**Abbreviations used in the table include the following: CC: County Council report; Crismart: reports by the National Center for Crisis Management Research and Training at the Swedish National Defence College; FOI: Reports by the Swedish Defence Research Agency; HaV: Report by the Swedish Agency for Marine and Water Management; JAIC: Reports by the Joint Accident Investigation Commission (Sweden, Estonia, Finland); Kamedo: Reports by the Swedish Disaster Medicine Study Organization at the National Board of Health and Welfare; MA: Municipal Administration report; MSB: Reports by the Swedish Civil Contingencies Agency; NBHW: Reports by the National Board of Health and Welfare; SAIC: Reports by the Swedish Accident Investigation Authority; SEA: Reports by the Swedish Energy Authority; SEMA: Reports by the (now defunct) Swedish Emergency Management Agency; SEPA: Reports by the Swedish Environmental Protection Agency; SOU: Reports by the Swedish Public Commission Inquiry; SPF: Reports by the now defunct Board for Psychological Defence; SRSA: Reports by the (now defunct) Swedish Rescue Services Agency; SVK: Reports by the Swedish National Grid.

national crises (Hartoft and Nilsson, 1999; Sandefeldt, 2005; MSB, 2009; Krisinformation.se, 2013).

Before we go into the results, a few caveats with the chosen approach should be mentioned. Firstly, the list does not claim to be exhaustive. Rather, it suggests some of the most comprehensive crises experienced in Sweden over the last 20 odd years. The list aims to serve as a basis for reflection on what kind of events are likely to affect citizens and propel authorities into a crisis mode in a EU member state with no immediate serious risks vested in its geographical location. Secondly, as previously mentioned, crises are phenomena that are difficult to define and categorize. A crisis typically affects many sectors and transcends several categories making it hard to place the crisis in a specific typology. A crisis may occur in one category while the actual consequences may place the event in a second category. For instance, the Southeast Asian tsunami of 2004 was a natural disaster of monumental proportions. It led to infrastructure breakdown in the affected countries. For some European states, it was also a psychosocial crisis. For the Swedish public agency response, however, the main challenge was in the initial stages and the task to manage a crisis from a remote location, thus the event could also be categorized as a consular crisis. In addition, the lapse crisis management in the first few critical days led to a reputational crisis for the government. Hence a crisis causes ripple effects and often-cascading consequences.

Correlating crises experience and diverse learning processes

According to Table 8.1, over the last two decades at least 36 events qualify as events that 'affect[s] many people and large parts of society, and threatens fundamental values and functions' (Proposition 2007/08: 92, p. 7), thus necessitating key members of government authorities to make critical decisions amidst time pressure and highly uncertain circumstances (Rosenthal et al., 1989, p. 10). Out of these crises, 25 were caused by some sort of human intervention. Only seven were natural accidents or disasters (the cause of the Tyresta forest fire in 1999 remains unknown), while the 2008 financial crisis, and the two cases of communicable diseases (the 2006 Bird Flu and the 2009 New H1N1 Influenza) do not fit into the rather crude dichotomy of the man-made crisis versus natural accident or disaster. When further broken down into crisis types based on the consequences of each case, 15 of the events sort under the major accident heading, while 21 were other types of crises such as natural accidents, communicable diseases or psychosocial crises such as riots, terrorist attacks or mass shootings.

In terms of crisis consequences, loss of life and injuries among citizens are the most serious ones. Fifteen cases led to deaths among citizens. Some of these crises led to the loss of no more than one life. Cases of crises only causing the loss of one life are the murder of Foreign Minister Anna Lindh in 2003 and the terrorist bombing in Stockholm 2010 in which the perpetrator was the sole victim. Other cases led to larger numbers such as the tsunami in which 543 Swedish citizens died, the 1994 Estonia disaster (501 deaths), the 1998 Gothenburg fire (63 deaths), the 2009 H1N1 New Influenza (31 dead and 11,000 infected), the 2001 Scandinavian Airlines air crash at Linate Airport in Italy (20 deaths) or Hurricane Gudrun in 2005 (18 deaths in the storm and the recovery work following the storm). Another three cases led to injured or infected citizens. Examples of crises with large numbers of injured or infected but without any dead are the 2010 Jämtland water crisis (20,000 infected) and the 2001 Gothenburg riots (130 injured). Consequently, 17 crises did not cause direct harm to citizens. This does not indicate that consequences were insignificant. For instance, the cases of derailed trains carrying dangerous substances caused evacuation of citizens. Others caused disturbances in critical infrastructure, such as the five cases of power cuts and the volcanic ash plume that spread over Europe in 2010. Some cases caused damages to the environment, such as the Hallandsås environmental scandal in 1997, the 1999 Tyresta Forest wild fire and the 2001 Bohuslän oil spill. Some cases caused financial loss and turbulence such as the 2008 financial crisis. Others caused widespread public fear such as the anthrax scare of 2001 and the 2006 bird flu.

Most of the 36 crises were subjected to a national and official post hoc investigation. In fact, there were only five exceptions. The first exception is the 2010 volcanic ash plume contingency when a volcano in Iceland erupted and a plume of ash spread over European skies disturbing and effectively cancelling air traffic over the continent. The event and its management has not been followed up specifically by a national official government agency inquiry or evaluation dedicated solely to this specific crisis and its management. It should be mentioned, however, that the Air Navigation Services of Sweden, which was possibly the most affected agency in a national context, conducted an internal organization evaluation of the natural accident and its consequences (Luftfartsverket, 2010). This evaluation was not published or made public to a larger audience. The case was also investigated in a report commissioned by the Swedish Civil Contingencies Agency as one of three cases of networks for information coordination and communication during crises (Johansson et al., 2013). In addition, the impact of the ash cloud crisis has been investigated by the European Organization for the Safety of Air Navigation (Eurocontrol).

The second event without an official national post hoc investigation is the 2010 Stockholm suicide terrorist bombing. There are at least three possible explanations for the absence of an investigation. One is the fact that this crisis was the subject of a criminal investigation for a long time, which effectively hindered public investigations into the issue.[1] Another reason may be the overall sensitivity involved in terrorist attacks and national security crisis. A third reason could be the framing and perception of the case as a 'near miss' rather than a crisis as the bombing did not lead to mass casualties.

Interestingly enough the group of cases that have not been investigated according to the traditional national and public investigation also includes a few bona fide accident cases. Transportation accidents occurring abroad or on foreign waters have not been investigated by the traditional Swedish accident commission. Three such cases are included in the table. The first is the Estonia disaster of 1994, which was investigated by a Joint Accident Investigation Commission made up of commissions in the three most affected countries Sweden, Estonia and Finland. The second is the 1993 Jan Hewelius ferry disaster, which was investigated by a national Polish commission, and the third is the 2001 Linate air crash, which was investigated by a national Italian commission as the event occurred in Italy.

Only seven of 36 cases were investigated according to a systematic method within the framework of the Swedish Accident Investigation Authority. Only one of these cases was a natural accident (the Vagnhärad landslide in 1997). The remaining six were major man-made accidents involving transportation such as trains, buses, boats or airplanes. These reports deal with the technical root cause of the accidents, rather than the management of the most significant consequences of the accident. Moreover, they do not proportion blame on involved parties. The second most common way of organizing post hoc crisis investigation is through the National Public Commission Inquiry. Among these cases we find national crises with political repercussions. These events challenged the trust in government and agencies alike. Examples include the Estonia disaster (two SOU investigations), the 1998 Gothenburg fire, the 1997 Halland ridge environmental scandal, the 2004 Southeast Asian tsunami, the murder of Foreign Minister Anna Lindh[2] and the 2001 Gothenburg riots. In fact, the only truly comprehensive national Swedish crisis that has not been subjected to a Public Commission Inquiry is the 2005 Hurricane Gudrun, which was investigated by a parliamentary report, which in turn is an unusual post hoc crisis investigation method in Sweden. Traditionally, most national crises that lead to political repercussions have been investigated by the Public Commission Inquiry. This does not mean, however, that they are investigated according to a systematic approach. Unlike the Swedish Accident Investigation Authority, the Public Commission Inquiry does not follow a given template or method. Rather they use an ad hoc approach regarding both selection of what cases to investigate, how the actual investigations are carried out, and regarding the issue of proportioning blame.

Besides the most commonly used arrangements for crisis investigations described above, the now defunct government agencies of the Swedish Emergency Management Agency, the Swedish Rescue Services Agency and the National Board of Psychological Defence investigated crisis events until 2009 when these agencies were merged into the Swedish Civil Contingencies Agency (MSB). The National Board of Psychological Defence conducted research oriented studies on crisis communication and the mass media's role in crisis management in seven of the crises depicted in Table 8.1. The Swedish Emergency Management Agency conducted investigations in three cases, the Swedish Rescue Services Agency in two and the newly established Swedish Civil Contingencies Agency in two cases. However, as these agencies all have had or have a key role in training and preparing agencies for crisis management, there may be self-interest generated biases in these investigations (cf. Christensen et al., 2005).

The bias challenge is also brought to the fore when local events are subjected to post hoc inquiry according to the method of self-assessment. Eleven cases were investigated by local authorities such as for instance the Municipal authority (the 2010 Jämtland water crisis, the 1998 Gävle snowstorm and the 2000 Arvika floods), the local fire department (1999 Tyresta forest fire and the Stockholm blackouts 2001 and 2002) or the local police investigation into the 2001 Gothenburg riots.[3] Another form of evaluation is carried out by Kamedo, the Disaster Medicine Investigation Committee led by the National Board of Health and Welfare, which investigated four cases on the list. Their investigations are not official national inquiries. They focus on lesson drawing for the medical health sector with special attention given to medical, psychological and organizational aspects of disaster. The National Board of Health and Welfare has also been in charge of crisis investigation into health aspects of major Swedish crises, including the 2004 tsunami, the 2009 New H1N1 Influenza and the investigation into the quality of the medical care of Foreign Minister Anna Lindh following the attack on her in a department store in 2003.

Other agencies with similar tasks and mandates that carry out post hoc investigations that fall under the self-assessment investigation heading are the County Councils (four cases). Bona fide self-assessment investigations were made by the Defence Research Establishment in the wake of the anthrax letter scare of 2001, by the Foreign Ministry after the evacuation of Swedish citizens from Lebanon in 2006 in the wake of sudden armed conflict between Hezbollah and Israel, and by the electricity utility Fortum after the 2002 Stockholm blackout. Other cases border on self-assessments as the agency in charge of the investigation also is tasked to monitor organizations in a specific sector. The Tidaholm prison riots were investigated by the Ministry of Justice (Government Report DS series). The two train accidents at the Borlänge railway depot were investigated by the former Railway Inspection Authority, the Swedish Police conducted investigations of the Malexander police murders and of the Gothenburg riots 2001. The County Board's investigation into Hurricane Gudrun 2005, the Swedish National Grid conducted two investigations after the Arvika floods and one after the 2002 Stockholm blackout, the Energy Authority conducted three investigations after Hurricane Gudrun, two after Hurricane Per in 2007 and one of both Stockholm blackouts 2001 and 2002. In all these cases, questions can be raised concerning the impartiality of the investigating body, as the accident investigating body was not fully separated from the regulator.

Crisis vs. Accident investigations: A systemic gap?

Experience of crisis management that goes beyond 'ordinary' emergency management or mediatized scandals requiring reputation management is relatively sparse in the Swedish public sphere. As Table 8.1 indicates, large-scale crises occur rarely in the case in question and overall Sweden looks like a relatively safe country. At the same time, the table demonstrates that crises in the pre-existing categories occur from time to time. However, relatively few of the most comprehensive crises originate in a major accident, and in even fewer cases, the Swedish Accident Investigation Authority (SAIC) has been in charge of the post hoc investigation. As a consequence, then, only a few crises have been investigated according to a systematic approach. There is thus a real risk that an organized structure of inquiry and a systematic method will only be used in a delimited share of cases. Some of the crises that may be categorized as infrastructure breakdowns or instances involving dangerous substances such as virus, poison or chemicals may be investigated within the SAIC framework as they may be rooted in a major technological accident. For instance, the 2011 Bohuslän oil spill came as a direct consequence of a collision of two vessels.

Other arrangements include the Swedish Public Commission Inquiry commissioned by the government. Formally, the commissions are government agencies. The events and processes investigated by the Public Commission Inquiry crises may be seen as a few really serious and national crises. Examples of these investigations are SOU 1998:137 on the environmental scandal at Hallandsåsen, SOU 2005:104 on the Southeast Asian tsunami and SOU 2002:122 on the Gothenburg riots. However, decisions on establishing such an investigation are made not on the basis of systematic and explicit planning, but on a case-to-case basis. On the other side of the continuum, we find a number of events that are in essence local events. There is an evident pattern here that such events, which are neither subjected to the SAIC nor the SOU arrangement, tend to be investigated in accordance with the method of self-assessment where the most affected and in many cases accountable organizations control the investigation (see, for instance, most natural accidents but also cases of power outages). Self-assessments are provided with extensive problems. Investigators conducting self-assessments tend to be exposed to internal and external pressures that can lead to the cover up of individual and organizational mistakes (Stern, 1997).

It seems then that our developed system for accident investigation does not automatically capture lessons learned from past crises. Without systematic reporting and investigation of crises, their causes and management, it becomes difficult to draw appropriate lessons from these events and to prevent similar incidents and mistakes from reoccurring. This lack of a structured arrangement regarding post hoc crisis investigations may therefore be damaging for long-term EU civil security. In addition, bridging this systemic gap is by no means easy as crises are unexpected, diverse and non-routine events with at times cascading consequences. Tied to the non-linear and interchanging nature of crises is the difficulty to effectively define them in advance. This also makes it difficult to define a standard crisis review procedure before the crisis occurs.

Conclusion

The study presented in this chapter has used database searches and previous research on crisis events in Sweden to draw a list of 36 national crisis events that occurred over the last two decades. As many as 86 per cent of these events were subject to some form of a national and official post hoc investigation. In fact, there were only five exceptions and four of these shared in common that the actual trigger causing the crisis occurred on the other side of state borders. This gives prima facie evidence for a strong review and learning culture in Sweden, which could be regarded as a model for other European countries. Only 19 per cent of the cases, however, were investigated according to a systematic method within the framework of the Swedish Accident Investigation Authority. Most of these were man-made major accidents. The second most common way of organizing post hoc crisis investigation was within the setting of the National Public Commission Inquiry. Self-assessments, or investigations conducted by agencies or organizations with close administrative ties to the subject of their investigations, were common. As many as 50 per cent of the cases were challenged by the issue of self-assessment bias as the investigations were conducted either by inspection authorities, principal regulators or by the organization mandated to deal with the crisis at hand. From this illustrative case study of past crises and post hoc crisis investigations in Sweden, this study has argued that the arrangements for post hoc crisis investigation as it is conducted in Sweden lack structure – which, by implication, is also likely to apply in other EU member states with similar crisis investigation arrangements. This systemic gap in civil security governance is likely to affect the learning capacities of government agencies and long-term societal resilience in a negative way.

In closing, let us discuss a few building blocks required to establish a more structured system for organizing lessons learned processes in response to crises. Both physical and intellectual arrangements are needed in this regard. In terms of physical arrangements, prerequisites include an organizational unit tasked to carry out the investigations. Such a unit should be dependent on achieving a high level of public trust, which, in turn, requires strong leadership and a clear mandate from the highest political level. An investigation unit does not need to be resource intensive or cumbersome to administer, rather it should be lean and flexible. Much like an investigation unit at the Swedish Accident Investigation Authority, a crisis investigation authority could be built around a core group of mandated investigators readily deployable at the event of a crisis. The core group may, in response to events, be expanded on the basis of a roster of broad expertise put together to cover different types of events.

In terms of the intellectual arrangements required for a post hoc crisis investigation unit, pre-established criteria for what type of events that should be investigated and how the investigation should be carried are critical factors. It is important that the criteria have some built-in flexibility, as crises are unexpected, surprising, dynamic and interchanging processes. Nevertheless, a base line for what kind of event that should be investigated needs to be established. This brings us back to the issue of what kind of event may be interpreted as a crisis. If we understand a crisis as something deviant breaking up a given and normal process or strategy, as has been suggested in this chapter, then a crisis can be characterized by an organization's inadequacy concerning ability and expertise required to handle an event. As most organizations are designed to deal with circumstances that do not include crisis situations, they tend to be inadequate when crises strike (Boin et al., 2005). A common way to deal with such inadequacy is to take steps to improve the fit between the situation at hand and the structures, capacities, resources and working ways of the organization by establishing some kind of crisis organization. In line with these ideas, then, a crisis investigation unit needs to monitor whether planned or special emergency organizations are launched in response to an event. When crisis organization is launched, it is reasonable to expect that a post hoc crisis investigation unit should investigate the management of that event. A professional and clearly mandated crisis investigation unit working in accordance with a systematic approach, as outlined in this chapter, should increase the potential for moving from rhetoric to real learning in the crisis aftermath. This, in turn, could prevent severe crises from seriously undercutting the legitimacy of the civil security governance system.

Notes

1. The Deputy Prosecuter closed the investigation almost four years after the event (Flores, 2014).
2. In this case the inquiry dealt with reforming the personal protection of members of the Cabinet, not with the actual cause of the crisis, nor with its management.
3. The latter case was also investigated within the Swedish Public Commission Inquiry arrangement (SOU).

References

Argyris, C. and D. A. Schön (1978) *Organizational Learning: A Theory of Action Perspective* (Reading: Addison-Wesley).

Birkland, T. (2009) 'Disasters, Lessons Learned, and Fantasy Documents', *Journal of Contingencies and Crisis Management*, 17, 146–156.
Birkland, T. (2006) *Lessons of Disaster* (Washington, D.C.: Georgetown University Press).
Boin, A., P. 't Hart, E. Stern and B. Sundelius (2005) *The Politics of Crisis Management: Public Leadership under Pressure* (Cambridge: Cambridge University Press).
Boin, A. and P. Lagadec (2000) 'Preparing for the Future: Critical Challenges in Crisis Management', *Journal of Contingencies and Crisis Management*, 8, 185–191.
Carley, K. M. and J. R. Harrald (1997) 'Organizational Learning Under Fire: Theory and Practice', *American Behavioral Scientist*, 40, 310–332.
Cedergren, A. and K. Petersen (2011) 'Prerequisites for Learning from Accident Investigations – A Cross-Country Comparison of National Accident Investigation Boards', *Safety Science*, 49, 1238–1245.
Christensen, T., P. Laegreid, P. G. Roness and K. A. Rövik (2005) *Organisationsteori för offentlig sektor* (Malmö: Liber).
Comfort, L. (1988) *Managing Disasters: Strategies and Policy Perspectives* (Durham: Duke University Press).
Dekker, S. and D. Hansén (2004) 'Learning Under Pressure: The Effects of Politicization on Organizational Learning in Public Bureaucracies', *Journal of Public Administration Research and Theory*, 14, 211–230.
Deverell, E. (2010) *Crisis-Induced Learning in Public Sector Organizations* (Stockholm: CRISMART).
Deverell, E. and E. K. Olsson (2010) 'Organizational Culture Effects on Strategy and Adaptability in Crisis Management', *Risk Management*, 12, 116–134.
Deverell, E. and J. Stiglund (forthcoming) 'Designing a Systematic Method for Organizational Crisis Investigation' in N. Schiffino, L. Taskin, J. Raone and C. Donis (eds.) *Organizing After Crisis: Public Management and Learning.* Forthcoming.
Elkjaer, B. (2003) 'Social Learning Theory: Learning as Participation in Social Processes' in M. Easterby-Smith and M. A. Lyles (eds.) *Blackwell Handbook of Organizational Learning and Knowledge Management* (Oxford: Blackwell), pp. 38–53.
Fiol, C. M. and M. A. Lyles (1985) 'Organizational Learning', *Academy of Management Review*, 10, 803–813.
Flores, J. (2014) *Utredningen av terrorattentatet i Stockholm läggs ned* (Dagens Nyheter), pp. 10–22.
Growth Analysis (2013) 'Strukturförändringar under finanskrisen – en kartläggning'. Working Paper, 07.
Hartoft, P. and A. Nilsson (1999) *Erfarenheter av övergripande ledning vid kris: En sammanställning av dokumenterade erfarenheter från kriser i Sverige under 1990-talet* (Stockholm: FOA).
Johansson, C., L. Jendel and A. T. Ottestig (2013) *Nätverk för kriskommunikation: Om myndigheters informationssamordning vid kriser* (DEMICOM Mittuniversitetet, MSB, the Swedish Civil Contingencies Agency), https://www.msb.se/RibData/Filer/pdf/26575.pdf, date accessed 11 November 2014.
Kingdon, J. (2003) *Agendas, Alternatives and Public Policies* (New York: Longman).
Krisinformation.se (2013) 'Tidigare händelser', http://www.krisinformation.se/web/Pages/SubStartPage____72907.aspx, date accessed 20 August 2013.

Lagadec, P. (2006) 'Crisis Management in the Twenty-First Century: "Unthinkable" Events in "Inconceivable" Contexts' in Rodriguez, E. L. Quarantelli, R. Dynes and W. A. Anderson (eds.) *Handbook of Disaster Management* (New York: Springer), pp. 489–507.
Luftfartsverket (2010) Utvärdering av LFV:s agerande vid vulkanutbrottet 2010.
March, J. G. (2010) *The Ambiguities of Experience* (Ithaca: Cornell University Press).
McConnell, A. (2003) 'Overview: Crisis Management, Influences, Responses, and Evaluation', *Parliamentary Affairs*, 56, 393–409.
McConnell, A. (2010) 'Success? Failure? Or Something In-Between? A Framework for Evaluating Crisis Management', *Policy & Society*, 30, 63–76.
Mitroff, I. I., M. C. Alpaslan and S. E. Green (2004) 'Crises as Ill-Structured Messes', *International Studies Review*, 6, 165–194.
MSB (2010) *Olyckor & kriser 2009/2010* (Karlstad: MSB).
Perrow, C. (1984) *Normal Accidents: Living with High-Risk Technologies* (New York: Basic Books).
Pfeffer, J. and G. R. Salancik (1978) 'External Control of Organizations: A Resource Dependence Perspective' reprinted in J. S. Ott, J. M. Shafritz and Y. S. Jang (eds.) *Classic Readings in Organization Theory* (Wadsworth: Cengage Learning Emea), pp. 520–531.
Proposition 2007/08: 92, *Stärkt Krisberedskap – För Säkerhets Skull* [Swedish Government Bill].
Resodihardjo, S. L. (2006) 'Wielding a Double-Edged Sword: The Use of Inquiries at Times of Crisis', *Journal of Crisis Management and Crisis Management*, 14, 199–206.
Rosenthal, U., M. T. Charles and P. 't Hart (1989) 'The World of Crises and Crisis Management' in U. Rosenthal U., M. T. Charles and P. 't Hart (eds.) *Coping with Crises: The Management of Disasters, Riots and Terrorism* (Springfield: Charles C. Thomas).
Rostis, A. (2007) 'Make No Mistake: The Effectiveness of the Lessons-Learned Approach to Emergency Management in Canada', *International Journal of Emergency Management*, 4, 197–210.
Sandefeldt, J. (2005) *Samverkan mellan offentlig sektor och näringslivet vid krishantering: En studie av kriser i Sverige 1993–2003* (Stockholm: Krisberedskapsmyndigheten, KBM:s temaserie 2005:6).
Savoia, E., A. Foluso and P. D. Biddinger (2012) 'Use of After Action Reports (AARs) to Promote Organizational and System Learning in Emergency Preparedness', *International Journal of Environmental Research and Public Health*, 9, 2949–2963.
Stern, E. (1997) 'Crisis and Learning: A Conceptual Balance Sheet', *Journal of Contingencies and Crisis Management*, 5, 69–86.
Stoop, J. and S. Roed-Larsen (2011) 'Public Safety Investigations – A New Evolutionary Step in Safety Enhancement?', *Reliability Engineering and System Safety*, 94, 1471–1479.
Sulitzeanu-Kenan, R. and Y. Holzman-Gazit (2013) 'Form and Content: Institutional Preferences and Public Opinion in a Crisis Inquiry', *Administration & Society* (OnlineFirst), DOI: 10.1177/0095399712469197.
Topper, B. and P. Lagadec (2013) 'Fractal Crises: A New Path for Crisis Theory and Management', *Journal of Contingencies and Crisis Management*, 21, 4–16.
Turner, B. A. (1976) 'The Organizational and Interorganizational Development of Disasters', *Administrative Science Quarterly*, 21, 378–397.

Part III
The Challenge of Cooperation and the Role of the EU

9
Exploring the EU's Role as Transboundary Crisis Manager: The Facilitation of Sense-Making during the Ash Crisis

Sanneke Kuipers and Arjen Boin

Introduction

In recent years, nation-states have encountered a rapidly changing environment marked by the onset of various threats. These threats range from terrorism to epidemics, from shifting international relations to the breakdown of the financial system, from climate change to cyber attacks. We live in a world where 'black swans' and 'mega crises' can strike any time (Taleb, 2007; Helsloot et al., 2012). These new threats and impending crises bring to the fore a specific set of political and administrative challenges that are hard to address (OECD, 2003, 2011; Boin et al., 2005; Boin, 2009).

Within the closely knit European Union (EU), a 'mega-crisis' typically affects multiple Member States. Many critical systems in Europe – those that sustain basic societal functions, such as energy grids, logistic networks, food distribution chains and financial flow structures – reach across national borders. An incident in one corner of the EU can easily cause a crisis in a region across the continent. We speak of transboundary crises, as they unfold across geographical and system borders (Boin and Rhinard, 2008).

The EU has faced several transboundary crises in the past (think of Chernobyl, the Mad Cow disease and the financial meltdown), which demonstrated the need for a joint response. The very idea of a transboundary response fits the core principles of subsidiarity (i.e. the EU should primarily initiate policies and capacity that member states could or would not develop on their own). In recent years, recognition of the need for transboundary crisis management capacities has grown steadily across EU institutions (Boin et al., 2013a; Bossong and Hegemann, introduction to this volume).

Transboundary crisis management requires international coordination, mutual assistance, information-sharing and joint decision-making (Ansell et al., 2010). But the civil security systems of the member states differ markedly in their organization of operational response, the (de)centralization of authority, the distribution of resources, the role of private actors and the military.[1] It is not easy to align all these different resources to facilitate a joint, transboundary response. The EU has begun to build capacities to facilitate a joint response to a disaster-struck area (Boin et al., 2013a).[2] But the EU still has limited capacities to facilitate a *joint* response to a *transboundary* threat that confronts *multiple member states*. There is 'no centralized department for transboundary crisis management; it is a field without a name (...) it is not even clear who in the EU is aware of all these available capacities' (Boin et al., 2013a, p. 130). This paper explores the EU's potential role in facilitating such a transboundary response. We are particularly interested to see how the EU can facilitate joint sense-making, one of the core functions of strategic crisis management (Boin et al., 2013b). We have two reasons for this particular focus.

First, a joint response to a transboundary crisis is undermined by the lack of a shared picture about the unfolding threat. The information required to fully understand what is going on during a transboundary crisis is usually spread widely across organizations, policy sectors and countries. Without such a shared picture, critical decisions will be uninformed and coordination is likely to be suboptimal at best (Boin and Bynander, 2015). Importantly, it will be hard to communicate an accurate message 'with one mouth' – a condition for effective crisis management in the media era. This is the challenge of transboundary sense-making (Weick, 1995; Ansell et al., 2010). Second, the EU does not have formal authority to *manage* a crisis response; it heavily relies on what member states will bring to the table (both in terms of granting authority and offering resources). The EU can therefore merely *facilitate* one. It is exactly in this area of transboundary sense-making that the EU can play a powerful and essential facilitating role (Boin et al., 2014).

We seek to illustrate this point by analysing a recent transboundary crisis: the volcanic ash crisis of 2010. We start by elaborating the concept of transboundary crisis. We then revisit the volcanic ash crisis and explore the EU's role in that crisis. We end by contemplating if and how the EU could enhance its role in providing capacities for joint sense-making.

Transboundary crises and the sense-making challenge

We speak of a 'transboundary crisis' when the functioning of multiple, life-sustaining systems or critical infrastructures faces an urgent threat that must be addressed under conditions of deep uncertainty (Ansell et al., 2010; cf. Rosenthal et al., 1989, 2001). Transboundary crises typically:

- affect multiple jurisdictions and challenge authorities at multiple levels of government (cities, regions, countries)
- require public–private cooperation
- undermine the functioning of multiple policy sectors and critical infrastructures
- escalate in unforeseen directions, exploiting linkages between functional and geographical domains.

The impact of a transboundary crisis can be felt far away from its epicentre: transboundary crises have no, or at least not one, Ground Zero. They have, of course, always existed (the Plague, invading marauders, and financial breakdowns are of all times). Modern vectors such as globalization, optimization of supply chains, increased mobility, tight coupling and complex interaction of technically advanced systems have increased systemic efficiencies that exacerbate the speed and scope of contagion (Turner, 1978; Perrow, 1984). This means that known hazards (floods, hurricanes, earthquakes) may have new and unanticipated effects (Boin, 2009).

It has always been hard to manage a crisis or disaster (Rosenthal et al., 1989, 2001; Boin et al., 2005; Rodriguez et al., 2006). At the strategic level of government, we can discern a set of critical tasks that senior policymakers and politicians are expected to fulfil during a crisis (Boin et al., 2005, 2013). They have to coordinate complex networks and make critical decisions; they must communicate with stakeholders; and they must account for their actions, preserving governmental legitimacy. But an effective fulfilment of these tasks requires one other and critical task: sense-making.

The *sense-making* challenge pertains to the recognition from vague, ambivalent and contradictory signals that a crisis is unfolding and how it is evolving. We define sense-making here in terms of collecting, analysing and sharing information on the causes, dynamics and effects of the crisis and its potential solution (cf. Weick, 1995). It is an essential task: if done well, it provides decision-makers with a *shared perception of what is happening*. All too often, it appears that decision-makers have different mental pictures of the crisis situation, which can and do lead to confusion, misunderstandings, irritation and, ultimately, misguided decisions.

We must make a distinction here between *detection* and *understanding* a crisis. *Detection* pertains to the recognition that a crisis has begun. Sometimes that is self-evident: an earthquake or tsunami is usually immediately and widely noticed. But, as a general rule, we know that the starting point of a crisis is much easier to pinpoint *after* a crisis, with hindsight knowledge, than *during* a crisis.

Understanding a crisis pertains to the causes, dynamics and consequences of an unfolding crisis. Again, what happens during a crisis may appear painfully obvious in hindsight. It is, however, rarely anywhere near evident in the midst of crisis. Policymakers typically find themselves confronted with an overload of seemingly useless information and a dearth of needed information. What may be clear at the operational level may be understood very differently at the strategic level.

To detect and understand unfolding crises, three interrelated processes are necessary:

1. Collecting information: defining what information is needed and gathering or requesting it
2. Analysing information: piecing together information from various sources, validating it and creating a 'complete' picture of a situation
3. Sharing information: communicating the emerging picture of the situation with internal and external partners, while specifying what is known for sure and what is merely suspected.

Sense-making may be one of the hardest challenges that crisis managers face. In the literature, we find at least three types of explanation for the limited sense-making capacity that we so often witness during a crisis. First, psychologists have shown that most people find it very hard to correctly process information when they experience high levels of stress (Reason, 2008; Kahneman, 2011). Second, the difficulties of information processing under stress can easily be amplified by certain group processes, which typically emerge when a group must act under time pressure (Vertzberger, 1990; 't Hart et al., 1997). Third, the processing of information can be hindered or even undermined by existing tensions that play up between organizational units (Turner, 1978; Rosenthal et al., 1991; Preston and 't Hart, 1999).

One only has to read the official reports on the response to Hurricane Katrina and the subsequent flooding of New Orleans (in the summer of 2005) to find telling illustrations of the findings summarized above (Brinkley, 2006; Cooper and Block, 2006). The most essential information about breaking levees and the location of survivors took what in hindsight appears an incredibly long time to reach the strategic level (and not all critical information reached that level). Academic research strongly suggests that this is a normal occurrence, especially if the organization of sense-making is not properly prepared.

The characteristics of transboundary crises compound the challenges of sense-making (Ansell et al., 2010). More actors become involved who have to communicate across vertical and horizontal boundaries. A wide variety of organizations will have to share information and somehow arrive at a shared picture of the situation. This multiplies the organizational and political interests; it also increases transaction costs. Emerging appraisals are easily thwarted by unexpected interacting developments and hidden interdependencies, which requires intense and continuous cooperation between organizations that never have worked with each other before. They must somehow understand the technical language of other sectors and appreciate cultural differences. When crises stretch across national boundaries, the challenge becomes even harder.

The sense-making challenge became particularly evident during the volcanic ash crisis of 2010. The case is a text-book example of a transboundary crisis. It caused an unprecedented mobility crisis due to an air space closure and aviation standstill of a full week. It has been well studied, but not from a transboundary perspective with a specific focus on the EU's role (Tindall, 2010; Alemanno, 2011; Brannigan, 2011; Budd et al., 2011; Macrae, 2011; O'Regan, 2011; Lee and Preston, 2012; Alexander, 2013; Christensen et al., 2013; Hutter and Lloyd-Bostock, 2013; Nohrstedt, 2013; Parker, 2014). Whereas most other studies of the Eyjafjallajökull crisis focus on preventing the next volcanic ash crisis, we are particularly interested in the role that the EU played in facilitating a transboundary response.

The Icelandic ash case

On 14 April 2010, the volcano Eyjafjallajökull on Iceland erupted, sending an ash cloud several miles high into the atmosphere. The eruption, though relatively small-scale, unexpectedly turned into a crisis for air traffic dependent industries, travellers and governments across the world as the ash cloud hovered over Europe for days on end. The Volcanic Ash Advisory Center (VAAC) in London registered high concentrations of airborne ash in the early morning of 14 April. A warning was forwarded to the European Organization for the Safety of Air Navigation (hereafter called Eurocontrol), which posted a message on the Open Network Portal, indicating possible implications for European air traffic.[3] Later in the afternoon, Eurocontrol organized a videoconference with participating National Air Traffic Services (NATS) discussing possible closing of air space.

The Norwegian Air Traffic Control centre was the first authority to impose flight restrictions in the late evening of 14 April. Sweden, Finland and the UK followed shortly thereafter as the ash cloud spread southeast during the night. The ash cloud continued spreading during the following day, causing Ireland, Denmark, the Netherlands and Belgium to impose flight restrictions. Initially, restrictions were announced on an hourly basis by local airport management. When national weather forecast services announced that westbound winds would continue for days, the first definite closure was announced at London Heathrow Airport in the morning of 15 April. Meanwhile, Eurocontrol recommended closure of national air space in Northwestern Europe. Eurocontrol recommendations are not obligatory, but countries complied. National Air Traffic Control agencies in Belgium, the Netherlands and France took subsequent action on the same day. Germany, Switzerland, Poland and the Czech Republic followed on 16 April.

In closing their airspace, authorities were acting on guidelines established by the International Civil Aviation Organization (ICAO, a UN organization). These guidelines prescribed a no-fly zone when volcanic ash is detectable in air space (a no-tolerance threshold at 200 μg). Though volcanic ash was a known hazard in the aviation sector, surprisingly little was known about the impact of ash particles on aircraft engines. The only data readily available was old – instances of high, localized concentrations of volcanic ash affecting the technology of 20 years ago. The ICAO guidelines were based on this old data.[4] Other guidelines or standards for safety being absent, the only guarantee for flight safety was to completely avoid ash clouds (Alemanno, 2011, p. 6).

The situation thus combined (1) an absence of reliable and accurate data detailing the composition, dispersion and changing location of the ash cloud with (2) a lack of consensus among manufacturers, airlines, regulators and engineers of what constituted a safe threshold for aviation. The default reaction amounted to a 'safety first' approach: first do not cause any harm. The across-the-board embrace of the safety first approach had immediate and unforeseen consequences.

Consequences

European aviation came to a grinding halt. Europe is one of the busiest air spaces in the world, with 150,000 air routes, 150 airlines and 9.5 million annual flights (O'Regan, 2011). On 16 April, air traffic volume in Europe had dropped by over 80 per cent (Eurocontrol, 2010). European air traffic reached its lowest point on 18 April at only 15 per cent of the scheduled air traffic.

The effects of the crisis rippled through the system, with a cancellation of 108,000 flights, a stranding of 10.5 million passengers and lost revenue of 1.7 billion US dollars in the airline industry alone (Eurocontrol, 2010). The member states with a significant tourism sector suffered. Industries dependent on air cargo (medicine, manufacturing, perishable goods) and 'just in time' delivery schemes experienced disruptions and delays. A survey by Chatham House among business executives revealed that 'had the disruptions continued for a few days longer, it would have taken at least a month for their companies to recover. One week seems to be the maximum tolerance of the "just-in-time" global economy' (Lee and Preston, 2012). For the airline industry, the crisis came with exceptionally bad timing. Global recession had already pressed private operators to the margin, and the grounding of all flights for several days brought significant losses. In the summer of 2010, 13 airline companies went bankrupt in the UK only.

Yet, a joint, transboundary response to the crisis was not forthcoming. Europe[5] consists of 38 countries, including the 27 EU member states, each with independent national authority over their own air space. National authorities tried to bypass ICAO regulations by offering their own interpretations of the VAAC-produced maps and charts of the ash cloud's location and density (O'Regan, 2011, p. 25). Countries applied different rules on Visual Flight Rules (VFR) at lower altitudes (Johnson and Jeunemaitre, 2011, p. 60).

The persistent application of the ICAO guidelines outraged the airlines. The weather forecasts predicted stable weather, allowing the cloud to remain in place for days, if not weeks. The economic costs of indefinite closure would be staggering (Brannigan, 2011). In response, several commercial airlines launched[6] test flights through the ash cloud area and reported no problems. British Airways CEO Willie Walsh joined a test flight to demonstrate publicly his confidence in aviation safety under the circumstances (Sawer and Mendick, 2011). Pressure on engine manufacturers to come forward with available data on their engine's ash tolerance levels mounted (Hutter and Lloyd-Bostock, 2013).

Making sense of an ash crisis

The Eyjafjallajökull ash cloud posed serious challenges to the many countries and organizations that were affected by it. However, the national authorities found it hard to agree on a common approach towards solving the transportation crisis. Underlying this decisional paralysis was the absence of a shared understanding with regard to the nature of the problem and potential solutions. Uncertainty played out along three dimensions.

First, there was uncertainty about the cloud. Experts remained unsure of the cloud's exact location and content (Brannigan, 2011, p. 109). As Budd et al. (2011, p. 32) observed: 'On the ground, confusion reigned. No one knew which sectors of the sky might be closed, when or the length of time they would remain shut.' This made it hard to agree on solutions. The lack of accurate guidelines and the dispersion of authority in the aviation safety domain produced a deadlock among international public and private actors. Pressures soon mounted to reopen air space, as millions of passengers got stranded.

Second, there was uncertainty about the consequences of the meltdown. As decision-making on aviation safety arrived at a standstill, so did logistical chains all over Europe. Many companies rely on cargo flights for high value and low weight products such as medicine, ICT manufacturing parts and automated machinery parts (Lee and Preston, 2012). Passengers stranded at airports all over Europe were left to themselves. Governments did try to bring them home, but the options were limited and at least passengers were safe on the ground. The airlines had no formal influence on the decision not to fly and did not consider it their responsibility to provide passengers with accommodation or compensation. Some airports, such as Schiphol Amsterdam, did provide sleeping space to stranded passengers. Industries and travellers soon began to voice their frustration through the media and through interest group lobbies. The ash crisis was becoming a full-blown political crisis.

But an escape from this dead-end situation required a joint reinterpretation of the threat. The no-tolerance policy was clearly not feasible, but individual governments could not take individual steps to deviate from the ICAO no-tolerance policy (Eurocontrol, 2010). Actors had to come to an agreement on how to overcome this gap by other means than applying the zero tolerance rule.

Third, uncertainty stretched to the question of responsibility: who was in charge here? Who could be held accountable for the consequences (revenue losses, bankruptcies, competition disadvantages)? Who should take care of the stranded citizens, particularly those with no means at subsistence level or special needs? Consular affairs? Airlines? Reception countries? Airports? Most importantly, it remained unclear who could or should decide on the zero-tolerance rule that paralysed air traffic in Europe. The ash cloud affected many countries and many sectors. As a result, an effective solution required the involvement of a variety of actors:

- National governments and their regulating authorities had the ultimate authority to open or close national air space. Each country had its own decision-making structures in place to cope with air space related crises (Lee and Preston, 2012).
- Eurocontrol facilitated cooperation between Air Traffic Management Systems by providing national Air Navigation Service Providers with information to estimate their capacity, and to plan and prepare their routing schema. Eurocontrol is a non-governmental agency at the European level, a functional cooperation between the aviation sectors of 40 involved countries without decision-making authority.
- The EU has had no authority with regard to (the closure of) air space. Since 2004, the EU had tried to gradually centralize air safety authority in the European Aviation Safety Agency (EASA), which was meant to become 'a "one-stop-shop" for managing the 27 member bloc's air space by promoting and regulating the highest common standards and environmental protection in civil aviation' (O'Regan, 2011, p. 23).
- At the international level, the ICAO sets the standards, procedures and protocols for aviation safety to which countries and airlines voluntarily comply.
- The ICAO, together with the World Meteorological Organization, also set up a global system for monitoring and advising on the presence of atmospheric ash. The London-based Volcanic Ash Advisory Center played a crucial role in this particular case. Its main task was to provide measurements of atmospheric ash concentration and dispersion, and recommendations in accordance with ICAO guidelines.

- Airlines, airports, travel agents and manufacturers, while major players in the aviation sector, had no formal decision-making authority in this case.
- Scientific experts on volcano eruptions, geophysics and meteorology had a crucial influence in providing information, models and predictions regarding the location, dynamics, composition and density of the ash cloud, but no decision-making authority.

The crisis was international and transboundary, but national authorities had to decide. The transnational nature of the ash crisis exposed an authority vacuum. There was no mechanism (such as majority rule, weighing of votes, solidarity clause, fallback arrangements) for decision-making among independent authorities, especially when interests and responsibilities clash. In addition, the participants in decision-making were largely unfamiliar with each other and each others' procedures (Brannigan, 2011, p. 110). O'Regan (2011, p. 25) therefore argues:

> Since it was unclear who had authority over what, European-wide institutions only offered the illusion of control without taking the initiative to 'govern' the closures and produce outcomes leading to the resumption of flights. The available governance tools were unable to help policy makers find a way out of the decision to close air space.

The search for an acceptable solution was further inhibited by different approaches towards risk assessment. Airlines felt commercial pressure to resume flying, but they would commercially suffer the consequences if something went disastrously wrong. The air traffic control agencies saw safety as their primary concern. Manufacturers (who held the key to more accurate and updated knowledge on engine safety tolerance levels), lawyers and insurers had a primary concern in avoiding liability. National aviation authorities sought to maintain trust and legitimacy.

Sticking to the precautionary principle in a situation of profound uncertainty may save lives. At the same time, a 'comparative analysis of expected costs and expected benefits of precautionary measures could serve as a useful check against overreaction to incidents' (Alemanno, 2011, pp. 8–9). This suggests that 'the precautionary principle was designed in part at least to make it clear that those who propose a technical activity bear the burden of proof of safety. In a crisis environment such principles can disappear under the weight of economic and political considerations' (Brannigan, 2011, p. 102). But there were no rules for how to resolve inconsistent and competing scientific evidence (Johnson and Jeunemaitre, 2011, p. 56).

The greatest step in uncertainty reduction was the redefinition of the acceptable risk, based on political and economic considerations (Lawless, 2011). When realization sunk in that the zero-tolerance approach would keep air traffic grounded for an indefinite time period, pressure grew to somehow lift the threshold without compromising aviation safety. As uncertainty lingered, the decision process shifted from the technical expert setting to the public arena. Political leaders had to decide and explain why it was now safe to fly in the same cloud. Uncertainty had been reduced to some extent by engine manufacturers providing test data on alternative tolerance levels (Macrae, 2011) and airlines and military operators conducting test flights; the latter argued that flying was possible within defined corridors. But all this evidence was not scientifically validated.

In time, a fundamental paradigm shift could be witnessed from strictly adhering to the precautionary principle centred on passenger safety to re-opening skies in favour of commercial and political interests (Brannigan, 2011, pp. 104–105, cf. Brannigan, 2010; Hutter and Lloyd-Bostock, 2013, p. 399). Uncertainty on the duration of the crisis and the chaos on the ground had become far more important than ash-related uncertainty: 'The general public imperative was to restore air travel back to normal rather than seek absolute assurances for safety' (Burgess, 2011, p. 76).

The U-turn in risk assessment and safety approach cleared the way for ending the crisis. The protracted air space closure had not only increased political and economic pressure on decision-making, it also had increased public impatience. Travellers seemed more than willing to fly near the end of the ash crisis. Then it happened: 'a twenty-year old safety regime governed by experts was overthrown in a two-hour meeting packed with politicians and airline executives' (Brannigan, 2010, p. 113). It is to this meeting that we turn next.

Facilitating transboundary sense-making: The EU takes charge

Europe has a fragmented air space. Air traffic control was (and still is) closely associated with sovereignty, and hence confined within national borders (Alemanno, 2011, p. 7). The limits of national problem-solving were painfully exposed by the ash crisis. The EU helped national actors to arrive at a common understanding of the crisis, which facilitated a speedy, joint and ultimately effective response.

The EU Commission, together with the Spanish presidency of the European Council, took a first crucial step on 17 April by asking Eurocontrol to work out a coordinated European crisis management plan. During the weekend of 17–18 April, the European Commission, with the assistance of Eurocontrol, coordinated a series of meetings with representatives from national aviation authorities, air traffic control services, the airlines, airports and scientists (European Commission, 2010a). The purpose of these meetings was to 'coordinate air space management without compromising safety' (European Commission, 2010a).

The participants to these meetings had to find an agreement, based on available but fragmented scientific evidence (on ash cloud conditions, on engine tolerance levels and on meteorological measurements and prospects) on technical solutions for stronger European cooperation to maximize available airspace. Based on these meetings, the plan developed by Eurocontrol would offer possible strategies for flying restrictions that could be adopted by the member states. These could be implemented by Eurocontrol immediately (European Commission, 2010a). The new plan relied both on pre-existing risk assessment models of Eurocontrol and inspection results from the aircraft industry regarding the results of test flights and engine ash tolerance levels (Nohrstedt, 2013, p. 970).

The EU Commission proposed the Eurocontrol plan to the EU ministers of transport (the European council of transport ministers) on 19 April. In the words of Commission president Barosso: 'I will present the results of this meeting to European transport ministers at 15:00 this afternoon. I hope that this will provide ministers with the basis of an agreement on the way forwards' (European Commission, 2010a). The Commission, Eurocontrol, ICAO and national aviation authorities participated in this meeting.

The ministers of transport agreed on a common approach for flying through ash that same day. In a press statement, EU Transport Commissioner Kallas declared:

> This evening, I am pleased to report that we have made real progress. On the basis of a recommendation agreed unanimously by the national authorities and experts of the 38 Members of Eurocontrol, transport ministers have agreed to intensify European co-ordination

and risk assessment of airspace management. The new air control measures come into effect from 0800 CET Tuesday morning.

(European Commission, 2010b)

The Eurocontrol plan was adopted. A three-zone division was implemented in all EU member states with no-fly restrictions for high-ash concentration levels, controlled flying at lower-ash concentration levels and unlimited flying in no-ash areas.[7] The immediate result of this EU-initiated and coordinated decision was that airlines could resume flying the next day almost anywhere in Europe.

The new strategy was implemented in all EU member states on 20 April at 8:00 CET. Air traffic resumed immediately and two days later schedules were back to normal. The head of the British Civil Aviation Authority noted that 'we achieved what often takes years in 96 hours' (Lawless, 2011, p. 240). The EU Commissioner for Transport, Kallas, summarized the role of the Union: 'faced with this crisis, the first priority of the Commission was to intervene to facilitate the opening of airspace under strict safety conditions so that millions of stranded passengers could get home and to ensure that EU passenger rights are fully respected' (European Commission, 2010c).

Following the crisis, existing policy changes were accelerated and new plans were adopted (Alemanno, 2011, p. 8). Most of these reforms had been prepared and discussed long before the ash crisis, but now a sudden increase of political support paved the way for their swift adoption and implementation (Nohrstedt, 2013). The process of European integration of air space policy had previously 'been stalled by EU member states' reluctance to give up control over national airspace' (Nohrstedt, 2013, p. 974). On 4 May 2010, the Transport Council of Ministers decided to give the Single European Sky initiative highest priority. This meant that:

- EU coordinators would facilitate the quick creation of Functional Airspace Blocks (FAB), nine in number, based on operational requirements. The FABs should optimize and integrate the provision of air navigation services and related ancillary functions, regardless of state boundaries (European Commission Memo, 2011).
- A central European Network Manager was designated to coordinate European Air Traffic Control on a daily basis. This allows for a more harmonized and coordinated approach to risk and flow/capacity assessment.

- The European Aviation Crisis Coordination Cell (EACCC) was established. This is exactly what the EU lacked during the crisis (Alemanno, 2011, p. 8). The EACCC, when activated, is chaired by the Commission and Eurocontrol, and includes participation from the EU presidency, air navigation service providers, air space users and airports as well as other relevant stakeholders. This cell is designed as an additional support structure for the Network Manager (above) in a crisis situation. The new EACCC has been effectively tested during the 2011 Grímsvötn eruption (Parker, 2014).
- The EU Commission decided to accelerate the implementation of the European Aviation Safety Agency's (EASA) competences in air traffic management safety. EASA's greater role in regulating common safety standards further enhanced a harmonized European air traffic control approach.
- Commissioner Kallas established an Aviation platform of high level officials and executives from the aviation sector for long-term strategic advice regarding a sustainable future for air transport and for a competitive future of the aviation industry (European Commission, 2011, p. 3).

Conclusion: The EU as transboundary crisis manager

The ash crisis revealed modern society's intensifying dependence on air travel (O'Regan, 2011, p. 26). It showed to what extent fully integrated markets that operate at full capacity and with last-minute delivery schemes depend on seamless mobility. However, the crisis episode also exposed what can happen when national authorities are confronted with a transboundary crisis and fail to put together a transboundary response. Finally, the crisis revealed how the EU can play a role in facilitating a transboundary response.

The Commission initiative to bring together all stakeholders to develop a strategy to safely resume flying was crucial to overcome the deadlock. That joint plan was based on a redefinition of risk: the zero tolerance approach was replaced by a more differentiated approach that was supported by both the industry and its regulators. The decision to relax airspace restrictions was not so much the result of new knowledge but the result of revised perceptions among safety regulation experts on engine tolerance levels to volcanic ash (Nohrstedt, 2013, p. 972).

This paradigmatic shift, in turn, required joint sense-making: all actors had to agree that the approach in place was neither effective nor legitimate. Such a seemingly simple decision required a political rationale. The unanimous decision to implement this plan in their respective national air spaces by the European Ministers of Transport in the extraordinary meeting of the Council provided precisely that rationale. Without such a harmonized and coordinated solution, no individual national authority was willing or able to unilaterally open its air space.

The EU played a critical role in facilitating the orchestrated and joint revision of national risk perceptions. It did so without a clear legal basis. In fact, the EU Commission insisted that it did not have authority over national air spaces: 'there is no EU competence for air traffic management or in relation to decisions taken to open or close air space i.e. the EU Commission and European Parliament have NO role – it is for the individual member state governments to decide' (European Commission, 2010b). However, given the crisis – 'we are faced with an unprecedented shutdown of Europe's airspace. This situation is not sustainable. It is now clear that we cannot just wait until this ash cloud dissipates' – the Commission assumed a transboundary role to facilitate joint solutions (European Commission, 2010a).

The question, then, arises how the EU could do what member states did not manage to accomplish? We offer three reasons for the success of the EU in facilitating a transboundary crisis response in the ash crisis. First, the EU offered a trusted and proven venue to solve wicked problems. The European Transport Council was a venue where decisions on aviation policy were regularly made (Nohrstedt, 2013). Even if decisions to open or reduce airspace were normally national decisions, it was easy for the member states to use a Council meeting to coordinate their decisions and decide unanimously. The legitimacy for the EU's role and the plan it devised together with stakeholders was confirmed by the unanimous agreement on the final solution and its rapid implementation. Also, additional policy changes (the Single Sky initiative) to coordinate and integrate aviation policy at the EU level were endorsed by the member states in the slipstream of the crisis (Nohrstedt, 2013).

Second, the EU offered a natural platform for experts to convene and discuss a common technical approach. The EU has long provided a forum in which experts can work together to prepare decisions that have political repercussions (see for instance the EU's role in preparing risk regulation and health-related policies). In this case, the EU convened engine manufacturers with their scarce data on engine ash tolerance levels. Allegedly, manufacturers were hesitant to do so because of liabilities (Macrae, 2011). It collected the available results from the over 40 test flights done by several airlines and the air force of several member states. The EU provided a forum for scientists (meteorologists, geologists), aviation regulators and industry representatives on 'neutral' ground – focusing the agenda on opening air space without compromising safety.

Third, the EU provided cover for decisions that are unpopular or potentially contested at home. In this case, member state authorities were eager to resume flying. At the same time, politicians must have worried that they would be held accountable for negative consequences of a premature decision. The EU has played this role for the longest time, but increasingly in the management of transboundary crises (think of the financial crisis). National leaders are happy to agree behind closed doors to common-sense decisions, only to loudly protest those same decisions back home. In similar vein, we can see how the EU provides political cover for risky decisions.

What does this mean for the future? In the introduction of this chapter, we pointed at an intriguing paradox: the EU has the least capacities in the area where it matters most (Boin and Rhinard, 2008). The findings of this chapter suggest the EU can play an important role in facilitating a transboundary response to a transboundary threat. In closing, we offer a few suggestions what the EU could do to further its role as a transboundary crisis manager.

To increase awareness of transboundary risks and the required response capacity, the EU could be more explicit about its potential roles. A common vision among member states is required, both on transboundary crisis management and the EU's role therein. Articulating such a vision would be an important first step to meet the challenges ahead. This vision should tie in with an encompassing vision on the EU's role in providing civil security (Bossing and Hegemann, introduction to this volume).

In preparing to meet such challenges, the EU can find natural allies in other international organizations, such as NATO and responsible UN divisions, which are by definition transboundary in their setup and response capacity. How do they increase compatibility and standardization among the systems of their respective members? How do they organize fast decision-making when a crisis escalates? And how can international organizations complement instead of cross each other's efforts in the transboundary crisis response? These are the types of questions that international organizations should not address by themselves, but in a dialogue with one another.

Sense-making is perhaps the most pivotal task in transboundary crisis management, because of the cross-border fragmentation of causes and effects. It is also the most feasible task, both from a functional and a political perspective. Though building a coherent operational picture of the ash crisis and preparing a shared diagnosis, the Commission managed to turn the tide during the ash crisis. The EU can build on this success.

The EU can and perhaps should be the go-to venue for transboundary crisis management efforts. National actors do not get together easily or naturally. The EU has the infrastructure in place to serve and exploit such gatherings. The EU needs to prepare to speed up the process of information sharing and the search for a common interpretation of escalating events (see Boin et al., 2014). By creating a true focal point for expertise, data collection, information sharing and international decision-making, the EU can become a hub for transboundary crisis management.

Notes

1. See, for instance, the recent comparative study on 22 European states conducted by the ANVIL consortium (http://anvil-project.net).
2. The EU coordinates member-state efforts to support an overwhelmed member state in dealing with a national disaster. The EU also coordinates member-state assistance to disaster stricken areas in other parts of the world (think of Haiti).
3. Eurocontrol is an independent international organization, founded in 1960. It is composed of 39 European member states and the European Community (which became a member in 2002). It coordinates air traffic flows across member states and support air traffic regulation (https://www.eurocontrol.int/about-eurocontrol, retrieved October 2014).
4. The ICAO policy was based on two previous experiences with attempts to fly through ash; the first one occurring in 1982 where a BA 747–200 (jumbo jet) flew into an ash cloud caused by the eruption of the volcano Mount Galunggung in Indonesia, causing temporary loss of all four engines. The second event occurred in 1989 where a KLM jumbo approaching Alaska flew across volcanic ash from the Redoubt Volcano, also resulting in the temporary failure of all four engines. None of these two events caused any loss in human life. The airlines that would accuse the authorities and scientists for being overly cautious had themselves been rather reluctant in the past decades to commission studies on the accurate thresholds (Alemanno, 2011, pp. 5–6).
5. Defined here in aviation terms (38 refers to the countries that were members of Eurocontrol, the organization that serves to facilitate air traffic management in European air space, at the time of the Volcanic Ash crisis).
6. KLM/Air France, British Airways, Lufthansa and Austria Airlines.
7. Unanimously, the transportation ministers of the member states adopted a differentiation of zones based on a new threshold of ash concentration at 2,000 μg per m^3, instead of the previous 200 μg. The zone between 200 and 2,000 μg constituted a controlled air space where certified aircraft could fly under conditions of regular engine inspection. A density above 2,000 μg would still

be a no fly zone, and anything under 200 μg would be considered normal air space (Nohrstedt, 2013).

References

Alemanno, A. (ed.) (2011) *Governing Disasters: The Challenges of Emergency Risk Regulation* (Cheltenham: Edward Elgar).
Alexander, D. (2013) 'Volcanic Ash in the Atmosphere and the Risks for Civil Aviation: A Study in European Crisis Management', *International Journal of Disaster Risk Science*, 4, 9–19.
Ansell, D., A. Boin and A. Keller (2010) 'Managing Transboundary Crises: Identifying the Building Blocks of an Effective Response System', *Journal of Contingencies and Crisis Management*, 18, 195–207.
Boin, A. (2009) 'The New World of Crises and Crisis Management: Implications for Policymaking and Research', *Review of Policy Research*, 26, 367–377.
Boin, A. and F. Bynander (2015) 'Explaining Success and Failure in Crisis Coordination', *Geografiska Annaler*, 97, 123–135.
Boin, A., M. Ekengren and M. Rhinard (2013a) *The European Union as Crisis Manager: Patterns and Prospects* (Cambridge: Cambridge University Press).
Boin, A., M. Ekengren and M. Rhinard (2014) *Making Sense of Sense-making: The EU's Role in Collecting, Analysing and Disseminating Information in Times of Crisis* (Stockholm: National Defence College).
Boin, A., P. 't Hart, E. Stern and B. Sundelius (2005) *The Politics of Crisis Management: Public Leadership under Pressure* (New York: Cambridge University Press).
Boin, A., S. Kuipers and W. Overdijk (2013b) 'Leadership in Times of Crisis: A Framework for Assessment', *International Review of Public Administration*, 18, 79–91.
Boin, A. and M. Rhinard (2008) 'Managing Transboundary Crises: What Role for the European Union?', *International Studies Review*, 10, 1–26.
Brannigan, V. (2010) 'Alice's Adventures in Volcano Land: The Use and Abuse of Expert Knowledge in Safety Regulation', *European Journal of Risk Regulation*, 1, 107–113.
Brannigan, V. (2011) 'Paradigms Lost: Emergency Safety Regulation under Scientific and Technical Uncertainty' in A. Alemanno (ed.) *Governing Disasters: The Challenges of Emergency Risk Regulation* (Cheltenham: Edward Elgar), pp. 101–114.
Brinkley, D. (2006) *The Great Deluge: Hurricane Katrina, New Orleans and the Mississippi Gulf Coast* (New York: William Morrow).
Budd, L., S. Griggs, D. Howarth and S. Ison (2011) 'A Fiasco of Volcanic Proportions? Eyjafjallajökull and the Closure of European Airspace', *Mobilities*, 6, 31–40.
Burgess, A. (2011) 'Representing Emergency Risks: Media, Risks and "Acts of God" in the Volcanic Ash Cloud' in A. Alemanno (ed.) *Governing Disasters: The Challenges of Emergency Risk Regulation* (Cheltenham: Edward Elgar), pp. 65–79.
Christensen, T., M. Johannessen and P. Laegreid (2013) 'A System under Stress: The Icelandic Volcano Ash Crisis', *Journal of Contingencies and Crisis Management*, 21, 71–81.

Cooper, C. and R. Block (2006) *Disaster Hurricane Katrina and the Failure of Homeland Security* (New York: Times Books).
European Commission (2010a) *Press Statement by Commission Vice-President Siim Kallas, Responsible for Transport*, EC MEMO/10/136, 19 April 04 2010, http://europa.eu/rapid/press release_MEMO-10-136_en.htm, date accessed 28 November 2014.
European Commission (2010b) *Volcanic Ash Crisis: Frequently Asked Questions*, EC MEMO/10/143, 20 April 2010, http://europa.eu/rapid/press-release_MEMO-10-143_en.htm, date accessed 28 November 2014.
European Commission (2010c) *Volcanic Ash Cloud Crisis: Commission Outlines Response to Tackle the Impact on Air Transport*, EC MEMO/10/152, 20 April 2010, http://europa.eu/rapid/press-release_MEMO-10-152_en.htm, date accessed 28 November 2014.
European Commission (2011) *Volcanic Ash Disruption: One Year On and Crisis Preparedness*, EC MEMO/11/235, 12/04/2011, http://europa.eu/rapid/press-release_MEMO-11-235_en.htm, date accessed 28 November 2014.
Eurocontrol (2010) *Ash Cloud Impact on Air Traffic*, http://www.eurocontrol.int/sites/default/files/article/attachments/201004-ash-impact-on-traffic.pdf, date accessed 01 December 2014.
't Hart, P., E. Stern and B. Sundelius (1997) *Beyond Group Think: Political Group Dynamics and Foreign Policy-making* (Ann Arbor: University of Michigan Press).
Helsloot, I., A. Boin, L. Comfort and B. Jacobs (eds.) (2012) *Mega-Crises* (Springfield, IL: Charles C. Thomas).
Hutter, B. M. and S. Lloyd-Bostock (2013) 'Risk, Interest Groups and the Definition of Crisis: The Case of Volcanic Ash', *The British Journal of Sociology*, 64, 383–404.
Johnson, C. and A. Jeunemaitre (2011) 'The Risk and Role of Scientific Input for Contingency Planning' in A. Alemanno (ed.) *Governing Disasters: The Challenges of Emergency Risk Regulation* (Cheltenham: Edward Elgar), pp. 51–64.
Kahneman, D. (2011) *Thinking Fast, and Slow* (New York: Farrar, Straus and Giroux).
Lawless, C. (2011) 'The Fallout from the Fallout: Hazards, Risks and Organizational Learning' in A. Alemanno (ed.) *Governing Disasters: The Challenges of Emergency Risk Regulation* (Cheltenham: Edward Elgar), pp. 233–245.
Lee, B. and F. Preston (2012) 'Preparing for High-impact, Low-probability Events: Lessons from Eyjafjallajökull', *Chatham House Report*, January 2012.
Macrae, D. (2011) 'Which Risk and Who Decides When There Are So Many Players?' in A. Alemanno (ed.) *Governing Disasters: The Challenges of Emergency Risk Regulation* (Cheltenham: Edward Elgar), pp. 13–24.
Nohrstedt, D. (2013) 'Advocacy Coalitions in Crisis Resolution: Understanding Policy Dispute in the European Volcanic Ash Crisis', *Public Administration*, 91, 964–979.
OECD (2003) *Emerging Risks in the Twenty-First Century: An Agenda for Action* (Paris: Organization for Economic Cooperation and Development).
OECD (2011) *Future Global Shocks: Improving Risk Governance* (Paris: Organization for Economic Cooperation and Development).
O'Regan, M. (2011) 'On the Edge of Chaos: European Aviation and Disrupted Mobilities', *Mobilities*, 6, 21–30.

Parker, C. F. (2015) 'Complex Negative Events and the Diffusion of Crisis: Lessons from the 2010 and 2011 Icelandic Volcanic Ash Cloud Events', *Geografiska Annaler: Series A, Physical Geography*, 97, 97–108.

Perrow, C. (1984) *Normal Accidents: Living with High Risk Technologies* (New York: Basic Books).

Preston, T. and P. 't Hart (1999) 'Understanding and Evaluating Bureaucratic Politics: The Nexus between Political Leaders and Advisory Systems', *Political Psychology*, 20, 49–98.

Reason, J. (2008) *The Human Contribution: Unsafe Acts, Accidents and Heroic Recoveries* (Farnham: Ashgate).

Rodriguez, H., E. L. Quarantelli and R. Dynes (eds.) (2006) *Handbook of Disaster Research* (New York: Springer).

Rosenthal, U., A. Boin and L. K. Comfort (eds.) (2001) *Managing Crises: Threats, Dilemmas, Opportunities* (Springfield: CC Thomas).

Rosenthal, U., M. Charles and P. 't Hart (eds.) (1989) *Coping With Crises: The Management of Disasters, Riots and Terrorism* (Springfield, IL: Charles C. Thomas).

Rosenthal, U., P. 't Hart, and A. Kouzmin (1991) 'The Bureau-Politics of Crisis Management', *Public Administration*, 69, 211–233.

Sawer, P. and R. Mendick (2011) 'Volcanic Ash Cloud: Test Flights Raise Hope for European Air Traffic', *Telegraph*, 18 April 2010, http://www.telegraph.co.uk/travel/travelnews/7603908/Volcanic-ash-cloud-test-flights-raise-hope-for-European-air-traffic.html, date accessed 28 November 2014.

Taleb, N. N. (2007) *Black Swan: The Impact of the Highly Improbable* (New York: Penguin Books).

Tindall, K. (2010) *Sense Making and Sense Giving during the April 2010 Volcanic Ash Crisis*, Research Paper, Department of Psychology, Australian National University.

Turner, B. (1978) *Man-Made Disasters* (London: Wykeham).

Vertzberger, Y. (1990) *The World in Their Minds: Information Processing, Cognition and Perception in Foreign Policy Making* (Stanford: Stanford University Press).

Weick, K. (1995) *Sense Making in Organizations* (Thousand Oaks, CA: Sage).

10
The EU as a Regulator of Civil Security across Europe[1]

Han Dorussen, Evangelos Fanoulis and Emil Kirchner

Introduction

The emergence of civil security governance as a transnational policy area in the European Union (EU) remains contested, and it is undisputed that the national governments of the member states still have a central role in protecting citizens and the environment against natural disasters and man-made threats (Monar, 2010; Boin et al., 2013). However, the EU and the member states define civil security broadly, bringing it under the remit of a large number of EU institutions. Accordingly, civil security remains a hybrid policy area drawing on both the Area of Freedom Security and Justice (AFSJ) and the field of Civil Protection (CP). Natural disasters (including infectious diseases) and transportation and industrial accidents have traditionally fallen under CP (Article 196 of the Treaty on the Functioning of the European Union, TFEU) (Ekengren, 2008; Matzén, 2008; Boin et al., 2013). Terrorism (including critical infrastructure failures caused by cyber attacks) is in the domain of Justice and Home Affairs (JHA, Article 74 of TFEU) (Bossong, 2008; Argomaniz, 2009; Kaunert, 2010). EU civil security is also closely related to the Solidarity Clause in the Lisbon Treaty (Article 222 of TFEU) and the EU Internal Security Strategy (EU ISS), which aims at a comprehensive approach to EU internal security (Council of the European Union, 2010). As also argued by Bossong and Hegemann in the introduction, civil security governance is a hybrid cross-cutting field that includes civil protection in a classic sense but also covers other kinds of risk management. Accordingly, we define civil security more broadly than civil protection to encompass crisis management against natural disasters, public health dangers (for example, pandemics), transport accidents, industrial accidents, critical infrastructure failures and also terrorist attacks (including cyber attacks and CBRN offences).[2]

Accordingly, multiple EU institutions and provisions concern themselves with the delivery of civil security. Traditionally most attention has been given to the EU Civil Protection Mechanism and the Emergency Response Coordination Centre (ERCC), operating within the context of the European Commission's DG ECHO, and to the EU Integrated Political Crisis Response arrangements (IPCR) that stay with the Council of the European Union. The intergovernmental nature of both arrangements has been emphasized in the literature. Yet, the Civil Protection Mechanism (CPM) and the AFSJ only cover part of the EU civil security policies. Internally, DG SANCO provides the Commission with important authority regarding food safety and public and consumer health, while the Commission can intervene in external crises of civil security nature by means of humanitarian aid (DG ECHO) and development aid (DG DEVCO). In these areas, it is possible to identify instances where the Commission has the authority to set a common policy and even to regulate policies in the member states (Kirchner et al., 2014).[3] A complete analysis of the EU role in civil security governance therefore needs to encompass a broad spectrum of crises, not only because civil security is a cross-cutting hybrid field, but also to consider the full set of institutions involved in providing civil security. Therefore, our analysis includes crises ranging from public health to environmental protection in order to recognize the network of actors (public and private at the EU, national government and regional level) involved in civil protection.

Several studies emphasize the role of transgovernmental networks in civil security governance (Hollis, 2010; Boin et al., 2013; Ekengren, in this volume). The value of such explanations is that they recognize the multiple actors involved in civil security governance and the limits of sovereignty both at the national and supranational level. A concern is, however, that they portray the process as rather 'ad hoc', responding to particular crisis events, and non-political, driven by efficiency and effectiveness (see also Ehrhart et al., 2014). The argument seems also contradictory; on the one hand, national governments are assumed to jealously guard their sovereignty because civil security is seen as their core responsibility, but simultaneously they 'outsource' the responsibility to transgovernmental networks involuntarily creating security governance at the EU level. For example, Boin et al. (2008) describe the emergence of EU civil security as a nearly autonomous process: 'the emergence of new threats has compelled the member states to delegate new security responsibility to the EU almost against their own will' (Boin et al., 2008, p. 26).

In contrast, we argue that a crucial insight of civil security governance is that political agency matters. The actions of the European Commission and the various committees and agencies are best understood as bureaucratic politics (see also Rhinard and Boin, 2009; Zwolski, 2014).[4] In particular, we explore two arguments. First, the nature of the crisis – whether it is internal, transboundary or external, or whether it is extremely severe or significant ('signature crises') – should matter less than the political opportunities that a crisis creates. In the context of the EU, it should matter particularly whether (the handling of) the crisis affects core EU policies. Secondly, although the expertise of national and supranational agencies provides them with an important source of power, other sources of power (hierarchy, status and funding) in the relations among the European Commission, the member states and the agencies cannot be ignored. To substantiate these claims, we consider a broad set of crises and institutions and we trace the process by which the EU and agencies have acquired a regulatory role.

The next section derives the key hypothesis about the importance of comitology in defining an EU regulatory role in civil security governance from a principal-agent perspective. Subsequently, we analyse agency slack within the context of six civil security crises and conclude with an evaluation of our central hypothesis. In short, the analysis below aims at unpacking the black box of EU regulation in civil security. Moreover, in this chapter, regulation is not restricted to the legal capacity to impose supranational legislation by means of Community regulations. Rather, it has a broader meaning, namely to demonstrate how EU institutions, committees and agencies participate and play a crucial role in coping with civil crises situations and the formation of EU secondary legislation.

Expanding the role of the EU in civil security

The key question to consider is how crises in civil security have promoted EU-wide standards in civil protection and EU authoritative actions? We are particularly interested in identifying the deliberative initiatives of political actors as part of EU civil security governance.[5] Principal-agent(s) models provide a useful conceptual framework (Hawkins et al., 2006; Gilligan and Johns, 2012). In our application of this framework, the principals are ultimately European citizens and, more directly and depending on the context, the governments of the member states. Their objectives are to maximize the level of civil protection, and especially for national governments to maintain their autonomy. The agents are the European Commission and the various EU agencies and committees. They aim to maximize their role in the delivery of civil security. Crucially, the principals and agents do not necessarily agree on the precise content of civil security policies. Agency slack is the core idea of a principal-agent model. Simply put, principals rely (at least in part) on agents to implement policies, but the agents may use their autonomy to advance their own agenda. Principal-agent theory thus aims to identify the conditions under which principals delegate authority to agents, and relatedly the conditions under which the agents are able to implement policies they prefer rather than the principals.

The existence of agency slack is important to understand bureaucratic politics. In the context of EU politics, member states have delegated regulatory powers to the European Commission around the core policy area of the internal market. Rhinard and Boin (2009, p. 8) also observe that even though in the EU the division between national and supranational policy levels is 'continuously evolving and often bitterly contested', '[i]ssues such as competition policy and agricultural management are recognized as supranational competences'. The European Commission thus has maximum agency slack in relationship to this policy area and increased authority whenever the rules of the internal market are somehow endangered. Civil security impinges to varying degrees on the functioning of the internal market, and the Commission and the various agencies can maximize their autonomy and influence over the member states by linking civil security to the freedom of movement of goods, services, capital and people (Christiansen and Dobbels, 2012). The testable hypothesis becomes that *EU agencies and committees will develop more regulatory capacity if the crisis is more closely related to the functioning of the EU internal market.*

EU comitology and civil security

Acknowledging that civil security governance is a hybrid field where actors often work within transnational networks, it becomes particularly important to carefully identify the key actors and their roles across a broad spectrum of crises. Over the last 20 years, a number of EU committees and agencies have been particularly active in policy areas related to civil security. These committees and agencies are part of the EU system of comitology centred on civil security.[6] Table 10.1 identifies the relevant policy areas and the respective committees and agencies.

Table 10.1 EU committees and agencies active on civil security matters

Policy area	EU committees/agencies
Animal health and food safety	• Standing Veterinary Committee (later Standing Committee on Food Chain and Animal Health) • (multiple) Advisory Scientific Committees (later European Food Safety Authority) • Consumers, Health and Food Executive Agency (previous Executive Agency for Health and Consumers)
Transport and infrastructure	• European Aviation Safety Agency • European Aviation Crisis Coordination Cell • European Maritime Safety Agency • Water Information System for Europe • European Environment Agency
Environmental protection	• European Environment Agency • European Maritime Safety Agency
Public health	• Health Security Committee • European Centre for Disease Prevention and Control • European Medicines Agency • Standing Veterinary Committee (later Standing Committee on Food Chain and Animal Health)
Justice and home affairs	• Standing Committee on Operational Cooperation on Internal Security (COSI) • Europol • Eurojust • European Network and Information Security Agency • EU Agency for Large-scale IT Systems • European Monitoring Centre for Drugs and Drug Addiction

Source: Research conducted by the authors in the frame of the ANVIL project.

Interestingly, some committees and agencies have multiple roles and hence their mandate benefits more than one policy areas.

Further, Europe faced a number of severe often transboundary civil security crises in the period 1990–2010. For us it is particularly relevant that they not only led to an emergency response on behalf of national competent authorities but also motivated EU involvement. In other words, from an EU perspective, they can be considered to be signature crises, where the involvement of EU institutions (in particular of

Table 10.2 Signature crises in Europe (1990–2010)

Crisis	Year(s)
BSE/mad cow disease	1996–1997
Foot-and-mouth disease	2001–2002
Danube river flooding	2002
Avian flu (H5N1) pandemic	2004–2007
Swine flu (H1N1) pandemic	2009
Irish oil spill	2009
(Icelandic) volcanic ash cloud	2010

Source: Research conducted by the authors in the frame of ANVIL projects.

EU committees and agencies) was necessitated by the occurrence of the crisis. This EU involvement solidified in EU secondary legislation that extended the authority of the EU committees and agencies that had been initially considered essential for the management of the crises. The preparation of the EU secondary legislation drew upon advice, meetings, proceedings, studies, surveys, opinions, statements of these EU committees and agencies, and in some cases even depended on their approval. Table 10.2 lists the most representative signature civil security crises in Europe between 1990 and 2010.[7]

The empirical analysis of the next section follows a simple methodology. Drawing upon Tables 10.1 and 10.2, we selected signature crises in Europe with a confirmed involvement in their management of at least one EU committee or agency. This allowed us to reduce the amount of available qualitative data, leaving a sample of six crises where we could trace the engagement of EU committees and agencies over time. By means of qualitative process tracing, we investigate the response of EU committees and agencies to these crises. We focus on the incidents and events in which EU committees and agencies played an explicit role in the formation of secondary legislation. The objective is to see whether and how the capacities of EU committees and agencies evolved over time and to what extent the policy area matters for this evolution. In particular, we test whether agency slack explains how EU agencies and committees have developed more regulatory capacity in crises that more closely affect the functioning of the EU internal market.

BSE/mad cow disease (1996–1997)

The mad cow disease (Bovine Spongiform Encephalopathy, BSE) preoccupied the EU and its member states for most of the 1990s. The crisis was linked to the areas of food safety, public and consumer health, animal health and the functioning of the internal market. It had a great impact on the UK economy and signified a time of turbulence in the relations of the UK with the EU institutions and some member states. As shown below, the crisis was particularly relevant for increasing the importance of two types of EU committees in civil protection, namely the Standing Veterinary Committee (regulatory committee) and the scientific committees related to animal health and food safety (advisory committees).

Concerns about BSE outbreaks in the UK dated back to late 1980s, with the EU adopting supranational legislation to temporarily forbid beef imports from the UK. This was followed by a period of EU inertia for the first half of 1990s, because the UK government resisted controls by EU inspectors. It submitted national studies that supposedly confirmed the safety of British beef and argued that the control of bovine products in the UK remained a domestic responsibility. Grönvall (2000) notices that the lack of EU controls in the UK may also have been due to the very limited number of EU inspectors qualified for such veterinary controls. In the European Parliament (EP), members of the European Parliament (MEPs) kept raising the issue by means of posing related questions to the EU Commission during most of early 1990s (Grönvall, 2000, pp. 34–36).

In 1996, with clear involvement of a number of committees and agencies, the EU Commission decided an overall embargo on beef imports from the UK. Following unilateral bans by a large number of member states on beef imports from the UK, the Commission asked from the Scientific Veterinary Committee (ScVC) – an advisory committee consisting of independent experts – to convene and discuss the matter in March 1996. The issue was subsequently discussed in the Standing Veterinary Committee (SVC) – a regulatory committee manned with member states' representatives with scientific expertise – and it accepted a proposal by the Commission to ban British beef from the internal market. In the meantime, in a move applauded by the EP, the Commission had adopted emergency measures. In fact, in March 1996 legislative drafts went back and forth between the Commission and the ScVC, which provided the necessary expertise for a draft proposal, and the SVC, which had a clear regulatory capacity and represented the voice of the member states.

Between April and June 1996, there were a number of significant meetings of EU committees. The Chief Medical Officers (CMO), a health-related committee constituted by national representatives of the member states, met with the SVC to ensure coordination of restrictive measures. The Scientific Food Committee, the Scientific Committee for

Cosmetics and the ScVC – all of them advisory expert committees and affiliated with the EU Commission – met and discussed particular concerns about gelatine from British beef. These meetings resulted in a Commission proposal on gelatine, forwarded in May 1996 to the SVC. To showing discontent with the Commission's decision to stop the circulation of British gelatine, the UK blocked at the same time decisions in the EU Civil Protection Council. The SVC eventually approved an emergency response plan on eradicating BSE from the UK, confirming once more the regulatory responsibility of the SVC, and corresponding decision of the Commission was passed.

In 1996 and 1997, the EP created a scrutiny committee to check whether the EU Commission and the member states had promptly reacted to the crisis. The EP's Committee of Inquiry into BSE concluded that the Commission had complied with most of the EP recommendations asking for more transparency in the workings of the advisory scientific committees. Subsequently, the Commission took two important actions. First, the number of relevant scientific committees was expanded from six to eight in order to provide more focused expertise. Secondly, the scientific committees on food safety and animal health merged into an umbrella committee, the Scientific Steering Committee, promising stronger independent expertise. The Steering Committee has the responsibility to alert the Commission about the emergence of consumer health issues, showing certain level of independence of action.

The BSE crisis led to further restructuring of the committees on consumer and animal health and food safety. In January 2002, the European Food Safety Authority (EFSA) was created. The EFSA temporarily absorbed the Scientific Steering Committee, which ceased to exist from April 2003, and took on board the scientific committees with expertise on food, feed and animal/plant health. EFSA has recruited a large number of scientific experts and closely collaborates with the national authorities of the member states. Whereas previously scientific committees had been largely dependent on the Commission for their activation, EFSA is an EU Agency with more autonomy, and not only the Commission but also the EP and the member states can request its opinion. Further, with the regulation 178/2002 the EU established a Rapid Alert System on Food Safety, a transnational information and early warning network, in which EFSA participates. According to the same regulation, the Agency participates in any ad hoc crisis units set up by the Commission in response to food crises, giving it an important advisory and technical role during crises.

As the BSE crisis evolved, the EU was increasingly engaged in the emergency response and contributed to the containment of the disease. The EU could play an important role because the BSE crisis directly affected EU agricultural policies as well as the functioning of the internal market. It was essential that contaminated British products stopped being circulated in order to protect public health. At the same time, national and uncoordinated efforts to this effect undermined the integrity of the single market. The BSE crisis shows firstly how dependent the European Commission but also the national authorities are upon the concentrated scientific expertise that the EU advisory committees bear; secondly, how authoritative a voice EU regulatory committees can have during a crisis that threatens the single market; and thirdly, how essential a role both types of EU committees and agencies (advisory, regulatory) play in the production of EU secondary legislation. The EU advisory committees did not only provide scientific expertise in the form of an epistemic community (Haas, 1992), but also acted as agents or even interest groups acting as main drivers for spillover promoting a supranational approach to decision-making in their specific area of expertise (Haas, 1964; Majone, 2000).

Foot-and-mouth disease (2001–2002)

Having still fresh the lessons learnt from the BSE crisis, the EU experienced in early 2000s yet another crisis related to animal health. The foot-and-mouth-disease (FMD) crisis not only had an impact on animal health, but also serious consequences for affected farmers and the functioning of the internal market. Once more EU committees were strongly involved in the emergency response. In February 2001, the UK alerted the EU Commission about animals infected with FMD. The Commission informed all other member states and imposed a temporary ban on the mobility of cattle in affected areas. Capitalizing on national scientific expertise and its proximity to the member states, the SVC gave its opinion about an ensuing Commission decision to prolong the ban and about the circulation of 'germinal products'.

In March, the SVC issued further opinions which informed Commission decisions on banning firstly the mobility of cattle in the UK and in France (where cases of FMD had now been found), and secondly the circulation of 'germinal products'. In the same month, the Netherlands and Ireland reported cases of FMD. The SVC issued respective opinions, allowing the EU Commission to prohibit transportation of cattle in these countries as well. The SVC met several times during March and

April 2001 to discuss the Dutch request first for suppressive vaccination and then for protective vaccination of animals, the extension of Commission decisions limiting the mobility of animals, and the UK's request for protective vaccination. In all cases, SVC opinions informed respective Commission decisions, pointing to the regulatory capacity of the SVC. On 10 April 2001, the SVC proposed to allow the consumption of Dutch meat. Yet in mid-April, new cases were reported in the Netherlands and the UK, leading to new Commission decisions. The latter were taken in haste and therefore without previous advice from the SVC.

The crisis started to wane in May 2001 with again an important role for the SVC, because it met to discuss the relaxation of measures. The ensuing Commission decisions certified the de-escalation of crisis, proving the significance of SVC meetings, proceedings and opinions. In the period June–September 2001, the SVC issued opinions about the 'traceability and dispatch of meat' and about methods to compensate farmers for economic losses because of the destruction of cattle. Further, the SVC discussed allowing meat exports from the UK but also the continuation of 'movement restrictions of FMD-susceptible species in the EU'. In October 2001, the SVC issued opinions on allowing the gradual circulation of fresh pork and beef in the UK and on the exports of lamb and goat meat from the UK. The Commission respected all of the SVC's recommendations while drafting corresponding decisions. Finally, in February 2002 the SVC suggested to amend and repeal some of the existing Commission decisions. Clearly indicating the regulatory capacity of the SVC, the Commission once more accepted the opinion of the SVC.

From the perspective of principal-agent models it is noteworthy that the foot-and-mouth crisis prompted two institutional innovations that clarified and enhanced the role of committees in responding to animal health crises. As in the case of BSE crisis also during the foot-and-mouth crisis, the EP held meetings and hearings to scrutinize the reactions of EU institutions and member states to the crisis. For this purpose, the EP established the EP Temporary Committee on FMD that judged the Commission's reaction to the crisis as appropriate (European Parliament, 2002). Moreover, following the crisis, the SVC was redefined as Standing Committee on Food Chain and Animal Health (SCFCAH), giving it a much more precise mandate. One of the first actions of the SCFCAH was to provide an opinion and amend an existing Commission decision hence prolonging precautionary measures against FMD until the end of 2002.

Avian influenza (2004–2007)

The EU responded to the avian influenza (or H5N1), which was an animal and public health crisis of global dimensions. The first case of H5N1 was diagnosed in the Republic of South Korea in December 2003. In 2003, the EU Commission closely followed H5N1, but got alarmed in early 2004. In January and February the SCFCAH, established following the FMD, met to discuss the spread of H5N1 in South East Asia and agreed to propose to the EU Commission to forbid imports of birds (everything but poultry) from South East Asia. The SCFCAH also took the initiative to propose new supranational legislation. The decision of the EU Commission to accept the proposal highlights the regulatory capacity of the SCFCAH. Following the spread of H5N1 in North America in March and April 2004, the SCFCAH discussed the suspension of bird imports from the USA. In this case, the EU Commission asked for milder measures, to which the SCFCAH eventually agreed.

The Commission mostly concerned itself with coordinating member states' responses to the escalation of the avian flu in South East Asia in 2005. It asked the member states to provide information about any national plans for dealing with H5N1, and the opinion of EFSA on avian influenza and food safety. In October 2005 the Commission, the WHO and the newly established European Centre for Disease Prevention and Control (ECDC) jointly organized an expert conference on pandemic preparedness. In the meantime, suspicious cases were traced in North Italy, Romania (and later in Bulgaria); the Commission sent an expert team to Romania, keeping the SCFCAH informed. All this scientific activity informed a resultant Council directive for measures controlling further spread of the disease (Council, 2005). When in 2006 cases of contaminated birds increased across Europe, the *Health Security Committee* (HSC), consisting of national representatives, EU Administrators from DG SANCO and other Commission DGs and experts from the ECDC and the newly minted European Medicines Agency (EMA) held another extraordinary meeting.[8] At the meeting, the member states renewed their commitment to exchange information about the development of the avian flu and about measures taken. The Commission prepared a directive for the migration of wild birds and potential dangers due to avian influenza and communicated a draft Commission decision to be discussed by SCFCAH in June 2006. In late 2006, the Commission suggested preventive vaccination to zoo birds; the Directorate General Environment of the European Commission (DG ENVI) met with SCFCAH in order to review bird surveillance measures and to discuss bio-security. The role of EU committees and agencies in the crisis management of avian flu remained substantial in 2007, the last year of the crisis. The SCFCAH would constantly meet and exchange scientific views. It worked on opinions for draft Commission decisions and consented to Commission decisions on response measures.

Spring 2004 was a pivotal moment for the EU agencies related to public health. Coinciding with the beginning of the avian flu crisis, the EU institutions and member states revised the mandate of the European Agency for the Medicinal Products, now renamed EMA. EMA became a centre of scientific expertise, giving opinions on marketing authorizations for medicinal products for humans and animals. Showing the regulatory nature of the Agency, requests for marketing authorizations are directly submitted to the EMA.[9] The EU also established the ECDC, which became fully operational in 2005. The ECDC offers independent scientific advice and assessment on communicable diseases and their threat to human health. This points to an advisory, facilitating responsibility. However, in the case of an unknown disease 'the Centre shall act on its own initiative until the source of the outbreak is known' (European Parliament and Council, 2004). Further, the member states are obliged to provide the ECDC with data on contaminations and spread of diseases and the Centre advises the Commission about which type of medicinal research is mostly salient and hence needs to be prioritized. The ECDC thus has a clear leverage in the domain of public health with a mandate that gives it a regulatory rather than a mere facilitating role. In addition, the ECDC manages the Early Warning and Response System (EWRS) and, related to the avian flu crisis, coordinates the European Influenza Surveillance Network (EISN). In 2013, the EU decided to give full responsibility to the ECDC on issues of surveillance of public health (European Parliament and Council, 2013). To summarise, the avian flu crisis contributed to the institutionalization of the EU capacity to deal with public health crises and simultaneously upgraded the role of EU committees and agencies from coordinating to potentially regulatory. As observed similarly for the veterinary crises, the EU advisory committees did not only provide scientific expertise, but also positioned themselves as primary actors within a supranational approach to decision-making in their specific area of expertise.

Swine flu (2009)

In 2009, the EU and the member states had to confront yet another crisis related to public health, the swine flu caused by a virus known as H1N1. Unlike the avian flu that mainly contaminated animals, the swine flu also infected humans, putting the EU Commission immediately on high alert. The ECDC published a report on the state-of-art of H1N1 in Europe, asking supranational and national competent authorities to stay vigilant. A joint meeting of the HSC and EWRS was held to appreciate the situation. In May, the Council of Ministers issued conclusions on H1N1 and adopted a common case definition. At the same time, EMA published guidelines on the use of antivirals. In June, the ECDC surveyed to options available to fight H1N1 and proposed mitigation and delaying strategies. Subsequently, the Council of Ministers mandated the HSC to discuss vaccination strategies. In addition, the HSC took over the overall coordination of measures against the swine flu in the EU and operated as an information platform for health workers and citizens, constantly monitoring the spread of the disease. The sequence of actions shows the important capacity of EU committees and agencies in civil crisis management: the ECDC offered the scientific evidence upon which the Council based its eventual decision to ask from the HSC to consider different counter-measures. In the same month H1N1 was declared a pandemic, enabling EMA to initiate a pandemic crisis management plan. The latter depicts the Agency's own actions for monitoring the spread of a pandemic as well as the acceleration procedure for authorizing vaccines for the member states (EMA undated).

Throughout the crisis cycle, the advisory and technical assistance of ECDC was crucial. For example, in July 2009 it released a 'third pandemic risk assessment', while a joint HSC/EWRS meeting was responsible to review national measures against the spread of H1N1. In August 2009, the ECDC announced the gradual de-escalation of the pandemic and in the framework of lessons learnt issued a report on the difficulties that surveillance of public health faced. The HSC and the EWRS published a series of statements on school closures and on travel advice, whereas their joint meeting issued the common statement 'vaccination strategies: target and priority groups'. Finally, the Commission adopted a 'strategy paper on pandemic H1N1' in September 2009. Interestingly, the swine flu crisis did not prompt any further institutional innovations, but instead the EU member states and the Commission applied the institutions that had been put in place in earlier health crises in a functionalist way. At the same time, committees, such as the HSC and the ECDC, took a central role in the supranational management of the crisis and contributed to secondary EU regulation.

Irish oil spill (2009)

In February 2009, the leakage of the Russian aircraft carrier Admiral Kuztsenov in the waters between Ireland and the UK caused a brief crisis (Office of Emergency Planning, 2012). Even though relatively small in scope, the crisis mobilized the Irish and British Coast guards and involved diplomatic communications between the Irish government and the Russian Republic. For these reasons and because the EU got involved as well, it can be considered as a signature crisis in the areas of maritime safety in Europe and environmental protection.

The European Maritime Safety Agency (EMSA) played a significant role in the management of the Irish oil spill. CleanSeaNet, the Satellite Oil Spill and Monitoring Service managed by EMSA, had detected the oil spill close to the Irish West Cork coast, prompting EMSA to inform the Irish authorities.[10] The Irish government timely activated the EU Civil Protection Mechanism, and as the spill expanded, it asked EMSA for assistance. Via the EU Civil Protection Mechanism, EMSA made available a cleaning vessel while it kept monitoring the movement of the oil spill. As the spill dispersed quickly, the Irish government did not have to make use of the cleaning vessel.

Instead of prompting institutional innovation, the oil spill allowed the EU and affected member states to make use of an existing agency. EMSA had been created in 2002 (regulation 1406/2002) with a clear mandate in the field of maritime safety and the prevention of maritime pollution from shipping. EMSA experts pay regular visits to the various member states to check compliance with the 'Community port State control regime'. EMSA experts work closely with the member states but report back to the Commission. EMSA also advises the Commission on the EU's standing in the different relevant international fora (Article 2 of the Regulation). In 2004 the mandate of EMSA was reinforced (regulation 724/2004), when EMSA was allowed to possess the means for taking action in maritime safety. More precisely, apart from maintaining expert teams and managing the CleanSeaNet service, EMSA was now also authorized to recruit cleaning vessels in case of an environmental crisis on sea. The Irish oil spill in effect allowed the agency to implement these newly acquired powers.

Volcanic ash cloud (2010)

Between April and June 2010, the European aviation was paralysed by the eruption of Iceland's Eyjafjallajökull volcano. The resulting ash cloud had a great impact on aviation safety, transport and the functioning of the internal market. The International Civil Aviation Organization (ICAO), the EU institutions and various European governments got involved in the response to the crisis (see also Kuipers and Boin, in this volume). The European Commission was quickly informed about the increased volcanic activity in Iceland and the contingency of escalation. Two organizations proved to be particularly germane. Firstly, the European Organization for the Safety of Air Navigation (Eurocontrol) was monitoring the spread and movement of the volcanic ash cloud and was informing its country members. Eurocontrol is a regional intergovernmental organization whose membership also includes the EU. Secondly, the European Aviation Safety Agency (EASA) provided the EU institutions with the scientific expertise and necessary technical assistance informing the overall response of the EU to the volcanic ash cloud crisis. EASA is an independent EU Agency constituted by representatives from the member states and the Commission.

The authority and capabilities of EASA evolved significantly during the volcanic ash cloud crisis. At the beginning of the crisis, EASA focused on technical issues, for example, certifying that airplanes were able to fly given low levels of volcanic ash in the air.[11] When a number of member states suspended flights, the Council of the EU held an extraordinary meeting on 19 April 2009, asking from the EU Commission and Eurocontrol to work on a 'coordinated European response' to the crisis. Based on the scientific expertise of EASA, the Commission presented measures to the Council of the EU in mid-May 2009. The latter included among others the adoption of a common European methodology on evaluating the risks from closing and re-opening airspaces and the creation of a crisis coordination cell. EASA's competences were also revised and increased in matters of monitoring airspace and providing technical assistance on air safety. The fact that the Council agreed upon the Commission's suggestion to reinforce EASA is a telling example of how the progress of a crisis can increase the authority of an EU committee/agency.

The cooperation of EASA with the European member states can be characterized as 'gently pushing'. During the volcanic ash cloud crisis, EASA would work closely with national 'aircraft operators, owners, and maintenance organizations' for the safety of flights, issuing both recommendations and requests. For example, the Agency recommended that the European countries respect the Volcanic Ash Safety Risk Assessments of each other and requested the feedback of the EU member states on the implementation of the safety recommendations issued by EASA (EASA, 2010).

The Commission had created an ad hoc working group from the start of the volcanic ash cloud crisis. However, in May 2009, a permanent committee was formulated following the decision of the Council of the EU. Comparable to a crisis task force, the European Aviation Crisis Coordination Cell (EACCC) brings together representatives from different institutions (the Presidency of the Council of the EU, the Commission, EASA, Eurocontrol and other air navigation stakeholders) for the sake of effective crisis management.

By late May 2009, the volcanic ash cloud crisis had largely passed. Nevertheless, the EASA capitalized on lessons learnt from the crisis to increase its competence in aviation safety both towards the EU institutions as well as the member states. EASA presented an action plan to the EU Commission on new technical standards that aircrafts should meet in order to deal safely with volcanic ash incidents. The Commission acknowledged that EASA's technical involvement is necessary when the Commission consults with ICAO. As a significant development, the EASA presented the Commission with two opinions – EASA Opinions 02/2010 and 03/2010 – for regulations related to aviation safety. The Commission based future draft legislation upon these opinions. In the aftermath of the volcanic ash cloud crisis, the EASA succeeded in becoming a crucial executive voice in air navigation.

Conclusion and discussion

As the six cases demonstrate, EU committees and agencies succeeded in enhancing their authority and responsibilities during times of crisis. As also noted by Rhinard and Boin (2009, p. 3) bureaucratic politics continues during crisis episodes, and 'government officials and public agencies may become more concerned about their authority and prestige in the face of crisis'. Tracing developments during crises, three features of the process stand out. First of all, there is a lot of institutional activity; new agencies and committees are put in place with generally newly formulated mandates, but also existing agencies are consulted by the European Commission, which largely depends upon their expertise for proposing implementing decisions are 'put to the test'. Secondly, agencies and committees take initiative to extend their role and competencies, but are also encouraged to do so by supranational institutions, in particular the EU Commission and the Council. The EU institutions behave like this because they understand a renewed, more focused mandate of EU committees and agencies as more robust scientific expertise and by extension as more efficient policy- and decision-making. Finally, even though agencies and committees represent national expertise, they insist on their technical independence as a path for providing effective opinions for EU secondary legislation. The just described conduct, either of the EU institutions or of the EU committees and agencies, reinforces our argument about the agency slack of the latter.

The nature of the committee or agency and its area of expertise matters to some extent. Committees and agencies of *advisory* nature (the scientific committees related to animal health developing into EFSA after the BSE and FMD crises or the EMSA) play a quintessential role during emergency response. Their expertise and technical assistance enable the EU Commission to take urgent executive measures or submit draft legislation to the member states (via the Council of the EU) and the EP. For example, Christiansen and Polak (2009, p. 9) demonstrate how dependent the European Commission is upon the expertise of EFSA for the circulation of genetically modified organisms (GMOs) in the internal market, an issue that also closely relates to food safety, reaching the point to argue that '[...] in practice the Commission's decisions have largely confirmed the opinions given by the EFSA. This suggests that not the Commission, but rather EFSA itself may in a sense be seen as the de facto risk manager'. Committees and agencies of *regulatory* nature – the SVC, the Chief Medical Officers and even the EMA – rather represent national (member states) interests and expertise. Both advisory and regulatory committees can be treated as agents, but the Commission (and to a lesser degree the EP) are the immediate principals of advisory committees, whereas the member states (and the Council of the EU) are more immediate principals of regulatory committees. However, in times of crisis, regulatory committees are the first to liaise with the European Commission in the preparation of secondary EU legislation. In principal-agent theory terms, the European Commission appears to be the main principal, having both the right to information – flowing from the EU committees and agencies – and the institutional power to propose EU secondary legislation and control its progress, hence maintaining a gatekeeping function in face of civil security crises with a clear linkage to internal market.

Regulatory committees tend to be more powerful than advisory committees, but the strong representation of national interests makes it also more difficult to extend their mandate and authority further. Simply put, regulatory committees are powerful but static. Rebranding occasionally appears the only opportunity for change as illustrated by the renaming of the SVC into the SCFCAH following the BSE crisis. In contrast, in the cases examined above, advisory committees and agencies underwent true metamorphoses. Scientific committees exploited the need for independent, focused and highly specialized expertise. The scientific committees of DG SANCO provide the best example. Following the BSE and FMD crises, they first consolidated into a Scientific Steering Committee and then into the European Food Safety Agency.

The advisory or regulatory nature of the committee or agency is however not the sole factor affecting their evolution. With the exception of the Irish oil spill, all signature crises analysed above directly affected the internal market and the freedom and security of movement (goods, people, and services) in the EU area. By linking the handling of the crises to the Single European Market, the European Commission was able to initiate more authoritative actions (see also Christiansen and Polak, 2009). At the same time, the Commission still had to justify its authoritative action politically to the Council of the EU (that is, the member states) and the EP. Moreover, the Commission had a clear interest to respond quickly and effectively to the emergencies (and definitely was watched carefully by the EP). For both these points, the Commission had good reasons not only to consult with advisory and regulatory committees and agencies, but also to strengthen their authority as manifested by the comparative analysis of the empirical cases above.

Technical expertise and the linkage to common EU policies provide the agencies and committees with a considerable amount of 'agency slack' as their expertise becomes vital to effectively tackle civil security crises by minimising the uncertainty these crises entail. Finally, it also matters whether the agencies and committees are able to seize upon these opportunities to promote their autonomy. Process tracing suggests that bureaucratic politics are indeed relevant; for example, in the wake of the volcanic ash cloud crisis, the EASA did not hesitate to propose to the Commission to revise its mandate. Similarly, the ECDC managed to extend its authorities in public health to the point where it now holds sole responsibility for public health surveillance.

Based on the study conducted above, there is clear evidence that the system of comitology enables the EU to respond more effectively to civil security crises and in a more transgovernmental manner. At the same time, this has come about largely via bureaucratic politics and 'agency slack', raising once more the issue of the democratic legitimacy and transparency of EU committees and agencies; the latter are not elected political actors, therefore unaccountable, which have been endowed with a considerable executive say in the EU policy-making (Bellamy and Castiglione, 2011; Christiansen and Dobbels, 2012). Notably, the

European Parliament has begun to set up committees to scrutinize the unelected political agents in the various agencies and committees (Hix, 2000); for example, the EP's Committee of Inquiry into BSE and Temporary Committee on FMD examined the response of the European Commission and the member states. At the same time, the authority of the EP is not only limited compared to some of the committees. In general, future research may not only have to highlight the authority – justified or not – of EU committees and agencies that operate under the auspices of the European Commission and the Council, but could also take a closer look at the different EP committees.

Notes

1. Research on this article was partly conduced in the project 'Analysis of Civil Security Systems in Europe' (ANVIL). ANVIL was funded under the EU's Seventh Framework Programme, grant no 284678.
2. See also the official definition of the ANVIL project for civil security, http://anvil-project.net/anvil-glossary-of-terms/, date accessed 10 November 2014.
3. Kaunert (2010) and Kaunert and Léonard (2012) argue that the European Commission and, to a lesser extent, the Council Secretariat are policy entrepreneurs in AFSJ.
4. Bureaucratic politics (Downs, 1967; Niskanen, 1971) studies the interaction between units in complex bureaucracies. The emphasis is generally on the competition between units, assuming bureaucrats to be self-interested and status maximizing rather than neutral and efficient implementers of policies. Here our concern is primarily the agency of bureaucracies and less with the possible inefficiency of policy output.
5. The focus on agency does not imply that we hold principal-agent models to be the only explanation for the emerging role of the EU as a regulator. Here, we are mainly interested in exploring the added value of studying agency in the context of EU politics as complementary to alternative explanations, such as functionalism or constructivism.
6. Christiansen and Kirchner (2000) provide a good introduction to the EU system of comitology.
7. The Madrid (2004) and London (2005) bombings are excluded, because we could not find any evidence of the involvement in EU committees and agencies in the response. See Rhinard and Boin (2009) for an assessment of EU bureaucratic politics in the preparation for such crises.
8. National experts were involved throughout the crisis; for example, national influenza coordinators and the MS representatives on the Early Warning and Response System (EWRS) also participated in this meeting, and national delegations of SCFCAH kept informed the rest of the Committee.
9. The EU Commission however decides to grant eventual authorizations (Article 4, regulation 726/2004).
10. See http://www.emsa.europa.eu/news-a-press-centre/press-releases/item/144-emsa-press-releases-archive.html, date accessed 11 November 2014.

11. See https://www.easa.europa.eu/newsroom-and-events/press-releases/volca
nic-ash-%E2%80%93-safety-information-bulletin, date accessed 12 November 2014.

References

Argomaniz, J. (2009) 'Post-9/11 Institutionalisation of European Union Counterterrorism: Emergence, Acceleration and Inertia', *European Security*, 18, 151–172.
Bellamy, R. and D. Castiglione (2011) 'Democracy by Delegation? Who Represents whom and how in European Governance', *Government and Opposition*, 46 (1), 101–125.
Boin, A., M. Ekengren and M. Rhinard (2008) 'Future Crises and Supranational Responses: Towards a New Paradigm for the EU?' in A. Boin, M. Ekengren, and M. Rhinard (eds.), *Security in Transition: Towards a New Paradigm for the European Union* (Stockholm: Swedish National Defence College), pp. 13–38.
Boin, A., M. Ekengren and M. Rhinard (2013) *The European Union as Crisis Manager: Patterns and Prospects* (Cambridge: Cambridge University Press).
Bossong, R. (2008) 'The Action Plan on Combating Terrorism', *Journal of Common Market Studies*, 46, 27–48.
Christiansen, T. and M. Dobbels (2012) 'Comitology and Delegated Acts after Lisbon: How the European Parliament Lost the Implementation Game', *European Integration online Papers (EIoP)*, 16, http://eiop.or.at/eiop/texte/2012-013a.htm, date accessed 18 November 2014.
Christiansen, T. and E. Kirchner (eds.) (2000) *Europe in Change: Committee Governance in the European Union* (Manchester: Manchester University Press).
Christiansen, T. and J. Polak (2009) 'Comitology between Decision Making and Technocratic Governance: Regulating GMOs in the European Union', *EIPASCOPE*, 2009/1, 5–11.
Council of the European Union (2005) Council Directive 2005/94/EC of 20 December 2005 on Community Measures for the Control of Avian Influenza and Repealing Directive 92/40/EEC. *Official Journal of the European Union* L10/16.
Council of the European Union (2010) *The EU Internal Security Strategy in Action: Five Steps towards a More Secure Europe*, Brussels, http://eur-lex.europa.eu/LexUriServ/LexUriServ.do?uri=COM:2010:0673:FIN:EN:PDF#page=2, date accessed 14 November 2014.
Downs, A. (1967) *Inside Bureaucracy* (Boston: Little, Brown and Co.).
Ehrhart, H.-G., H. Hegemann and M. Kahl (2014) 'Towards Security Governance as a Critical Tool: A Conceptual Outline', *European Security*, 23, 145–162.
Ekengren, M. (2008) 'EU Civil Protection: An Ascending Sector' in A. Boin, M. Ekengren and M. Rhinard (eds.) *Security in Transition: Towards a New Paradigm for the European Union* (Stockholm: Swedish National Defence College), pp. 47–62.
EASA (2010) 'Flight in Airspace with Contamination of Volcanic Ash', *EASA Safety Information Bulletin*, No: 2010–17R5, 1–9.
European Medicines Agency, EMA (undated) *Pandemic Influenza*, http://www.ema.europa.eu/ema/index.jsp?curl=pages/special_topics/general/general_content_000267.jsp, date accessed 11 November 2014.

European Parliament (2002) *REPORT on Measures to Control Foot and Mouth Disease in the European Union in 2001 and Future Measures to Prevent and Control Animal Diseases in the European Union* (2002/2153(INI)), Brussels.

European Parliament and Council of the European Union (2004) Regulation (EC) 'No 851/2004 of the European Parliament and the Council of 21 April 2004 Establishing a European Centre for Disease Prevention and Control', *Official Journal of the European Union* L142/1.

European Parliament and Council of the European Union (2013) *Decision of the European Parliament and of the Council of 22 October 2013 on Serious Cross-border Threats to Health and Repealing Decision o 2119/98/EC*, Strasbourg.

Gilligan, M. J. and L. Johns (2012) 'Formal Models of International Institutions', *Annual Review of Political Science*, 15, 221–243.

Grönvall, J. (2000) *Managing Crisis in the European Union: The Commission and 'Mad Cow' Disease* (Stockholm: CRISMART, Swedish National Defence College).

Haas, E. (1964) *Beyond the Nation-state: Functionalism and International Organization* (Stanford: Stanford University Press).

Haas, P. M. (1992) 'Introduction: Epistemic Communities and International Policy Coordination', *International Organization*, 46, 1–35.

Hawkins, D., D. Lake, D. Nielson and M. Tierney (eds.) (2006) *Delegation and Agency in International Organizations* (Cambridge: Cambridge University Press).

Hix, S. (2000) 'Parliamentary Oversight of Executive Power: What Role for the European Parliament in Comitology?' in T. Christiansen and E. J. Kirchner (eds.) *Committee Governance in the European Union* (Manchester: Manchester University Press), pp. 62–78.

Hollis, S. (2010) 'The Necessity of Protection: Transgovernmental Networks and EU Security Governance', *Cooperation and Conflict*, 45, 312–330.

Kaunert, C. (2010) 'The Area of Freedom, Security and Justice in the Lisbon Treaty: Commission Policy Entrepreneurship?', *European Security*, 19, 169–189.

Kaunert, C. and S. Léonard (2012) 'Introduction: Supranational Governance and European Union Security after the Lisbon Treaty – Exogenous Shocks, Policy Entrepreneurs and 11 September 2001', *Cooperation and Conflict*, 47, 417–432.

Kirchner, E. J., E. Fanoulis and H. Dorussen (2014) 'Civil Security in the EU: National Persistence versus EU Ambitions?', *European Security*, http://dx.doi.org/10.1080/09662839.2014.968133, date accessed 4 December 2014.

Majone, G. (2000) 'The Credibility Crisis of Community Regulation', *Journal of Common Market Studies*, 38, 273–302.

Matzén, N. (2008) 'EU Health Security Sector: An Ascending Sector' in A. Boin, M. Ekengren, and M. Rhinard (eds.) *Security in Transition: Towards a New Paradigm for the European Union* (Stockholm: Swedish National Defence College), pp. 63–78.

Monar, J. (ed.) (2010) *The Institutional Dimension of the European Union's Area of Freedom, Security and Justice* (Brussels: P.I.E. Peter Lang).

Niskanen, W. A. (1971) *Bureaucracy and Representative Government* (Chicago: Aldine-Atherton).

Office of Emergency Planning (2012) *A National Risk Assessment for Ireland*. http://www.emergencyplanning.ie/media/docs/A%20National%20Risk%20 Assessment%20for%20Ireland%20Published.pdf, date accessed 11 November 2014.

Rhinard, M. and A. Boin (2009) 'European Homeland Security: Bureaucratic Politics and Policymaking in the EU', *Journal of Homeland Security and Emergency Management*, 6, 1–19.

Zwolski, K. (2014) 'How to Explain the Transnational Security Governance of the European Union?, *Journal of Common Market Studies*, 52, 942–958.

11
What Can EU Civil Security Governance Learn from the Common Security and Defence Policy and the European Defence Agency?

Magnus Ekengren

Introduction

The EU has since the beginning of the new millennium rapidly expanded its competences and increased the number of assistance interventions in the field of civil protection – a core area of civil security governance (Boin et al., 2013). As a way to strengthen the legal and institutional basis of this development, the EU established an Emergency Response Coordination Centre (ERCC) and adopted a new Union Civil Protection Mechanism and legal framework in 2013 (European Parliament and the Council, 2013). The objective is to support the member states when their capacities are overwhelmed by a crisis. The legal framework establishes a European Emergency Response Capacity (EERC) consisting of 'a voluntary pool of pre-committed response capacities of the member states' and prescribing when these are to be used:

> [t]he Capacity shall be available for response operations...following a request for assistance through the ERCC. The ultimate decision on their deployment shall be taken by the Member States...When domestic emergencies, force majeure or, in exceptional cases, serious reasons prevent a Member State from making capacities available, this member state shall inform the Commission as soon as possible.
> (European Parliament and the Council, 2013: paragraph 7)

The question is whether this new legal basis can overcome the non-binding ad hoc coordination of national resources that has made the EU's civil protection response unpredictable and the EU member states insecure with regard to what kind of EU assistance they can expect in times of crisis (Boin et al., 2006; Ekengren, 2007a; Åhman and Nilsson, 2009; Boin et al., 2013: chapter 2). Will the Union, in addition to being a non-war security community,[1] develop into a *secure community* in which the members are integrated to the point that there is real assurance that they will assist each other in times of crisis and disaster (Ekengren, 2007b)?

Unfortunately, the new legal framework neither solves the question as to what extent the member states are obliged to assist each other nor specifies the kind of resources that they are expected to provide to the 'voluntary pool' of ERCC. In the negotiation of the new civil protection mechanism, many member states for reasons of sovereignty concerns resisted stronger legal commitments, so the issue of under what circumstances and with what resources they are bound to help each other remains.[2] Traditionally, the member states have emphasized the need to respect national sovereignty and the principles of subsidiarity and warned against any EU capacity that does not add value to their own national civil protection capacities. Many member states have been against EU specifications of national provisions because they think civil protection resources need to be as flexible as possible in a situation where future disasters are 'unknown'. This flexibility can, according to most member states, only be safeguarded with a strong autonomy for national authorities to make judgements on the most appropriate means for assistance and what future capacities are needed (European Commission, 2005, p. 11; Friedrich, 2013).

This chapter shows that the challenges of striking a balance between national sovereignty, flexibility and predictable and effective EU capacities are very similar to ones encountered within the Common Security and Defence Policy (CSDP). But it also describes how the CSDP ever since 1998 has been able to reconcile the objectives of building flexible joint capacities and preserving national sovereignty with the help of new methods of coordination and compliance, such as provisional 'EU capacity goals', joint evaluations of member state fulfilment and recurrent revision of the EU objectives. The goal has been to make the member states' capacities converge for more efficient EU cooperation despite the great difficulties of predicting future needs and setting precise political and capacity objectives. This method of coordination has resulted in the creation of EU visions on long-term needs, EU earmarked national military resources and standing joint military capacities as well as a peer pressure induced convergence of national norms in the defence field (Andersson, 2006; Oikonomou, 2012; Cross, 2014; Ekengren, 2015).

The method has been very similar to the so-called 'open method of coordination' – a method also called experimentalist governance, used in many other areas of EU cooperation such as employment and environmental cooperation (Sabel and Zeitlin, 2010). This chapter will use the experiences in the security area as analytical point of reference. The open method of coordination has been suggested as a way to implement the goals of the Solidarity Clause of the Lisbon Treaty (Ekengren, 2006). Bossong has investigated the impact of EU peer reviews, as a central element in experimentalist governance, on the counterterrorism policies of the EU member states (Bossong, 2012). Nance and Cottrell have examined the use of experimentalism in the field of preventing nuclear proliferation (Nance and Cottrell, 2014).

The aim of this chapter is to explore how the EU's capacity building in the field of civil protection can learn from the CSDP experiences. The chapter first reviews these experiences. While there has been some criticism, this chapter gives a rather positive summary of achievements and progress. Second, it describes the evolution of EU policies in civil security governance and identifies central challenges for the development of joint capacities in the field. Finally and on this basis, it then asks what EU civil protection and security governance can learn from the CSDP case.

Common security and defence policy: Experimenting with new modes of governance

The search for new methods of governance

In the same period as the emergence of a field of civil security governance, 1999–2014, the EU has established CSDP and developed military crisis management capacities for external use (Howorth, 2014). The so-called Petersburg tasks were included in the 1999 Amsterdam Treaty (article 17) encompassing peacekeeping, peacemaking and humanitarian and rescue operations. At the beginning of 2015, around 25 military and civilian CSDP missions had been or were being carried out around the globe, ranging from border control in Gaza to peacekeeping missions in the Democratic Republic of Congo and police and military training programmes in Kosovo and Afghanistan and Mali.[3]

Like in the civil protection field, the search for a balance between the EU and the national level that could guarantee effective joint capacities was in CSDP initially hampered by EU member states' fear of losing sovereignty (Hyde-Price, 2012; Dyson and Konstadinides, 2013). It was soon realized, however, that the traditional EU institutions and methods of cooperation would not be enough for creating the military capacities needed. The strong practical requirements for efficient military crisis management and clear chains of command resulted in new EU organs and capacity generating methods (Mattelaer, 2013).

Already at the Saint-Malo meeting in 1998, it was decided that the CSDP needed to develop an autonomous capacity for action backed up by credible military capabilities. In order to create a momentum for the provision of joint resources, new forms of EU cooperation were deemed necessary. The Union established the so-called Helsinki Headline Goals declaring that member states by 2003 must be able to provide for 60,000 troops that could be deployed within 60 days, stay at least one year in the crisis region and be self-sustaining (Shearer, 2000). The specific numbers were calculated in the light of the experiences in Kosovo 1999 and on the basis of estimated requirements for a European force that could operate independently from the US. These objectives, however, were quickly revised in the aftermath of 9/11 and the 2003 Iraq War. The EU saw the need for new types of military operations and extended the list of tasks to disarmament, military advice and assistance, post-conflict stabilization, conflict prevention and the fight against terrorism, including third country cooperation. This list was later included in the 2009 Lisbon Treaty. The next revision was an outcome of the lessons learned from natural disasters and failed states in the early years of the new millennium. To the capacity goals for Kosovo-type and counterterrorism operations were added civil-military and civilian objectives for the management of humanitarian, evacuation and security-sector reform tasks. 'The Civilian Headline Goal 2008' aimed to pool police, rule of law administrators and civil protection resources (Howorth, 2014).

In order to meet the Headline Goal 2010, the EU battle group concept was adopted by the European Council in 2004 (Gowan, 2005; Andersson, 2006). EU battle groups were designed as truly multinational forces (1,500 troops) formed by a 'framework nation' or a multinational coalition of member states, deployable within 5–10 days and able to stay 30–120 days. The background to this were the 'lessons learned' of early CSDP missions, such as that in the Democratic Republic of Congo in 2003 where EU member states experienced the need for quicker availability of forces and transport facilities ('deployability') (Lindström, 2007). The goal was to create multinational standby forces for EU missions ready for use from 2007 onwards. The generation of national force contributions to these forces was guided by three framework objectives that were translated into distinct qualitative and quantitative indicators: 'interoperability', 'deployability' and 'sustainability' (Council of the European Union, 2004). Criteria were also set for 'evaluation and certification'.

National implementation: Plans and benchmarking

The CSDP Headline Goals are implemented by EU capacity guidelines directed at the national administrations and in the form of separate agreements ('Memoranda of Understanding') between member states and their armed forces. Originally, the capacity build-up was organised within 'Military Capability Commitment Conferences' taking place every 12–18 months. In reality, these were only political milestones on work that was going on continuously within each equipment area in specialized committees ('panels' and 'project groups' of national experts) that define the military benchmarks and criteria to be reached by member states in order to fulfil the tasks of the 'scenarios' painted in the Headline Goals. This work is today included in the Capability Development Plans (CDP) aimed at monitoring progress and endorsed by the EU governments on a regular basis. The CDP is developed by the European Defence Agency (EDA)[4] led by a Steering Board of 27 Defence Ministers (meeting around six times per year),[5] the EU Military Committee and the EU Council General Secretariat in a process headed by the EU High Representative for Foreign Affairs and Security Policy (Oikonomou, 2012).

The CDP sets the objectives for the member states' own capabilities planning. The aim is not, in the words of former High Representative Javier Solana, 'to replace national defence plans and programs but to support national decision making' (European Defence Agency, 2008). The plans are developed on the basis of the EDA's 'Long-Term Vision 2025', which defines military priorities and objectives aimed at making member states 'converge towards a more common understanding of military needs in the 21st century' (European Defence Agency, 2008). The CDP is regularly reviewed and updated on the basis of changes made by the Military Committee's capability development priorities, reassessments of the programs conducted by the member states and lessons learned from CSDP operations.

European Defence Agency

By creating EDA in 2004, the EU wanted to avoid a system that allows member states overly broad options in their contributions to the list of capabilities required to achieve the Union's Headline Goals. The feeling was that member states had not provided the capacities deemed most necessary from a European perspective, but rather equipment, sometimes outdated, that they did not need for their national defence. In the EU 'Capability Improvement Chart', published every six months, the progress or shortcomings of hundreds of 'capabilities' are presented. In 2004, the Chart showed that only 7 out of 42 shortfalls could be defined as solved (Biscop, 2005, p. 90). The explicit philosophy of the EDA is to bring together military planners, research, armaments authorities and industry for a comprehensive approach throughout the planning and capacity-building process. The aim is to combine the longer-term planning – that is the 2025 vision – with immediate needs.

The dynamics of the revision and implementation of CSDP framework objectives are the result of a close interaction between EU institutions and the increasingly intensive networks of lower levels of national administrations fostered by the system of specialized capacity committees and the EDA's work. In the words of a senior official at the EDA:

> The agency works with a balance of top-down pressure and bottom-up experts work – both are needed to move forward. Therefore, the personal involvement of ministers of defence is essential. They sit in EDA's Steering Board. But without the input from experts (bottom-up) it would never work. EDA operates directly with experts in capitals, through meetings but also through electronic communication tools. These expert networks are crucial. EDA itself can initiate, stimulate or catalyse activities, but at the end of the day the member states have to contribute and invest, as defence remains a bastion of national sovereignty.[6]

The working groups of national experts, including capacity committees, constitute the basis for the EDA's activities. Their role within the EDA is to systematize information on member states' military equipment and procurement, deployment of troops and research and development. By including national expertise and keeping its activities on a very technical level, the agency has gained legitimacy in the eyes of the member states and been seen as a guarantee of their influence vis-à-vis the European Commission, which also plays a role in creating a European market for defence equipment (Leroux, 2009/2010, p. 69).

The EDA evaluates how far the EU criteria are met by the member states' capability commitments and reports regularly to EU governments, leading to periodic adjustments of the CDP itself. The evaluation criteria have been developed as benchmarking systems to facilitate comparisons between member states. Since 2006, when the first big shortfall was published, the agency has collected data on the defence spending of each individual member state and reported the result to the Ministerial Steering Board on an annual basis. The aim has been to reveal national differences with regard to absolute spending on personnel, equipment procurement, research and development and operations, as well as the relative distribution of total member state spending on the same categories (Zandee and Horrocks, 2009). The data has laid the ground for the elaboration of benchmarks by the Steering Board that member states should strive to meet in their *collective* defence investments. The EDA homepage displays data for each and every member state with regard to the development of spending on European collaborative projects over the years.[7] There is no obligation to turn EU benchmarks into national targets or timelines for realizing benchmarks. The homepage only shows indicators of the evolution towards the collective benchmarks. The former EDA Chief Executive calls the EDA's task of scrutinizing the member states' record a 'scorecard-work' (Bátora, 2009, p. 1084).

The Lisbon Treaty strengthened the EDA's role in the evaluation of member states' European commitments by introducing the so-called permanent structured cooperation in the area of security and defence. Article 42–46 stipulates that '[t]hose member states whose military capabilities fulfil higher criteria and which have made more binding commitments to one another in this area with a view of the most demanding missions shall establish permanent structured cooperation'. The EDA's annual report is intended to serve as a basis for Council recommendations and decisions. So far (December 2014) there are no examples where permanent structured cooperation has been established in practice. More important, perhaps, will be the EDA's role in elaborating cooperative proposals within the member states' programme for pooling and sharing military capabilities in the context of financial austerity and European economic crisis (Council of the European Union, 2012).

Challenges and achievements of joint capacity building

The process of provisional goals and recurrent revisions has received some criticism, but this section argues that also produced results that might be a reasonable model for civil security governance. In particular, it has been criticized for being too reactive and lacking strategic thinking. One explanation is that the setting of capacity goals has not been accompanied by a discussion among the member states of the principles and long-term purpose of the EU's global role (Howorth, 2010, 2014). Another explanation is that the EU has tended to fall into the same trap as the member states it attempts to transform: instead of being innovative it has planned its capacities in the light of the most recent war or crisis (Ekengren, 2007a).

The effects of EDA evaluation of national implementation of the CDP are difficult to measure. So far there has been no systematic research on this issue. It is clear, however, that the coordinated process conducted by the EDA puts pressure on the member states to respect their commitments. The agency's reports 'flow directly into the ongoing Headline Goal implementation process' and in this way strengthen the political pressure on the member states (Bauer, 2005, p. 4). From 2006 to 2007, the total spending of EDA member states on collaborative defence research and technology rose from 9.6 per cent to 13.6 per cent (benchmark 20 per cent) (Zandee and Horrocks, 2009, p. 22). There are also drawbacks to such European peer pressure. Keohane points to the pressure 'to buy European' when it comes to defence equipment, which, according to him, does not necessarily mean the best quality (Keohane quoted in Batora, 2009, p. 1089).

It is also unclear to what degree the EU's coordination has served to improve the basis for a better division of labour among the member states in the provision of national contributions to the joint capacity. It is not clear whether the EDA has contributed to an improved burden sharing between member states through increased specialization in the capabilities creation and procurement. This uncertainty is one of the reasons behind the introduction of the concept of 'pooling and sharing'. The idea is to find a better division of labour by making one or several member states 'pool their resources' in areas where they have comparative advantages and make these capacities available for common use by all participating states. The concept was introduced in the crisis years of 2007–2008 and found legal support in the Lisbon Treaty clause on permanent structured cooperation which, as already mentioned, allows deepened cooperation for groups of high capacity countries and thereby creates incentives for others to pool their resources so as to be included in these groups (Bogzeanu, 2012). The chairman of the European Union Military Committee has called for more innovative defence cooperation. He has proposed setting aside an increasing share of national defence budgets for common European purposes and the translation of the top-down peer pressure from the European Council and the Commission into a strengthened vertical pressure within each armed forces led by the Chiefs of Defence and national plans for the implementation of European goals (Syrén, 2012).

Moreover, the existence of joint EU capacities is no guarantee for the efficient use of these capacities – the most salient question for all policy fields of security governance. The CSDP is firmly based on intergovernmental decision-making. It is however interesting to note how the joint military capability-building generates a development towards binding commitments among the member states and the avoidance of the 'veto-power' of all 27 member states through 'structured cooperation' for a selected number of states.

The challenges for the new coordination method – experimentalist governance – in CSDP echo the shortcomings in other areas where it has been used. Bossong found that the experimentalist peer pressure process in EU counterterrorism strengthens mutual trust but it is doubtful whether it has an impact on the national compliance to EU norms and rules in the area (Bossong, 2012). Nance and Cottrell conclude that the experimentalist way of implementing the Financial Action Task Force on Money Laundering and the UN Security Council Resolution on the nuclear non-proliferation regime has served the purpose to expand and engage the wide range of actors required to solve this security problem. However, Nancy and Cottrell are less ready to draw conclusions on whether the process has led to change in actor behaviour (Nance and Cottrell, 2014). In fact, the question of the impact of EU guidelines on national policies and systems has been a key question in all research on experimentalism (Heidenreich and Zeitlin, 2009). Despite these difficulties, the comparative advantages of experimentalist forms of coordination have been strong in the security area and underlined by the great national diversity in the field (Norheim-Martinsen, 2013).

The former Czech Defence Minister points out several areas in which the EDA is achieving things where, for example, NATO for decades has failed. This holds not only for the development of military capabilities, where NATO proved unable to integrate European and US defence industries. Perhaps most important, according to the Minister, is that EDA has created 'incentives that encourage Member States to opt for European solutions' to their capability shortfalls: 'Member States regard the EDA as a more effective framework than NATO for mobilizing political will'. In addition it has broadened defence cooperation beyond military areas to a wide range of civilian and 'soft-power' fields through close cooperation with the European Commission (Parkanová, 2009). The EDA develops capacities and tools that are useful for today's security, such as nation-building and post-conflict reconstruction (Howorth, 2014). The EU is seen as institutionally better equipped than NATO to push the necessary transformation of national security and defence thinking needed for the 'paradigmatic' challenges of the 21st century (Thiele, 2006). The recursive revision of CSDP goals has been a sign of the EU's capacity to adapt and learn (Ekengren, 2015).

Thus, many observers have emphasized the long-term effects of EDA's work, rather than rapid national change and adaptation. The new experimentalist type of coordination has been able to set long-term EU capacity goals and create a momentum in the joint capacity building on the basis of scenarios of common crisis situations. By providing a platform for EU institutions and member state experts, common practices and goals are created. The broad and constant national participation in the joint capacity building has strengthened the 'supranational' pressure on member states to follow the objectives set in common. In this perspective, the EDA plays a key role in the Europeanization of the European defence space (Leroux, 2009/2010). Moreover, to advance mutual learning and socialization, the EDA has created common strategies for sharing best practices. In 2008, it presented the European Armaments Cooperation Strategy including a Guide to Armaments Cooperation Best Practice and Best Practice Standardization Management.[8] The search for useful 'best practice' has long been a driving force in bilateral military cooperation initiatives. It has been a way to circumvent one of the biggest obstacles to cooperation in this field, namely the lack of instruments and authority of NATO and the Western European Union (WEU) to force European states to keep their armaments commitments (Keohane, 2002, pp. 29–32). Even though there is national resistance to implement the norms created by EDA, the agency has built up a supranational pressure that gives the member states no other choice than to accept these in the longer run (Cross, 2014).

Though the EU battle groups reached full operational capability at the beginning of 2007, they have never been deployed in action to date (December 2014). However, the battle groups concept has played an important role for the long-term convergence of national capacities. Many member states officially recognize that the main importance of the creation of the battle group has been its function as an 'engine' and 'competence bearer' in the transformation of national armed forces from a one-sided focus on territorial defence to a more flexible expeditionary capacity (Swedish Government Proposition to the Parliament, 2012, pp. 9–10).

Overall, the positive experiences in joint capacity building outweigh the negative, or rather unclear, aspects and justify the exploration of the ways EU civil protection can learn from CSDP and EDA.

EU civil protection cooperation

The limits of the 'legal' method of capacity building

As mentioned in the introduction, EU civil protection relies entirely on EU member states capacities (voluntary pooled or not). There exists no method or system that can contribute to a convergence of national resources to make them better adapted for joint use. The EU has no capabilities of its own that it can call on. The lack of a real assurance of European assistance and knowledge of what kind of assistance that can be expected makes it extremely hard for national authorities to streamline national resources in relation to a common capacity, let alone to find comparative advantages and a division of labour among the member states. The new legal basis of EU civil protection, referred to in the introduction, does not clarify the subsidiarity issue of what level provides for what capacities. The resistance from member states to a principled and predictable role for EU capacities is still strong.

The strong sovereignty concerns are reflected in the fact that EU civil protection mainly uses the Union's traditional 'legal' method for capacity building which restricts the EU's role to the coordination of existing national resources. The first EU legal competence in the civil protection field was established in 1997. It took the form of an action programme aimed at the pooling of member state expertise and mutual assistance (Council of the European Union, 1997). In October 2001, in the aftermath of 9/11, the EU developed its legal competence through a Council Decision establishing a Community mechanism for civil protection to facilitate reinforced cooperation in civil protection assistance interventions (Council of the European Union, 2001). In the legal basis of the cooperation from 2001, it was stated that 'the Member State in which the emergency has occurred shall notify those Member States which may be affected by the emergency'. Member States 'shall...identify in advance intervention teams which might be available for such intervention' (Council of the European Union, 2001, Article 2). In 2007, the Union further developed the Community mechanism and set the parameters for the development of a European rapid response capability based on civil protection modules of the member states. The modules were earmarked national resources that the member states offered on voluntary ground for EU use on a case-by-case basis. The modules were streamlined in accordance with EU standards (Council of the European Union, 2007). In 2013 the EU, as mentioned, through a Decision of the European Parliament and the Council, established the ERCC and the EERC (European Parliament and the Council of the European Union, 2013). According to the former Commissioner for crisis management, Kristalina Georgieva, the difference between the earlier voluntary ad hoc offers of national assistance and modules and the EERC is that the latter is based on a pre-identified pool of member states' response assets, so-called civil protection intervention modules. The member states can if they want put some of their capacities on standby in the voluntary pool (Georgieva, 2013).

Member states discuss and steer policies in this field through the responsible Council formations and committees. The Commissioner for international cooperation, humanitarian aid and crisis response is responsible for EU civil protection. She or he heads the ERCC which coordinates the EERC based on pre-agreed contingency plans. The Centre, which is part of the EU's Humanitarian Aid and Civil Protection department (ECHO), coordinates existing national rescue and intervention teams for prevention and immediate responses to disaster, both outside and inside the Union. Through this mechanism, national authorities in need can appeal to a single information and coordination centre instead of having to activate a whole range of bilateral contacts if their own preparedness should prove insufficient. No single member state, particularly not among the smaller countries, possesses the expertise and the specialized intervention teams that are often needed in major emergencies.[9] The ERCC also operates a 24/7 communication and rapid alert network between the Commission and national services called the Common Emergency Communication and Information System (CECIS). Provision has been made for interlinking this information system with other existing networks for radiological, health and biological and chemical emergencies. In addition, the ERCC consists of a series of elements and actions which include the identification of intervention and assessment teams, as well as training programmes.

The Council of Ministers have adopted EU law in the sector such as Council Resolutions and Decisions. The Commission has issued communications. This civil protection *acquis*, in turn, are framed by the Maastricht Treaty's principle of subsidiarity. EU regulations can be grouped into two main categories; one related to the Community mechanism, and another related to the Community action plan. The former concerns the response phase of a disaster and involves the pooling of civil protection resources among the 28 member states plus four non-EU states (Croatia, Iceland, Lichtenstein and Norway). The latter provides the legal basis for cooperative preparation activities in the EU, including workshops, training courses and major projects related to disaster management. The total legal output in the sector increased significantly in the period 1998–2002 and remained at similar level in the following years (2003–2007) (Ekengren, 2008).

The shortcomings of the 'legal' method for joint capacity-buildings have been clear. Few member states have made use of the Community mechanism when overwhelmed by crisis. The EU's civil protection capacities have not been adapted to the domestic security needs of the member states. This mismatch was reflected after the bombings in Madrid in 2004 and London 2005 where the Spanish and the British authorities did not consider using the mechanism (Boin et al., 2013, pp. 43–45).

The challenges for joint capacity building

The EU has in recent years attempted to overcome the capacity shortcomings by prescribing the EU's role vis-à-vis its member states more clearly in the Union treaty. In the Lisbon Treaty, civil protection cooperation is framed under Article 176c. It states that the EU shall encourage cooperation between the member states in order to improve the effectiveness of systems for preventing and protecting against natural and man-made disasters. However, the Article warns against an extended use of the 'legal' method: the Union should exclude 'any harmonisation of the laws and regulations of the Member States' (Article 176C § 2). The prescription of what the Union can do and with what resources, however, is still vague. The Union has the right to adopt 'co-ordinating, complementary and supporting measures' but it remains unclear what these concepts mean in practice with regard to national resources and the EERC.

Furthermore, only so much improvement is possible through ERCC coordination if the underlying longer-term challenge is not addressed: European fragmentation of civil protection capacities. The EU's response is handicapped by a system in which 28 member states have 28 distinct civil security systems and sets of national rules (Bossong and Hegemann, in this volume). The purpose of ERCC and the voluntary pool is to enable a better management of existing national resources not to make national capacities converge or create EU-owned capabilities.

There are some elements of new thinking in sub-areas of EU civil protection that point in the direction of the innovative coordination methods used in CSDP. Elements of experimentalist governance are emerging in the field of disaster and risk management. There are now European Commission guidelines on risk assessment covering all major natural and man-made risks affecting the Union. The EU guidelines provide a general assessment framework for all natural and man-made disaster risks. The aim is to help EU member states develop a capacity for producing national risk assessments which can be aggregated into an EU-wide risk overview, as a way to complement the law making in the civil protection area. The Commission has also suggested that member states draw up national disaster risk management plans (DRM) to describe how they cope with their risks. The aim is to provide common standards and methods for the EU member states' development of national actions plans to make them comparable and facilitate mutual learning and the sharing of best practice (European Commission, 2010). The Commission sponsored exchanges of experts is another element that contributes to the process of mutual learning (Hollis, 2010). The Commission's conviction is that civil security in Europe is strengthened through the sharing of experiences and a more integrated view of different types of risks, including better planning systems that allow for more efficient cooperation. In 2014, the Commission presented an integrated European risk overview on the basis of the national risk assessments. According to this overview, the biggest European risks are flooding (17 member states noted this risk), earthquakes (19) and catastrophes caused by extreme weather (15) (European Commission, 2014). The aim is also to propose good practice guidelines (that will be available at ECHO website).

To put pressure on the member states to fulfil guidelines, the EU has established a system of peer review of national systems for disaster management and resilience. The first review (on the UK) was carried out by EU representatives from Finland, Sweden and Italy together with the UN (Office of Disaster risk Reduction, UNISDR) and OECD and published in 2013 (UNISDR, 2013). Finland went through this peer review process in 2014. The system has similarities to the EU's peer reviews of national policies in the fight against terrorism. In this area the lack of a systematic and institutionalized approach to mutual learning has led to only marginal changes within the security authorities of EU member states (Bossong, 2012, pp. 532–533).[10]

EU guidelines for member states already exist in the area of home affairs and internal security. The Commission has asked the member states to draw up national programs focusing on EU internal security priorities. In the area of home affairs and internal security, the Commission has recently introduced Funds for Internal Security and Asylum and Migration and proposes that member states set up national programmes focusing on a number of strategic Union priorities (European Commission, 2011a, 2011b).

However, currently the EU guidelines and national plans in the areas of risk management and internal security lack a clear follow-through on the EU level. The method is today mainly built on positive 'carrots' of EU help with funding of implementation of EU guidelines and targets. But the Council and the Commission have not established a system for joint evaluation of national plans and, if necessary, the issuing of recommendations to member countries that are not doing enough to meet the EU's guidelines.

In summary, the EU has just started its search for new instruments and methods that can strengthen the joint capacity building in civil protection. The EU is still searching for a legitimate balance between effective and flexible EU capacities and national sovereignty. The role of the ERCC is to support, coordinate and complement existing national resources, not to contribute to joint capacity building. Sub-areas such as risk assessment contain new elements for a more efficient coordination, but are still not advanced enough to make sure that joint evaluations lead to mutual learning and national compliance to EU guidelines and norms (see the counterterrorism field).

As seen, the challenges are extremely similar to the ones that the CSDP for nearly two decades has relatively successfully met with new methods of governance. How can EU civil protection learn from the CSDP and EDA experiences to achieve convergence and genuine *Union* resources?

Conclusion: What EU civil protection can learn from CSDP and EDA

By comparing the achievements and challenges in the two policy-fields, it is now possible to answer the question of what EU civil protection can learn from CSDP and EDA. The objective of this conclusion is to translate the lessons from CSDP and EDA into concrete recommendations for EU civil protection capacity building.

The EU's civil protection should in the setting of joint capacity goals draw on the scenario and long-term visionary thinking within CSDP. This would create momentum in the joint capacity building and ensure that the resources made available for EU use are adapted to the threats that the member states have in common and European transboundary threats. We could here think of scenarios of both overwhelmed states (floodings, forest fires, terrorist attacks) and transboundary crisis (migration flows, epidemics, disruptions of transport systems and critical infrastructure).

The work on EU civil protection capacity goals can build on the EU guidelines on risk assessment and the national DRM plans. The European risk overview of 2014 can constitute a ground for the elaboration of scenarios and a discussion of what tasks that needs to be performed in common. The joint capacity goals could be elaborated on the basis of this discussion.

To make the goal setting as well informed and updated as possible, and open to learning and revision, the EU should engage national civil protection authorities and experts on a regular basis. Like in the CSDP, a combination of a top-down and bottom-up approach, giving civil servants and experts responsibility for working out the joint criteria and resources that could fulfil political 'visions' and scenarios, would create legitimacy for the process in member states. The method would build trust over a longer period of time by setting longer-term goals on the basis of continuous national needs assessment and updated contributions and commitments. It has been easier for European governments to adopt long-term EU visions ('2025') within CSDP knowing that their officials would defend the national interest throughout the implementation process and that goals could be easily revised, than to reach agreement on binding commitments in the form of EU civil protection legislation.

In order to implement the goals and fulfil the joint criteria emanating from the scenarios, the EU should help the member states to develop Civil Protection Capacity Plans (CPCP) to be included in their own capacity planning. The plans should be regularly revised within EU committees and the EU should help the member states to monitor progress. The CPCP should be annually endorsed by the ministers of defence and interiors.

The non-binding character of the experimentalist method of coordination gives the member states the freedom to ultimately do what they want, or at least just to follow the guidelines they choose. That makes it very important that also the evaluation of national compliance in the form of CPCP implementation should use a combination of a top-down and bottom-up approach that guarantee uniform EU assessment standards but also take into account the great variation of national conditions for implementation.

By creating a broad and constant national participation in the joint capacity building, EU civil protection would strengthen the 'supranational' pressure on member states to follow the objectives set in common. Systems of benchmarking and peer pressure would make the member states go in the same direction towards collective capacity goals. EU capacity goals would be publicly more visible tools than EU laws and could thus function as driving force that could put political pressure on member states to work for more integrated capacities. This would enhance the pressure on member states to change and contribute to the European common good. EU goals and evaluations would make the naming and shaming of member states that do not fulfil the objectives a powerful tool for change. We could here think of the strong public and peer pressure to implement EU capacity goals that could emerge after natural disasters (e.g. forest fires) that show that there is an acute need for EU capacities.

Given the strong law making tradition in EU civil protection, the adding of experimentalist forms of coordination may make supranational law making and intergovernmental coordination through objectives complementary. One way forward towards complementarity of the 'legal' and 'new' method in the civil protection field would be to develop EU law more clearly for the coping phase of crisis management – prescribing how decisions should be taken for the activation of EU capacities, leaving EU experimentalism for the prevention, capability-preparedness and learning phases. The two EU methods of cooperation may even converge as they have done in the field of EU defence cooperation, where experimentalist elements have led to a convergence of the traditional community method (the Commission is responsible for key areas such as market aspects of procurement) and the intergovernmental CSDP into a new hybrid governance form with the potential to overcome longstanding blockages to cooperation (Lemmens, 2011).

The civil protection intervention capacity created by ERCC, which today consists of national modules, could be developed in the direction of the battle group concept. The capacity could be transformed into multinational modules for a coherent, predictable and legitimate European response. This kind of EU modules would give national civil protection first responders and experts the opportunity to train and exercise together on a regular basis. The multinational modules could be put on standby on the basis of a rotating scheme similar to the one of the battle groups. Like the battle group concept, the EU modules could also guide national civil protection reforms.

The ERCC could elaborate risk and crisis scenarios and EU tasks related to these. The member states could on this basis decide on EU CPCP to be implemented through 'EU civil protection preparedness guidelines' directed to national authorities. The Centre could also help the member states to establish National CPCP, including criteria and benchmarks to be reached by member states to fulfil the identified EU tasks. The national plans could be evaluated on a yearly basis together with officials from the EU institutions. ERCC could elaborate proposals for EU recommendations (decided by the Council) to member states that do not fulfil the criteria and benchmarks set by the EU. The Centre could also formulate indicators (minimum levels, reform requirements) for comparisons between member states and within individual countries over time. In this way, ERCC would be able to respect national diversity at the same time as it promotes the longer-term development of common outlooks, resources and trust. Similar to EDA, the ERCC should constitute the institutional memory of the joint capacity building and contribute to the member states' learning process through recurrent revisions of goals in the light of the experiences of EU civil protection operations and changes in the security environment.

The ERCC could also lead the work of formulating longer-term visions (10–20 years) in the field. The visions could generate EU long-term guidelines. These guidelines should be elaborated in the light of generic requirements for efficient crisis management capacity and deep knowledge of national systems. Guidelines could include standards for interoperability between national systems, goals that a certain percentage of national preparedness plans should be 'EU compatible', objectives for adequate professional skills and exercises. In effect, the ERCC and EU should aim to support domestic reforms, build-up trust and a culture of mutual assistance and remove the obstacles to a more integrated *European* civil security governance system. Gradually, national systems would gain common features, a European mind-set would develop, and the capacity to respond to major domestic and transboundary threats would become more robust. In the end, the reflex of mutual assistance within the EU will be domestic-like. EU Guidelines and National Preparedness and Capacity Plans might be for the new EU civil security paradigm what EC legislation and national implementation by law was for the old paradigm.

This work should be carried out within the framework of the Solidarity Clause of the Lisbon Treaty together with the new External Action Service, the Commission's DGs for home affairs and crisis management. With an expansive view of the Clause, it could mean that member states should be able to rely on each other to the point that they fully take the collective European civil protection capacity into consideration when building their own national capability (Ekengren, 2008).

It could conceivably give rise to a joint capacity which integrates 28 civil security systems for domestic, transboundary and global crisis management. This may require levels of mutual trust reminiscent of the 1950s when a select group of nation-states created the European Community (Deutsch, 1957).

Notes

1. A 'security community' as defined by Karl Deutsch (1957, p. 6) is 'a group of people that is integrated to the point that there is real assurance that the members of that community will not fight each other physically, but will settle their disputes in some other ways'.
2. Interview with officials at the Swedish Civil Contingencies Agency and the European Centre for Disease Prevention and Control, February 2014.
3. http://www.eeas.europa.eu/csdp/missions-and-operations/, date accessed 15 January 2015.
4. EDA was established in 2004 to support the Council and the member states in their efforts to improve European defence capabilities in the field of crisis management. It has four tasks: defence capabilities development; armaments cooperation; strengthen the European defence technological and industrial base and defence equipment market; support research. EDA was created through a so-called CFSP *Joint Action* Decision (Council Joint Action 2004/551/CFSP of 12 July 2004).
5. All EU member states except Denmark which is not part of the CSDP.
6. Interview senior official EDA, 17 September 2009.
7. EDA, Defence data, http://www.eda.europa.eu/DefenceData/Benchmarks, date accessed 16 August 2013.
8. http://www.eda.europa.eu/aboutus/whatwedo/eda-strategies/Armaments, date accessed 16 August 2013.
9. Interview with Head of Cabinet for Kristalina Georgieva, Commissioner for International Cooperation, humanitarian aid and crisis response, Brussels, 4 December 2013.
10. The influence of EU guidelines and peer reviews on national reforms – in the form of the Open Method of Coordination – has also been examined in the area of employment and welfare policies (Heidenreich and Zeitlin, 2009).

References

Andersson, Jan Joel (2006) *Armed and Ready? – The EU Battle Group Concept and the Nordic Battle Group*, Report, Swedish Institute for European Policy Studies (SIEPS), 2006: 2.

Åhman, T. and Nilsson, C. (2009) 'The Community Mechanism for Civil Protection and the European Union Solidarity Fund' In Olsson, S. (ed.) *Crisis Management in the European Union: Cooperation in the Face of Emergencies* (New York: Springer), pp. 83–107.

Batora, J. (2009) 'European Defence Agency: A Flashpoint of Institutional Logics', *West European Politics*, 32, 1075–1098.

Bauer, T. (2005) *Defence Agency vs. Commission? Claims and Realities of a Comprehensive European Armaments Policy Strategy*, http://www.cap.lmu.de/download/spotlight/Reformspotlight_06-05_de.pdf, date accessed 11 December 2014.

Biscop, S. (2005) *The European Security Strategy: A Global Agenda for Positive Power* (Aldershot: Ashgate).

Bogzeanu, C. (2012) 'NATO-EU relation from the perspective of the implications of "Smart Defence" and "Pooling and Sharing" Concepts' *Strategic Impact*, 44, 33–40.

Boin, A., M. Ekengren and M. Rhinard (2006) 'Protecting the Union: Analysing an Emerging Policy Space', *Journal of European Integration*, 28, 405–421.

Boin, A., M. Ekengren and M. Rhinard (2013) *The European Union as Crisis Manager: Patterns and Prospects* (Cambridge: Cambridge University Press).

Bossong, R. (2012) 'Peer Reviews in the Fight Against Terrorism: A Hidden Dimension of European Security Governance', *Cooperation and Conflict*, December, 47, 519–538.

Council of the European Union (1997) *Council Decision of 19 December 1997 Establishing a Community Action Programme in the Field of Civil Protection (98/22/EC)*, Official Journal of the European Union L 8/20.

Council of the European Union (2001) *Council Decision of 23 October 2001 Establishing a Community Mechanism to Facilitate Reinforced Cooperation in Civil Protection Assistance Interventions (2001/792/EC, Euratom)*, Official Journal of the European Union L 297/7.

Council of the European Union (2004) *Military Capability Commitments Conference: Declaration on European Military Capabilities*, 22 November 2004, http://www.consilium.europa.eu/uedocs/cmsUpload/MILITARY%20CAPABILITY%20COMMITMENT%20CONFERENCE%2022.11.04.pdf, date accessed 16 August 2013.

Council of the European Union (2007) *Council Decision of 8 November 2007 Establishing a Community Civil Protection Mechanism (2007/779/EC, Euroatom)*, Official Journal of the European Union L 314/9.

Council of the European Union (2012) *Council Conclusions on Pooling and Sharing of Military Capabilities*', 3157th Foreign Affairs Council Meeting, 22 and 23 March, http://www.consilium.europa.eu/uedocs/cms_Data/docs/pressdata/en/esdp/129162.pdf, date accessed 11 December 2014.

Cross, Davis M. (2014) 'Norm Resistance & The European Defence Agency', *paper*, ARENA Centre for European Studies, retrieved at the ARENA website, 11 December 2014.

Deutsch, K. W. (1957) *Political Community and the North Atlantic Area: International Organization in the Light of Historical Experience* (Princeton: Princeton University Press).

Dyson, T. and T. Konstadinides (2013) *European Defence Cooperation in EU Law and IR Theory* (Basingstoke: Palgrave Macmillan).

Ekengren, M. (2006) 'New Security Challenges and the Need for New Forms of EU Co-operation', *European Security*, 15, 89–111.

Ekengren, M. (2007a) 'The Internal-External Security Challenge for the EU', *Studia Diplomatica*, 60, 81–106.

Ekengren, M. (2007b) 'From a European Security Community to a Secure European Community: Tracing the New the Security Identity of the EU' in H. G. Brauch et al. (eds.), *Globalisation and Environmental Challenges: Reconceptualising Security in the 21st Century* (Berlin: Springer).

Ekengren, M. (2008) 'EU Civil Protection: An Ascending Sector' in Boin, A., M. Ekengren and M. Rhinard (eds.) *Security in Transition* (ACTA SERIES, Acta B 41) (Stockholm: Swedish National Defence College), pp. 47–61.

Ekengren, M. (2015) 'Extending Experimentalist Governance in Crisis Management' in Zeitlin, J. (ed.) *Extending Experimentalist Governance: The EU and Transnational Regulation* (Oxford: Oxford University Press).

Ekengren, M., N. Matzén, M. Rhinard and M. Svantesson (2006) 'Solidarity or Sovereignty? EU Cooperation in Civil Protection', *Journal of European Integration*, 28 (5), December, 457–476.

European Commission (2005) *Consultation on the Future Instrument Addressing Prevention of, Preparedness for and Response to Disasters: Issue Paper*, 31 January 2005, http://ec.europa.eu/echo/files/civil_protection/civil/pdfdocs/consultation_paper_civpro.pdf, date accessed 12 December 2014.

European Commission (2010) *Commission Staff Working Paper: Risk Assessment and Mapping Guidelines for Disaster Management*, SEC(2010) 1626 final, 21 December 2010.

European Commission (2011a) *Proposal for a Regulation of the European Parliament and of the Council Establishing, as Part of the Internal Security Fund, the Instrument for Financial Support for External Borders and Visa*, COM(2011) 750 final, 15 November 2011.

European Commission (2011b) *Proposal for a Regulation of the European Union and of the Council Laying Down General Provisions on the Asylum and Migration Fund and on the Instrument for Financial Support for Police Cooperation, Preventing and Combating Crime, and Crisis Management*, COM(2011) 752 final, 15 November 2011.

European Commission (2014) *Disaster Risk Management: ECHO Factsheet*, http://ec.europa.eu/echo/files/aid/countries/factsheets/thematic/disaster_risk_management_en.pdf, date accessed 12 December 2014.

European Parliament and the Council of the European Union (2013) *Decision No 1313/2013/EU of the European Parliament and of the Council of 17 December 2013 on a Union Civil Protection Mechanism*, Official Journal of the European Union, L 347/924.

European Defence Agency (2008) *Press Release: EU Governments Endorse Capability Plan for Future Military Needs, Pledge Joint Efforts*, 8 July, http://consilium.europa.eu/uedocs/cmsUpload/080708-PR_Capability_plan.pdf, date accessed 12 December 2014.

Friedrich, H.-P. (2013) 'The EU's Civil Protection Policy Versus National Interests', Interview with Dr. Hans-Peter Friedrich, German Minister of the Interior, *The European Security and Defence Union*, Special Edition: Civil Protection (pp. 6–8), www.magazine-the-european.com.

Georgieva, K. (2013) 'The European Emergency Response Centre', *The European Security and Defence Union*, Special Edition: Civil Protection (p. 5), http://www.ifreact.eu/_uploads/site_downloads/The_European.pdf, date accessed 15 May 2015.

Gowan, R. (2005) 'The Battle Groups: A Concept in Search of a Strategy', in Biscop, S. (ed.) *E Pluribus Unum: Military Integration in the European Union*

(Egmont papers 7) (Brussels: Royal Institute for International Relations), pp. 13–19.
Heidenreich, M. and J. Zeitlin (eds.) (2009) *Changing European Employment and Welfare Regimes: The Influence of the Open Method of Coordination on National Reforms* (London: Routledge).
Hollis, S. (2010) 'The Necessity of Protection: Transgovernmental Networks and EU Security Governance', *Cooperation and Conflict*, September, 45, 312–330.
Howorth, J. (2010) 'The EU as a Global Actor: Grand Strategy for a Global Grand Bargain?', *Journal of Common Market Studies*, 48, 455–474.
Howorth, J. (2014) *Security and Defence Policy in the European Union* (Basingstoke: Palgrave MacMillan).
Hyde-Price, A. (2012) 'Neorealism: A Structural Approach to CSDP' in Kurowska, X. and F. Breuer (eds.) *Explaining the EU's Common Security and Defence Policy: Theory in Action* (Basingstoke: Palgrave Macmillan).
Keohane, D. (2002) *The EU and Armaments Co-operation*, Centre for European Reform, http://cer-live.thomaspaterson.co.uk/sites/default/files/publications/attachments/pdf/2011/wp408_armaments-2288.pdf, date accessed 12 December 2014.
Lemmens, T. (2011) *Governance Relationships in European Defence Procurement Policy: From Rivalry and Complementarity to a Hybrid Future?*, Master Thesis Political Science – International Relations, University of Amsterdam.
Leroux, A. (2009–2010) *The Institutionalisation of the European Defence Space: The European Defence Agency,* Seminar Europe another Way (Rennes: Sciences Po).
Lindström, G. (2007) *Enter the EU Battle Groups*, Chaillot Paper, No. 97, February, http://www.iss.europa.eu/uploads/media/cp097.pdf, date accessed 12 December 2014.
Mattelaer, A. (2013) *The Politico-Military Dynamics of European Crisis Response Strategy* (Basingstoke: Palgrave Macmillan).
Nance, M. T. and M. P. Cottrell (2014) 'A Turn Toward Experimentalism? Rethinking Security and Governance in the Twenty-first Century', *Review of International Studies*, 40, 277–301.
Norheim-Martinsen, P. (2013) *The European Union and Military Force: Governance and Strategy* (Cambridge: Cambridge University Press).
Oikonomou, I. (2012) 'The European Defence Agency and EU Military Space Policy: Whose Space Odyssey?', *Space Policy*, 28, 102–109.
Parkanová, V. (2009) 'In Some Ways, the European Defence Agency is Stronger than NATO,. http://europesworld.org/2009/02/01/in-some-ways-the-european-defence-agency-is-stronger-than-nato/#.VIqz_clp0xI, date accessed 12 December 2014.
Sabel, C. and J. Zeitlin (eds.) (2010) *Experimentalist Governance in the European Union: Towards a New Architecture* (Oxford: Oxford University Press).
Shearer, A. (2000) 'Britain, France and the Saint-Malo Declaration: Tactical Rapprochement or Strategic Entente?', *Cambridge Review of International Affairs*, XIII(2).
Swedish Government Proposition to the Parliament (2012) *Den nordiska stridsgruppen 2015* (*Nordic battle group 2015*), Regeringens proposition 2011/12: 84, http://www.riksdagen.se/sv/Dokument-Lagar/Forslag/Propositioner-och-skrivelser/Den-nordiska-stridsgruppen-201_GZ0384/?text=true, date accessed 12 December 2014.

Syren, H. (2012) 'Facing realities – in Search of a More European Mindset' Keynote Speech at Conference Pooling and Consolidating Demand, Organized by the Cyprus Presidency, the EDA and Egmont in Brussels on 19 September 2012. http://www.regards-citoyens.com/article-facing-realities-in-search-of-a-more-european-mindset-keynote-speech-by-general-h-kan-syren-bru-110945957.html, date accessed 12 December 2014.

Thiele, R. (2006) 'Plug to Operate: Command and Coordination of Armed Forces in Europe in Time of Transformation' in Hauser, G. and F. Kernic (eds.) *European Security in Transition* (Aldershot: Ashgate), pp. 115–134.

United Nations Office for Disaster Risk Reduction (2013) *Peer Review Report United Kingdom 2013. Building Resilience to Disasters: Assessing the Implementation of the Hyogo Framework for Action (2005–2015)*, http://www.unisdr.org/files/32996_32996hfaukpeerreview20131.pdf, date accessed 12 December 2014.

Zandee, D. and P. Horrocks (2009) 'EDA Defence Data: Reaching Maturity' *EDA Bulletin*, 10 (February), 22.

12
Who Cares? The Relevance of EU Crisis Cooperation for EU Scholars
Mark Rhinard

Introduction[1]

A curious development is underway in the process of European integration. The European Union, long accustomed to taking decisions that lead to slow, incremental steps towards common policies, is being asked to take urgent, decisive steps during extreme events. In contrast to the early years of the EU, today hardly a day passes without a news report of EU involvement in what might generically be called a 'crisis': a possible pandemic, a major cross-border flood, a cyber-attack, a looming energy shortage, a civil war, a chemical spill, a volcanic eruption, or, of late, a debt-driven financial breakdown. These are all very different kinds of events and the EU's involvement varies. However, they conform to the generic definition of a crisis as an unexpected, acute disruption to normal societal functions that must be handled quickly and under conditions of uncertainty (Rosenthal et al., 1991). A crisis is intriguing – from a scholarly perspective – because it shines a spotlight on the governance capability of a political-administrative system. It reveals a system's coordination capacity, leadership arrangements, power sharing potential, communication effectiveness, and degree of legitimacy in the eyes of citizens. The EU is increasingly being asked to tackle crises according to this definition on a fairly regular basis and is developing capacities to do so (Boin et al., 2013). Not only does this development offer an intriguing angle into which to view the EU's civil security governance as highlighted by this book, but it also suggests a rich vein of research agendas and theoretical development opportunities for scholars.

This chapter speaks to scholars of European integration who have largely neglected the EU's 'crisis' role in civil security governance. The reasons for this neglect are varied but can be attributed to some of the same causes outlined in the introduction to this book; namely, that this particular empirical phenomenon does not fit neatly into entrenched topics or sub-disciplines. Reacting collectively to different kinds of crises, and the emerging capacities associated therein, is an EU activity that crosses empirical boundaries. To list but a few examples: EU CFSP scholars are narrowly focused on foreign policy and/or operational missions; EU AFSJ scholars tend to focus on borders, immigration or justice cooperation *per se*; those studying EU development policy tend to focus only on the longer-term impacts of crises; finally, scholars with their attention in other EU sectors and issues tend to see safety and security questions as tangential to the main thrust of a dominant policy or political goal.

Greater attention to developments in this area would yield two main benefits to scholars. The first and most obvious benefit is empirical. Few scholars, especially in the EU studies community, have understood the considerable amount of data accumulating in past years on this kind of European cooperation (cf. European Commission, 2009; Boin et al., 2013). That data offers new opportunities for applying and testing traditional analytical frameworks used to study the EU, to reveal new insights to what the EU 'is' as an organization, how it works legally, politically and organizationally, and with what implications for European governance. The second benefit is theoretical rather than empirical. As this chapter will show, existing theories will need to be developed further or complemented by other approaches if they are to remain relevant to studying this growing area of EU cooperation.

The chapter first sketches the range and nature of the EU's activities in this area, for example the empirical phenomenon in focus (section two), and summarizes some general empirical patterns (section three). The chapter then reviews several analytical dimensions worth further exploring (section four) before summarizing the unique traits of European cooperation on crisis management and outlining how several mainstream approaches may need to be developed further to account for this cooperation (section five). It concludes by highlighting broader questions about what developments in the EU's 'crisis' role mean not only for the EU but also for how we study and understand the EU (section six). As such, this chapter is less about explaining developments per se and more of a call to action to use, adapt and develop further the mainstream approaches used in European integration studies to this intriguing new empirical area.

The EU and crises

The EU is not completely new to decision-making on 'crisis' issues. For instance, the Commission and member states have had to make unexpected price adjustments to commodities regulated by the Common Agricultural Policy, where billions of ECU (or later, Euro) were at stake as global commodity prices shifted overnight (Ackrill, 2000). Moreover, the process of comitology – by which the Commission has been granted authority to make swift decisions subject to varying degrees of member state oversight – supplies us with a number of examples of decision-making under pressure (see Dorussen et al., in this volume). Since 1992 and 1998, when the Common Foreign and Security Policy Common Security and Defence Policy were established, respectively, the EU has had to react swiftly to events with an external security or political 'edge'. Indeed, the term 'crisis management' in EU circles is normally reserved for CSDP missions in which troops are sent to monitor peace agreements or rebuild infrastructures, to name just a few crisis management tasks (Smith, 2004).

However, these examples represent just a fraction of situations in which the EU is being asked to make acute decisions under conditions of uncertainty and urgency. Several studies have emerged in recent years providing descriptive inventories of where, when, why and how such decision-making has occurred (Olsson, 2009; Boin et al., 2013) and official documents, albeit fairly few, have emerged which document the range of crisis-related activities taking place (see, for instance, European Commission, 2009). A brief overview of developments at the levels of policy, operations, treaty/strategic and institutional illustrates the point.

Policies

On the policy side, a few EU policy sectors are without some focus on real and potential crises. The language of 'all hazards' preparation is trendy (Paton and Jang, 2011), but a closer look reveals a more pragmatic concern to officials: breakdowns. What happens when something goes wrong in a policy sector that the EU has helped to integrate? This question animates new policy attention in virtually all sectors. For instance, the EU has long been active in facilitating Trans-European Transport Networks; more recently, focus in the Commission's DG Transport has included what happens when those networks break down owing to, say, a chemical spill, a recurring road accident or a bomb in the port of Rotterdam. Regional policy and cohesion policy officials have questioned the sustainability of previous local development initiatives (especially in the light of earthquakes, forest fires and floods in Europe) and instead focus on projects that both help to develop a region and build resilience to disasters and emergencies. The same kind of dynamic operated in the 1990s regarding animal health: having allowed and regulated, through the internal market, the free movement of animal by-products, attention was given to what happens when the system breaks down: a major disease spread, for instance. Actual disease outbreaks then prompted a substantial 'crisis' response and subsequent preparations to manage them more effectively next time. Jumping to a very different example brings us to monetary union. Having built a single currency system to improve transaction costs within (most of) the internal market, some attention – but clearly not enough – was placed on the EU's role when (not if, as it turned out) that system broke down. The chapter returns to the theoretical implications of these trends below; for now, let it suffice to show how new crisis-oriented policies are emerging from functional breakdowns in regulatory regimes and common policies.

One policy area in which the EU has taken a somewhat more deliberate role is civil protection. The EU's cooperation in civil protection cooperation dates back to 1985, when an environmental ministerial meeting in Rome agreed to investigate a community role for improving member states' collective response to natural disasters. From that initiative, which mainly involved investigations, studies and research programmes, a variety of legal bases and policy instruments have been put into place. In 2001, a Civil Protection Mechanism was created to fortify participation in civil protection cooperation, via four main instruments operated by the Commission: a monitoring and coordination centre staffed 24/7 by Commission officials, which was renamed the European Response Coordination Centre (ERCC) in 2013 (see below for more on the ERCC); a Common Emergency Communication and Information System (CECIS) for reporting contributions and coordination measures; a variety of cross-border training initiatives; and sets of stand-by resources at national levels available for deployment when requested by the Commission and following an official request from a stricken country – stand-by resources that have been reorganised and strengthened since 2008 and that now take the form of multinational 'modules' (see Council of the European Union, 2014a). The Civil Protection Mechanism was recast in 2007 and a financial instrument was adopted by the Council that same year, representing a major boost to both the funding and operations of civil protection cooperation in the EU.

Consolidating the Commission's civil protection responsibilities, the Lisbon Treaty introduced, for the first time, a clear legal basis for civil protection cooperation (Article 196, TFEU). While the TFEU provisions reserve civil protection as a national competence, they give the Commission a clear coordinating role and provide a firm foundation for new initiatives. As part of its civil protection responsibilities, the Commission gathers information on what is available in member states for coordinated deployment and keeps databases of information on supplies and equipment available to affected states. This enables it to undertake civil protection activities in the immediate relief stage after a disaster. These activities usually involve the coordination of national experts and national resources and are deployed in the service of such activities as search and rescue, firefighting and the provision of emergency medical assistance, temporary shelter and food and water. The Civil Protection Mechanism was triggered (thus setting in motion a Commission-coordinated response) 21 times in 2012 and 16 times in 2013.

The Council, concerned as to how it might make effective decisions in a crisis, has created a set of protocols and procedures for decision-making in times of crisis. The Integrated Political Crisis Response (IPCR) arrangements (previously called the Crisis Coordination Arrangements, but renamed in 2013) directs the Council in how to put itself on a 'crisis footing', including allowing member state ambassadors at the highest level (COREPER II) to make decision on behalf of national governments and requiring them to assemble in Brussels within two hours when triggered the arrangements are tested roughly one a year in a scenario implicating most member states and all the EU institutions. The 2012 and 2013 scenarios were 'Hurricane Katrina'-like event in the Mediterranean, killing thousands and knocking out power supplies to much of Europe, and a hostage situation involving EU diplomats in the Baltic Sea, respectively.

Treaty/strategic

In terms of treaty/strategic developments, the Lisbon Treaty contained several new legal provisions related to the EU's role in crises. Civil protection (Article 91, TFEU), health security (Article 220, TFEU) and humanitarian aid (Articles 208–214, TFEU) are just some examples.

Moreover, the EU now has a treaty-enshrined 'Solidarity Clause' obligating EU member states to: jointly prepare for crises; to come to one another's aid when asked; and, to coordinate amongst themselves using EU institutions (Article 222, TFEU). The means to be used include both

'Union instruments' and national resources (including military means) while the threat envisioned is wide-ranging, including accidents, natural disasters and terrorism. The Solidarity Clause can reasonably be contrasted with the more traditional security defence guarantee of Article 42.7 TEU, which is focused on 'territorial incursions' and is mainly intergovernmental in focus. The origins of the Solidarity Clause are found in the European Convention debates on a draft constitution for the EU (2002–2003). Delegates contemplating the Western European Union's mutual defence clause (which eventually became Article 42.7 TEU) felt the EU also needed a 'solidarity' approach to a range of new threats confronting Europe. There were two lines of thought in support for a new kind of solidarity obligation. For some members of the convention, the threat of 'armed aggression', although politically relevant, was out-of-date. With 11 September 2001 fresh in their minds, and with debates underway regarding a draft European Security Strategy, the threat spectrum needed to be broadened. Moreover, some members felt a mutual defence clause could not, and would not, leverage the full range of crisis and disaster response capacities available to the EU. A broad clause would offer an alternative way of showing solidarity, in contrast to that required by the mutual defence clause.

The Solidarity Clause begins with a broad proviso: 'the Union and its members states shall act jointly in a spirit of solidarity' when an attack or disaster strikes. This formulation demonstrates the supranational intent of the Solidarity Clause, making it more than an intergovernmental obligation (as is the case with the mutual defence clause). The use of the words 'the Union and its Member States' make explicit the fact that EU institutions should be involved alongside member states in cooperation. The clause also focuses on the mobilization of resources, obligating 'the Union' to 'mobilise all the instruments at its disposal, including the military resources made available by the Member States'. It states that if a member state is the object of an attack or disaster, 'the other Member States shall assist it'. The last paragraph of the clause mandates the European Council (not the Council of Ministers) to 'regularly assess threats facing the Union' in order to allow the Union and its member states 'to take effective action'.

In short, the Solidarity Clause places several obligations upon member states. First, the clause establishes a duty of the Union and member states to 'act jointly' if an attack or disaster takes place. This obligation stands in contrast to previous references on solidarity within the treaties and applies to joint action between member states and the EU institutions. Second, the clause establishes a duty of the Union to 'mobilise all instruments at its disposal'. This obligation suggests the EU institutions must be capable of drawing upon instruments in a coherent, coordinated and effective fashion. Third, the clause establishes a duty of member states to 'assist' a stricken member state. It prescribes that member states make assistance available, in addition to acting jointly.

The Solidarity Clause has recently been 'implemented' via a Council decision (Council of the European Union, 2014b), defining its terms and spelling out its implications. The debate over implementing the Solidarity Clause once featured opinions emphasizing the importance of the instrument as a stand-alone mechanism with its own response role and capacities versus opinions focused on the clause as a 'trigger' to launch other, existing capacities in the EU (Myrdal and Rhinard, 2010). In the actual implementation, the latter perspective won out, meaning that the Solidarity Clause has been largely downplayed as a significant, legal instrument. In any case, however, the Solidarity Clause takes its place alongside a growing list of treaty provisions focused on the EU's obligations during moments of emergency, disaster, crisis and hazards – all terms which are used interchangeably but which are part of a growing conceptualization of activities in this field. The most well known is the 'risk society' perspective (Beck, 2002) that suggests, and helps to explain, the EU's growing role in managing crises, a theme returned to later in this chapter.

One might also include in this category the EU's Internal Security Strategy from 2010 (Council of the European Union, 2010). The subtitle of the ISS suggests the EU should move 'Towards a European Security Model', a concept subsequently defined as a 'set of common tools' and a commitment to a long list of normative 'principles' including solidarity, inclusion of relevant actors, a commitment to civil liberties, and prevention work in addition to addressing 'sources of insecurity'. The text begins with a list of threats and challenges, listed as terrorism, serious and organized crime, cyber-crime, cross-border crime, violent itself, natural and man-made disasters as well as phenomena such as road traffic accidents. It then shows the responses that are taking place – and which ostensibly should take place – such as prevention work, improving response capacities, coordinating EU agencies and roles more effectively, improving information sharing based on mutual recognition and improving evaluation and follow-up activities.

After outlining the normative principles that constitute a European Security Model (principles largely corresponding with the European

Charter of Fundamental Rights), the document concludes with a set of 'strategic guidelines for action'. A list of ten objectives follows, which overlap with the 'responses' described above and which could be described as a 'christmas tree' of wishes in a number of disparate working areas and at different operational levels: more intelligence-led policing, better focus on democratic freedoms, more integrated border control and improved information exchange, to name some examples (Council of the European Union, 2010).

The ISS has been criticized for being wide-ranging and unfocused (Horgby and Rhinard, 2013) and has not been a driving force behind policy change amongst member states (Bossong and Rhinard, 2013a). However, the ISS has prompted further action and consolidation by the European Commission where it has been used strategically to justify some new ventures (see European Commission, 2014, for instance).

Institutional

We might also look at the institutional aspects of these developments. There is a rising number of 'crisis units' and 'coordination centres' in the EU institutions. Most are housed in the Commission where, especially between 2005 and 2010, Directorates-General seemed to be competing to build the most lavish crisis operations room. The earliest and most well known was the MIC (the Monitoring and Information Centre) in DG Environment, which from 2012 was merged with the crisis room in DG ECHO and is now known as the ERCC. It contains round-the-clock staff, high-tech information and communication systems, and three operational centres to coordinate the EU's role in up to three simultaneous events. THE ERCC normally focuses on coordinating the EU's role in disasters (floods, fires, earthquakes) but officially handles anything ('all hazards') both inside and outside of Europe. Other operational centres include DG SANCO's HEOF (Health Emergencies Operations Facility), which is intended to monitor and respond to pandemic outbreaks, and DG Home's STAR (Strategic Analysis and Response Centre) for risk assessment and, during an internal security crisis, for situation assessment and response coordination. The European External Action Service has its Situation Room, formerly the Situation Centre in the Council's General Secretariat and the product of a merger with DG RELEX's crisis 'platform'. Space constraints do not allow for discussion of the other locations for crises room: EU agencies, including Frontex and Europol.

Also of note is a new Crisis Coordination unit in the Commission's Secretariat-General which, since 2005, has been tasked by the Commission President to bring actors across the Commission's DGs to identify overlaps and possible synergies in the emergence of these new Commission competences.

Main empirical patterns

The discussion above offers a hint of the rich empirical material now available in a field traditionally neglected by EU studies scholars. However, what more are we to make of it? What broader empirical patterns are worth drawing out? Three are identified below before the subsequent section assesses their analytical significance.

One is the varying nature of the EU's activities in this area. Sometimes the EU is deeply involved, such as during a food disease outbreak in Europe or a crisis of the Eurozone. Other times, the EU is tangentially involved. Much of this has to do with the legal basis, of course, on which cooperation is premised. In the area of animal health or agriculture-based diseases, the EU is a significant area since these are areas of 'Union competence'. In other areas, the EU has a few – or unclear – legal competences to act independently. Managing the effects of the Ash Cloud crisis in 2010 presented one such dilemma. A meeting of the College of Commissioners at the time featured a tense debate over whether the Commission as a whole should 'step in' and help manage the cross-border effects of the event, or rather it should 'stay out' and let any individual DGs directly implicated take their own action. In other cases, the legal basis is less important. For decades, the EU developed its now-fairly robust civil protection cooperation structures without a firm legal basis; the Lisbon Treaty's inclusion of a treaty basis simply codified what already existed. In typical fashion, then, EU cooperation is varied and fragmented across different sectors of this broader empirical field.

A second empirical pattern is the varying rationales behind the EU's involvement. For some kinds of events, the EU has become involved by 'choice': a decision has been made, normally by the Council and Parliament, to help coordinate oil-spill clean-ups, to deploy disaster aid or to send civilian crisis management missions abroad. In other situations, the EU has been dragged in to reacting. This is mainly because of the potential impact of a crisis on the internal market: the Icelandic volcano eruption (2010), which grounded both flights and supply chains, or the Austrian power outage (2006), which affected a wide swath of Europe through direct and indirect effects. Similarly, the EU has been forced to develop crisis management facilities owing to the unintended (or underappreciated) consequences of other policies: creation of the EU's common external border has generated a number of tragedies, such as that at Lampedusa (2013), which prompted new calls for joint EU action. Even though that action has been slow to follow, the question has reached high-level agendas and the EU, in the case of the Lampedusa, follow-up, launched its own 'Frontex plus' search-and-rescue mission in 2014.

One last pattern is the different types of 'crisis' activities in which the EU is involved. Interestingly, not all of the EU's activities in this area are focused on the response phase of a crisis outbreak. Using the traditional 'crisis management' stages-heuristic, we also detect activities in the area of analysis and prevention, preparation and recovery – in addition to response. For instance, a considerable amount of EU activity is directed at prevention: steps that might stop an impending problem from becoming an acute one. There at least 80 types of 'rapid alert systems' which allow for early crisis communication between capitals and the EU institutions, on such issues as chemical or biological threats, radiological leaks, food disease outbreaks and possible oil spills (Boin et al., 2014) . The EU is involved in risk analysis activities, as well, such as running 'stress tests' on its energy distribution system (in the event of a Russian gas shut-down) and on its banks. The scenario-based crisis exercises taking place in different sectors, and EU-wide in the case of the ICPR, suggests a degree of preparation underway. Such activities more developed in sectors with a history of experiencing crises, such as food safety and health security (Boin et al., 2006). Finally, the EU is also involved in recovery: offering resources to help rebuild affected locations through the European Solidarity Fund.

Analytical dimensions

The empirical overview and patterns described in the previous sections clearly prompt a variety of analytical questions. This section discusses some of those questions and highlights relevant theoretical perspective that could be applied by EU scholars.

What is driving these developments?

A classic query in European integration studies, this question has many possible, intertwining answers.

Actual Crises. The role of sudden, attention-grabbing events in generating pressure for policy change is well studied within political science (Kingdon, 1995). In the case of the EU's expanding role in managing different types of crises, the role of such 'focusing events' appears to be a critical variable. For external crisis management, the Balkans break-up and subsequent conflict served to concentrate minds on the need for independent capacity for sending military missions abroad. For civil protection, the Seveso toxic chemical release and increasingly severe Italian forest fires prompted newfound attention to the importance of cooperation. For transboundary crises, SARS and 11 September provided the 'shock' necessary to raise concerns and prompt new initiatives in crisis cooperation. Arguably, it is the increasing prevalence of transboundary crises more generally (from H1N1 to energy supply failures, and from climate change to the financial crisis) that helps to explain the EU's growing role in those kinds of crises.

Political Symbolism and Council Voting Dynamics. At some point in time, every EU member state will be the victim of a crisis. Public concern rises and frightening vulnerabilities are highlighted by commentators. National leaders are under pressure to 'do something' to demonstrate lessons-learned, and this often includes calls for increased supranational cooperation. The UK did exactly this after the 2005 London Transport bombings – which led to the Crisis Coordination Arrangements and EU Counter Terrorism Strategy largely under UK policy. Other member states are obliged to stand symbolically 'shoulder-to-shoulder' in response and usually agree to take new initiatives or unblock old ones. Even leaders firmly against further integration find it hard not to stand alongside European colleagues to denounce terrorism, to combat disease, to protect infrastructures or to stop suffering. Of course, these may be largely political and symbolic declarations, but they nevertheless start the 'wheels turning' and encourage actors – from the Commission to the Council Secretariat, and from motivated member state officials to civil society – to ramp up cooperation.

Institutional Entrepreneurism. The role of the European Commission as a drive of policy developments in this area should not be ignored. Far from the average international secretariat, the Commission is a legally independent institution with the power to initiate policies, hold governments to account and to 'breath life' into the treaties (Vahl, 1997; see also Nugent and Rhinard, 2015). In the aftermath of focusing events, the Commission is in the position to present new initiatives and provide 'substance' to Council declarations. The Commission seizes upon such opportunities, of course, to push its own agenda and stake out new policy ground. During the everyday process of policy-making, the Commission is expected to carry through projects focused on boost the security and safety of European citizens. The Commission thus provides momentum and, when needed, legal muscle, behind the EU's push towards crisis management on a continuing basis. In so doing, the Commission serves as an 'entrepreneur' in pursuit of policy change reflective of its interest (Kaunert, 2010) and the same can be said about the Council Secretariat (Bossong, 2012). Although it is too crude to define such interest as 'more Europe' (as was traditionally done within academia), the Commission measures its performance in terms of common policies and EU-managed programs (Rhinard, 2010).

Spillover. The rise of European cooperation in the face of different kinds of crises can also be explained in terms of 'spillover', a well-established explanation for progress in European integration (Niemann, 2010). In this topic area, spillover plays a particularly powerful role. The question of safety and security, while not the primary concern for building a single market, became increasingly connected to the project throughout the 1990s. Building a single market means lowering borders, eliminating obstacles, de-regulating at the national level and re-regulating at the European level. This process generates new interdependencies, many with positive aspects (such making all states reliant on an interconnected set of energy networks to increase the reliability of supply). This process also generates negative externalities (such as the ability of criminals to easily cross borders) and highlights new regulatory gaps (since national security regulations may not apply to transboundary infrastructures). The previous chapters made frequent reference to the effects of spillover in generating new policies, or 'flanking measures' to use the Brussels terminology (Armstrong and Bulmer, 1998). In the case of transboundary crises, the steady, if scattered, growth of capacities related to managing those crises can be traced back to efforts to 'make safe' many of the initiatives associated with building the Schengen zone, the Single Market, the Single European Sky and other projects.

Evolving Security Conceptions. As the concepts used to understand modern threats, and the means by which to respond to them in a complex threat environment, undergo change, the European Union has moved to the centre of security discussions. Concepts such as 'human security' (Kaldor, 2007), 'societal security' (Boin et al., 2007), 'functional security' (Sundelius, 2005) and, albeit more critically, the 'risk society' (Beck, 2002) take in a much broader range of threats to the individual and key societal functions. The effect of this move has been to legitimize the EU as a security provider in Europe, a role once considered the exclusive province of NATO, and to hasten new and broader ranges of security initiatives (Ekengren, 2008). From one perspective, the EU is the only cooperative arrangement with the policy competences required to address a broadening threat spectrum. The EU has thus accumulated new security and safety responsibilities by default, since no better cooperation option exists. From another perspective, the EU has led the way in addressing a more complex threat environment by choice, since many of the security interdependencies it has responded to are of its own making.

What are the effects of these developments?

Clearly there are a significant number of drivers pushing developments forward in this area, although the variation in empirical patterns discussed in section three suggest that developments do not proceed in a straight line nor are do they reflect the same depth of cooperation. Indeed, one major effect of these developments is a highly varied degree of cooperative momentum – and thus cooperation itself. The Council voting dynamics discussed above, for instance, are common in the immediate aftermath of a crisis but may not always lead to practical, operational cooperation. Indeed, member states are sometimes more keen to declare their support for cooperation in this area than to actually cooperate (Bossong and Rhinard, 2013b).

Nevertheless, the effect of these developments is a highly varied and richly textured set of cooperation dynamics that suggests more cooperation it taking place (albeit sometimes in the shape of coordinating, networking, etc. than in true sovereignty pooling) than is normally thought. It also suggests the EU has more operational capacity for handling extreme events (albeit imperfectly) than is widely understood. For those scholars assuming a strategic, linear development sanctioned regularly by political authorities – for instance, scholars who usually study domestic emergency management systems – they are likely to be surprised by the ad-hoc, incremental nature of developments underpinning the EU's role in managing crises. This is the case despite the increasingly effort – the effects of which are thus far unclear – to structure developments here through a greater resort to legal bases, strategy and planning. The Solidarity Clause and Internal Security Strategy stand out in this regard and partially reflect a political acknowledgement of how far matters have developed in this field and a need to provide some direction and explicit oversight.

Implications for EU studies

The discussion above already revealed some intriguing implications of this expanding cooperation area for EU scholars. At one level, developments in this area provide new fodder for use by theorists employing traditional analytical frameworks to study the EU, its activities and its outputs. At another level, these developments challenge the ability of prevailing frameworks to provide adequate explanations for why they have taken place and with what effect. As shown below, this area of EU cooperation is not an 'easy case' for most prevailing theoretical or conceptual approaches. The management of crises reflects a fundamentally different kind of activity in which the EU traditionally engages. Instead of deliberative bargaining in inclusive networks over time, for instance, this activity involves split-second decision-making amongst a core group of actors. Instead of managing large, redistributive cohesion and agricultural policies, for example, crisis management involves operational horizon scanning, threat prioritization and early warning tools. And rather than relying on questions of treaty competence to distinguish roles, this kind of activity prioritizes decision efficiency, information reliability and general degrees of trust to drive cooperation *in the moment*, and when cause-effect relations on what is happening and what should be done may be unclear (see Kuipers in this volume).

These are just some of the unique characteristics of this cooperation area that may lead us to question the efficacy of existing frameworks used to the study the EU from different perspectives. By way of brief example, three sets of conventional approaches are examined below.

Integration theories

The first approach involves traditional integration studies, namely the dichotomy between supranational institutionalism (Sandholtz and Stone Sweet, 1998) and intergovernmental approaches (Moravcsik and Schimmelfennig, 2009). The former set of theories, including those associated with neofunctionalism, have much to explore in the emerging data on the EU's crisis management role, not least considering the historical focus on 'integration by crisis' (Weiler, 1999). While supranationalism and neofunctionalism are normally best at explaining integration outside of issues touching on core national sovereignty – thus excluding security and crisis questions – a new generation of neofunctionalist scholars have revived the notion of different kinds of functional pressure leading to additional integration, including: functional spillover, political spillover, cultivated spillover, exogenous spillover and social spillover (Niemann, 2010, pp. 29–47), which can account more systematically for integration in a broader number of policy areas. Indeed, neofunctionalism may provide a central analytical framework for explaining the developments outlined in this chapter. However, it cannot explain all of them. Neofunctionalist accounts tend to be sweeping and general, and unable to explain some setbacks and fine-grained variation in integration (the stunted evolution of the EU's rapid response for migration in the Mediterranean, for instance, or the lack of any robust cooperation in cyber security are both developments which neofunctionalists might struggle to explain).

Further, the operational and urgent decisional aspects of the EU's role in crisis management may challenge neofunctionalism. Can it also explain moments of intense cooperation (e.g. during crises, when situations dictate) but immediate rollback (e.g. when the crisis fades, and sovereignty concerns return)? The *social* spillover dynamic, which has been explored the least amongst the various functional pressures, may be most appropriate here since crisis-driven reflexive learning and socialization often seems to be at play. This relates to the long-standing research agenda of socialization processes in European integration (see, for instance, Checkel, 2007) which could test assumptions of whether socialization can take place on sensitive security topics such as civil defence and managing crises. Still, neofunctionalism in general includes an implicit, long-term temporal change assumption that may not fit cases featuring swift crisis dynamics.

Intergovernmentalists would no doubt emphasize the fact that, in crisis management, 'real' authority remains with national governments. They would emphasize that crisis management as an emerging EU activity is characterized by some degree of 'spill back', likely caused by domestic political changes, diversity amongst member states and generally negative integration climates. A high profile example is that of EPCIP – the European Programme for Critical Infrastructure Protection – which was launched with great fanfare but languishes (at the time of writing, early 2015) in relative stasis (for background, see Fritzon et al., 2007). They might try to explain successful cooperation in the area of crisis management as the result of a cost/benefit calculation by national governments, something that is no doubt accurate in some cases (Moravcsik and Schimmelfennig, 2009). However, is it accurate in all cases, in various sectors? A focus on national government and competence is in some respects myopic, since information management and the control of knowledge in the immediate aftermath of a crisis is how power and authority is wielded – regardless of by whom (Comfort, 2007).

Public policy approaches

A second set of approaches used in EU studies that might require reassessment comes from the field of public policy analysis. Public policy-oriented scholars in EU studies would have much to work with in this new area of research, perhaps focusing on the role of crises as 'focusing events' which open up new opportunities for policy change as mentioned in the previous section. The role of policy entrepreneurs, such as sufficiently motivated member states, the European Commission or Council Secretariat, to expand collective policy-making would be of great interest (see, for instance, Kaunert and Della Giovanna, 2010; Bossong, 2012). What has not been examined yet – but with obvious relevance to public policy research – is the role of different policy (epistemic) communities operating in this domain, albeit in different professional jurisdictions. Tensions can arise between disaster relief experts and humanitarian aid providers, for instance, both in Brussels and in the field. Because the EU's approach to crisis management is cross-sectoral, conflicting worldviews and professional orientations often come to the fore (for a related political sociology argument, see Bigo, 2002).

Still, other public policy approaches would be challenged to explain developments in this area. The research orientation of policy agenda setting, for instance, tends to view crises only as focusing events – moments when Kingdon's three streams come together, connecting existing solutions to newly perceived problems (1995). Yet this perspective treats crises as exogenous to the explanation – a temporary moment independent of the long-standing and more important stream of policy-making. What must be explained in the EU is not only the development of policies but also the development of operational and functional capacities focused on crises decision-making, for instance. This touches again upon the long-term, temporal bias implicit in public policy analysis (exemplified by the frequent pairing of historical institutionalism with public policy analysis). Similarly, research on Europeanization – focused partly on measuring the effect of EU policy change in domestic settings – would be challenged to explain the operational (not simply policy) effects of EU capacity building in the area of crisis management (Börzel and Risse, 2003). Much of what this chapter describes implicates national executives and central decision-making processes, for instance. There are no doubt 'downloading' and 'uploading' pressures (Börzel, 2000), but how are national capitals changing as the result of EU developments which are largely tactical and operational, rather than policy or legal in nature?

Security governance approaches

The security governance approach – as this book attests – is increasingly employed to understand the security 'steering' aspects of European cooperation. It offers a nuanced, empirically-driven approach to explaining some of the classic questions of EU studies, including the quality of relations between actors and their mutual influence, the way in which sovereignty is pooled in non-obvious ways and the constellation of public, private actors, national and supranational interests in any one policy area (see Bossong and Hegemann in this volume). While useful, governance approaches might be hard pressed to explain some of what is happening in this empirical area. First, scholars interested in the EU's security identity (Wivel, 2005; Anderson, 2008; McDonagh, 2014) and security communities (Adler and Barnett, 1998; Ekengren, 2008) could find an expanded array of evidence to work with here. That said, the question of the EU as a security 'actor' would need to be adjusted to the EU's crisis management capacity building (see Ekengren, in this volume) since the EU's role in managing crises varies both internally and externally (Eriksson and Rhinard, 2009; Wolff et al., 2013). Similarly, work on the EU's security 'actorness' (Koops, 2011) would need updating. Actorness is normally applied to EU action outside of its own borders, but its main analytical dimensions – context, coherence, capability and consistency (Brattberg and Rhinard, 2013) – might be applicable to domestic crises as well. If not, the utility of the approach could be questioned in an era of 'transboundary' crises (see Kuipers and Boin, in this issue).

Second, security approaches to understanding the EU, especially those which emphasize processes of 'securitization' might be challenged. As has been oft-noted, the EU is a unique kind of security actor pursuing a unique set of goals (or 'referent objects'). Much work has been done on the securitization of issues beyond the security sphere, such as in environmental (Brown et al., 2007) or immigration policy (Boswell, 2007) and the approach could be usefully applied to issues like civil protection, emergency management, pandemics and transport safety in order to see the extent to which these issues have, or have not, been subject to processes of securitization. Moreover, the move towards complementing 'speech acts' with actual practice when studying securitization processes, along with the trend of examining the effects of speech acts on the audience (for an overview, see Balzacq, 2010), could be usefully applied in the area of crisis management developments in the EU. However, much of the EU's crisis management capacity building has been done behind closed doors, without need for public justification. The explosion of crisis rooms and rapid alert networks, for instance, are done quietly, without committing substantial resources, by using technical rationales and without setting in train the dynamics of securitization as traditionally understood. This may represent a different type of securitization, but its parameters and dynamics need to be specified and elaborated.

The claims made above are preliminary, of course. It remains to be seen whether existing frameworks used to study the EU need to be developed, or whether with minor adaptation they can suffice. In that respect the discussion above reflects a call for action, new attention and further research. The arguments do suggest, however, that our traditional approaches to studying the EU may need to be adapted or supplemented to account for a kind of European cooperation that is qualitatively different than most previous examples. Drawing from other theoretical traditions and academic fields to explain an activity that must be addressed under conditions of urgency, uncertainty and complexity may well be in order.

Conclusion

This chapter has sought to bring light to an underexplored area of European cooperation. The EU's role in preparing for, trying to prevent, and helping to respond to various 'crises' has grown over the years to the extent that it not only demands attention for its own sake – to improve our understanding of what is taking place and why – but also for what it tells us about how we study the European Union. Are existing conceptual and analytical frameworks capable of, and appropriate for, explaining these kinds of developments? Do these developments reveal aspects of the EU that challenge conventional wisdom? This chapter has reflected upon several such aspects that deserve future study. One such aspect is the nature, operation and dynamics of the EU's political system. Designed for incremental, inclusive and methodical joint decision-making, the EU's political system is being asked to make swift, controversial and operational decisions that in some cases are a matter of life-or-death – and clearly reaching into a 'core state function' to the extreme. The practical challenges of such situations are only the start of the discussion: the normative questions strongly beckon as well. What does it mean for democratic legitimacy when such decisions are being made collectively and multilaterally, amongst decision-leaders with responsibilities for populations other than those directly affected (to suggest just one problematic scenario) and how can they be held responsible?

The EU's emerging role also casts the rationale for cooperation into sharp relief. The notion of the modern 'risk society', the hazards of living in an interdependent and networked world, and the prevalence of 'transboundary' crises are all narratives creeping into the public discourse (both at national and EU levels, in should be noted) and seemingly serve as a strong justification for further integration in Europe. Events appear to support such claims, as when we are faced with an attack on a transport system, a breakdown in an energy grid or an influenza pandemic. In some cases (Barroso, 2014), the modern risk society and the need for cooperative crisis management is even being trumpeted as the new *raison d'être* for European cooperation, suggesting there is a certain inevitability of these developments. Without overstating the case, it seems clear that the EU's role in crisis management provides a strong incentive for the EU studies community to review its our empirical, theoretical and normative understandings of European integration in new light.

Note

1. The author is grateful for research assistance provided by Aras Lindh of the Swedish Institute of International Affairs and for helpful comments from the editors of this volume. The central argument in this chapter was inspired and developed within a broader research project carried out together with Arjen Boin and Magnus Ekengren.

References

Ackrill, R. (2000) *The Common Agricultural Policy* (Sheffield: Sheffield Academic Press).
Adler, E. and M. N. Barnett (eds.) (1998) *Security Communities* (Cambridge: Cambridge University Press).
Anderson, S. B. (2008) *Crafting EU Security Policy: In Pursuit of a European Identity* (Boulder: Lynne Rienner Publishers).
Armstrong, K. A. and S. Bulmer (1998) *The Governance of the Single European Market* (Manchester: Manchester University Press).
Balzacq, T. (2010) *Securitization Theory: How Security Problems Emerge and Dissolve* (London: Routledge).
Barroso, J. M. (2014) *Barroso Speech, Chatham House*, 20 October, http://www.euractiv.com/content/barroso-speech-chatham-house, date accessed 22 January 2015.
Beck, U. (2002) 'The Terrorist Threat: World Risk Society Revisited', *Theory, Culture and Society*, 19, 39–55.
Bigo, D. (2002) 'Security and Immigration: Toward a Critique of the Governmentality of Unease', *Alternatives: Global, Local, Political*, 27, 63–92.
Boin, A., M. Ekengren and M. Rhinard (2006) 'The Commission and Crisis Management' in Spence, D. (ed.), *The European Commission* (London: John Harper Publishing), pp. 481–501.

Boin, A., M. Ekengren and M. Rhinard (2013) *The European Union as Crisis Manager: Patterns and Prospects* (Cambridge: Cambridge University Press).

Boin, A., M. Ekengren and M. Rhinard (2014) *Making Sense of Sense-Making: The EU's Role in Collecting, Analysing, and Disseminating Information in Times of Crisis*, Research Report Presented to the Swedish Civil Contingencies Agency, March 2014.

Boin, A., M. Ekengren, A. Missiroli, M. Rhinard and B. Sundelius (2007) *Building Societal Security in Europe: The EU's Role in Managing Emergencies*. EPC Working Papers, 27.

Bossong, R. (2012) *The Evolution of EU Counter-Terrorism: European Security Policy After 9/11* (London: Routledge).

Bossong, R. and M. Rhinard (2013a) 'The EU Internal Security Strategy: Towards a More Coherent Approach to EU Security?', *Studia Diplomatica*, LXVI, 45–58.

Bossong, R. and M. Rhinard (2013b) 'European Internal Security as a Public Good', *European Security*, 22, 129–147.

Boswell, C. (2007) 'Migration Control in Europe After 9/11: Explaining the Absence of Securitization', *Journal of Common Market Studies*, 45, 589–610.

Brattberg, E. and M. Rhinard (2013) 'Actorness and Effectiveness in International Disaster Relief: The European Union and United States in Comparative Perspective', *International Relations*, 27, 356–374.

Brown, O., A. Hammill and R. McLeman (2007) 'Climate Change as the "New" Security Threat: Implications for Africa', *International Affairs*, 86, 1141–1154.

Börzel, T. A. (2000) 'When Europe Hits Home: Europeanization and Domestic Change', *European Integration Online Papers*, 4, 1–13.

Börzel, T. A. and T. Risse (2003) 'Conceptualizing the Domestic Impact of Europe' in Featherstone, K. and C. Radaelli (eds.) *The Politics of Europeanization* (Oxford: Oxford University Press), pp. 57–80.

Checkel, J. T. (2007) 'International Institutions and Socialization in Europe: Introduction and Framework' in Checkel, J. T. (ed.) *International Institutions and Socialization in Europe* (Cambridge: Cambridge University Press), pp. 3–31.

Comfort, L. K. (2007) 'Crisis Management in Hindsight: Cognition, Communication, Coordination, and Control', *Public Administration Review*, 67, 189–197.

Council of the European Union (2010) *Draft Internal Security Strategy for the European Union: Towards a European Security Model*, Brussels, 8 March, 7120/10.

Council of the European Union (2014a) *Council Conclusions on Multinational Modules under the Union Civil Protection Mechanism*, Justice and Home Affairs Council Meeting, 5–6 June.

Council of the European Union (2014b) *Implementation of the Solidarity Clause*, Luxembourg, 24 June, 11270/14.

Ekengren, M. (2008) 'From a European Security Community to a Secure European Community Tracing the New Security Identity of the EU' in Brauch, H. G., Ú. O. Spring, C. Mesjasz, J. Grin, P. Dunay, N. B. Chadha, B. Chourou, P. Kameri-Mbote and P. H. Liotta (eds.) *Globalization and Environmental Challenges* (New York: Springer), pp. 695–704.

Eriksson, J. and M. Rhinard (2009) 'The Internal-External Security Nexus: Notes on an Emerging Research Agenda', *Cooperation and Conflict*, 44, 243–67.

European Commission (2009) *Inventory of Crisis Management Capacities in the European Commission and Community Agencies*, Internal Report by the Secretariat-General, Brussels.

European Commission (2014) *Communication from the Commission: The Final Implementation Report of the EU Internal Security Strategy 2010–2014*, COM (2014) 365 final, Brussels, 20 June.

Fritzon, Å., K. Ljungkvist, A. Boin and M. Rhinard (2007) 'Protecting Europe's Critical Infrastructures: Problems and Prospects', *Journal of Contingencies and Crisis Management*, 15, 30–41.

Horgby, A. and M. Rhinard (2013) *The EU's Internal Security Strategy: Living in the Shadow of Its Past*, UI Occassional Papers #24. Swedish Institute of International Affairs.

Kaldor, M. (2007) *Human Security* (Cambridge: Polity Press).

Kaunert, C. (2010) 'The Area of Freedom, Security and Justice in the Lisbon Treaty: Commission Policy Entrepreneurship?', *European Security*, 19, 169–189.

Kaunert, C. and M. Della Giovanna (2010) 'Post-9/11 EU Counter-Terrorist Financing Cooperation: Differentiating Supranational Policy Entrepreneurship by the Commission and the Council Secretariat', *European Security*, 19, 275–295.

Kingdon, J. W. (1995) *Agendas, Alternatives, and Public Policies* (New Haven: HarperCollins).

Koops, J. A. (2011) *The European Union as an Integrative Power? Assessing the EU's 'Effective Multilateralism' Towards NATO and the United Nations* (Brussels: Brussels University Press).

McDonagh, K. (2014) ' "Talking the Talk or Walking the Walk": Understanding the EU's Security Identity', *Journal of Common Market Studies* (Online First).

Moravcsik, A. and F. Schimmelfennig (2009) 'Liberal Intergovernmentalism' in Wiener, A. and T. Diez (eds.) *European Integration Theory* (Oxford: Oxford University Press), pp. 67–87.

Myrdal, S. and M. Rhinard (2010) *The European Union's Solidarity Clause: Empty Letter or Effective Tool?*, UI Occasional Papers.

Niemann, A. (2010) *Explaining Decisions in the European Union* (Cambridge: Cambridge University Press).

Nugent, N. and M. Rhinard (2015) *The European Commission* (Basingstoke: Palgrave Macmillan).

Olsson, S. (2009) *Crisis Management in the European Union: Cooperation in the Face of Emergencies* (Dordrecht: Springer).

Paton, D. and L. Jang, L. (2011) 'Disaster Resilience: Exploring All Hazards and Cross-Cultural Perspectives' in Miller, J. R. (ed.) *Community Disaster Recovery and Resiliency: Exploring Global Opportunities and Challenges* (Boca Raton: CRC Press), pp. 81–89.

Rhinard, M. (2010) *Framing Europe: The Policy Shaping Strategies of the European Commission* (Boston: Martinus Nijhoff).

Rosenthal, U., P. 't Hart and A. Kouzmin (1991) 'The Bureau-Politics of Crisis Management', *Public Administration*, 69, 211–233.

Sandholtz, W. and A. Stone Sweet (1998) *European Integration and Supranational Governance* (Oxford: Oxford University Press).

Smith, M. E. (2004) *Europe's Foreign and Security Policy: The Institutionalization of Cooperation* (Cambridge: Cambridge University Press).

Sundelius, B. (2005) 'Disruptions: Functional Security for the EU' in Missiroli, A. (eds.) *Disasters, Diseases, Disruptions: A New D-Drive for the European Union* (Paris: Institute for Security Studies, European Union), Chaillot Paper No. 83, pp. 67–84.

Vahl, R. (1997) *Leadership in Disguise: The Role of the European Commission in EC Decision-Making on Agriculture in the Uruguay Round* (Aldershot, UK: Ashgate).

Weiler, J. H. H. (1999) *The Constitution of Europe: 'Do the New Clothes Have an Emperor?' and Other Essays on European Integration* (Cambridge: Cambridge University Press).

Wivel, A. (2005) 'The Security Challenge of Small EU Member States: Interests, Identity and the Development of the EU as a Security Actor', *Journal of Common Market Studies*, 43, 393–412.

Wolff, S., N. Wichmann and G. Mounier (2010) *The External Dimension of Justice and Home Affairs: A Different Security Agenda for the European Union?* (London: Routledge).

13
Conclusion: European Civil Security Governance between Consolidation and Contestation

Raphael Bossong and Hendrik Hegemann

Introduction

This edited volume aimed to raise our empirical and conceptual awareness of European civil security governance and stimulate a sustained and critical engagement with this phenomenon from different analytical perspectives. For long, social science research on international politics and European integration had disregarded the prevention of, preparation for, response to and recovery from crises and disasters as a largely technical, epiphenomenal issue beyond the realm of 'high politics' that was largely left to officials and experts (see also Rhinard, in this volume). Particularly when moving beyond national levels of analysis, the study of the political drivers and consequences of this field was found to be 'marginalised and largely invisible' (Hannigan, 2012, p. 7) and political scientists proved to be 'hardly interested' (Attinà, 2012b, p. 21). This has begun to change; partially due to the experience of 'new' or 'unconventional' transboundary security challenges, such as during the Indian Ocean Tsunami or the Fukushima nuclear disaster, but also because international organizations have been equipped with new, more substantial competences and instruments. This is reflected by a growing literature on global and regional activities to enhance humanitarian assistance, reduce the risks of disasters and improve overall resilience in vulnerable societies (Attinà, 2012a; Hannigan, 2012; Hollis, 2015). The European Union (EU) has been a special frontrunner in this field. A number of recent contributions, therefore, highlighted that the comprehensive management of crises and disasters increasingly infiltrates many areas of EU integration and seems to be establishing itself as a distinct and dynamic area of European integration (Boin et al., 2006, 2013; Attinà, 2013).

To contribute to this nascent, but dynamic area of academic research and political practice, this edited volume was guided by a number of propositions captured by the notion of European civil security governance. In particular, it suggested that 'civil security' – though a fuzzy term – is in the process of establishing itself as a cross-cutting policy-field for the comprehensive management of diverse, civilian crises and disasters in Europe. Moreover, it started from the assumption that 'governance' would be a useful framework concept for the analysis of the fluid and fragmented civil security field with its emphasis on diverse, multi-actor and often informal multilevel arrangements. Finally, it was especially interested in what this means for the functional opportunities and normative desirability of the EU's role as provider of civil security.

This volume contributed to clarifying and substantiating these assumptions, but also confirmed the sense of a highly mixed picture outlined in the introduction to this book. As shown by the chapters in this volume, we are simultaneously confronted with, on the one hand, new shared security challenges and parallel institutional and conceptual processes in civil protection systems since the end of the Cold War and, on the other hand, a complex empirical picture that underlines the importance of national and regional path-dependency in the make-up of different security systems. Civil security governance remains a useful notion to cast a net over a wide range of transformation processes in contemporary security policy in Europe and possibly also beyond, which previously escaped attention or fragmented into narrow or technical perspectives. Yet the observable level of difference underlines the need to refrain from simplistic functionalist arguments that call for 'necessary' adaptations of national security systems under a new paradigm.

To illustrate, threat exposure varies considerably even among smaller regional blocks, while we also have to appreciate the importance of different social and cultural expectations vis-à-vis the organization of political authority across Europe. Such institutional, cultural and social differences also apply to subgroups, such as the 'new' EU member states that could be assumed to have undergone a strongly convergent transformation of their security sectors in the post-communist and EU-accession period (Matzcak et al., in this volume). Furthermore, seemingly shared discourses on changing risks and the importance of an all-hazards approach to security provision can overlay the difficulties and divergent approaches to putting such notions into practice.

A supposedly common and strongly transboundary crisis or challenge, such as the H1N1 pandemic, provides a perfect example of the possible range of reactions and response patterns, particularly when including political and public debates on the legitimacy and appropriateness of security measures (Brazova and Matczak, in this volume). And also at transnational levels – where we might expect a less pronounced influence of cultural and institutional path-dependence or a stronger focus on functionalist cooperation – the EU is embedded in wider overlapping regime complexes and continues to represent a unique case of regional integration that is not easily emulated on the basis of rationalist criteria (Petz and Hollis, in this volume).

This remaining conclusion reviews these main trends or patterns and discusses them in light of broader empirical and theoretical debates. It finally suggests some building blocks for a wider and interdisciplinary research agenda on European civil security governance, adding to the research gaps in EU studies that have been aptly identified by Rhinard in this volume.

Civil security as an unconsolidated, but dynamic field

Security studies scholars have long highlighted that the way security governance is organized and executed strongly depends upon the underlying representations and understandings of 'security', including respective prefixes (Christou et al., 2010). Framing security in specific ways shapes the political and public assessments of pressing threats, responsible actors and reasonable solutions. For example, the advancement of security research agendas under the label of 'civil security', such as in Germany and the EU, clearly serves the legitimation of involved actors by stressing the non-military, purportedly technical nature of research funding in a controversial area in which states strictly guard their sovereignty. Hence, the concept of civil security is not just academic navel-gazing, but it is also put into practice by political actors. It could hence be seen as 'new security thinking in practice' (Boin et al., 2006, p. 412).

Various chapters illustrated the relevance of many features of the concept of civil security that were discussed in the introduction to this book. First, most authors accepted the trend towards more diverse, civilian risks where the potential damage to societies – understood as the central security reference object – becomes more important than the concrete source of a threat. While military scenarios have seen a dramatic revival after the onset of the Ukrainian crisis, which could not be reflected in the research conducted for this volume, we maintain that this larger trend remains in place. This is not to say that official and societal risk perceptions do not diverge significantly when looking at details in various European countries. Second, these changing threat perceptions or framings are accompanied by an increasingly dominant response mode across countries and policy-fields. This mode revolves around increasingly networked, integrated or 'joined-up' thinking where different actors from different levels are supposed to join forces against complex risks. The military can contribute to these efforts during especially severe crises, but has come under clear civilian leadership. Yet again, this does not mean that this shared trend should blind us to significant cross-country differences and obstacles to implementation, as taken up further below.

So at a relatively high level of abstraction civil security highlights and connects important dynamics of contemporary security policy in Europe. However, we remain confronted with a variety of different labels and policy discourses at different levels of governance (see again the introduction to this volume), which revolve around similar ideas on the need to rethink and reform the provision of public security in response to crises. For instance, Hollis traces the spread of UN-supported notions of disaster risk reduction, while Prior et al. historically embed the turn towards 'resilience', which seems to establish itself as a global 'meta-narrative' for appropriate risk management all the way down to the local level. In fact, civil security is not widely used as an explicit concept by political and administrative actors in Europe, even though their actions and responsibilities might fit its meaning. This adds to the fact that many policy labels, including seemingly traditional ones such as civil protection, do not neatly translate across languages and always need to be seen in the context of national legal and institutional frameworks. For instance, Scandinavian countries share the term 'societal security' while Germany and Switzerland have coined the fixed expression 'protection of the population' (*Bevölkerungsschutz*) to describe their attempts for a comprehensive, integrated response to diverse crises beyond military-focused civil defence. Within the EU, Dorussen et al. also show how EU regulation and decision-making for crisis management expands across various policy areas, but without becoming integrated under a single headline. In sum, there is substantial evidence for the emergence of a common field of civil security based on such broadly shared institutions and ideas. However, this field still lacks a clear narrative and remains 'fluid and unsettled' (Hannigan, 2012, p. 4), so that we cannot claim that civil security will emerge as a dominant label for practitioners and policymakers.

The multilevel politics of civil security governance

The second major premise of this volume is that 'governance' serves as useful framework to highlight precisely these fluid and fragmented patterns of cooperation and coordination beyond fully consolidated policy regimes. Thus, various contributions have applied the notion of governance in fruitful as well as diverse ways. Deverell, for instance, shows that the challenges of post-crisis learning in complex, multi-actor settings can well be captured by the notion of civil security governance. This difficult task requires flexible, both formal and informal arrangements for the development and exchange of knowledge and expertise. In another case, Ekengren argues that the EU's Common Security and Defence Policy's (CSDP) experience with new or experimental forms of governance by 'benchmarks' and 'headline goals', rather than supranational legislation, might be the most suitable role model for furthering EU capacities for civil protection and crisis management. And Dorussen et al. utilize the idea of civil security governance to analyse the role of individual and bureaucratic agency within the diverse net of different decision-making and consultation bodies in the EU system of comitology.

However, civil security governance as analysed in this volume diverges from other major trends in contemporary security governance (Krahmann, 2003; Webber et al., 2004). In particular, we found a nuanced picture that speaks against categorical claims about a shift from 'traditional' models of disaster management and public security provision to a general condition of 'security governance', if narrowly understood as a retreat of the state or privatization of security. This adds to recent debates on implicit assumptions of security governance as an analytical approach, and the need for more systematic, case-specific empirical inquiry (Hameiri and Jones, 2013; Ehrhart et al., 2014). Especially when looking at the national level, traditional government-centred and largely hierarchical structures for security provision remain at the forefront, although the entrenched role of civil society actors, such as the Red Cross, in civil protection and disaster management may also be read as evidence for governance networks (in the form of corporatism). One needs to recognize that many European states face difficulties to sustain such wider civil security governance systems under conditions of dynamic social and economic change. Conscription, which contributed to the societal embedding of civil defence systems, has been abolished in almost all European countries, while one can point to declining membership in civil society organizations that is not (yet) compensated for by more spontaneous forms of civic mobilization and participation that can be channelled through social media. But returning to dominant notions of security governance, the first part of this volume could not make out a significant trend to outsource emergency response and civil security tasks to private actors – at least if one moves beyond conventional legal regulations for industrial and product security. Prior et al. also demonstrate how conceptions of security provision are subject to major historical transformation and swings, with resilience serving as a focal point for reemphasizing the role of citizens as responsible societal actors. But again, this should not be read as proof of a general retreat of the state and public authorities for civil security provision.

Instead, we could confirm the importance of emphasizing the multilevel nature of civil security governance, understood as an increased layering and cross-cutting interdependence of still dominantly public actors. To begin with, the second chapter by Bossong and Hegemann outlined homologous pressures across countries to strike a new balance between decentralized response capacities and national special emergency platforms to respond to new and increasingly transboundary risks. Disaster management and civil security remain a vital responsibility at local and regional levels of governments or of first responders, whereas various platforms, centres and institutions at higher government levels have been created or reformed over the last decade. And as shown by Hollis and Petz, such reforms or re-balancing efforts have also been promoted by international organizations and high-level discourses on improved disaster risk reduction. In a nutshell, civil security governance helps us to look beyond functional boxes as well as hierarchical levels that structure traditional thinking on civil protection, disaster management and various technical aspects of crisis management.

Yet, once again, when decreasing the level of abstraction and focusing on empirical findings we underline the extensive and persistent degree of national diversity. Despite shared security notions or new cooperation instruments, as outlined by Ekengren, one can at best discern the beginnings of 'experimental governance' whereby the European and international networks would lead to regular reform or benchmarking of national policy regimes (for example compared to education and research policy). Hollis similarly highlights the 'gap' between international discourses and local practices on disaster risk reduction including the ambivalent role of the EU in this regard. Finally, when looking at review processes – as in Sweden and or the H1N1 pandemic that are discussed in this book –, we see that that crises might often be too diverse and complex to translate into easily transferrable, standardized 'lessons'. In any case, national institutional processes and political obstacles to reform have to be tackled first before any substantive learning can take place.

The contested role of the EU in civil security governance: Still towards an ever closer union?

However, even if we need to critically review the impact of transnational civil security governance to date, we maintain that governance is particularly helpful to explore the increasingly operational – rather than just ideational or experimental – role of the EU in this area. As summed up by Rhinard, we should take note of a wide range of policies, instruments and flexible initiatives that have partially adapted the EU to the time-sensitive demands of crisis management (see also Boin et al., 2013). Of course, national sovereignty, or the principle of voluntary cooperation and member state control over material assets, remains fundamental to understanding the operational capacities of the EU. However, one can rightly point to moderate successes in the area of external and partly military crisis management that could further inspire related EU civil protection and civil security activities (see Ekengren in this volume). Petz, in his chapter, already shows on the basis of a logical set of indicators why the EU constitutes the leading transnational organization for civil security and crisis management, which has moved beyond general policy declarations. Meanwhile, Dorussen et al. demonstrate how familiar processes from EU integration, namely spill-over, creative use of legal regulatory competences for single market matters and bureaucratic politics, have over time created a substantial regime for regulation and decision-making in times of crises. Boin and Kuipers add to this analysis from a perspective that is less familiar to EU researchers, but highly significant for students of disasters. That is, bureaucratic entrepreneurship and the use of windows of opportunities for policy-making after crisis should not only be understood as a rational game for extending EU policy competences. If the EU steps in during a crisis, it may also answer the widely perceived need to re-establish rationality and direction under conditions of extreme uncertainty. Aside from questions of subsidiarity and formal institutions the EU may, therefore, acquire increasing professional authority and respect to interpret the meaning of, and best response to, various civil security challenges.

How then should we understand this evolution of multilevel civil security governance in Europe and by the EU from a normative perspective? The research presented in this volume does not lend support to strong theses or critiques about an ever-expanding securitization of social and political life in Europe, as identified by critical security scholars in other areas like policing and migration (Bigo, 2002; Huysmans, 2008). There are some technocratic tendencies for an inscription of new forms of insecurity and security provision, such as transnational risk maps or an increasing role for little-known regulatory committees (see Dorussen et al. and Ekengren, in this volume). However, we could neither identify a universal trend towards exceptional politics in the face of purportedly existential threats, nor a decreasing space for democratic processes of debate and decision-making. The observed structural diversity at the national level, the overall minor role of the military and the simultaneous tendencies for centralization and decentralization in national civil security governance system all speak against such overriding critical arguments.

This leaves us with debating the role of the EU, which, depending on perspective and political conviction, should further expand its role in transboundary crisis management or needs to reflect upon its limits in the nascent policy space of civil security. From a sceptical perspective, we would underline the lack of a self-evident spill-over or teleological integration process and point to numerous non-functionalist drivers for EU integration in this issue area, such as bureaucratic entrepreneurship and symbolic politics (compare again Rhinard, in this volume). Many concrete threats and vulnerabilities, or natural disasters, take place on lower geographical scales than the EU as a whole, whereas other threats, such as pandemics, might rather require global governance responses. In that sense, the appropriate location of authority has to remain permanently contested. It is not enough to posit a conventional conflict between national sovereignty and progressive supranational integration leading to the inevitability or illusionary comfort of a 'secure community' (Ekengren, 2008). Rather, there is no convincing or widely accepted model for the organization of this core political responsibility. In this perspective, the EU may be an important player that can fulfil sense-making and coordination functions in transboundary crisis management. But the EU continues to play alongside, and cannot supplant or conceptually transcend, a large number of actors in the multilevel field of civil security governance, such as regional authorities, global international organizations or national crisis management centres and ministries.

After all, civil security governance needs be understood as a field of 'civil' politics. This should include extensive opportunities for debate in civil society and participation of, or at least oversight by, democratic institutions. The wider literature on contemporary and participatory risk management provides an important point of reference here (Klinke and Renn, 2014). However, the ideal of open deliberation among a diverse set of stakeholders often comes under pressure, and not only due to the demands of crisis decision-making that classically concern security scholars. New or rarely experienced security challenges, such as the H1N1 or ash could crisis discussed in this volume, generate dilemmas about appropriate risk communication (Palttala and Vos, 2012). And as mentioned above, post-crisis review and learning processes remain difficult to design and of questionable impact.

Nonetheless, we would not subscribe to a fundamentally alarmist or critical analysis of the state of civil security policy and governance in Europe. European member states that were analysed in this volume seem to enjoy relatively high, if often only implicit, support of their citizens (compare chapters 2 and 3 in this book) when it comes to varied responsibilities of protection and emergency management. This support for still dominantly public structures and authorities for civil security (see above) may even be read as precisely the shared, 'thick' sense of security that is the best means to 'civilize' it – or to contain the problematic and excessive tendencies of some forms of contemporary security governance (Loader and Walker, 2007). This core achievement of civil security provision in Europe needs to be preserved, both by regular reform processes to ensure the continued desired effectiveness and by critical attention to the evolving multilevel governance system to maintain responsibility and accountability. Wherever the master-discourse of resilience might ultimately lead us when one follows the long-term perspective set out in the chapter by Prior et al., it cannot mean a return towards fatalism or only support supranational technocratic governance that is decoupled from local practice and democratic deliberation.

What's next? Implications for future research

We conclude this volume by briefly outlining further areas of research that should support this sustained political and scholarly engagement with European civil security governance. Reflecting the disciplinary background of the editors and most contributors, this exploratory research agenda is catered towards what has been called 'strategic-political perspectives' rooted in international relations, EU integration studies and (critical) security studies, rather than a 'technical-managerial perspective' often dominating discussions among policy-oriented security experts or professionals of crisis management ('t Hart and Sundelius, 2013, pp. 447–49). Hence, this discussion is not so much concerned with the practical operational and administrative challenges of organizing effective prevention and response in case of actual crises than with the political and social drivers and consequences of the observed multilevel space of European civil security governance. Hence, we pay special attention to questions surrounding the 'disaster-politics-nexus' (Hannigan, 2012).

Following our previous discussion, we can identify four main sets of questions. First, our findings call for intensified research on the political usages, meanings and ramifications of 'civil security'. In line with wider comparative and critical research agendas on the concept of security (Zedner, 2003; Balzacq, 2014), we need to learn and debate more about what civil security means, what it encompasses and how it relates to other terms. The more extensive conceptual literature on resilience (Prior and Hagmann, 2014) suggests that this is a difficult task and requires further empirical research on the application of the term in concrete instances. There are already some attempts that apply discursive and sociological approaches to understand and disentangle overlapping and/or competing discourses in areas like crisis and disaster management (Hannigan, 2012; Hollis, 2014). It has also been suggested elsewhere that we need to reflect more how specific representations and logics of security shape specific modes of governance, such as securitized, politicized or functional forms of security governance (Christou et al., 2010). The broadly constructivist orientation of critical security studies offers a rich toolkit for the analysis of respective security discourses and practices and their manifest political and normative implications that can be brought to be bear on the study of EU civil security governance.

Second, the multilevel governance perspective advanced by this book demands not only increased attention by EU scholars (see Rhinard, in this volume), but also by students of International Relations and Global Governance. To begin with, existing research on global and regional processes of convergence and diffusion in disaster risk response should be taken further and linked to debates on the more specific case of the EU (Hannigan, 2012; Hollis, 2014, 2015). The sociological-institutionalist framework that is typically taken by these studies also seems a reasonable basis to assess how specific aspects and understandings of civil security governance emerge as global 'best practice' and how this emanates from and trickles back down to the regional and national levels. The established literatures on comparative regionalism and the diffusion of the EU model of regional integration (Jetschke and Lenz, 2013) as well as on the EU's global role in multilateral and interregional fora (Söderbaum and van Langenhove, 2006; Jørgensen, 2009) may offer helpful insights. From a theoretical perspective, it might be useful to explore whether civil security governance can and should be conceptualized as a 'regime complex' (Raustiala and Victor, 2004), 'organizational field' (Bremberg and Britz, 2009; Dingwerth and Pattberg, 2009) or 'community of practice' (Adler, 2008; Bremberg, 2010) in order to move beyond the narrow focus on single organizations and actors and take a broader look at cross-cutting institutional and ideational developments in this field.

Third, the specific role of the EU and its interaction with national civil security governance systems, or the 'supranational-national interface' (Rhinard et al., 2006, p. 523), could also be explored further in cultural and sociological directions. The diversity of member state approaches that has been identified here awaits more detailed analysis on specific patterns and conditions. One thing that stands out from the analysis is the crucial role played by cultural and historical traditions. Here, research relying on the concept of strategic culture, which has already successfully been applied to security governance in the more military-oriented realm of CSDP policy (Norheim-Martinsen, 2013), could be a welcome addition to approaches drawing on cultural and psychological studies on risk perception (Rothstein et al., 2013). Taking up attempts to integrate the 'practice turn' in social science into research on strategic culture (Neumann and Heikka, 2005), studying how different approaches to civil security manifest and reproduce themselves in specific material practices, such as risk assessments or joint exercises, might also be useful to better understand the social and ideational underpinnings of European civil security governance at its different levels.

Fourth and finally, we can envisage further debates on security governance that draw on these empirical insights and applications. We underline again that even though civil security governance primarily takes place among security policymakers, practitioners and other 'stakeholders' beyond public scrutiny, it is not a mere technical question. A security governance approach can involve contentious questions (e.g. costs of protection, responsible levels of authority) and delicate trade-offs (e.g. efficiency vs. sovereignty). Civil security governance can lead to significant conflict and require further political and scholarly debate about underlying risk perceptions, goals to be pursued, measures to be taken and costs to be distributed (Hameiri and Jones, 2013; Ehrhart et al., 2014). This should entail further debate on the intended and unintended consequences of civil security governance (Daase and Friesendorf, 2010), for example in the form of institutional competition and duplication in international disaster management or collective action problems in European capacity-sharing (Rhinard et al., 2012). Moreover, the findings of this book lend further credence to the argument that security governance needs to leave behind its exclusive focus on the analysis of specific actors within a European context. Rather, more is to be discovered about the system-level qualities of civil security governance and the interactions between organizations and networks at different – global, regional and national – layers of security governance (Adler and Greve, 2009; Sperling and Webber, 2014).

References

Adler, E. (2008) 'The Spread of Security Communities: Communities of Practice, Self-Restraint and NATO's Post-Cold War Transformation', *European Journal of International Relations*, 14, 195–230.

Adler, E. and P. Greve (2009) 'When Security Community Meets Balance of Power: Overlapping Regional Mechanisms of Security Governance', *Review of International Studies*, 35, 59–84.

Attinà, F. (ed.) (2012a) *The Politics and Policies of Relief, Aid and Reconstruction: Contrasting Approaches to Disasters and Emergencies* (Basingstoke: Palgrave Macmillan).

Attinà, F. (2012b) 'Disaster and Emergency Policies at the International and Global System Levels' in Attinà, F. (ed.) *The Politics and Policies of Relief, Aid and Reconstruction: Contrasting Approaches to Disasters and Emergencies* (Basingstoke: Palgrave Macmillan), pp. 21–41.

Attinà, F. (2013) *Merging Policies as Strategy against Emergency Threats: The EU's Institutional Response to Disasters, Risk and Emergencies*, ReShape Online Papers Series 01/13 (Catania: University of Catania).

Balzacq, T. (2014) *Contesting Security: Strategies and Logics* (London: Routledge).

Bigo, D. (2002) 'Security and Immigration: Toward a Critique of the Governmentality of Unease', *Alternatives: Global, Local and Political*, 27, 63–92.

Boin, A., M. Ekengren and M. Rhinard (2006) 'Protecting the Union: Analysing an Emerging Policy Space', *Journal of European Integration*, 28, 405–21.

Boin, A., M. Ekengren and M. Rhinard (2013) *The European Union as Crisis Manager: Patterns and Prospects* (Cambridge: Cambridge University Press).

Bremberg, N. (2010) 'Security, Governance and Community Beyond the European Union: Exploring Issue-Level Dynamics in Euro-Mediterranean Civil Protection', *Mediterranean Politics*, 15, 169–188.

Bremberg, N. and M. Britz (2009) 'Uncovering the Diverging Institutional Logics of EU Civil Protection', *Cooperation and Conflict*, 44, 288–308.

Christou, G., S. Croft, M. Ceccorulli and S. Lucarelli (2010) 'European Union Security Governance: Putting the "Security" Back In', *European Security*, 19, 341–59.

Daase, C. and C. Friesendorf (eds.) (2010) *Rethinking Security Governance: The Problem of Unintended Consequences* (London: Routledge).

Dingwerth, K. and P. Pattberg (2009) 'World Politics and Organizational Fields: The Case of Transnational Sustainability Governance', *European Journal of International Relations*, 15, 707–744.

Ehrhart, H.-G., Hegemann, H. and M. Kahl (2014) 'Towards Security Governance as a Critical Tool: A Conceptual Outline', *European Security*, 23, 145–162.

Ekengren, M. (2008) 'From a European Security Community to a Secure European Community: Tracing the New Security Identity of the EU' in Brauch, H. G. et al. (eds.) *Globalization and Environmental Challenges: Reconceptualizing Security in the 21st Century* (New York: Springer), pp. 695–704.

Hameiri, S. and L. Jones (2013) 'The Politics and Governance of Non-Traditional Security', *International Studies Quarterly*, 57, 462–472.

Hannigan, J. (2012) *Disasters without Borders: The International Politics of Natural Disasters* (Cambridge: Polity Press).

't Hart, P. and B. Sundelius (2013) 'Crisis Management Revisited: A New Agenda for Research, Training and Capacity Building within Europe', *Cooperation and Conflict*, 48, 444–461.

Hollis, S. (2014) 'Competing and Complimentary Discourses in Global Disaster Risk Management', *Risk, Hazards & Crises in Public Policy*, 5, 342–363.

Hollis, S. (2015) *The Role of Regional Organizations in Disaster Risk Management: A Global Strategy for Resilience* (Basingstoke: Palgrave Macmillan).

Huysmans, J. (2008) *The Politics of Insecurity: Fear, Migration and Asylum in the EU* (London: Routledge).

Jetschke, A. and T. Lenz (2013) 'Does Regionalism Diffuse? A New Research Agenda for the Study of Regional Organizations', *Journal of European Public Policy*, 20, 626–637.

Jørgensen, K. E. (eds.) (2009) *European Union and International Organizations* (London: Routledge).

Klinke, A. and O. Renn (2014) 'Expertise and Experience: A Deliberative System of a Functional Division of Labor for Post-Normal Risk Governance', *Innovation: The European Journal of Social Sciences*, 27, 442–465.

Krahmann, E. (2003) 'Conceptualizing Security Governance', *Cooperation and Conflict*, 38, 5–26.

Loader, I. and N. Walker (2007) *Civilizing Security* (Cambridge: Cambridge University Press).

Neumann, I. and H. Heikka (2005) 'Grand Strategy, Strategic Culture, Practice: The Social Roots of Nordic Defence', *Cooperation and Conflict*, 40, 5–23,

Norheim-Martinsen, P. (2013) *The European Union and Military Force: Governance and Strategy* (Cambridge: Cambridge University Press).

Prior, T. and J. Hagmann (2014) 'Measuring Resilience: Methodological and Political Challenges of a Trend Security Concept', *Journal of Risk Research*, 17, 281–298.

Palttala, P. and M. Vos (2012) 'Quality Indicators for Crisis Communication to Support Emergency Management by Public Authorities', *Journal of Contingencies and Crisis Management*, 20, 39–51.

Raustiala, K. and D. G. Victor (2004) 'The Regime Complex for Plant Genetic Resources', *International Organization*, 58, 277–309.

Rothstein, H., O. Borraz and M. Huber (2013) 'Risk and the Limits of Governance: Exploring Varied Patterns of Risk-Based Governance in Europe', *Risk & Regulation*, 7, 215–235.

Rhinard, M., M. Ekengren and A. Boin (2006) 'The European Union's Emerging Protection Space: Next Steps for Research and Practice', *Journal of European Integration*, 28, 511–527.

Rhinard, M., S. Hollis and A. Boin (2013) 'Explaining Civil Protection Cooperation in the EU: The Contribution of Public Goods Theory', *European Security*, 22, 248–269.

Söderbaum, F. and L. van Langenhove (eds.) (2006) *The EU as a Global Player: The Politics of Interregionalism* (London: Routledge).

Sperling, J. and M. Webber (2014) 'Security Governance in Europe: A Return to System', *European Security*, 23, 126–144.

Webber, M., S. Croft, J. Howorth, T. Terriff and E. Krahmann (2004) 'The Governance of European Security', *Review of International Studies*, 30, 3–26.

Zedner, L. (2003) 'The Concept of Security: An Agenda for Comparative Analysis', *Legal Studies*, 23, 153–176.

Index

Note: The locators followed by 'n' refer to note numbers.

African Union (AU), 98
air space policy
  actor's involvement, 199–200
  common approach, 198–9
  Eurocontrol plan, 180, 196–7, 199, 202–4, 225–6
  International Civil Aviation Organization (ICAO) guidelines, 196–7, 199, 202
  risk assessment, 200–1
  zero-tolerance rule, 199
all-hazards system, 1, 8, 11, 16, 31, 45–6, 64, 69, 279
Analysis of Civil Security Systems in Europe (ANVIL), 75, 118, 126, 129
Andean Community of Nations (CAN), 111 n. 6
Area of Freedom, Security and Justice (AFSJ), 3, 19, 211–12, 257
ASEAN Coordinating Centre for Humanitarian Assistance (AHA Centre), 100
Association of Southeast Asian Nations (ASEAN), 100, 120
avian influenza
  comparative analysis (OMS and NMS), 57
  EU agencies' role, 222
  global dimension, 221
  national plans, 221
  preventive vaccination, 221
  Standing Committee on Food Chain and Animal Health's (SCFCAH) action, 220–2

battle groups (EU), 236, 242, 249
benchmarks, 43–4, 46, 237, 239–40, 249–50, 282–3

bird surveillance measures, 221–2
  see also Standing Committee on Food Chain and Animal Health (SCFCAH)
BSE/mad cow disease (1996–1997)
  DG SANCO's role, 228
  emergency response, 219
  EP recommendations, 218, 220, 227–9
  EU committees, meeting, 217–18
  UK economy, impact on, 217
bureaucratic politics, 3, 45, 63, 213–14, 226, 228, 282, 284–5

Capability Development Plans (CDP), 237–8, 240
Caribbean Community (CARICOM), 100, 102–3, 111 n. 6, 125
Caribbean Disaster Emergency Management Agency (CDEMA), 102
Central American Integration System (SICA), 100, 103, 111 n. 6
Centre for Research on the Epidemiology of Disasters (CRED), 111 n. 4
Chernobyl disaster, 105–6, 147, 191
Chief Medical Officers (CMO), 217
civil defence
  civil protection vs., 126
  crisis management (EU), 270
  in European countries, 32, 41, 45, 283
  federalist traditions, 35
  military vs. civil-led systems, 12, 29, 31, 37, 281
  9/11 attacks, 7
  nuclear war consequences, 6
  Oslo guidelines, 102
  post-ColdWar period, 1
  public–private partnerships, 40

rescue operations, 41
war on terror, 5
war time, 33
Civil Protection Capacity Plans (CPCP), 248–50
Civil Protection Mechanism (CPM)
  2013 revision, 105
  2014 version, 121
  BSEC vs., 108
  disaster modules, 102
  DRM research, 108, 110
  protection modules, 104
  regional funding for DRR, 101
  security policies, 212
civil security governance system (CSGS)
  capacity building challenges, 41–2, 235–7, 239–43, 245–7
  cooperation challenges, 18–20, 243–5
  CSDP and EDA (joint goals), 247–51
  definition and redefinition, 4–5
  disaster distribution, 53–61
  diversity challenges, 14–16
  evaluations and reviews, 43–5
  institutional aspects, 34–6, 263–4
  multilevel governance perspective, 282–4, 287–8
  principal-agent(s) models, 213–14
  stability and change, 51–3
  state-society relations, 38–40
  treaty/strategic developments, 260–3
civilian crises, 1, 32, 41, 279
CleanSeaNet service, 224
Committee of Permanent Representatives (COREPER II), 260
Common Emergency Communication and Information System (CECIS), 11, 103–4, 244, 259
Common Foreign and Security Policy (CFSP), 2–3, 257–8
Common Security and Defence Policy (CSDP)
  capacity goals, 234–5, 237, 243, 247–9
  coordination method, 241, 245–6
  governance methods, 235–7, 247
  revision dynamics, 238, 242
comprehensive security, 2, 28, 35
Council of Europe (CoE)
  DRM issues, 99, 102
  European boundaries, 97
  member countries, 105–6
  regional organization's DRM indicators, 103, 108–10
Country Council (CC), 171, 174–5, 177
crisis investigation
  harmful events, 160
  level of complexity, 163
  policy change and reform, public sector, 166–7
  post hoc, 160–1, 165, 168, 180–1, 183–5
  prevention and societal resilience, 18
crisis management
  air space, 202
  all-hazards system, 64
  avian flu, 222–3
  challenges in Europe, 18, 44, 77, 105
  citizen's role, 65
  civil protection, 211, 249
  civil security, 5
  civilian missions, 12, 264
  classic legal frameworks, 31–2
  communication's role, 87–90, 181
  concepts, 162–4, 168–9
  contemporary concerns, 46
  CSDP missions, 258
  EERC module, 244, 250
  epidemic, 78
  EU activities, 265–6, 269–72, 274
  formal procedures, 33
  global, 251
  influenza pandemic, 85
  institutionalism, 20, 34–5
  media and the medical staff (H1N1), 87
  military capacities, 41, 235–6
  national and regional level, legal frameworks, 33
  peacetime, 33
  private actor's role, 40
  public health laws, 75–6
  special dimension, 28
  strategic concept, 13

crisis management – *continued*
 transboundary, 9, 18–19, 192, 206–7
 values and functions, 178
 volcanic ash cloud, 226
 war legacies (Croatia), 67

Directorate-General for External Relations (DG RELEX), 263
Directorate-General for Health and Consumers (DG SANCO), 212, 221, 228, 263
Directorate-General for the Environment (DG ENVI), 221
Directorate-General Humanitarian Aid and Civil Protection ((DG ECHO), 11, 105, 212, 263
disaster management (DM)
 budget, 121
 CoE and OSCE in, 108
 global ideas, 125–8
 HFA goals, 128–9, 131–2
 indicators, 100–4
 information system, 101
 institutional change, 128–30
 norm diffusion, 122–5
 regional organizations (RO's), 105
 type of centres, 100
 use of terminology, 98
Disaster Preparedness Programme of the EU Humanitarian Aid and Civil Protection (DIPECHO), 120
disaster risk management (DRM)
 BSEC's activities, 107–9
 CoE's, 108
 European and Mediterranean (EUR-OPA), 105–6
 European Commission guidelines, 246, 248
 European organizations, 104–5
 indicators, 99–100, 103–4, 109–10
 natural hazard management processes, 149
 OSCE's role, 107
 regional funding, 101
 technical cooperation (ROs), 102
 use of terminology, 98
disaster risk reduction (DRR)
 Capacity Development Methodology (UNDP), 129

European civil security concept, 134
European Forum for DRR (EFDRR)
 surveys, 118
 global prescriptions and norms, 117–18, 122–3, 125
 HFA goals, 129, 131–2
 intergovernmental meetings, 104
 international advocacy, 119
 national platform reviews, 130, 132
 prevention strategies (global community), 119–20
 RDM framework, 99
 regional funding, 101
 regional organizations (ROs) role, 99, 109, 111, 127
 SADC's definition, 125
 sites of diffusion, 123–4, 126
 supragovernmental frameworks, 153
 use of terminology, 98
 world conference, 130, 133

Early Warning and Response System (EWRS), 222–3
Ebola virus pandemic, 1
Economic Community of West African States (ECOWAS), 98, 101
emergency management
 accident investigations, 165
 in Canada, 167
 citizen support, 286
 EU domestic system, 268
 military capacity, 41
 national organization's role, 38–9, 134
 regional organizations (ROs), 102
 resilience approaches, 151–2
 in Sweden, 181–2
 US federal system, 33
Emergency Response Coordination Centre (ERCC)
 civil protection capacities, 11, 233, 245, 247, 249
 civil security, 212
 crisis management, 2, 104
 disaster management, 263
 establishment, 244
 EU recommendations, 250
 renaming, 259, 263
 voluntary pool, 234

environmental protection, 2, 38, 199, 212, 224
EU integration, 10, 278, 284–5, 287
EU Military Staff (EUMS), 103
EU policies, 2, 8, 10–11, 19, 27, 213, 228, 235, 258, 271, 284
Eurocontrol
  air traffic policies, 196–7, 199
  national air space, closure, 196
  national aviation authorities meeting, 202
  new strategy (airspace plan), 203
  volcanic ash cloud, 180, 226
  zero tolerance rule, 199
European and Mediterranean Major Hazards Agreement (EUR-OPA), 102, 105–6
European Aviation Crisis Coordination Cell (EACCC), 204, 226
European Aviation Safety Agency (EASA)
  air space standards, 199, 204
  crisis task force, 226
  volcanic ash cloud crisis, 225, 228
European Centre for Disease Prevention and Control (ECDC), 221–3, 228
European Commission
  advisory or regulatory nature, 228–9
  bird surveillance measures, 221
  BSE crisis, 219
  civil security concerns, 212–14
  collective policy-making, 271
  cooperation with EDA, 241
  crisis management, 226–7
  defence equipment, 238
  definition of resilience, 150
  European crisis management plan, 202–4
  governance processes, common guidelines, 43
  Green Paper, 100
  institutional entrepreneurism, 266
  intergovernmental practices, 19
  ISS ventures, 263
  risk assessment guidelines, 246
  transboundary crisis response, 205
  volcanic activity in Iceland, 225

European Community Humanitarian Office (ECHO). *see* DG ECHO
European Currency Unit (ECU), 258
European Defence Agency (EDA)
  areas of achievement, 241
  capacity building aspects, 243
  CDP development, 237, 240
  civil protection *vs.*, 247–8
  ERCC comparison with, 250
  Europeanization of defence space, 242
  member state data, 239
  scorecard-work, 239
  Union's Headline Goals, 237–8
European Emergency Response Capacity (EERC), 120, 233, 244–5
European Food Safety Authority (EFSA), 218, 221, 227
European Forum for DRR (EFDRR), 118, 129, 132
European Influenza Surveillance Network (EISN), 222
European integration studies
  decision-making issues (EU), 258
  developmental effects, 268
  EU policy sectors, 258–60
  evolving security conceptions, 267–8
  institutional aspects, 263–4, 266–7
  public policy analysis, 270–1
  security governance approach, 271–3
  treaty/strategic developments, 260–3
European Maritime Safety Agency (EMSA), 224, 227
  see also Irish oil spill
European Medicines Agency (EMA), 221–3, 227
European Organization for the Safety of Air Navigation, *see* Eurocontrol
European Parliament
  BSE crisis, 220, 229
  civil protection framework, 233, 244
  disaster management approach, 133
  embargo on beef imports, 217
  establishment of ECDC, 222
  expansion of scientific committees, 233, 244

European Parliament – *continued*
foot-and-mouth crisis, 220
national risk perceptions role, 205
regulatory nature, 227–8
European Platform for Disaster Risk
Reduction (EPDRR), 124
European Union (EU)
armaments commitments, 242
battle group concept, 236–7
civil protection module, 243–4
civil security governance, 211–12
common policies, 256
cross-border training initiatives,
259, 263
defence cooperation, 240
disaster management, 121
formal norms and institutions, 2
geographical definition, 97
national pandemic strategies, 73
political system, 273
security conceptions, 267
societal functions, 191
Solidarity Clause, 262
Europeanization, 52, 69, 242, 271

foot-and-mouth disease (FMD
2001–2002)
emergency response, 219
principal-agent model perspectives,
220
Standing Veterinary Committee's
(SVC) role, 219–20
Fukushima nuclear disaster, 1, 138,
278
Functional Airspace Blocks (FAB), 203

genetically modified organisms
(GMOs), 227
Global Facility for Disaster Risk
Reduction (GFDRR, World Bank),
95, 117, 119
Global Network for Disaster Reduction
(GNDR), 120
globalization, 1, 94, 143, 156, 193

H1N1 influenza
administrative management, 77–9
antiviral vaccines, priority groups,
79–81

common case definition, 223
consequences, civil security
governance, 83–5
crisis management, challenges,
14–15
ECDC's role, 223
governmental (over)reactions, 81–2
HSC and EWRS, joint meeting, 223
Media's role, 87–8
Poland (exceptional case), 82–3
Stakeholder's involvement, 85–7
transboundary risks, 14
WHO declaration, 74
see also swine flu
HaV (Swedish Agency for Marine and
Water Management), 172, 177
Health Emergencies Operations
Facility (HEOF), 263
Health Security Committee (HSC),
221, 223
homeland security (US), 2, 5, 7–8
Humanitarian Activities in Complex
Emergencies (United Nations
HACE), 102
Hurricane Katrina, 7, 138, 195, 260
Hyogo Framework for Action (HFA),
11, 17, 117–20, 122, 124–5,
128–33, 149

Integrated Political Crisis Response
arrangements (IPCR), 212, 260
International Civil Aviation
Organization (ICAO), 196–7, 199,
202, 225–6
International Commission for the
Protection of the Rhine (ICPR),
265
International Decade for Natural
Disaster Reduction (IDNDR), 117,
119, 125, 133
International Disaster Response Laws,
Rules and Principles (IDRL),
103–4, 108–9
International Federation of the Red
Cross and Red Crescent Societies
(IFRC), 95, 97, 103, 117, 120, 127
international relations, 191, 287

Irish oil spill
  EU committees and agencies role, 228
  European Maritime Safety Agency's (EMSA) role, 224
  maritime safety protection, 224
isomorphism, 14–15, 28, 46, 125

Joint Accident Investigation Commission (JAIC), 170, 177
Justice and Home Affairs (JHA), 211

Kamedo (Swedish Disaster Medicine Study Organization at the National Board of Health and Welfare, 170, 174–5, 177, 181

L'Aquila earthquake, 38, 46
League of Arab States (LAS), 97, 111 n. 6, 120
Lisbon Treaty, 211, 235–6, 239–40, 245, 250, 260, 264
Local Environmental Knowledge (LEK), 139, 147
Local Government Self-Assessment Tool (LGSAT), 129
London bombings (2005), 38

Mad Cow Disease, 147, 191, 216–19
Médecins Sans Frontières (MSF), 131
members of the European Parliament (MEPs), 217
Military and Civil Defence Assets (MCDA), 102
Ministry of Defence (MoD), 64, 80
Monitoring and Information Centre (MIC), 263
MSB (Swedish Civil Contingencies Agency), 172, 177, 178, 181
Municipal Administration (MA), 173, 174, 177

National Air Traffic Services (NATS), 196
National Board of Health and Welfare (NBHW), 174, 177
National Center for Crisis Management Research and Training at the Swedish National Defence College, 170–1, 177
national disaster management organizations (NDMO), 99, 102
natural disasters
  capacity generating methods (EU), 236, 249
  civil security governance, 10, 73, 211
  crisis management, 32, 169, 285
  Eurobarometer data, 37, 57
  in Europe, 53
  fatalistic interpretations, 2
  in late Middle Ages, 141
  new member states (NMS), 68
  old member states (OMS), 68
  policy instruments, 259, 261
  regionalism, 95, 105, 107
  security challenges, 1
  society-wide distribution, 151
natural hazard management
  20th century risk precision, 145–9
  21st century transformation, 140, 147, 154
  2013 revision of the European CPM, 105
  adaptive mechanisms, 139
  challenges, 153
  cherry-pick elements, 138
  comprehensive management, 16, 148
  culture of prevention, 124
  direct response, 142
  DM centres, 100
  explicit risk-based planning, 42
  history, 140–3
  in medieval period, 142–3
  International Decade for Natural Disaster Reduction (IDNDR) agreement, 117
  modern practices, 139, 143–5
  quantitative approaches, 139
  regional organizations (ROs) role, 94–8
  resilience, 17, 149–51, 156
  risk assessment, 145
  social consequences, 140–1
  technical approaches, 138–9

new member states (NMS)
  civil security governance systems development, 15, 61–6
  control mechanisms, 75
  convergence and divergence factors, 51
  Croatian case study, 66–8
  disasters types, 55
  levels of concern, 38
  national policy-making, 50
  number of volunteers, 39
  outsourcing, civil security tasks, 40
  responses to H1N1 crisis, 84–5
  risk-based forward planning, 30
  types of risk, 59
non-governmental organizations (NGOs), 53, 63, 65, 69, 86, 97, 120, 124, 133, 156
North Atlantic Treaty Organization (NATO), 67, 70, 206, 241–2, 267

old member states (OMS)
  civil security governance systems (CSGSs), 64, 68–70
  disaster types, 53, 55
  man-made disasters, 59
  NMS comparison with, 51, 54–6
  post-communist *vs.*, 61
  threat perceptions, 57
  types of risk, 59, 60–2
Organization for Black Sea Economic Cooperation (BSEC)
  DRM issues, 99, 107–10
  IDRL treaty, 103
Organization for Security and Cooperation in Europe (OSCE)
  DRM meetings, 99, 107
  institutional regime, 106
  natural disaster issues, 110
  notions of the boundaries, 97
  organization fulfilling indicators, 103, 108–10
Organization of American States (OAS), 103, 111 n. 6
Oslo guidelines, 102
Oslo/Utøya attacks, 38

path-dependent practices, 123, 126, 134

pooling and sharing, 239–40
post-crisis investigations (public sector policy change and reform), 166–7
post hoc (crisis investigation), 160–1, 165, 168, 180–1, 183–5
prevention
  authorities, 166
  concept, 119, 134
  crime, 43, 144
  crisis, 163, 249, 265, 278, 287
  disaster, 34, 107, 118, 120–2, 132–3, 244
  European Security Model, 262
  global culture, 17, 124–5, 129
  hazard, 149, 152
  individual crimes, 8
  maritime pollution, 224
  natural and man-made risks, 50, 100
  opportunity cost, 130
  organizational crisis, 18, 117
  risk, 141
  stakeholders involvement, 85
  terrorism, 236
principal-agent(s) models, 213–14, 220, 227, 229 n. 5
public policy, 43, 270–1

regional cooperation, 16, 67, 69, 94, 100, 107
regional organizations (ROs)
  comprehensive civil security programs, 105
  disaster risk management, 97, 99–104, 108, 110–11
  DRM activities, definition, 98
  global picture, 108
  indicators, DRM work, 99–102, 109
  public relations, 109
  research resources, 106
  threat management functions, 96
resilience
  civil security provision, 283
  concept, 46
  decentralized societal, 2, 7, 18, 131–3, 184
  HFA principles, 128
  long-term perspectives, 286–7
  natural hazards, 117, 139, 149–56
  oft-used concept, 138

risk management and disaster, 11, 16–17, 106, 118–21, 132, 134, 140, 246, 259, 278, 281

Scientific Veterinary Committee (ScVC), 217–18
Secretariat of the Pacific Community (SPC), 100, 103, 111 n. 6
Seventh Framework (FP7) Programme, 47 n. 1
Severe Acute Respiratory Syndrome (SARS), 266
Signature crises (EU policy areas)
 civil security governance's role, 213
 EU committee's involvement, 216
 Irish oil spill, 228
 L'Aquila earthquake, 38, 46
 London bombings (2005), 38
 Oslo/Utøya attacks, 38
 secondary legislation, 19, 215–16
Single European Market, 228
Solidarity Clause, 2, 11, 200, 211, 235, 250, 260–2, 268
South African Development Community (SADC), 111 n. 6, 120, 125
South Asian Association for Regional Cooperation (SAARC), 100, 111 n. 6
Standing Committee on Food Chain and Animal Health (SCFCAH), 220–2, 227, 229 n. 8
Standing Committee on Operational Cooperation on Internal Security (COSI), 215
Standing Veterinary Committee (SVC), 217–20, 227
Strategic Analysis and Response Centre (STAR), 263
Swedish Board for Psychological Defence (SPF), 170–5, 177
Swedish Defense Research Agency (FOI), 173, 177
Swedish Emergency Management Agency (SEMA), 170, 175–7
Swedish Energy Authority (SEA), 171, 174, 177
Swedish Environmental Protection Agency (SEPA), 173, 177

Swedish National Grid (SVK), 177
Swedish National Investigation Authority (SAIC), 170–3, 177, 182–3
Swedish Public Commission Inquiry (SOU), 170, 172, 174–7, 180, 183
Swedish Rescue Services Agency (SRSA), 174, 177
swine flu, 14–15, 28, 73–84, 86–90, 177–9, 181, 216, 223, 266, 280, 284, 286
 see also H1N1 influenza

terrorist attacks, 1, 7, 10, 37, 58, 160, 178, 180, 212, 247
transboundary crises
 air space policy, 197–8, 201–4
 detection, 194
 EU's role, 201–7
 joint response, 192–3
 known hazards, 193
 sense-making challenge, 193–5, 201–4
 subsidiarity principle, 191–2
 understanding, 194
 volcanic ash crisis, 192–3, 195–201
transnational cooperation, 9–10, 27
Treaty on the Functioning of the European Union (TFEU), 211, 260
tsunami, 1, 95, 138, 278

United Nations Development Programme (UNDP), 129
United Nations Office for Disaster Risk Reduction (UNISDR)
 diffusion norms, 124–6
 disaster risk management, 95
 emergency response agency work, 13
 on HFA goals, 131, 149
 peer review process, 246
 protection culture, 117, 129
 resilience concept, 150
 risk identification capabilities, 148
 standardized reports, 128
US Department of Homeland Security (DHS), 7

USA (United States of America), 80–1, 106, 221
see also homeland security

Visual Flight Rules (VFR), 197
Volcanic Ash Advisory Center (VAAC), 196–7
volcanic ash crisis
  cooperation challenges, 224–6
  EASA Opinions, 224–6
  EU committees and agencies' role, 226–9
  flight restrictions, 196
  ICAO guidelines, 196, 199
  in 2010 (Europe), 179, 192
  safety regulations, 204–5
  sense-making challenge, 195

war on terror, 5, 8
Western European Union (WEU), 242
World Bank, 95, 117, 119, 126–7
World Health Organization (WHO), 15, 73–4, 82–3, 221

zero tolerance rule, 199, 201, 204